Monika Otter
New York, March 1991

Medieval assumptions about the nature of the representation involved in literary and historical narratives were widely different from our own. Writers and readers worked with a complex understanding of the relations between truth and convention, in which accounts of presumed fact could be expanded, embellished, or translated in a variety of accepted ways. Ruth Morse's book explores how these assumptions operated in a broad range of genres, including romance, history, and biography. The book recovers the rhetorical principles which governed the creation and interpretation of such writings, and demonstrates their educational centrality in medieval Europe. Drawing upon this background, *Truth and Convention in the Middle Ages* examines in detail the diverse ways in which ostensibly 'historical' narratives established their legitimacy, notably through their invocation of earlier textual authorities or 'sources'. In analysing these complex processes of narrative reconstruction, the book itself reconstructs medieval habits of reading and writing, and raises far-reaching questions about language and representation.

# TRUTH AND CONVENTION IN THE MIDDLE AGES

# TRUTH AND CONVENTION IN THE MIDDLE AGES

## RHETORIC, REPRESENTATION, AND REALITY

### Ruth Morse

*Fellow and Lecturer in English*
*Fitzwilliam College, Cambridge*

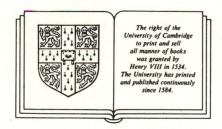

*The right of the University of Cambridge to print and sell all manner of books was granted by Henry VIII in 1534. The University has printed and published continuously since 1584.*

CAMBRIDGE UNIVERSITY PRESS

Cambridge

New York   Port Chester

Melbourne   Sydney

Published by the Press Syndicate of the University of Cambridge
The Pitt Building, Trumpington Street, Cambridge CB2 1RP
40 West 20th Street, New York, NY 10011, USA
10 Stamford Road, Oakleigh, Melbourne 3166, Australia

First published 1991

Printed in Great Britain at
the University Press, Cambridge

*British Library cataloguing in publication data*
Morse, Ruth
Truth and convention in the Middle Ages: medieval
rhetoric and representation.
1. European literatures. Rhetoric, history
1. Title
808.009

*Library of Congress cataloguing in publication data*
Morse, Ruth
Truth and convention in the Middle Ages: medieval rhetoric and
representation / Ruth Morse
p.     cm.
ISBN 0 521 30211 0
1. Rhetoric, Medieval.   2. Narration (Rhetoric)   1. Title.
PN185.M6   1991
808'.009'02–dc20   90–1752 CIP

ISBN 0 521 30211 0 hardback

To Stefan Collini

Par ce que c'estoit luy; par ce que c'estoit moy

'. . . and things only seems to be things . . .'

Henry Reed, 'Lessons of the War'

# CONTENTS

List of plates                                                   *page* xi

Preface and acknowledgements                                          xiii


Introduction                                                            1

1   Meaning and means                                                  15
    The rhetorical approach to education                               16
    Learning through commented texts                                   24
    Imitation of speech, style, and action                            45
    The exercises of rhetorical invention                             63

2   The meaning of the past                                           85
    Historical fictions                                               92
    Exercising historical invention                                  105

3   Let us now praise famous men                                     125
    Encomiastic lives                                                125
    Models of sanctity                                               138
    Exercising biographical invention                                158

4   Traitor translator                                               179
    Reference and representation                                     179
    The conventional wisdom of translators                           185
    Sacred wisdom                                                     191
    Words and deeds                                                  209

5   Texts and pre-texts                                              231
    Invention and representation                                     231
    Convention and invention                                         238
    Truth and convention                                             244


Notes                                                                249

Index                                                                289

# PLATES

1 *Aeneid* Book I with annotations compiled from Servius, Donatus, and other Commentators by J. Ascensius (Paris, 1507), reproduced from CUL Ta.54.2.     *page* 25

2 The opening of the Book of Genesis with the Glossa Ordinaria, from CUL Ff.2.19 (twelfth century).     28

3 The opening of Psalm 23 from *The Interpreter's Bible: The Holy Scriptures in the King James and Revised Standard Version with General Articles and Introductions, Exegesis, Exposition for each book of the Bible*, ed. G. A. Buttrick et al., vol. IV (NY and Nashville, Tenn., 1955), p. 123.     37

4 The final stanza of and the beginning of the Notes to 'September' from Edmund Spenser, *The Shepheardes Calender* (London, 1579) reproduced from CUL Syn.7.64.61 (1586).     77

5 A *divisio* of tropes and schemes from Johannes Susenbrotus, *Epitome troporum ac schematum et grammaticorum & Rhetorum, ad Autores tum prophanos tum sacros intelligendos non minus utilis quam necessaria* (London, 1562), reproduced by CUL Aa★.5.31.     79

6 A page from the *Summa Dictaminis* of Laurentius de Civitate Austriae, from CUL Add. 3312, a fourteenth-century manuscript.     115

7 The *divisio* which precedes Thomas Speght's Life of Chaucer in his edition of the *Workes* (London, 1598), reproduced from CUL s★2.29.     131

8 The opening verses of the Twenty-third Psalm in Rolle's Translation and Commentary. Reproduced from Sidney Sussex College, Cambridge, MS 89 (unfoliated).     208

9 An extract from the Introduction to Douglas's *Aeneid*, with a fragment of his accompanying commentary. Reproduced from Trinity College, Cambridge, MS Q.3.12.     224

# PREFACE AND ACKNOWLEDGEMENTS

To paraphrase Pascal, if I had had more time, I would have written a shorter book. It began in 1980 and was first sketched as undergraduate lectures at the University of Leeds, when I was trying to introduce students to the assumptions of rhetoric. It developed slowly when I was a Summer Fellow at the Humanities Research Centre of the Australian National University, where I was delayed by the enthusiasm and erudition of Graeme Clarke, Ian Donaldson, and R. St C. Johnson. I failed to complete it in the year I was a Research Fellow at Clare Hall, Cambridge, where my editor, Michael Black, gave me the courage of his convictions, and, while never failing to urge me to try new things, never forgot to nag me about old ones. Had he not insisted I answer his questions and deal with his reservations, a quite different book would have been finished much sooner; and it would have been the worse without him. How much I owe him he neither suspects nor, perhaps, would acknowledge. The book was finally completed while I was Leathersellers' Fellow in English at Fitzwilliam College, Cambridge. The relief I express in reaching, if not the finish, at least the laying aside, was well put by Caxton at the end of his translation of the *History of Troy*, 'for as moche as in the wrytyng of the same my penne is worn, myn hande wery and not stedfast, myn eyen dimmed with overmoche lokyng on the whit paper, and my corage not so prone and redy to laboure as hit hath ben, and that age crepeth on me dayly and febleth all the bodye, and also because I have promysid to dyverce gentilmen and to my frendes to adresse to hem as hastely as I myght this sayd book'. If the fulfilment of that promise has an air of *festina lente* about it, I can only hope to be excused by Patricia Williams, who helped so much at the beginning, and Barry Windeatt, who, at the end, cheerfully shouldered burdens we had meant to share. Roger Ray encouraged me at an early stage of my research, and fifteen years later found time to read what, without his acumen, might have been the final version. Successive drafts were read and reread, as always, by Helen Cooper and

Stefan Collini; and the first of the rhetorical tropes in this book expresses my gratitude for their patience, care, and humour – it must be right that my first example of rhetorical convention should none the less be true. Writing, like the authors with whom this book is concerned, under correction, I was constantly aware of them as my first, most demanding, and most generous, readers. Through all the peripatetics, and *peripeteia*, of the last decade, their astringent affection has sustained me: for this relief, much thanks.

I am grateful to the Syndics of the University Library, Cambridge, for permission to reproduce Plates 1, 2, 4, 5, 6, 7 from books and manuscripts in their possession; to the Master and Fellows of Sidney Sussex College, Cambridge for Plate 8; and to the Master and Fellows of Trinity College, Cambridge for Plate 9. Plate 3 is reproduced by kind permission of the publishers, the Abingdon Press.

This last acknowledgement is the first sentence – in the course of two books and many issues of *The Cambridge Review* – to have escaped the vigilance of Susan Beer, Capital Copy-Editor.

# INTRODUCTION

When the early-fifteenth-century Augustinian Friar, John Capgrave, wrote that the corpse of Henry I (who had died in 1135) stank horribly, he expected his readers to understand a moral criticism. Because it had long been an agreed proof of sanctity that the deceased holy person's body resisted decomposition so far as to smell sweet rather than to putrefy, a corpse that stank might be taken as evidence of the opposite kind of life. Not John Capgrave, but Nature herself, revealed the dead king's character. Capgrave was not in a position to know for certain what a particular twelfth-century corpse smelled like; dependent upon what he himself had read, he embellished his sources according to his knowledge (from oral and written sources as well as from his own and common experience) and the picture he wanted to draw. A question such as, 'But did Henry's corpse *really* smell?', might have seemed to him to miss the point of his description. One or more authorities said so. It might have done. He writes with a presumption of truth, for no one would deliberately write what he knew to be false. Or at least, true according to his lights and not false except under certain special circumstances. His Lives of Illustrious Henries were examples of the large genre, *encomium*, patterned on earlier accounts which his learned medieval readers, familiar with the literary traditions of praise and blame, could recognize. Finding out whether or not something had happened was a difficult business, and the sources and authorities upon which he depended varied in quality and reliability. He deferred to the authority of his twelfth-century predecessor, Henry of Huntingdon (whom he quoted and acknowledged). Other twelfth-century historians, among them Orderic Vitalis and William of Malmesbury, make no mention of any offensive putrefaction (though Orderic tells a similar story about the corpse of William the Conqueror). Capgrave could defer to, choose among, question, or reinterpret earlier authorities. His attitudes to those authorities further complicates his intention – one among many competing ambitions – to transmit his interpretation of earlier interpretations of the past. As soon as he began to

turn his perception of King Henry I into words, and into a shaped narrative
for Latinate readers, readers who enjoyed their prose interspersed with
elegant hexameters, other dynamics came into play. By similar kinds of
conventional allusion, a depiction of a murdered monarch (the Anglo-Saxon
Edward, say, or the French Henry IV) in the guise of a martyred saint might
suggest an interpretation of the monarch which claimed sanctity for him, or
a satirical portrait which rejected the implied claim, or a range of possibilities
in between.

For medieval writers of long narratives, for medieval historians above all,
the 'embellishments' of words bore a complex relationship to the 'truths'
they depicted. This book explores some aspects of the complicated
relationship between the claim to be telling the truth about the past, about
historical actors and events, and the conventional representations in which
such truths were expressed. It considers what appear to be claims to accurate
representation, both of word and of deed. But to ask how medieval writers
represented the deeds which had taken place in the past is not to ask simply
how they shaped their narratives, it is to ask how they re-shaped them. An
inevitable intertextuality pervades the study of the range of texts which
described themselves as historical. Medieval writers did not suddenly create
their historical methods out of nothing; they inherited a large and ever-
growing body of 'historical' narratives whose conventional patterns and
styles suggested a range of meanings. The omission of part of a narrative
which ought to have been included, the turning of historical events to
recognizable narrative patterns, the insistence that agents did or said things
which accorded with ideas about their status, or reign, or character – all these
possibilities could be manipulated in order to convey complex impressions
of the past and its relevance to the present. The rise of empiricism in the
seventeenth century, that great watershed in western culture, has erected
barriers between us and the Middle Ages, here as in so many other ways. To
ask why medieval writers claimed that what appears to us obviously
'invented' material was 'true' is another reminder of the incommensurability
of our cultures – however much ours owes to, and descends from, theirs.
Among the questions uniting the disparate texts which will come under
scrutiny in the following chapters are: What is it they mean when they
appear not to mean what they say? Can we tell when that is? If
representations are not literally true, how are they true?

Perhaps, in the late twentieth century, our own self-consciously sophisticated post-empiricism puts us at an advantage over some of our

scholarly predecessors because we expect to recognize a diversity of non-literal meanings. If medieval interpretations proceeded by recognition of context, of suitability of linguistic register and stylistic decorum, of the detailed description which exploited, adapted, and modified a complex textual inheritance, then we must recapture context, especially the texts which formed that context. The descriptions both of the decomposing corpse and the martyred king depend upon audience ability to evaluate a particular instance against habitual readings of similar ones, but neither description is automatic or necessitated by any *zeitgeist*; rather, each is learned and manipulated by authors within cultures. Both examples assume multiple reference: to the events that the text represented and to the text as a kind of expression which imitated other texts representing prior events. Not true/false only, but 'authorized', 'exemplary', and, inevitably, 'persuasive', and these in relation to other beliefs and practices of their writing culture. To put it another way, historical events could be written about in poems which themselves belonged to a tradition of historical poetry, often – and perhaps misleadingly – categorized as 'epic'. Such poems could be read by potential authors who expected to be able to extract their 'historical' matter for new compositions. In turn, depending upon a subsequent author's will and skill, representations of past events which also referred to past texts would emerge, sometimes claiming a direct relationship with the past which in some unexplained way jumped the intervening textual tradition. Were there not large scope for manipulation there could be no irony, no parody, no development – only imitation and pastiche, or the repetitive reproduction of earlier authorities. And understanding these manipulations implies an audience with different expectations about how texts represent and refer from those which many modern readers would bring to their reading.

The basic argument of this book thus stems from an observation already familiar to many modern scholars of different disciplines: medieval (and many renaissance) readers and writers seem to have thought they could read through or across conventional styles, narrative types, and languages to a kind of prelinguistic core of truth that lay underneath. Rhetoric is thus a prolegomenon to what follows because it grounds the habits and assumptions which pervaded medieval writing in an even older intellectual milieu. In the analyses which follow, I hope that by juxtaposing texts of different kinds, it will become possible to find underlying patterns where before there were separate insights. If something might be said to have united the many different kinds of writing in which medieval authors engaged, that

something might be derived from a version of the assumptions and practices
of classical rhetoric. What words and pictures represented, what kinds of
things or ideas they referred to, depended not only upon experience, but also
upon some familiarity with a complex system of signs (or conventions)
whose content and methods were acquired initially as part of a process of
learning to read. Medieval writers were themselves often troubled by the
contradictions between the principles enshrined in their prefaces and
included as a matter of course in their texts and their habitual practice
(especially, it must be said, other writers' habitual practice). Within a few
sentences of a claim – or what appears to be a claim – to follow the strictest
criteria of accurate representation or transmission they launch themselves (or
catch others launched upon) an expansion, an elaboration, an insertion
which confounds their previous self-description.

*but could*
*there have*
*been a*
*contradiction*
*for them?*

   Allegorical imagery is an extreme case of habits which permeated
medieval representations of many kinds. Aesopic Fable, which depicts lambs
as talking beasts, is similar, since the lambs have to be recognized as sharing
human as well as animal traits; but the limits of interpretation are drawn
differently, controlled by assumptions that grow from the reading of fables,
which seldom ask readers to think of their lambs as God. At least in non-
verisimilar fictions, where readers can be certain that the things depicted
could not have happened, there is a predisposition to look for other
meanings. The punning representation of 'a' lamb as 'the' Lamb of God,
Christ as the sacrifice, is a central occurrence of a common habit. It depends
not on knowledge of sheep, but on familiarity with a textual tradition in
which they play an important part, and such interpretation assumes an
acceptance that what is represented also refers to a reality beyond what is
depicted. It also encompasses verbal style, so that an author's use of shepherds
(the low style of life and art) signifies something about God's willingness to
humble himself. The words which embody the symbol are chosen in order
to convey values. The tale is told for a purpose other than conveying
information. This is straightforward enough; more difficult to recognize is
the use of this transforming kind of representation when the narrative is or
claims to be a verisimilar account of the past. Readers coming to medieval
historians for the first time may be perplexed to find patent fictions presented
as part of a true account; readers of medieval fictions may wonder why
invented stories are offered as 'true'. Historians appear at least inconsistent;
writers of romances hypocritical. Beginning from the observation made
above about reading 'through' narratives, I shall try to elucidate some of the

complicated implicit patterns behind otherwise inexplicable inventions and inconsistencies. Medieval authors depended upon shared habits of reading in order to convey their views and beliefs to their audiences. The implications of that initial observation are complex, and lead outward in many different directions. To castigate translators for failing to achieve a particular kind of close verbal correspondence, to demand a clear, dependable dividing line between 'history' and 'fiction' is to begin with modern categories; useful as they are, they need to be related to other ideas about composition in a different culture.

How to interpret, and then how to express, core meanings, in order to move and persuade an audience, were the central concerns of rhetorical education in antiquity. Medieval readers and writers did not have to inherit the actual education in rhetorical declamation which had been the achievement of antiquity in order to inherit some of the categories of thought and of composition which underlay, for example, the depiction or dramatization of direct speech which appeared in histories and poems. They inherited the literature which was written in those categories, and which came accompanied by commentaries which emphasized the achievement of great writers in such identifiable terms as metaphoric language, dramatic and persuasive speeches, and moving descriptions of many kinds. Christianizing imitations of the categories preserved them, however much they succeeded in substituting newer, and morally more acceptable, texts for the dangerous literature of pagan antiquity. As long as classical compositions survived, ambitious writers would return to them for models of inspiration; classical literature remained a challenge, problematic but undeniably *there*, suggesting — but not compelling — varieties of creation and interpretation.

Both the examples with which I began, the reprobate king and the saintly one, presume knowledgeable audiences, since they depend upon a relation to something assumed but not stated within the particular work. And the relation of a particular work to its genre, to the kinds of books which it resembles (from which assumptions about how to read it may primarily be drawn) must be expanded to include at least potential comparison to quite different works. Saintly kings or kingly saints are not the only innovating mixtures that medieval writers created. Kings might become lions (or lions kings). The kinds of adventure that are usually found in the narratives classed as 'romances' or even the low-life anecdotes found in 'fabliaux' could be — and were — adapted for the apparently higher genres of history and the saint's life. The interpenetration of genres in the Middle Ages assumed that readers

Yes — although this is
not altogether
beyond

were familiar with different styles of expression, and that they would recognize them for what they are. Yet 'genre' can itself raise as many problems as it solves, because the definitions which the Middle Ages inherited from antiquity scarcely fitted the kinds of text which were common.

'History' was the central secular category of long verisimilar narrative. Though it appeared to be obvious what 'history' meant, the breadth and variety of narratives, in verse and in prose, that described themselves (or were described by readers) as histories suggests that complex processes were at work and that playing within the definitions of history occupied many writers. Calling a text 'historical' might have a legitimating function. It might defend the embroidering of a narrative based on another narrative (which had been extracted from a text defined as 'historical'), like so many of the expansions created in the course of the twelfth century and after to tell the stories of Thebes or Troy, King Arthur or Charlemagne, or to celebrate a saint, a relic, a religious house. 'Historical', though, might be thought of as an exemplary narrative based upon events which had occurred at some point in the past, told in order to move and persuade its audience to imitate the good and eschew the evil, a 'true tale about the past' which included a vast range of what modern readers would regard as invented material and inappropriate, if implicit, moralizing. What was the place of anecdotal material in history or biography? How did the need for certain kinds of illustration or expansion inspire – and control – the use of invented, or dubious, or even true, material? What is the relation of the historical narrator to his subject, and to the traditions of historical narrators?

In the different conceptual space of the Middle Ages, 'true' might mean 'in the main' or 'for the most part' true, or even, 'it could have happened like this'. The problems of factuality were not resolved by medieval writers, even late-medieval legal writers, and the constant elaboration towards fiction created tensions between some recognizable, even extractable, central claims and narrative methods of conveying the author's sense of how the past was to be interpreted. In this sense history was a broad church, teaching by precept and example.

The corpus of classical historical texts, preserved and imitated, could be read at first hand, or through imitations and adaptations of many kinds. 'History' was an umbrella term for many different kinds of narrative, united by their being, or posing as, verisimilar reports of events which had happened in the past. Different writers, creating different kinds of works for different kinds of audiences in a climate ostensibly hostile to ambition, literary or otherwise, were constrained by explicit commitments to the truth, whole and unadulterated, which coexisted with implicit expectations about how to elaborate and embroider in order to write elegantly and move and persuade. Medieval historians seldom explained that a section of their work was entirely their own invention, yet they seemed to approach other writers' works knowing that such distinctions could be made, and assuming that they could distinguish truth from embellishment when choosing what to preserve and how to convey it. Internal consistency and verisimilitude appeared to count among the highest criteria for subsequent readers and writers, who only rarely had external validation to turn to. This in turn meant that attitudes to the authors' authority were crucial, in medieval societies in which 'authority' itself posed another unresolvable problem.

The classical Latin expositions of the idea of 'history', the corpus of Ciceronian and pseudo-Ciceronian texts, the description of an Orator's training by Quintilian, and the late-Latin commentators and expositors of their teaching, were not always available to medieval readers and writers, nor always fully understood when they were available, nor even completely approved by those who owned them, read them, analysed them, and made use of them (for their own purposes). Like so much of the inheritance from classical antiquity, rhetoric was a two-edged sword, less an education in oratory than an incitement to the study of potentially disturbing poets such as Virgil and Ovid and Statius, and a stimulus to emulate their secular tales of politics, war, family, reputation, human friendships and illicit love. However much medieval readers thought they were studying classical texts in order to learn the techniques of writing well (in order to apply those techniques to holier purposes), they were still exposing themselves to the extraordinary persuasive powers of great poetry, which convinces – against the odds – that *this* might have happened, in this way; that, had we been there, we too would have acted as these characters acted. The historian Macaulay's envy of the novelist Scott's ability to convey an immediate impression of the past is well worth carrying in mind. As long as Latin texts survived, however sanitized by accompanying moral commentary, rhetorically sophisticated works remained to tempt as well as to teach medieval readers. The glosses, commentaries, and dialogues which explicated these texts explicated them in terms of the rhetorical skills, from the verbal ornaments of the 'tropes' and 'schemes' to the invention of speeches and the

creation of plots and characters. These in turn pointed back to a system of
education whose basic assumptions about style and the ways styles could be
varied without affecting the assumed core meaning survived with the
classical texts which embodied them.

The model texts taught that writing should be metaphoric and figurative,
full of the decorative additions which characterized Latin poetry and prose;
that it should embody the set pieces of the model authors, and increase their
number and scope where possible. The creations of recognizably intertextual
*topoi*, the set pieces of medieval composition, which called attention to their
place in a long tradition of creative imitation and cross-reference, were part
of writerly ambition whatever the type of text being produced – where the
writers were educated enough to know what and how to imitate. To be able
to recognize an epic simile or a high style description; to expatiate upon a
description of a city, storm at sea, praise of a man's ancestors; to appreciate a
good death, or two friends vying to outdo each other in bravery; to
dramatize the arguments in defence of a course taken or for and against love;
all these are part of a literary inheritance that is also the way that medieval
writers expressed their understanding of events and agents. It means that
different sections of the same text may employ apparently inconsistent
standards of veracity, and that quite different adaptations and translations
could claim to represent the same original text. This book attempts to restore
some large-scale (as well as small-scale) patterns which can be thought of as
deriving from rhetorical attitudes to writing.

Rhetoric was itself a vexed category; at different times it was – in so far as
it was one thing – the subject of debate about its content (even whether or
not it had one), its legitimacy, its status, its place in the educational syllabus.
In the late Middle Ages its relation to grammar and logic was often a
problem, and it probably only reassumed its classical pre-eminence with the
Renaissance. Rhetoric could be rejected (sometimes ostentatiously) by those
who fled to the cloister, or modifed for the use of Christians, and
hagiography is one route of that modification. The Psalter could replace
Virgil in the classroom. But one of the things it replaced Virgil for was the
teaching of just those rhetorical skills of which Virgil had been the great
master. Changing the model did not change all the questions. The need to
move and persuade remained, even if biblical texts were supposed to
supersede pagan ones. But Virgil did not disappear, and the desire to study
the works that had meant so much to Church Fathers such as Augustine and
Jerome, themselves rhetoricians of great skill, led generation after generation

back to the classics. Rhetoric could be a scheme of study, or it could be, more pervasively but perhaps more intangibly, a habit of mind, a set of assumptions about how words represent the world – or other words.

In antiquity, the process of education which familiarized generations of students with these habits of interpretation was organized as an education in oratory. In the schools of antiquity, boys who could already read and who had already begun to study (and to learn by heart) their cultures' great texts, trained themselves to apply the lessons of those texts to their own compositions, especially to speeches of persuasion, of defence of a course of action, of praise and blame. It is common to call this a 'literary' education, and that is correct. Indeed, I have already invoked 'literary' ambitions as if they were commonplace among medieval writers. But 'literary' may now imply ideas of creative writing, of free-standing independent fictions. It is clear that in the Middle Ages the delineation of such a category raised many problems. 'Poetry' was the word often used to identify texts which contained large proportions of 'invented' material. Medieval resistance to the free-standing fiction was frequently expressed, although its continued existence is perpetual testimony to the human impulse to tell stories, to write and sing about feelings not altogether consistent with the pursuit of salvation. 'Literature' was everywhere and nowhere, because learning to write, whatever the style or content, was based on the acquisition of certain well-defined basic rhetorical skills. Ambitious historical writing was rhetorically sophisticated; so was poetry. Historical poetry was possible, and so was poetical history. In this sense 'rhetoric' might have meant the concatenation of skills which contributed to the analysis of texts: of what they meant and how they moved their readers. Verisimilar literary creations were problematic, and the longer and more ambitious they were the more pressing became the question of their legitimacy. What proportion of a text could be added by the poet, and how did that change the status of his new text? If he claimed higher truths for his additions what kind of hierarchy was he invoking? How were subsequent readers to know that his additions were his? What is the relation between a re-telling, or adaptation, or translation, and an original text or texts? What controlled these additions or embellishments or decorations? Reconstructing rhetorical habits of mind can go some way to providing answers to these questions.

The desire among medieval authors for rhetorical training might appear to be a dangerous impulse, at best a distraction from, and at worst a betrayal of, any commitment to preserving the truth of true tales about the past. Yet

scholars of the calibre of Bede, whose pedagogic reforms meant so much to
monastic educators and writers of all kinds, absorbed both precept and
example from rhetorical texts, and supplied new writing which had digested
the lessons of rhetoric for Christian historians, exegetes, and poets. It is one of
the striking testimonies to the hold of classical antiquity on the changing
circumstances of the Middle Ages, that the more talented, the more
ambitious, the more skilful the medieval writer, the more likely he was to
know something about rhetorical methods of interpretation and expression.
Whether this knowledge came from textbooks or from model authors may
not make, in the last analysis, much difference. 'Rhetoric' might be a
curriculum of study, the name of the discipline which enabled students to
move and persuade, or the manipulations of style they acquired from
handbooks, glossed or commented texts, and ambitious imitations of great
classical works (which illustrated those manipulations at their best).

In dealing with what was similar, with what made variety of expression
possible, it is difficult to avoid generalizations which may seem to suggest a
'Middle Ages' in which no changes occurred for a thousand years. One
generalization of which I am – sometimes painfully – aware, is that although
I discuss individual writers who were women, by and large the educated,
Latinate class who form the focus of this book were men. When I write 'he', I
usually mean 'he'; but the 'he' I describe is only a tiny subsection of medieval
manhood, the curious group whose lives revolved around writing. That
changes occurred, and that they were spurred by, among other things, the
dramatized depictions of character and motive created by great writers, is a
*leitmotif* of this book. Literature is profoundly a form of knowledge. But in
the mental space of the Middle Ages that was an argument medieval
interpreters could scarcely confront head on, because it glorified fiction.
Medieval resistance to fiction may have been well founded, and it may be
art, rather than science, which was the greatest threat to religion, because it is
multivalent and multivocal, because it celebrates (even while, even by,
ostensibly condemning) experiences and behaviour anathema to religious
dicta, and perhaps because, by its very existence, it creates a higher escapism
bound to distract even the most reverent from contemplation of the ineffable
to the particularities of the great human desires: love, revenge, ambition.

The history of the study of rhetoric in the Middle Ages is still at an early
stage. Historians and literary critics who are unlocking the traditions of
commentary and debate have found a rich ambivalence to classical learning;
my debt to their work is great, and is, I hope, amply acknowledged in the

notes to the following chapters. If I have made what must seem to specialists like wild generalizations across a millennium and for too many of the countries of western Europe, I can only hope that by juxtaposing early and late medieval writing, and the writing of genres often studied separately, within separate fields of modern specialization, I have raised questions worth discussing. She who concentrates on similarities must also apologize for insufficient attention to difference: to how things changed, and why.

The scope of this book is an exploration of the variety of imaginative historical writing in western Europe in the high and late Middle Ages. But in order to situate the discussion of an eclectic range of Latin and vernacular texts, I begin in antiquity, and to illustrate the last gasps of medieval (in contrast to Gothic Revival) ways of writing about the past, I make the occasional foray into the seventeenth century. I have claimed that a lively sympathy with rhetoric must underly the analysis of what controlled historical invention. Therefore, Chapter 1 is a heuristic description of a rhetorical education in learning to read, interpret, and write. In describing a possible medieval education, I do not pretend for a moment that it ever existed in quite this form. This long description attempts to establish patterns of transformation, to show the ways that the same things could be imagined to be expressed by quite different styles of expression, and to suggest categories more complex than the yes/no, true/false patterns that might seduce a reader who has never met medieval styles of writing before to think that a narrative is either historical or not, according to modern ways of thinking and modern criteria of assessment. It attempts to lay groundwork for the analysis of latitudes of invention and embellishment, to suggest the larger patterns which support and generate the multiplicity of *topoi*.

Thinking about literary habits of expression and learning about the *topoi*, the set-piece subjects such as descriptions of towns or storms at sea or atrocities during wars, that is, applying the techniques of literary analysis to medieval historical texts, informs Chapter 2. In a way, 'history' might be thought of as a particularly privileged kind of plot, suggesting themes upon which medieval writers created their own narrative variations. History's true tales about the past represented agents and events, but also referred to other texts which had previously represented them, or agents and events similar to them. The claim that historical narratives are susceptible to literary analysis is not startling in itself; as in the first chapter, I attempt to give examples which will help identify patterns of literary manipulation, and elucidate styles of representation and reference, so that, to give another simple example, 'realism' is not assumed to guarantee truth, but is perceived as a style. To succeeding generations of writers, what once had claimed to be revolutionary innovation, or root and branch eradication of corruption and accretion for the sake of restoring a pristine state, rapidly assumes an appearance of weak variation, of mere reaction which succeeds only in preserving what it pretended to overcome. Chapter 3 takes 'biography' as a continuation of historical writing, but – in what might be thought of as a 'literary' term – emphasizes the representation of character rather more than plot. Chapter 4 concentrates on linguistic transfer from one literary language to another, but considers this as part of a pattern of imitation and reference; I look at translations as varieties of 'referring' texts, and at their methods of reference both to earlier texts and to the events represented in those texts. For any medievalist, translation of the Bible must be of paramount importance, and I consider something of the variety of biblical transformations, perhaps beyond the boundary of what is habitually classified as translation. Chapter 5 suggests how, in looking at medieval writing, we might wish to broaden our ideas of what constitutes literature, and how criteria of elegance and eloquence are supported by the rhetorical traditions which have been the subject of the earlier chapters. While this book concentrates on the high and late Middle Ages in Western Europe, its earliest examples reach back beyond Sulpicius Severus to Cicero and Quintilian; its most modern include archaizing texts as late as *Paradise Lost*. One of the educational strains in this story is the increasing distance between the source-culture language, Latin, and the literary languages of the increasingly nationally defined European vernaculars, especially English, French, and Italian. Love and ambition can also be focussed on books, and the desire to emulate the literary successes of the past is one of the main motive forces for medieval and renaissance writers.

In writing for an audience of scholars as well as students coming to pre-seventeenth-century writing for the first time, I have been conscious that some of the exposition is likely to seem tedious to the learned. In addressing two disparate learned audiences, professional historians and literary critics, I hope that while the former will tolerate the application of the habits of literary analysis, the latter will be intrigued by the breadth of what passed as history. Because my own intellectual formation is in a literature-based discipline, and my experience of reading is mainly in English and French, readers with similar backgrounds may find many of the examples in the first and fourth chapters familiar. I hope that the section headings will facilitate judicious selection, and that by restricting the bibliography and polemic to the footnotes I have managed not to bore those for whom the book was originally intended, who

> don't know much about the Middle Ages –
> look at the pictures and turn the pages.

Allegory has been well served by students of the Middle Ages, and I discuss it only in passing. For the opposite reason, I say little about one of the basic parts of any training in oratory: delivery. There is very little on what medieval texts must have sounded like. It is a profound limitation of this book, as book, that words in the mind read faster than words addressed to the ear, that paronomasia (sound effects) cannot easily be discussed when we habitually read silently, so that our experience appears to negate generalizations about the normal experience of readers whose reading was not silent. The importance of repetition, of rhythm, assonance and alliteration, all the sound chimes, cannot be overemphasized as a pseudo-logical effect. Arguments are not just reinforced, they are sometimes created – or at least the impression of an argument is created – however meretriciously, by sound, and the sense of an ending may move profoundly because of shifts in rhythm which bring the hearing reader to a halt. By supplying quotations in the original languages as well as in translation, I have tried to invite readers to think about these possibilities.

# I

# MEANING AND MEANS

Besides it would be absurd that, while incapacity for self-defence is a
reproach, incapacity for mental defence should be none; mental effort
being more distinctive of man than bodily effort. If it is objected that an
abuser of the rhetorical faculty can do great mischief, this, at any rate,
applies to all good things except virtue, and especially to the most useful
things, as strength, health, wealth, generalship. By the right use of these
things a man may do the greatest good, and by the unjust use, the
greatest mischief.

Style will have propriety, if it is pathetic [emotional], characteristic, and
proportionate to the subject. This proportion means that important
subjects shall not be treated in a random way, nor trivial subjects in a
grand way; and that ornament shall not be heaped upon a commonplace object . . . Passion is expressed, when an outrage is in question, by
the language of anger; when impious or shameful deeds are in question,
by the language of indignation and aversion; when praiseworthy things
are in question, by admiring language; when piteous things, by lowly
language – and so in other cases. The appropriateness of the language
helps to give probability to the fact; the hearer's mind draws the
fallacious inference that the speaker is telling the truth, because, where
such facts are present, men are thus affected; the hearer thinks, then, that
the case stands as the speaker says, whether it does so stand or not, and
invariably sympathises with the passionate speaker, even when he is an
imposter.                    Aristotle, *Rhetoric*, 1355b, 1408a (trans. Jebb)

The poet is ranked with the scientist as authority for a purely scientific
proposition. This astonishing failure to distinguish – in practice, though
not always in theory – between books of different sorts must be borne
in mind whenever we are trying to gauge the total effect of an ancient
text on its medieval readers. The habit, like many medieval habits, long
outlived the Middle Ages. Burton is a notable offender. He illustrates
the physiological force of imagination from the *Aethiopica* of
Heliodorus as if that romance were a history . . .
     C. S. Lewis, *The Discarded Image* (Cambridge, 1964), pp. 31–2.

## THE RHETORICAL APPROACH TO EDUCATION

When the educational habits that were developed in classical antiquity devolved upon the countries of medieval Europe, they created standards and raised problems for the Christian West. Classical education had established the idea that the cultivated man knew (by heart) the best writing of his culture, and it nominated the texts; trained him to analyse with detailed care; to speak well enough to move and persuade his audience, and to write always with the mind's ear in his mind's eye, following the models of excellence that he had studied and imitated at school. Even if the Bible replaced Homer or Virgil, an education in rhetorical skills might still be a goal. When medieval writers argued over the suitability of such study for the godly, they defended the use of rhetorical skills on the grounds that Christians could not afford to relinquish oratorical advantages of persuasion to their adversaries. Sometimes they pointed out the undeniable rhetorical achievements of the Bible or the Church Fathers. The schools and practice of antiquity had set a curriculum but they had equally enshrined an interlocking complex of ideas. Medieval writers could refer to rhetoric, to rhetoric texts, to writers on rhetoric, without ever defining exactly what they meant. They continued to converse with what they took to be Antiquity's Rhetoric as a standard, a syllabus, or a discipline, without ever restricting the subject to a specific course of study. Today, when 'rhetoric' implies bombast, words without content, it is hard to recapture the all-encompassing richness of the classical rhetorical education, or the pervasiveness of its assumptions. Rhetoricians had trained the governing citizens of Athens, despite the reservations about their ostensible expertise which Plato expressed, and Romans imitated and adapted the schools of their predecessors. When Christianity, with all its complex and contradictory ambivalences about the value of worldly achievement, became dominant in late antiquity, rhetorically trained writers reinterpreted classical texts for Christian education and, despite their ambivalent view of their heritage, preserved it: Augustine, Jerome, Cyprian, and many others were rhetoricians before they were churchmen – and they were rhetoricians after, whatever they told themselves. If an apparently excessive dedication to their literary training sometimes led them to reproach themselves with too much concern with the culture, the literary achievements of this world, they justified that training, using it to raise the standard of their new, Christian culture in order that it might emulate and surpass pagan Greece and Rome. Medieval students of eloquence would find pagan writers at the base of their study, maintaining the prestige which accrued to 'founders' and 'inventors' of any skill; the same models of excellence retained their supremacy across the whole of Europe, in a language increasingly remote from those registers of spoken and written Latin in which educated people communicated. Later still, but still across the breadth of the continent, writers aspired to achieve in their vernacular languages poetry and prose that would stand comparison with the monuments they had inherited and studied either through precept or, implicitly, through example.[1] Thus their habits of argument, their delight in display, the unstated assumptions that they shared about writing or speaking well, informed their sermons, their historical and imaginative writing, and their letters. In this chapter I shall consider how models of reading became models of writing, and what kinds of conventions the model texts established as integral to composition and interpretation. Since textbooks written by Greeks could be translated by Romans and still used by English schoolboys, I make no apology for choosing my examples eclectically. And since texts analyse what great writers do, I use the analysis of literature as an indication of ways of reading or habits of writing which could be learned wherever commentary and interpretation were part of private or group study. Throughout this book it will be the typical (against which the unusual shows its surprises) that will be my concern, and the horizon to be plotted is a horizon of expectation.[2]

It is the argument of this book that the habits of reading and writing that were engendered by education according to a variety of rhetorical assumptions created a literary culture in which the meaning of a passage or even a whole work may ultimately depend on recognition of its place in a familiar scheme of categories of style, method, and organization. Acquaintance with the expectations, rules, and habits of mind that moved these writers is an important preliminary which will help modern readers begin to appreciate why medieval authors wrote as they did, what they intended – even if (perhaps especially if) they did not actually do what they meant to do, achieve what they intended to achieve. If medieval Europe was always a collection of bilingual cultures, it was at least in this way no different from Rome. This experience of a 'referring' culture, or of 'referring' texts, will continue to be an important theme. Greek texts defined the inherited categories in which men wrote, as well as providing standards of excellence. So Homer's epics created standards of writing about the past which included models of courage, beauty, ethics, arguments, behaviour – all the moral and aesthetic satisfactions that books provide. Emulating and surpassing Homer's achievement was a constant challenge to the writers who succeeded him, first in Hellenistic Greece and Egypt and then in Latin-speaking Italy. Greek plays set the canons of drama as Greek orations established the forms of forensic, or apparently forensic oratory; Greek historians showed the ways to write about the past.[3] Even at the earliest stages of learning a Roman schoolboy studied the animal fables attributed to a Greek slave, Aesop. Pride in things distinctly Roman came with the erotic sequences of Propertius, Catullus, and, above all, Ovid, and with the satires of Juvenal and Persius, and with this pride came a sense of cultural legitimation, of satisfaction with the achievements of the Latin language-culture, which we can watch being repeated in the European vernaculars in the centuries which followed. The idea of 'referral' is perhaps now so obvious that it is worth inserting a reminder of the efficiency of a shared culture which allows authors to evoke, extend, ironize, misunderstand, and legitimate both their own new work and the old works to which they address themselves, even if one takes the extreme view that whatever they think they are doing, they always misinterpret. Writers never stopped looking over their shoulders. There is something Janus-faced in the way they look back to situate their work, while their additions look forward, transforming the inherited stock of literature. It is one of the paradoxes of Modernism that T. S. Eliot was much concerned to remind his contemporaries of this process.

The aim of Greek education had been to create good citizens and good government for the community.[4] In theory, literary study was one of the ways that the 'right' values could be inculcated in young men; preparing them to analyse and argue was a political education.[5] Much of the argument over methods of education concerns the dangers of teaching the techniques of persuasion without ensuring that the speakers will use their power wisely; it was never clear why a good orator would also be a good man, though many asserted, with Quintilian, that there would of necessity be no good orator who was not.[6] In the Platonic dialogues Socrates may outargue the sophists, but it was the sophists, with their control of the skills of rhetoric and the schools which taught them, who triumphed. Education increasingly stressed the techniques of good speaking and writing until, with the end of participatory democracy in Greece, and, similarly, the end of the Roman Republic, those techniques were divorced from the political life that had once been their reason for being. Education is conservative, and its methods remained. In practice, of course, the study of literature, because it describes and dramatizes the behaviour of human beings in greater variety than moral treatises do, continually provides material for questioning 'right' values. In the Middle Ages the insistence that it was safe to study classical texts about the Passions (e.g. anger, fear, sorrow, desire) because knowledge would provide a prophylactic against them, was never entirely convincing; no accent on allegory ensured that the allegorical reading superseded the literal one, if only because medieval readers were alert to the multiplicity of interpretation which could be brought to bear on all kinds of texts. Indeed, it is often not clear where 'Rhetoric' comes in medieval educational schemes, or even what it implies beyond an ambition to write as well as the model authors of Antiquity. At times it appears to identify a classicizing (and therefore archaizing) impulse in a medieval author. As components of the trivium, the first part of medieval university study, 'Grammar', 'Rhetoric', and 'Dialectic' were never hard and fast categories. If, broadly speaking, rhetoric appears to be a controversial label for the arts of persuasion, that may suffice as at least a place to start.

Excellence in Roman school displays continued to be a route to success up to the time of Augustine and Jerome, if only to the prestige of being famous for those displays. Indeed, the less the declamations were grounded in the possibilities of real action, the more extravagant the speakers became: when the subject was imaginary, with no consequences dependent on its outcome, method and style became all. Excellence was a matter of moving and persuading the audience, so that attention concentrated upon ways of manipulating their emotions.[7] The audience was a listening audience, even when the text is written to be read; and even the private reader read aloud to himself, or listened as someone else read aloud for him.[8] Texts were studied in order to understand how authors created moving scenes; the more moving the text, the better it served as a model: Seneca's melodrama or Ovid's witty eroticism.[9] In principle, the study of great literary texts was also the study of conduct, good and bad, so that the youthful imagination could exercise itself upon the dangers experienced by heroes of the past, and scholarly commentary on Seneca or Statius or Ovid encouraged moral interpretation. Commentary must, simply by regularly calling attention to certain aspects of texts rather than others, emphasize those aspects of the texts at the expense of different ways of reading. Decorative language easily became an end in itself rather than a means. If emphasis on preparation for public life faded, concern for individual morality continued to occupy generations of pedagogues, pagan or Christian. At the same time, the texts from which moral lessons were to be extracted – at whatever cost to the general interpretation of the texts – were the more treasured for themselves. The moral ends of literature were advanced by the study of style. Like the point about the good orator being, as of nature, a good man, so there is an assumption that literature, too, leads us to desire the good, indeed, teaches us what the good is. What is evil is recognizable and repugnant. This assumes a trained reader.

The survival of rhetoric-training was never uncontested, nor was it unvaried. Attempts to preserve, renew, improve, and modify the classroom texts and exercises concerned teachers, especially devout teachers, from generation to generation, as historians of both rhetoric and education have emphasized. Textbook writers such as Donatus in the fourth century and Priscian about the year 500 themselves became the subject of extensive annotation, supplying in writing perhaps what had long been oral explication in the classroom. At the end of the period, when economic expansion, printing, and the need for more educated clerks for secular society coincided to free more children to study, there were new textbooks for young readers which ran into many editions and were adopted all over western Europe. Rhetoric once more assumed a recognizable shape as a curriculum of study based on the exercises of Aphthonius and Hermogenes and praised by Cicero and Quintilian. There is a famous bravura performance by Erasmus of two hundred ways to vary the simplest polite greeting; in trying to show what can be done he never questions the idea that the two hundred variations express one thing.[10] Education was a leg up, a process to be digested and transcended, but not forgotten. If we are unable to see the attraction of lists of tropes and schemes it may be because we fail to understand the place of such a list in the training of potential orators and writers. Tacitly, what was being conveyed was the belief that the many varieties of expression represented the same reality. That is, there was *a* reality to be expressed.[11] Even the representation of a text by transfer into another language also represented at one further remove the reality to which that original text had referred.

If books on rhetoric described the three kinds of speeches and their divisions and subdivisions, these same kinds could always have been found in many works of verse and prose. Again, it is important to remember that the point of these formulae for construction was to enable both the orator and his audience to follow the organization of a long speech: the *orality* of this convention made it important to signpost and to repeat, even by counting sections on their fingers, as one finds medieval preachers doing in manuscript illustrations. As with the modern instruction to school children that essays have introductions, bodies, and conclusions, if the pattern is approached from the outside, artificially, the material may have to be tortured into the right shape. Start with a fact; with a quotation from a dictionary; always illustrate your point with three examples; end with a citation from a poem, critic, historian, encyclopedia: we, too, learn our conventions and write according to preconceived plans. Any sense that one kind of essay structure is natural and inevitable evaporates when juxtaposed with the intellectual habits of another culture: French schoolchildren, for example, learn that essays come in two balanced sections. Such training leads to taking certain habits of mind for granted.

Before considering the basic examples available in this training, let me begin by looking at a poet reading a poet using them. This is a famous, and complex, example of misinterpretation, a Christian example which illustrates both that great cultural change in which expectations of depravity replaced expectations of a natural desire for the good and also a striking instance of literary old-fashionedness. When Blake reinterpreted Milton's *Paradise Lost* in his own *Marriage of Heaven and Hell* he remarked that Milton was 'of the Devil's party without knowing it'. Blake's reasons seem to have had to do with the power and strength Satan exhibits, and especially the moving quality of his language. Blake thought that the skill invested in Satan implied sympathy with Satan, whether Milton knew it or not. The epigraph to this chapter is a reminder that the pretence of sympathy, even imaginative sympathy, is not the same as moral sympathy. Certainly, Milton goes out of his way to make a brilliant rhetorician of the Devil, whose speeches can be used to illustrate many of the orator's tricks. But that it is *tricks* that the Devil is up to is crucial to Milton's poem: Satan's arguments are consistently specious, and they appeal to the basest desires of the already corrupted angels, and to Eve. That is, characters *in* the poem interpret, and we, the readers, interpret *like them*, what Satan says, and *not like them*, because we also interpret their interpretation. The reader, who knows who is speaking, (unlike Eve, who cannot, since she is inside the fiction, be alert as we can) will be on his guard because he knows that Satan, father of lies, can be expected to cheat and deceive. Indeed, we 'heard' him say he was going to do just that. His *ethos*, his moral authority, is bad. It is also worth remembering that unless Satan is an exceptionally powerful speaker no one who listens to him (on whichever side of the story) will succumb to his temptations. He must not appear to be bad. Though he puts the best case for evil that he can he is still wrong. We are, and ought to be, moved, since rhetoric is directed at our emotions. For readers to be moved by Satan is an experience which also concerns human memory, and implicates us all in the susceptibility of the individual, fallen, human will. It was mankind's fate once to be seduced by that temptation, and no doubt Milton would agree that men are daily seduced by similar arguments – but this does not and cannot mean that *he* would subscribe to them. Recognize their power, yes, but endorse them, never. To be convinced by Satan is to repeat Adam's fall. To understand courage in a bad cause, great rhetoric serving evil, is to make temptation tempting, and to make a *poem* not a sermon. The danger arises because poems require interpretation, and they invite discussion.

It may be argued that this is a special case, not only late in the period under consideration, but an epic. First, as I hope the rest of this book will show, Milton's Satan exhibits one aspect of standard rhetorical training: arguments to urge someone to a course of action, a speech-type central to rhetorical training. Second, that Milton wrote epic poetry is not licence from the methods of good writing that obtained across the range of literary genres. Third, Milton's imaginative recreation of biblical events contains claims to render a kind of truth that his readers would have accepted as indeed historical. His is a plausible account of what might have happened; it therefore invites categorization as history. In his attempt to write an *English* epic that would, however, deal with the episodes which determined all subsequent human history Milton was creating a capping work in a line that went back to Homer, in a competition in which national, linguistic, pride as well as personal greatness were the prizes. His pedantry, like Ben Jonson's, was a claim about both literature and his place among its great creators. He was translating, adapting, and amplifying from earlier texts.[12] Fourth, the anachronisms of Milton's cosmology provide a reminder that 'the renaissance' did not open like a window; literary periodization is a retrospective and problematic convenience. *Paradise Lost* was a backward-looking archaism which commanded respect in part because of the dignity and ambition of its subject. Milton exploited a linguistically conservative text – the English Bible – to reassert a morally conservative story – the Fall – by means of a high prestige, but already apparently outmoded genre – Epic Poetry. The resulting paradox, that the claim to tell the truth is expressed by dramatic and emotive fiction, reminds us not least of the complexities any interpretable text invited. Questions about the plausibility of the historical account in *Paradise Lost* could be deferred either because or in spite of its sacred subject. Books which now seem to belong to the category 'fiction' once belonged to the category 'history', even if modern readers no longer care even to study works that were once treasures of comfort and inspiration.

In generalizing about rhetorical training as a necessary preliminary, I am aware that the 'system' I elucidate may never have existed in any single time or place in exactly the forms I describe. Educational theory is always tidier than the classroom. This book is not meant as a survey of educational practice from Antiquity to the end of the Renaissance, but an introduction to the range of expectations engendered by training along rhetorical lines. And the training itself changed according to place and circumstance. Medieval attempts to substitute Christian poems for Classical ones were a tribute to the necessity to retain the techniques while finding morally suitable matter on which to refine them.[13] Actual teachers no doubt fell far short of the aspirations that they shared, and in the early Middle Ages books and parchment were scarce. Yet whenever men were able to organize centres of learning, they looked back to the schools of Antiquity for their models, and studied the same texts, with accretions of commentaries, the same masters of rhetoric. Medieval libraries contained hundreds of copies of Cicero's rhetorical works, often with the commentaries of Victorinus. To be articulate was to emulate the styles and methods of classical Latin literature, first in evolving Latin, then in the European vernaculars. This encouraged the idea of a standard of correctness impossible to emulate. Handbooks, rulebooks, even students' exercise books exist in enough numbers to assure us of the continuity of rhetorical aspirations and ideals. So do, more importantly, references – sometimes witty, sometimes denigrating – to the shared experience of schools texts and techniques (see below for an example from Francis Bacon). Although there are questions about the attention paid to classical rhetorical texts in the monasteries, recent scholarship confirms the suspicion that a larger number of ancient texts circulated than has hitherto been thought.[14] Articulate men were not common; the education I describe was, at its most sophisticated, relatively rare. At any time many of its lessons could be extracted by imitation of model texts, where commentators perpetually called attention to precisely those small-scale features which were the heart of detailed rhetorical instruction. A reassessment of rhetorical habits of mind may make it possible to appreciate – not least to understand – a range of medieval and renaissance texts which will otherwise remain at best quaint, at worst incomprehensible. Although it can be argued that some arts die and stay dead, even as this book is being written political speechwriters all over the world have rediscovered ancient rhetorical analyses, and have put them to use for modern speeches, using especially the topics and sound patterns which move audiences. This gives the re-educated modern orator a great advantage over relatively innocent audiences, whose emotions may be manipulated without their appreciating why. The ancient habit of analysing texts encouraged appreciation, but also created a defence.

Wherever it is found, rhetorical education emphasizes preservation and imitation. Masters like Donatus and Priscian, at the level of most basic grammarians, to Martianus Cappella (early fifth century) or Cassiodorus (early sixth century) at a more sophisticated level of educational theory, insisted that the student learn to read and comment upon an agreed corpus of Latin texts so that he could proceed from the appreciation of the masters' skills in rhetoric to the acquisition of his own.[15] This means quite a different approach to the 'set texts' from that we are accustomed to. For one thing, they looked different: the texts were mediated by commentaries, either in the margins, or as accompanying books. This created an impression of dialogue, almost of simultaneity: the poet's voice with constant accompaniment. This dialogue was a constant discussion of how to read. For a text to acquire a commentary became a mark of seriousness: not only classical poems, like the *Aeneid*, but classical rhetorical texts, like the *Ad Herrenium*, which was thought to be the work of Cicero, appeared with annotations. Commenting upon the sacred texts of Judaism or Christianity followed this model, as, later, did Arabic commentaries on Aristotle or the Koran. So, even later, did renowned secular texts, like Dante's *Commedia* as early as the thirteenth century, or Spenser's *Shepheardes Calender* in 1579, which was actually published with its commentary already provided. So, too, a quasi-legal text like the sixteenth-century description of the trial of 'Martin Guerre' could boast of its 111 annotations.[16]

### LEARNING THROUGH COMMENTED TEXTS

Plate 1 illustrates an early printed text of one of the most widely used commentaries on Virgil's *Aeneid*; this was a compendium of earlier commentaries, and not solely the work of Servius, the late-fourth-century scholar to whom it was ascribed.[17] This first example of what such texts looked like shows how their presentation discouraged continuous reading. Where commentaries were printed separately one would have constantly to look from one book to the other. Typically, Servius preserves grammatical

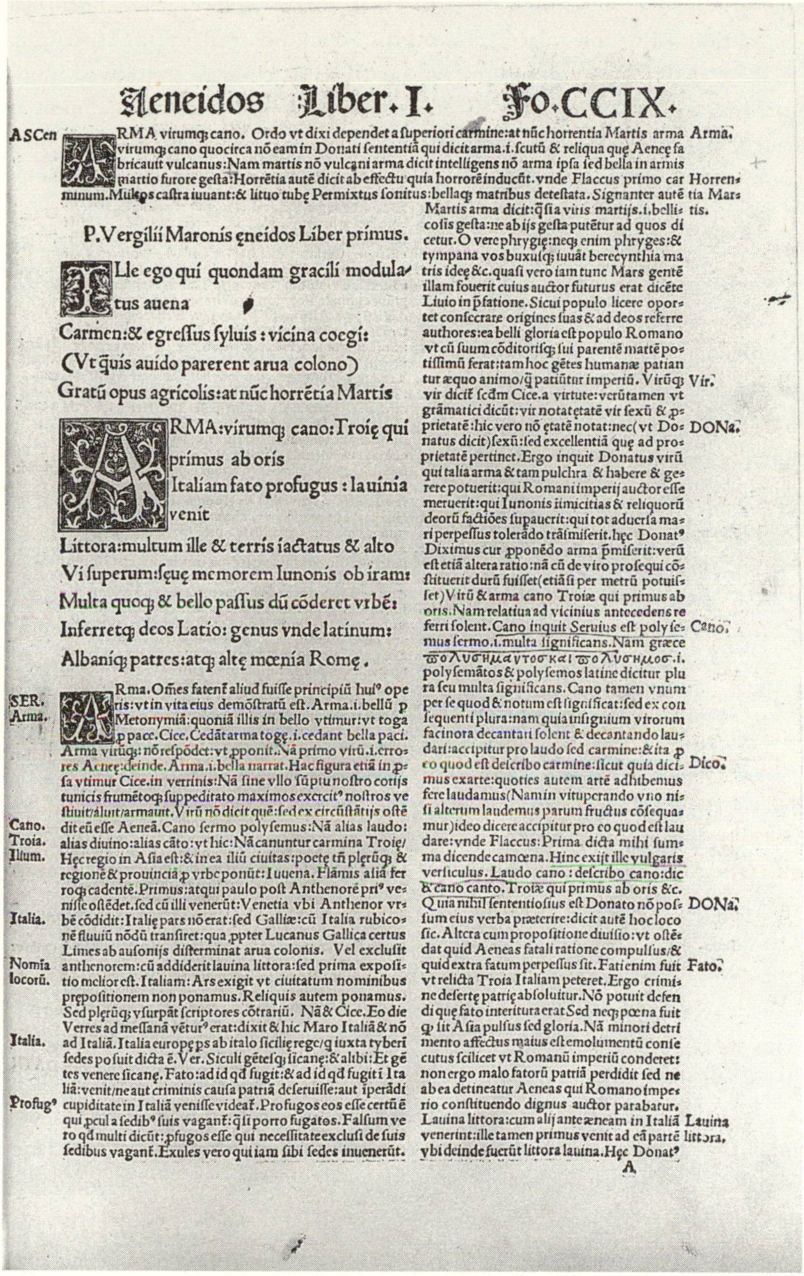

Plate 1   *Aeneid* Book I with annotations compiled (and labelled in the margins) from Servius, Donatus, and other Commentators by J. Ascensius (Paris, 1507).

and syntactic explanations of individual words and phrases, historical elucidations of people, places, and myths which the student might require, detailed analyses of the figures of speech which Virgil employed, and, infrequently, explanations of Virgil's characterization (often at the point at which an apparent inconsistency needs to be explained away). Such commentary emphasizes the detail almost to the exclusion of the larger issues of literary criticism which engage classical scholars working on the same texts today. Yet there was intertextual explication of Virgil's imitations and adaptations of earlier versions of his story as well as earlier epic models (telling different stories) for his poem. It is not enough to explain this approach to the model authors by the need to analyse and maintain a literary language, Latin, which became ever more alien to its readers. Of course they went to their authors for style, to learn the techniques of writing which were agreed to be the best for moving and persuading, but they also read epic for love of epic.

Even commentaries did more than one thing, and can illustrate the penetrability of genres. One of the most famous, contemporary with Servius, the *Saturnalia* of Macrobius, detaches itself from its subject, Virgil's *Aeneid*, and preserves, in its form, an example of a 'Dialogue', that is, a report of conversation among a group of learned friends.[18] The *Dialogues* of Plato were the model for Macrobius, but with the exception of the *Timaeus*, these were not available in the Latin-speaking West until the fourteenth century, which suggests that the philosophical dialogue was represented by texts which discussed other texts, and shows the way that a commentary could begin to move towards becoming a literary work in its own right. This is also true of another commentary by Macrobius, this time on only a section of a Dialogue by Cicero in which a dream is reported. 'Macrobius on the Dream of Scipio' is the only way in which this work survives, although 'survives' does nothing to convey the way the embedded dream appears, laden as it is with the weight of information about the theory of dreams.[19] This work in turn became a source for other authors, of whom Chaucer is probably the best known: his *Book of the Duchess* begins with a narrator reading this dream commentary, then dreaming himself, with an implied invitation to the reader to comment upon the new dream. The dream becomes a 'text' which invites commentary.

Commentaries attracted commentaries. The *Talmud* begins with the *Pentateuch*, upon which there is a first commentary, which itself became the focus for a later commentary, so that printed texts have three 'layers' for

study. In the High Middle Ages the *Sentences* of Peter Lombard, themselves
an exercise in biblical interpretation, attracted further commentary, formalized by the University of Paris as a subject which all students were
required to study and discuss.

The Bible is, of course, the most commented text, because it is both the
most important and the most difficult to understand. It also became a source
of stylistic examples for writers of rhetoric books who wished to substitute
morally unexceptionable rhetorical models for their students that would
keep them away from the dangerous pagan texts that were the focus of the
textbooks of Donatus and Priscian and the like.[20]

The existence and continued prestige of pagan literature posed a constant
challenge to medieval and renaissance Christians. Emphasis upon classical
literary texts as sources for imitation preserved the texts, whatever else it did,
and though they might be read as the commentators wished, they might be
read in other ways as well. The imaginative arts are always a threat, not only
because they encourage multiple interpretations of cause and motive (with a
concomitant urbanity which turns understanding to forgiveness), nor solely
because their dramatizations of questionable behaviour may enshrine the
very values they are meant to castigate (forgiveness turns to envy and
approval), but above all because the pleasures of story-telling, of going
somewhere else and becoming, even for an hour, someone else, complicate –
by their existence – our moral responses to experience. From Jerome's self-
accusation at the beginning of the period that he was a Ciceronian rather
than a Christian there was no question but that fascination with content and
style carried undeniable risks to the devout. Flirtation has not always
culminated in fastidious rejection. Augustine's arguments in *De Doctrina
Christiana* opened the door to centuries of classicizing Christians.[21] As the
children of Israel put the Egyptians' gold to better use, so Christians would
reinterpret pagan culture. Augustine's argument is, perhaps, vulnerable to
the reminder that the Children of Israel used their stolen gold to make the
Golden Calf, that symbol of whoring after false gods, as soon as Moses
turned his back. Augustine's habit of treating an analogy as a demonstration,
of reading one thing and interpreting it as another, remained a staple of
applied interpretation throughout the Middle Ages. He and Jerome were, in
effect, introducing a fifth column; by building into education the assumption
that the 'best' models and techniques were those of pagan Rome, they
authorized the argument that pagan writing should be preserved as an
integral part of a Christian writer's education. In 1513 Gavin Douglas was

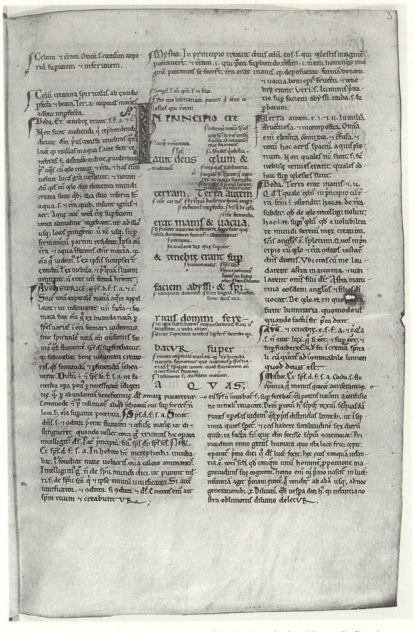

Plate 2    The opening of the Book of Genesis with the Glossa Ordinaria
(twelfth century).

still referring to Augustine's weeping over Dido. They built temptation into their educational methods: of the pagan party without knowing it. The justification is of particular importance in a culture ostensibly uneasy with fiction or poetry (which is invented) that either fails to direct readers toward God or actually celebrates worldly experience. If the study of classical 'models' did nothing else it preserved the category and prestige of 'poetry'. And 'poetry', because it is thought-provoking about human beings, remains a source of knowledge. Agreeing a standard of 'good style' also elevates the texts which embody it, and it is impossible to read those texts simply for 'good style'. This has many implications.

By the time medieval grammarians came to write their own textbooks, the incongruities of training future churchmen on a diet of Virgil's *pietas* or Ovid's lovers, or the martial ardour celebrated by pagan Romans, had become an ineradicable argument in the literary–philosophical heritage of Europe. Pagan examples may have been held up to new readers as examples of behaviour to eschew, but they were, necessarily, the examples discussed wherever method and style were discussed. Augustine's *Confessions* preserved – and legitimated – a serious reaction to Dido and made readers' reactions to her fate a pinnacle of emotive expressiveness, both for them and for aspiring writers. It is almost a piece of structural bad faith: it is all right to weep over Dido as long as you are aware that it is not all right to weep over Dido. There were attempts, of course, to replace pagan texts with Christian secular ones. But the context of Latinity and of belief – as well as the absence of genius – had changed too radically for this ambition to succeed for long; it is part of the power of the *Aeneid* that it, too, is a backward-looking text which preserves a kind of cultural archaeology. Theodulus wrote an early Christian pastoral in either the ninth or the tenth century, and John of Garland was still trying in the twelfth century.[22] Not only had the pagan texts greater prestige, since they formed part of the culture inherited from the greatest civilization the western world had known, but they were *better*. Great literature escapes strictures about *usefulness*. This question of quality will dog the following chapters.

Classical Latin maintained its appeal wherever there were readers capable of understanding (or misunderstanding) it. Such readers, who had progressed beyond the point of painfully deciphering the difficult and various styles to the level of reading them and loving them, were also the writers who would emulate classical achievements in their own writing. If, because of the changes in medieval Latin, they could no longer scan in quantitative measures, they could and did write stressed and rhymed poetry that won the admiration of their contemporaries. Medieval Latin was flexible, rich in philosophical and theological terms, and ultimately adequate to the writing of epic, history, and stylish letters, on the models of pagan antiquity, or as need and imagination developed.[23] It is easy to remark, though difficult to explain, that the most ambitious medieval writers were the likeliest to understand and imitate the lessons of classical rhetoric, to make something successful of it. Priority counts. 'Rhetoric' is not the name of an answer; it is the problem.

The prestige of classical literary forms ensured that, whatever adaptations were made to the models, as long as they survived they could remain points of reference for imitation, an agreed, generally known and acknowledged corpus of masterpieces for study and imitation. Renaissance schoolmasters in England asked their students to do a kind of double translation exercise, in which a passage of Latin verse was rewritten in prose, then transformed back into verse to the best of the student's ability. This was merely a case of doing twice what generations of schoolboys had done once, and translating one's own translation. Translation was a method of interpretation – and vice versa. (I shall look at a serious example of rewriting the same material in different styles in Chapter 3 and in more detail at translation as rhetorical transformation in Chapter 4.) The habit of transforming a model passage was integral to rhetorical education from the beginning. Putting a speech into leonine hexameters or elegaic couplets concentrates the student's mind on style, on synonymy and rhythm, certainly on bravura expression. It creates important and ineradicable habits and expectations in a reader's mind, too, since it encourages alertness to techniques that recommend themselves as imitable. This runs from the small-scale phrase which will fit a line of verse in the right place, or, better still, establish a model rhythm upon which other similar phrases can be generated (this came to be of great importance in the twelfth century when the *cursus*, or rhythmic sentence ending, became fashionable in the art of writing letters), to the sentence- or paragraph-long structural unit. Rhetorical questions, as we call them, provide a clear example of this method of organization and expansion. In a culture which is primarily oral, even when reading, they make that kind of useful repetition which helps the ear to recognize what is to come by a clear announcement of the topic (or sound) to follow. Even if one were asked to adapt pagan structure to a Christian subject, the result would be the twofold preservation of the pagan model as a reference for arbitration and emulation (because it continues to be the model for excellence) but, more insidiously, as a model of a subject which counts, that is, which provides the mark of what has to be superseded.[24] Churchmen who adapted in this way pagan or secular subjects risked enshrining just those models of behaviour and secular value that they would perhaps most have wished to denigrate. Heroic action, public debate, and the many and complex reactions to sexual passion, threatened to become a staple diet for aspiring writers, for whom one text often referred to another, earlier, text.

The dangers inherent in the study of pagan literature did not go unremarked; as the model of what was to be superseded pagan poets inspired Christian imitation until by the early twelfth century there was an abundant corpus of medieval Latin literature which could be studied without harm to the soul, even if it recapitulated pagan models. (That there was also an abundant corpus of medieval Latin literature which was secular in orientation and therefore reinforced those ambitions and experiences of most potential harm to the soul is another matter.) The arguments about how to use pagan gold, how to make pagan literature 'safe' for Christianity, were continual. One method already had deep roots in pagan culture itself: allegory. Allegorical interpretations which turned Aeneas's wanderings into the wanderings of the human soul, or Ovid's *Metamorphoses* into a Christianized struggle of good against evil, however extravagant, occupied the fertile minds of commentators who wanted to preserve the culture of pagan antiquity while putting it to use. This approach can be illustrated by this paragraph from a commentary on the *Aeneid* once attributed to Bernardus Silvestris:

Some poets (such as the satirists) write for instruction; some (such as the comic playwrights) write for delight; and some (such as the historians) write for both. Horace speaks about this: 'Poets aim either to benefit or to amuse or to utter words at once both pleasing and helpful to life' (Art of Poetry, 333–4). The *Aeneid* gives pleasure because of verbal ornament, the figures of speech, and the diverse adventures and works of the men which it describes. Indeed, anyone who imitates these matters diligently will attain the greatest skill in the art of writing, and he will also find in the narrative the greatest examples of and inspiration for pursuing virtue and avoiding vice. Thus, there is a double gain for the reader: the first is skill in composition which comes from imitation, and the second is the good sense to act properly which comes from the stimulus of examples. For instance, the labors of Aeneas are an example of patience; similarly, we are called to religion by Aeneas's piety toward Anchises and Ascanius, by this veneration of the gods and the oracles which he consults, by the sacrifices which he offers, and by the devotion and prayers which he utters. We are recalled from appetite for unlawful things by his immoderate love for Dido.[25]

The strength of this approach is the easier to understand if one thinks either of Jung, finding 'real' similarities between the most disparate cultures in order to uncover mankind's shared unconscious, or the witty punning of currently fashionable Deconstructionists. It depends upon the assumption that if the commentator can imagine something it must be there, and that the wealth of verbal free association will reveal something about the universe because words refer to real things, and that association must associate real things. The full-blown medieval allegorical approach, by which any pious equivalent can be inflicted on the events or persons of a narrative without regard to consistency, to tone, to the poetry thus distorted, can be seen at its most arbitrary in such works as the *Ovide moralisé*, from which, after all, many late-medieval readers learned their mythology.[26] What is striking about this approach to texts is the way it subordinates them to the interpretation to which they give rise; it elevates scholiast, commentator or critic above the original artist, who, for the pleasure and edification of his audience, clothed his true meaning in dark veils which only learned interpretation can remove. The shrine to Difficulty may be the most tenacious of Golden Calves.

While allegorizing commentary defused the dangers of the text, and preserved the habit of reading the text for something else, it safeguarded both the text and the method of interpretation. However much it became a convenience for the discussion of interpretations only tenuously related to the original, the original survived, and survived as 'essential reading'. William Caxton's version of this argument appears in his preface to his translation of a fifteenth-century Burgundian prose version of the *Ovide Moralisé*, which includes an interpretation of the title of Ovid's poem:

And thenne among the Latyn Poetes Ovyde of Salmonence is to be preysed and honoured hyely . . . His werke is ryghte excellent and notable. Of whyche bycause of the perycye and subtilte of the fables wherin is conteyned grete and prouffitable wysedom to them that knowe and understande theme, he imposed the name Methamorphose, which is asmoche to say as transmutacion of one fable into another interpretacion of theym. For he, seeng as wel the Latin Poetes as the Poetes of Grece that had ben tofore hym and hys tyme, hade touched in wrytyng many fables and them passed superfycyelly without expressynge theyre knowledge or entendement. The sayde Ovide hath opend unto the Latyns the way as wel in the fables of Grekes as in other, and hath them tyssued and woven by so gret subtyltee of engyne, charge, and solicytude in such wyse that one by that other that it myght be sayde very semblably that they depended one of another and that by such ordre that frome the creacion of the world unto hys tyme he had ordeyned hys sayengs, some by fable and some by hystorye only. And otherwyse tyssued and medled with fable and hystorye togidre, which is a thyng right subtil. And his dittes or sayengs ben not to be repudyed ne reproched ther as they ne conteyn but fable only.

For over and above theloquence whiche is right swete, under veyle or shadowe hyd, he compryseth the scyence and advertysement of grete partye of thingis comen or at leste by possybylite ben for to com. And yf the cronyclers of hystoryes had wryten by so cler and lyght style the gestes and feates of the noble and valyant men or of thynges possible to come, thenne eche man might at the first sight have conceyved and comprised theym, where they hade be holden thenne more for Phylosophers than for Poetes . . .

For whoso can discovre and take away the veyle or shadowe fro the fables, he shal see clerly sometyme poetrye and somtyme right hye phylosophye; under other scyence of Ethique, under other yconomyque, under other polytique; under other he shal fynde geste or hystorye comprysed, yf he wil entende and enploye hys tyme by aspre diligence.[27]

This is a secular version of the ways that the Bible had been interpreted, especially such awkward books as the *Song of Songs*, which collects a series of erotic poems, ensuring their place in the canon by attributing them to King Solomon and by allegorizing the eroticism away, into the 'higher' love of God for his chosen people (Hebrew tradition) or Christ and his church (Christian). Nevertheless, here, too, the literal meaning survives and is accessible to anyone who looks at it, despite structures from the commentators that the literal meaning is to be understood only in the context of the allegorical ones.

Long before 'Bernardus', Virgil had become a storehouse of ancient wisdom for his readers, and past veneration for him only increased with time: another way of safeguarding, if not making safe. The extract quoted emphasizes Virgil's importance as a model for all the styles and all the figures of speech that the aspiring writer might need. In the early, widely used Dialogue, the *Saturnalia* of Macrobius, the fourth book celebrates while it analyses Virgil's skills in the art of oratory. Two long quotations will illustrate the method:

Let us consider now how the pattern of a speech expresses and evokes emotion; and first let us ask what are the rules of rhetoric for such a speech. Being concerned with emotion the speech should certainly seek to express and arouse either indignation or pity . . .; and of these two emotions the *prosecution* is necessarily concerned with one, the *defense* with the other. To express and arouse indignation the opening of the speech must be abrupt, since a quiet opening would be ill fitted to its purpose. And that is why Vergil makes Juno, in her indignation, begin a speech as follows:

Why dost thou compel me to break my deep silence?        (*Aeneid* x.63)

Notice the way the commentary subsumes 'character' into a legal metaphor. This is itself an instance of the circularity of rhetorical habits of analysis, as will be clearer when I consider the debate-exercises in more detail. And Macrobius goes on to give five more examples, of which four are rhetorical questions like the one quoted. In the next section he writes:

Nor is it only the opening words that should follow the examples I have suggested, but, if possible, the speech as a whole should be calculated to express and arouse emotion, both by the brevity of the sentences and by the frequent changes of the figures employed, thus giving the impression that the speaker is, as it were, being borne to and fro amid surging waves of anger. Let us take, then, a single speech in Vergil as an example. It begins with an exclamation:

O hated race!

Then follow a number of short questions:

Did they fall on the Sigean plains? Could they, once captured, be held captive? Did the flames of Troy consume the Trojans?

Then comes the figure 'hyperbole':

Through the midst of armies in battle array, and through the midst of flames, they have found a way.

Then 'irony':

But, methinks, my divine powers lie spent at last, and flag; or I have sated my hatred, and now desist.[28]

Among the unstated assumptions which these extracts reveal is the stress on Virgil's skill as an *orator* (rather than a poet writing for the private reader), a master of the art of moving and persuading an audience in order to praise Augustus. Macrobius points out the common assumption that to raise anger the orator must simulate it himself. This sense of rhetoric as a complex *courtroom* skill was, indeed, all pervasive, and the approach to speeches within the poem as examples of ways to move an audience as if in court shows what Macrobius was looking for. The accent on strong emotions, like indignation or pathos, encouraged writers to imitate – and exaggerate – just such moments (Ovid's *Heroides*, like Seneca's plays, reinforced this by providing more passages of characters in the grip of overpowering emotion). Virgil is praised for exemplifying a series of rules, as if he had written his poetry with a checklist of figures in hand, and ticked each off as he used it; the student is encouraged in turn to read with his own mental checklist, making extracts as he goes. This is perhaps a pedagogic necessity: figures of speech happen naturally, but teaching them encourages an artificial feeling about 'discovering' them whenever they occur. This in turn emphasizes an artificial kind of composition, in which the search for metaphors displaces their natural occurrence. The decorative use of ever-more-extended epic similes (comparisons using 'like' to give analogies to the experiences described) are a notorious example. Classical epic similes were often taken from the animal world, characterizing by emblematic likeness: fierce as a lion might stand as shorthand, but there is a complex relationship here to the world of fable which is seldom explored. Epic similes are ornamental and appropriate to epic, and medieval writers imitated them in order to raise the register of their tales. In Statius' *Thebaid* x he describes a character fighting to protect the body of his friend in a style typical of this easily imitable author:

> Now he
> stands his ground, making his drawn sword a barrier;
> he turned to face all missiles, to kill or be killed.
> Alert as a lioness who protects her young
> when hunting Numidians trap her in her fierce lair,
> whose mind is torn, growling savage and pitiful –
> she could bite through missiles and sow confusion,
> but love of her cubs overwhelms her cruel feelings,
> and in the midst of her rage she looks around at
> them.                                   (11. 414-19, my translation)

Either this or some similar example lies behind Chaucer's analogy for Arcite's pursuit of his friend, Palamon, in the *Knight's Tale*, ll. 2626–9:

> Ther nas no tygre in the vale of Galgopheye,
> Whan that hir whelp is stole whan it is lite,
> So crueel on the hunte as is Arcite
> For jelous herte upon this Palamon.

Sometimes the comparisons grow incongruously, distractingly. Yet such extravagance was an achievement of sorts, compelling the reader to think about the skill of the presentation rather than the mimesis. Even if the classroom experience disappears, as long as the commentators survive the voice of the pedagogue is heard in the land, expounding, and, in his exposition, tacitly but powerfully insisting that these are the ways Virgil and Statius were and should continue to be read.

Epic was the place where poetry was at its most historical. For 'Bernardus Silvestris' Virgil is a writer of historical poetry who presents the reader with examples (both rhetorical and moral) for consideration, contemplation, even imitation. The extract quoted above approaches Virgil in familiar categories. He begins with the imitation of Virgil's fine writing, which he sees in terms not of structural characteristics or insight into character and situation, but of verbal ornament. The events of the poems exemplify something else: patience, piety, and restraint – or their opposites. 'Bernardus' reads as if Virgil's poem were a cipher which it is the reader's duty to break. He uses the etymology of names as a key to the 'true' meaning of the poem, which is an allegorical exploration of the development of the human soul. The *Aeneid* he makes safe for Christian readers is hardly an *Aeneid* we would recognize as Virgil's.

It is hard to recreate a sense of just how 'mediated' these privileged texts appeared; it is always difficult to recapture another habit of reading. The illustration (Plate 3) of The Interpreter's Bible takes 'mediated reading' to one modern extreme, lacking only a column of the original language. This book is meant to be used for detailed examination of the text. Unlike medieval commentaries, from which it descends, the modern explication assumes that the reader owns another, less heavily annotated copy of the same text. This is a reference book, intended to accompany, not to replace, the reader's usual Bible. (There will be detailed discussion of these points, especially the relations between 'accompaniment' and 'substitute' translations, in Chapter 4.) There is a tentativeness to this idea that the words indicate something beyond themselves that can be expressed in many other ways, which makes them counters, or symbols, into which a prelinguistic reality has been temporarily coded. Since medieval and renaissance habits of reading preceded and informed habits of writing (not least because they knew the allegorizing tendencies of some, at least, of their readers), it is worth making the effort.

The very scarcity of written texts of any kind meant that students memorized what they read, or what they heard read out to them. This meant, as well, that they proceeded only very slowly, since a few lines a day are all that can be absorbed on this method, whether one is memorizing the Psalter or Virgil. In the twelfth century, John of Salisbury, an early and exceptional classicizing scholar (and biographer of Becket) describes his own

A Psalm of David.

**23** The Lord *is* my shepherd; I shall not want.

A Psalm of David.

**23** The Lord is my shepherd, I shall not want;

---

### XXIII. The Goodness of the Lord (23:1-6)

In the course of the centuries this psalm has won for itself a supreme place in the religious literature of the world. All who read it, whatever their age, race, or circumstances, find in the quiet beauty of its thoughts a range and depth of spiritual insight that both satisfies and possesses their souls. It belongs to that class of psalms that breathe confidence and trust in the Lord. Such psalms resemble the concluding section or strophe of a lament, which ordinarily consists of a strong affirmation of faith in the loving care of the Lord. So here the psalmist has no preface of complaints about the pains of sickness or the treachery of enemies, but begins, as he ends, only with words of grateful acknowledgment of the never-failing goodness of the Lord.

---

Once again we must move on from the psalm to Christ.

Vss. 27-30 express in the form of a hymn the hope for a universal kingdom under the rule of God. They may well call to mind our own aspirations: **All the families of the nations shall worship before him** (vs. 27). **Yea, to him shall all the proud of the earth bow down** (vs. 28). **Posterity shall serve him** (vs. 30) would be a good slogan for the religious education departments of churches. A helpful suggestion is to link vs. 22 with vs. 30. **I will tell of thy name;** so will there be more likelihood that **posterity shall serve him:** "I" being especially a father or a mother. **Posterity** should be particularized. The thought of far-off generations has no power to hit home on the mind; **for us posterity** means our own children, or all children whom we can help. That does hit home on the mind, and helps us to change the mood of the verb **shall serve** from mere future to a future of purpose. **Posterity,** our immediate posterity, "shall serve him, God being our helper."

Was something of this same confidence in the mind of Jesus, even as he cried out in that

moment of dereliction? What was going on around him must inevitably have reminded him, for instance, of vss. 7-10. What vision broke on his closing eyes? (Cf. vss. 27-31.)

**23:1-6. Shepherd and Host.**—What is there about this psalm that makes it so beloved? For it is but a simple little lyric, artless and sunny, written by some godly Hebrew Robert Burns in a restful moment, when he sang because he must. Yet it is hardly too much to say that along with the Lord's Prayer it is the best-known passage in the Bible; and it has proved a mine for the expositor.

It is of some value to attempt an explanation of the unique affection with which people of all sorts and conditions regard it. Its brief simplicity is one reason. Here is no elaborate ode, smelling of midnight oil. Even for those who find a change of imagery from the shepherd to the host in vs. 5, an underlying unity is retained, with a meaning which he who runs may read. But the main point about it is its realism. This is no sundial recording only sunny hours: it faces faithfully the dark defile and the lurking foes. At the same time it honestly and thank-

123

---

Plate 3    The opening of Psalm 23 from *The Interpreter's Bible: The Holy Scriptures in the King James and Revised Standard Version with General Articles and Introductions, Exegesis, Exposition for each book of the Bible* (1955).

teacher, the famous Bernard of Chartres, reading and commenting – obviously at a fairly advanced stage of study – upon the texts that were the object of elucidation.[29] Bernard's comments identified the grammatical and syntactic structure of the language and explained the hard words; historical information further illuminated the passage, so that mythological allusions, historical actors, important events would become familiar to students removed in time and culture from the Latin of the texts. The beauties of the passage, labelled with their rhetorical names, were identified to help the students understand how the passage achieved its emotional effects. John says that at the end of each day students would compose and deliver sermons to each other (this was Christian training for twelfth-century clerics); this was probably a means of putting into practice the literary techniques they had been studying during the day. Turning literary study to Christian use by improving the students' ability to preach was both justification of literary study and demonstration of the use to which it was meant to be put. The preacher replaces the Orator.

John's description sounds like an advanced group of students who are already able to mix analysis and practice. The references to hard words and mythological and historical information suggest that the text under consideration may have been classical, perhaps Virgil. Obviously the young John of Salisbury did not start there. Much preparation was required before schoolboys could hope to understand the letter, let alone the spirit, of this greatest of poets. Similar difficulties attended the study of the greatest of prose masters, Cicero.[30] If these two authors represented the summit of Latin literature, brooding over the curriculum, there were slopes and foothills to be conquered along the way as students toiled up the mountain of eloquence that they called Parnassus. The cultivation of an orator began early in childhood with moral and literary training on texts more suitable to children than the wanderings of Aeneas. From the beginning the goals were clear, and when John came to write his own rhetorical textbooks he maintained them as he had been taught them: teach good Latin models, alert readers and writers to shared elements of style, inculcate virtue. It must always be remembered that 'grammar' was 'Latin grammar', and that these generations of schoolboys were educated in a language which they had to acquire at school, so that even memorizing rules added to their vocabulary, if the rules they memorized were themselves in the Latin they were learning.[31]

They began with the distichs of Cato.[32] Schoolboys memorized these Latin sayings for hundreds of years – a feature of Erasmus's commitment to education was his edition of a text of 'Cato' for use in schools. The distichs are simple phrases and couplets which were memorized and analysed, for their grammar, vocabulary, and wisdom. Their level of difficulty, at least at the early stages, corresponds to the hornbook rhymes from which English and colonial American children learned their alphabet:

In Adam's fall
We sinned all.

So young children learned by heart 'Deo supplica', 'Parentes ama', 'Cum bonis ambula'. These injunctions to worship God, love one's parents, and keep good company were so much part of what everybody who had been to school knew by heart that they could be referred to by medieval writers and poets with the assurance of instant recognition. In the collection of poems known as the *Carmina Burana* there is one that is a kind of joke sermon on the virtue of charity in which the author considers the importance of choosing a recipient worthy of the gift and the donor, and ends with the suggestion that he himself is the best choice for a patron's generosity. This is the second verse, where he is still building his case for careful selection:

Si legisse memoras
ethicam Catonis,
in qua scriptum legitur:
'ambula cum bonis',
cum ad dandi gloriam
animum disponis,
inter cetera
hoc primum considera,
quis sit dignus donis.

(If you remember reading Cato's ethics, we find written there, 'Keep good company'; now if your mind is disposed towards the glory of giving, above all your first consideration should be that the recipient is worthy.)

The irony is perhaps obvious, but the point is that the humour depends on the shared culture that some kind of shared rhetorical education created.[33] In a similar fashion one of the distichs is recalled in Chaucer's *Nun's Priest's Tale*, where Chanticleer the cock and his wife are arguing about the truth (or lack of it) revealed in dreams. 'Somnia ne cures', pay no attention to dreams, quotes the hen, trying to convince her husband that the nightmare he has just had has nothing to do with prognostication, and everything to do with what he had for dinner the night before. Here the 'little learning' of the birds is not only funny in the way that fables always are when animals ape the habits of humans, but also funny as part of a longer and more complex discussion of the value of authority as opposed to experience which appears and reappears throughout the course of Chaucer's story competition. Only a reader who recognizes the puerility of the textual authority Pertelote adduces will understand the irony of the reference. The ignorant will miss the joke.

It must not be thought that Cato's distichs were always quoted in order to be mocked, though certainly what is taken seriously for schoolboys looks different from the perspective given by age and increased literary sophistication. There were commentaries written on the Distichs, which called attention to grammar, vocabulary, moral parallels in other authors, and also stylistic parallels in harder texts to follow. In the prologue to Book II of the Distichs there is an anticipation of the pleasure and knowledge to come when the boys will find themselves tackling Virgil. There are other hills to be climbed first, however, and the simplicity of Cato was followed by longer – though still quite short – poems that continued to press home important moral doctrines, this time through the simple allegory of the beast fable (of which, of course, the Nun's Priest presents a superb example).

Avianus was responsible for one of the most popular versions of what we know as Aesop's fables.[34] These, like the Distichs, came accompanied by commentary. Yet even had they been taught unadorned, they would still have inculcated in their young readers the habit of interpreting the literal sense as an example of something else – in this case abstract moral precepts. The manuscripts which preserve the collections of fables, whether they be Avian's or Aesop's, are often quite clearly school anthologies. It is likely that the schoolmaster would prepare one of the fables for study: memorization and then imitation. Certainly in the Eastern Empire the fable was the first piece of writing which schoolboys practised, and there is no reason to think that the western schoolboy's experience was different. The roots of this tradition go back to Antiquity, and forward as well – French schoolchildren still memorize La Fontaine's French fables. Where the model fable was in verse, the schoolboy could be set to summarizing it in prose. He could expand it by the addition of description, dialogue, multiplication of examples, or expansion of the summarizing *moralitas* with which most fables ended. This kind of summary and concentration upon amplification was basic to the kind of education which children received. One measure of the seriousness with which these exercises were taken is the number of versions

of fables written by authors well known for their achievements in more
sophisticated forms of poetry and prose. Not just writers, either, since Plato's
*Apology* tells of finding Socrates versifying a fable on the night before his
execution. Socrates explained that his *daimon*, the inner voice he had always
obeyed, had told him to 'practise the art', which he had hitherto understood
to mean philosophy. Now he wondered if by 'the art' poetry were not
meant. What Plato would expect any reader to understand is that in
versifying a fable on the night before he was to die, Socrates demonstrated
the humility of starting at the beginning, like a schoolboy with all his life
before him.

In the Middle Ages fables were often recommended by prominent
churchmen, who were probably directly involved in the education of future
orators, so that there was every reason both to teach eloquence and to stock
the minds of preachers with fables that they would be able to use to instruct
their congregations. Modern readers perhaps tend to take fables much less
seriously, as stories only to be told to very young children, and then left
behind; the contrast with medieval esteem for the fable could not be more
marked. A list of the poets who wrote fables includes the late-twelfth- or
early-thirteenth-century Anglo-Norman Marie de France, better known
today for a series of exquisite *lais*, stories which celebrate the experience of
loving, but whose *Fables* represent more than half of her output (they are also
the earliest vernacular fable collection); the writers – from the twelfth to the
fifteenth centuries – who exploited the saga of Reynard the Fox; Chaucer,
who wrote one perfect beast fable for his *Canterbury Tales*; the fifteenth-
century poet, Robert Henryson, better known for his sequel to Chaucer's
*Troilus*;[35] and the sixteenth-century courtier-poet Thomas Wyatt, that most
moral and intellectual writer among the glittering circle who surrounded
Henry VIII;[36] and after our period one can add the names of other satirists
and critics like John Gay, better known for his *Beggar's Opera*; Lessing, and,
of course, La Fontaine, a selection of whose poems has recently been
translated into English by James Michie.[37] As late as the eighteenth century
fables might still be used with complete political seriousness: *The Fable of the
Bees* is the title of a treatise by Mandeville about the monarchical system of
government, a government apparently represented by the hive. Nor would
anyone wish to omit Orwell's *Animal Farm* from such a list.

Fables were taken seriously for their own sake, not only as a means of
alerting children to moral virtues, but also as a stock of wisdom to which
adults could refer. They were a cornerstone of medieval and renaissance

moral argument, however, and for centuries the apt quotation or reference
to a well-known fable retained its force. There was nothing automatic or
mechanical about this, and one has always to analyse how fables are used.
Part of the game Chaucer plays in his beast fable is that *within* it the beasts
quote authority, while the narrator, himself part of an encompassing fiction,
tells his fable to illustrate views about telling fables as authority, at the same
time as his fable is part of a story competition, which is framed by the
pilgrims and the other tales, told, in the end, by Chaucer, most knowing of
narrators. All this comes with the widest range of stylistic effects, the
language as rich and varied as anywhere in *The Canterbury Tales*. Among the
many jokes is the multiplication of moralities, so that the number of lessons
to be derived from the tale become part of the self-conscious, amused, and
humane variety of its content. To ask what the *Nun's Priest's Tale* means
entails the specification 'to which listener'.

In Shakespeare's *Coriolanus* when Menenius tells the mob the fable of the
body, he is making a serious political point; but that is not all that is going on.
He makes his point in the allegorical, more accurately 'fabulous' style
traditionally considered suitable to the level of a mob of uneducated men –
so that the context in which the fable is used is nicely judged, with the kind of
double sophistication that demands a smile of recognition for Menenius' skill
as a manipulator both from other characters within the play and from the
audience watching it. This association of fable with the rude level of learning
that can be expected of the uneducated or the rustic can be found in Spenser's
*Shepheardes Calender*. Interpretation involves wheels within wheels.[38] The
pretence of humility often masks ambition. These complexities already
indicate the range of ways in which rhetorical types, models, or habits could
be used. First, the fables were the instruments by which young boys learned
Latin and, at the same time, learned those moral precepts that would make
them good men and good orators. If children were the primary audience for
fables, certain other classes of audience who supposedly shared one or other
characteristic of the state of childhood – its innocence of complexity,
ignorance of learned reference, and general lack of literary sophistication –
were also likely to find fables appealing. Whoever the audience of the fable
might be, the telling appealed to a shared stock of moral aphorisms, a shared
world of moral belief, the invocation of which could be used as part of
arguments about politics, in the widest sense of agreement about social life
and individual action. This kind of complexity in apparent simplicity is also
available for potential fabulists. Fables are ostensibly modest exercises, but

since they are pedagogically crucial ones, their simplicity is no measure of their importance. As a primary exercise for young children learning a new language, there is a kind of humility in the level of style, the register, that can be expected: fables must be simple, clear, and concise. The most sophisticated writers might try their hands at meeting this challenge, both in order to present young students with good models, and also to perform a kind of paradoxical condescension. That is, for a writer (even a philosopher) at the height of his powers to perform this lowliest of exercises demonstrates the humility of the truly assured. It is, in its way, an indication of modesty *not* to try to write like Virgil, but to write like – but not too like – a child. In the case of someone like Marie de France, conscious as she was of being a woman author in a period when that was not only a rare but also a suspect activity for her to engage in, there is an added piquancy. For whom was this learned and innovative woman writing her fables? By recreating (or perhaps inventing in accordance with school experience of writing fables) the familiar stories in the Anglo-Norman vernacular of the English nobility, was she providing other women with a parallel education to the Latin learning that was the lot of young boys? Certainly Marie read Latin herself. Had she more literary ambitions for her compositions? When she refers, in one of her prologues, to Priscian, basic textbook writer that he was, is that part of a sophisticated use of the humility topos? If we cannot answer any of these questions, asking them at least alerts us to the possibilities that are raised by an author's choice of *this* form rather than that. We open ourselves to the nuances of her – or another's – performance by understanding the variety of effects that the author might create, and how these might be posited upon complex assumptions about audience.

From our understanding we can move to the perception of new effects, challenges to the conventions which the author may create. If Thomas Wyatt's earliest editor, Tottel, was right that the fable of the city mouse and the country mouse was addressed to Wyatt's friend John Poyntz, the apparent humility of his subject, source, and setting exploits what might be 'low style' to create a higher moral complexity and turn fable to court satire by the expedient of addressing, in a knowing way, his fable to an understanding reader. Since the dangers of life at Henry VIII's court had more than once brought Wyatt close to execution, his appeal to the store of common wisdom (he attributes the fable to his mother's maids, i.e. the group of young women placed in his mother's household to be brought up under her guidance) is in his version underlined by the autobiographical context. His choice of the middle style, his colloquial dialogue, the specificity of his description of the contrast between the poverty of the country mouse and the wealth of her sister in the town, build to a climax in which the actual fate of the mice is left unclear, pulling the reader back from too much sympathy with the poor four-legged creatures, and the grip of the tale, and redirecting them to attention to the reasons for telling it. His self-consciousness as narrator extends beyond the fable to an invitation to fabulize his own life, to see his life at court as itself an example of the common stock of wisdom.

If we look for a definition of fable, we find in the earliest rhetoric handbooks the idea of the fable as a kind of narrative that clearly could never have happened, a non-verisimilar narration.[39] Talking animals are the simplest example of the kind. A fabulous narrative invites allegorical or symbolic interpretation: mouse becomes man, the hive a whole society. The assumption that one reads for something other than the surface meaning of the story (i.e. that it cannot exist for its own sake, for the pleasure of the fantasy or the exercise of the imagination) is thus inculcated from the earliest lessons in reading and writing, and becomes a habit of mind. This self-conscious alertness to a whole range of possible effects was a source of great pleasure to readers who were able to appreciate the challenge of making the apparently simple into something witty, pithy, and forceful. Sometimes the very distance of moral from fable, the unexpectedness or unpredictability of the allegory, was the source of pleasure, as with a fable like Robert Henryson's Cock and Jasper, where the precious jewel (often set up to read as something a wise man disdains, as betokening only worldly value) is moralized as something distinctively precious which the cock fails to recognize. The effect of the moral is enhanced by surprise. The basic interpretative lesson is that the animals of fable are not just animals. They represent aspects of animal and of human experience, and they represent them simultaneously. From practically their earliest experience of hearing stories, then of reading, children learned to assume that the simultaneous meanings of a text might be analogies: 'things only seems to be things', as the epigraph to this book has it. This habit of reading analogically was preparation for the 'hard' texts, Virgil, and ultimately, if they were Christian children, Scripture, the code of God.

## IMITATION OF SPEECH, STYLE, AND ACTION

More is known about the analysis of great poets than of the first steps in learning to read. The master-texts of Antiquity retained the prestige that accrued to being the subject of analysis by many of the key writers on rhetoric, but the *value* of the study of secular texts never went unquestioned.[40] Arguments about 'canons' are familiar enough, as are questions of what should be studied at all. In Latin Antiquity Virgil above all, but also Ovid and Statius, reigned supreme among poets, Cicero and Seneca exemplified the highest achievements of prose style for the Latin-speaking West. The appreciation of masters of different genres meant that 'creative literature', oratory, and moral essays were grouped together in a looser, but still recognizable category of good writing for the potential writer, preacher, or orator. Together they formed a complete education, of a literariness which is today hard to recapture. It helps to remember that this curriculum was created for men whose 'work', if they had to do anything beyond managing the family estate, was public life. This is one of the reasons why training in the classics was thought to be sufficient qualification for running empires: 'training in the classics' is a modern gloss on what appeared simply to be *training*. While that strong sense of a curriculum disappeared in practice in the Middle Ages, its prior existence remained known. Thus there was always likely to be some kind of conversation between what *had been* the best education and what was now appropriate for Christian education.

The school curriculum owned works specially written for allegorical interpretation, where the 'correct' recognition of the author's meaning would reveal satisfying Christian doctrine. I have already mentioned the single *Eclogue* of Theodulus. This ninth- or tenth- century imitation of pastoral poetry taught classical mythology, metre, and mode while it inculcated acceptable moral lessons: the ideal use of Egyptian gold, if not the greatest poetry. The setting is the literary, classical, pastoral landscape: there is a description of the summer countryside, in which there is a challenge between a shepherd and a goatherd to a debate, a judge is agreed upon, there is a promise of prizes, then the contest, and the poem closes with nightfall. What makes the content distinctively Christian is that the debate is between a keeper of sheep whose name means 'truth' and a keeper of goats called 'liar'. The shepherdess is of the seed of David; the goatherd is an Athenian, i.e. a pagan. Their debate, judged by 'Wisdom', balances Christian descriptions of biblical stories with pagan legend. Not surprisingly, the victor's prize in the songmatch goes to Alithia, truth. The accent on the 'debate' motif is a departure from the practice of Virgil's own eclogues, but one with important consequences for subsequent writers, for whom the debate had particular attraction.[41] Even here pagan stories are still the ones to be defeated.

Still there remains a continual assumption that students should read a non-realistic literary genre which was intended for allegorical interpretation. With Theodulus the allegory is so straightforward as not to present any ambiguity; it is little more difficult, because of its specificity, than the abstract injunctions of the fables. Not only did such a poem offer itself for study and interpretation, it became a model for imitation in its turn. Because it came at a fairly elementary level of study, too, it further reinforced the idea of the scholar's progression towards Epic; that is, the single pastoral of Theodulus, like the pastoral efforts of Virgil himself, precede that Everest of literary study, the *Aeneid*. Textbook writers imitated Theodulus' example in order to provide illustrations of the rhetorical rules they explained. In John of Garland's thirteenth-century pastoral poem the nymph who is his heroine is seduced away from her true lover; she is meant to be understood as the Flesh, seduced away from Reason by Sin, each personified by a Shepherd in the verse. The point of writing such a poem, with classroom interpretation in mind, is to help young men to learn to read, interpret, and, eventually, write; all that is unusual about John is his ambition to demonstrate his own mastery of the common lessons by providing illustrations of his own composition. He is almost bound to point out his own felicities: choosing the appropriate level of style, the right amount of decoration in nicely chosen figures of speech. Pedagogues are easily parodied as pedants, and John of Garland and his ilk have suffered – with the scholastic method – at the hands of Rabelais and Shakespeare, but their influence is too great to ignore. Dante, after all, wrote for allegorical interpretation, and Petrarch wrote difficult, not to say obscure, pastoral poetry. They expected what they wrote to be incomprehensible to uninitiated – that is, unlearned – readers and understandable even to the learned perhaps only with the aid of a commentary. So did Spenser. It is just this sense of established route, of the writer's career as having known steps, that inspired classically educated writers like Spenser and Milton to imitate the Virgilian succession of literary types: early experiments in the pastoral mode before settling down to the important work of writing Epic. Even for the student who did not aspire to writing poetry of his own, and we may assume that this defined the majority of students, practice at imitating poetry was part of the course of study, study that was thought to be vocational. The students who analysed, interpreted, and imitated fables and eclogues were expected to go on to preach, to teach, and to write as servants of either the church, the king's government, or both. The analysis and creation of texts continued to be the focus of their work.

Reading had become training for both writing and speaking. The education of an orator had concentrated on the latter, and the idea of oratory had organized school practice. What had been categories of speeches made in court, or in court-like situations, were interpreted, especially by commentators for whom the original circumstances had long since been lost, as categories for writing of all kinds. The declamations of the schools, in which boys practiced *controversiae* and *suasoriae*, exercises of persuasion or defence, became types of speech for writers to emulate and to fit into their histories.[42] There were three categories of speeches, which may be traced back to Aristotle, but which were perhaps already traditional when he organized them in his *Rhetoric*: deliberative, judicial, and laudatory. Rhetoric as a classroom discipline for the training of orators existed for a long time under a variety of conditions, and the demands made upon the original classification changed with the educational and political changes of the societies in which Rhetoric was taught. The classical texts which survived often appeared with commentaries, as Victorinus on Cicero's *De Inventione*.[43] Still, theory remained more conservative than practice, and the three categories were retained by modifying their definitions, or by redescribing new kinds of writing in order to force them to fit the pre-existing categories. The speeches of oratory were transferred to dialogue within texts. Deliberative speeches concern decisions about a course of future action. Thucydides gives many examples of political deliberations, as for example the debate over the Sicilian expedition. Bede invented a dramatic representation of churchmen debating whether England should follow Irish or Continental practice over the dating of Easter which he located at the Synod of Whitby. In the Middle Ages, Geoffrey of Monmouth created one which many subsequent writers expanded when he made one of Arthur's knights argue the case for invading Europe. This opportunity for a deliberative debate, however brief, was seized upon by Geoffrey's translators.[44] Looking at three versions of this scene will not only illustrate what a deliberative speech was, but will also show how authors took advantage of an occasion to amplify arguments.

Behind the debate as we have it lurks a tradition of discussion of whether or
not peace makes men soft which medieval historians knew from their
reading of Lucan and Sallust. Geoffrey writes:

Ac dum gradus ascendere incepissent, Cador dux Cornubie, ut erat leti animi, in hunc
sermonem cum risu coram rege solutus est: 'Hucusque in timore fueram ne Britones
longa pace quietos ocium quod ducunt ignauos faceret famamque militie qua ceteris
gentibus clariores censentur in eis omnimodo deleret. Quippe ubi usus armorum
uidetur abesse et alee et mulierum inflammationes ceteraque oblectamenta adesse,
dubitandum non est ne id quod erat uirtutis, quod honoris, quod audacie, quod fame,
ignauia commaculet. Fere nanque transacti sunt .v. anni ex quo predictis deliciis
dediti exercitio martis caruimus. Deus igitur ne nos debilitaret segnicia Romanos in
hunc affectum induxit ut in pristinum statum nostram probitatem reducerent.

(As they started to climb the stairs, the light-hearted Cador, Duke of Cornwall,
laughingly said these words in the king's presence: I have been afraid up till now that
the long peace the Britons have enjoyed might over time make cowards of them and
weaken their military fame until they lost what everyone had admired. Certainly,
when it becomes clear that men no longer use their weapons, but throw dice and
consume themselves with women and other indulgences, then without doubt their
strength, honour, courage, and fame will be stained by cowardice. It is now about
five years that we have given ourselves over to these delights instead of the exercises
of Mars. It is therefore to deliver us that God had led the Romans into this anger, in
order to return us to our former pristine state.).[45]

When Robert Wace, the twelfth-century Anglo-Norman historian,
translated this passage into French verse he first expanded Cador's defence of
war by adding more general sentiments on the relative demerits of peace –
not, it should be said, especially relevant to the particular circumstances of
Arthurian foreign policy, but inserted to give shape to the speech. To be fair
to the issue, Wace added a few words on the benefits of peace, which he put
into the mouth of Gawain, who was not even present in the first version.
Wace is a good rhetorician, and makes Gawain praise the peace which
succeeds war, so that his implicit advice, too, is for Arthur to fight.

> Ja estoient sor les degrez
> Baron et conte lez a lez,
> Qant Cador dist an sozriant,
> Oiant le roi, qui ert avant:
> 'An grant crieme ai, dist il, esté,
> Et mainte foiz i ai pansé,
> Que par oidives et par pes

Devenissent Breton malvés.
Car oisdive atret malvestié
Et maint home a aperescié.
Oisdive met home an peresce,
Oisdive amenuise proesce,
Oisdive esmuet les lecheries,
Oisdive esprant les drueries.
Par lonc repos et par oisdive
Est jovante tost antantive
A gas, a deduiz et a fables,
Et a altres geus deportables.
Par lonc sejor et par repos
Poons nos perdre nostre los.
Piece avons esté andormi,
Mes Damedeus, soe merci,
Nos a un petit resveilliez,
Qui Romains a ancoragiez
De chalongier nostre païs
Et les altres qu'avons conquis.
Se Romain an aus tant se fient
Que ce facent que par brief dient,
Ancor avront Breton enor
De hardemant et de vigor.
Ja longue pes ne amerai
Ne onques longue pes n'amai'.
'Sire cuens', dist Gauvains, 'par foi,
De neant estes an esfroi.
Bone est la pes anprés la guerre,
Plus bele et miaudre an est la terre.
Molt sont bones les gaberies
Et bones sont les drueries.
Por amistiez et por amies
Font chevalier chevaleries.'[46]

(Then, on the steps, barons and counts side by side, Cador, hearing the king going ahead of him, said smiling, 'It has been a great worry to me, and I have often thought, that through idleness and peace the Britons were weakening. For idleness attracts weakness, and many men have become lazy. Idleness makes a man lazy; idleness weakens prowess; idleness wakes lechery; idleness encourages flirtation. By long rest and idleness youth becomes too attentive to pleasure, to delights and stories and other games. By a long stay and rest we lose our renown. We have slept a long time, but

thanks to Our Blessed Lady who has woken us a little by encouraging the Romans to
challenge our country and those we have conquered. If the Romans are confident
enough to do what they say in their letters, the British will again have honour,
audacity, and strength. I have never loved a long peace and I never will love a long
peace.'

  'Lord count,' said Gawain, 'fear nothing, by my faith. Peace is good after war: the
world is more beautiful and better. Pleasures are better, and so are flirtations. Knights
fight for friendship and for their friends.')

Poetry makes a difference, and the rhetorical figure, anaphora, in which
several lines begin with the same word or phrase, emphasizes 'oisdive',
leisure, so that the repetition itself increases the force of the criticism. So, too,
Cador's changes of tense emphasize what he doesn't love.

  When Laȝman translated this into English in the thirteenth century, he
dramatized it as a fully fledged debate, and incidentally suppressed any hint
of humour. His version gives Gawain an angry riposte which defends peace.

> Þa stod þer up Cador, þe eorl swiðe riche ær,
> and þas word sæide bifore þan riche kinge:
> 'Ich þonkie mine Drihte, þat scop þes dæies lihte,
> þisses dæies ibiden, þa to hirede is iboȝen,
> and þissere tidinge, þe icumen is to ure kinge,
> þat we ne þuruen na mare aswunden liggen here,
> for idelnesse is luðer on ælchere þeode;
> for idelnesse makeð mon his monscipe leose;
> ydelnesse makeð cnihte forleosen his irihte;
> idelness græiðeð feole uuele craften;
> idelness makeð leosen feole þusend monnen;
> þurh eðeliche dede lute men wel spedeð.
> For ȝare we habbeoð stille ileien – ure wurðscipe is ða lasse –
> ah nu ic ðo[n]kie Drihtne, þæ scop þas daȝes lihte,
> þat Romanisce leoden sunden swa ræie
> and heore beot makieð to cumen to ure burhȝes,
> ure king binden and to Rome hine bringen.
> Ah ȝif hit is soð þat men saið, alse segges hit telleð,
> þat romanisce leoden sunden swa ræȝe
> and sunden swa balde and swa balufulle
> þat heo wulleð nu liðen into ure londen,
> we heom scullen ȝarekien ȝeomere spelles;
> heore ræhscipe scal heomseoluen to reouþe iwurðen.
> For nauere ne lufede ich longe grið inne mine londe,

for þurh griðe we beoð ibunden and wel neh al aswunden.'
Þat iherde Walwain þe wes Arðures mæi,
and wraððede hine wið Cador swiðe þa þas word kende.
and þus andswærede Walwain þe sele.
Cador, þu ært a riche mon þine ræddes ne beoð noht idon.
for god is grið and god is frið þe freoliche þer haldeð wið.
and Godd sulf hit makede þurh his Godd-cunde.
for grið makeð godne mon gode workes wurchen.
for alle monnen bið þa bet þat lond bið þa murgre.[47]

(Then Cador, the noblest earl there, rose before the noble king and said these words: 'I thank my God, who made the daylight, that I have seen this day come, and the news it has brought to our king, that we no longer lie here sleeping. Because idleness is hateful for everyone; because idleness makes a man lose his manhood; idleness makes a knight lose his rights; idleness encourages many wicked arts; idleness makes the loss of many thousand men; few men succeed through easy deeds. We have lain still too long – our renown has diminished. Now I thank God who made the daylight that Roman men are so brave that they plan to come to our cities to bind our king and take him to Rome. If what men say is true, as they report, that the Romans are so brave, so bold, and so hostile that they mean to come to our London, we shall prepare an unpleasant tale for them; their bravery shall work their sorrow. For I have never loved a long peace in my country. For through peace we have been bound and well-nigh asleep.

Gawain, Arthur's kinsman, was angry when he heard what Cador said, and answered, 'Cador, you are a noble man, but your advice amounts to nothing. Peace is good, and freely-held treaties are good, which God himself made through his divinity. Peace makes a good man do good works; when the land is secure, everyone is better.'

Rhyme and repetition are at work again to make the speeches sound forceful. Cador's passing joke has become a formal exercise in which the king's advisers perform their traditional duty of advising their prince. Gawain, whose presence was Robert Wace's idea, has begun to acquire a critical tongue, and what appeared in French to be a neutral statement of an argument, now appears to be characterized by the way he replies, in the early English (and archaizing) heroic mould. This reverses what might be considered the direction of characterization: the arguments create the character rather than vice versa. Indeed, and this will be particularly important in Chapter 3, arguments may not be intended to *characterize* at all; they may be present for their own sake, with the speaker assigned as a secondary consideration. There is nothing unique about these scenes, or the expansions. A similar occasion, with a more serious outcome, occurs at the beginning of *The Song of Roland*, where Charlemagne's peers discuss the issue of whether or not to return to France, and what is the best way to deal with the pagan threat. Arguments are marshalled formally, but character is involved, too, and motive is ascribed. Here literature advances psychological exploration by suggesting that there are more reasons than disinterested advice for urging one course of action rather than another, not least by showing characters ascribing motives to each other and by using their misunderstanding to advance the plot. When Guido delle Colonne adapted the *Roman de Troie* of Benoît de Ste. Maure in the thirteenth century, or Lydgate adapted Guido in the fifteenth, similar expansions were made. They need not have been trained in formal debates, as Sallust was trained; as long as they could read model texts they would find the same lessons.

These examples are primarily instances of political deliberations. For the ancient orator, concerned ultimately with government, this was the height of achievement. He may have addressed fellow-citizens, his *polis*, senatorial colleagues, or his prince. As long as his advice was wanted – or tolerated – learning to make this kind of speech was important to his public career. But not all courses of action need be so closely involved in actuality, and other subjects and circumstances were used in schools for practice. When democracy in Greece, or later the republic in Rome, were replaced by other forms of government, more private deliberations became not only expedient, but also ends in themselves. The student might be set a historical subject: many schoolboys urged Julius Caesar to cross the Rubicon.[48]

The subject might not be a public one at all, and one favourite was the question of marriage. Tacitus tells us (*Annals* XII. 1–2) that the Emperor Claudius asked his freedmen to advise him on the choice of an empress, and that he listened carefully to their speeches, noting the arguments. This may be true; it may be a criticism of how Claudius wasted his time, and brought a venerable institution into disrepute. One of the long model orations contained in Wilson's *Art of Rhetoric*, a famous English handbook written over a thousand years after Claudius sat taking notes, rehearsed the same subject, which is obviously one of perennial interest.[49] The first seventeen of Shakespeare's sonnets are a series of arguments on this theme, but this time in verse. Wilson does something which is characteristic of the specificity of the situations which orators had to imagine and deal with: he describes a young man who is the only member of his generation in a position to marry (he has a sister, but she has become a nun), who is now presented with a wealthy, suitable, and desirable bride. Like the young man of Shakespeare's sonnets, Wilson's hesitates. Wilson claims that the speech he reproduces in his text is a 'real' speech. Generations of readers have assumed that the sonnets are addressed to a real young man. In neither case is there a sure way of knowing, nevertheless Wilson's speech seems to be a translation of a similar speech written by Erasmus for a Latin textbook which Wilson was pillaging. Wilson's speech is long and rather ponderous; the measure of Shakespeare's success is that so many people have been moved by what he wrote. Love and death provide the alert orator with endless opportunities to deliberate. Rhetorical training or example suggest appropriate forms in which to weigh the decision to be made. It is a literary skill to show – as in Epic poetry – characters misinterpreting each others' words and deeds. Whenever one character claims to know what another is thinking, or why the other character did or said something, we can begin to be sure that medieval writers are exploiting the breadth of interpretation, leaving room for argument about what the 'real' motives were or what was 'really meant': a certain amount of narrative indeterminacy creates space for audience discussion.

The second category of formal speeches, judicial or forensic oratory, which deals with past actions rather than future ones, is addressed more clearly to one audience: the judge or jury in a court of law. Some of the most famous orators in Rome – including Cicero and Quintilian – made their names as 'pleaders'. Judicial oratory received disproportionate emphasis in ancient handbooks, but there were good reasons for the sustained treatments. First, performances in court are highly susceptible to clear codification; second, even when political deliberation was possible the law courts claimed a large share of attention, a share which only increased as the governmental arena narrowed; third, the law courts provided a road to success for aspiring young men who wanted to attract public attention to themselves. Someone else's law case gives the pleader a recognized distance from the cause he argues, and a brilliant attempt which ends in defeat may work to the credit of the losing speaker. It may be noted in passing that a knowledge of the arts of persuasion was what was emphasized, and not a grounding in the law. For information, one went to a juris-consult.

That habits of mind were inculcated by reading these speeches is attested to by the number of court scenes in medieval and renaissance literature. They received a further impetus in the Renaissance theatre, which in turn encouraged the modification of literary prose towards conciseness. Shakespeare's fondness for them is obvious in speeches by Shylock and Portia, Hermione, Isabella, and other learned and unlearned pleaders. Ben Jonson's *Volpone* comes to its climax in court, where the wit and dexterity of its arguments are certainly absorbing as well as scarifyingly amusing, and his *Epicoene* has a wild send-up of a court case. Later in the seventeenth century, Corneille and Racine both exhibit what may be taken to be stylizations of rhetorical exercises. The *monologue intérieur* which developed in the hands of medieval writers of romance gave many familiar examples and methods to the writers of soliloquies. Not only in drama, but also in all kinds of narrative literature, a trial scene where speeches could be written with all the passion that came when a life is at stake provided writers with ideal opportunities to show what they could do, using the techniques they had been drilled in at school. Sidney's *Arcadia* ends with a situation straight out of Roman textbook extravagance: not only are characters pleading for their lives against a mistaken accusation of murder, but fathers who also happen to be rulers find themselves sitting in judgement upon defendants who are their apparently guilty sons. Victor Hugo used a variant of this situation (foster- or spiritual- father sentences his beloved son to the guillotine out of a misplaced sense of duty) in *Quatrevingtreize*, and Dickens, too, revelled in melodrama of this kind.

   This habit of thinking of speeches in terms of arguments manifests itself even when the scene is not a legal one. The illusion of 'court' was maintained by the pretence that the writer is deferring to the judgement of his audience. The so-called 'courts of love' took legal procedure as their model, as did the 'pui', the bourgeois poetry contests, now best represented in Wagner's *Die Meistersinger von Nürnberg*. Courts include princely courts, where the presiding 'judge' or 'prince' may be someone playing a role. So obvious an observation is this that it is easy to ignore what it implies: the possibility of organizing poetry and performance on the long-tested forensic model. The *demande d'amour* asked its audience to adjudicate between two positions, where the poem was meant to stimulate more arguments. These poems have multiple appeal, since the poet can describe his imaginary situation dramatically and at length, using the particulars of character and status to create carriers for a series of balanced or specious or biassed arguments. There are a pair of such poems by Guillaume de Machaut, Chaucer's great French contemporary, in which he poses the question whether it is better to lose one's lover through death or desertion. Judgement is requested from the

King of Bohemia in one poem, from the King of Navarre in the other; and
one poem is set up to support the ladies, the other the gentlemen. This is
argument as play, as relaxation, but the same techniques of argument are
used for love as for any other subject. When Chaucer used a similar device, a
parliament, in his *Parlement of Fowles* he provided a temptation for readers to
look for a real-life situation behind the playful judicial debate. Of course it is
the process which is of interest, and in Chaucer's poem there is no judgement
– 'sentencing' is deferred until the next St Valentine's day. These examples
assume that literature stimulates conversation and emphasize the continuing
orality of the cultures in which the texts were written. This social occurrence
could itself be imitated in writing, like Boccaccio's frame of the ten young
people who tell the tales of the *Decameron* or Chaucer's Canterbury Pilgrims,
who famously misinterpret each other's tales.

In the course of Robert Greene's sixteenth-century *The Carde of Fancie* the
young hero invents a dream in order to reveal his love to a lady to whom he
does not dare to speak plainly. The circumstances of the retelling are public:
he is with his beloved, but in the company of other young courtiers. He
describes how in his supposed dream he saw a beautiful woman standing on a
bare rock surrounded by a dangerous sea. He, the dreamer, found himself on
a cliff before a bridge so dangerous that to try to reach the Lady would mean
certain death. His question, addressed to his beloved, but equally to the
courtiers present, is

Whether it had beene better to have ventured upon the brickle bridge, and so either
desperately to have ended cares with death, or else valiantly to have injoyed desire
with renowne, or still like a fearfull dastard to have ended my dayes in lingering love
with miserie?[50]

For pages the arguments are canvassed, and each character in accordance
with his or her age, status, and position within the plot, weighs the possible
courses of action and their consequences. Though Greene's fictional court is
ducal, and the courtiers are playing, not 'trying', the character of the
speeches is formal, and their structure is that of the judicial oration. Knowing
how the formulae for such speeches are normally used is a prerequisite to
recognizing the reasons why they appear in the forms that they do – they
may not be revelations of character at all, though of course much may be
revealed by the use of the formulae, even by misuse or significant omissions.

I have sometimes referred to a 'client', as if judicial oratory were actually a
legal occasion, where plaintiff and defendant were represented by pleaders, if

they were not speaking for themselves. This is the convention, the habit of mind, but although the scheme of exordium-narratio-confirmatio-refutatio-peroratio was first based upon court practice, it was so soon extended to other uses that it is easy to forget where its basically argumentative structure came from. It is always worth remembering, too, that many of the most famous model speeches which survived from antiquity were not the *verbatim* accounts transcribed by court stenographers, but carefully *written* and revised expansions of speeches that might have been, or were, delivered. One of the most famous, Cicero's *Pro Milone*, was never made, since apparently Cicero was so put off by the sight of armed thugs ringing the court that he couldn't speak. One needs to imagine that the speeches one reads are to be read *as if* they were legal defences. So, too, the 'client' might not be a person at all, but, by extension, an abstract idea, like Liberty or Poetry. Sir Philip Sidney's *Defence of Poetry* is written in the form of a judicial oration; so is Milton's *Areopagitica*, which even enshrines the name of an Athenian court in its title.[51] It is one of the curiosities of literary history that authors constantly extend old forms to new uses, sometimes almost without seeing what they are doing or why. Intending to do one thing, authors create another. However deeply these judicial habits penetrated, they were no more *determining* of what was written than any other genre. Questions of the unity, the style, the characterization of a work may grow from the recognition that something unusual is (or is not) happening. The 'oral' could be extended to the written, as the written imitated an oral performance, so that there are not two independent categories. To remember that the so-called 'Debate' literature of the Middle Ages grew from this ostensibly forensic exercise thickens the texture of our understanding, by revealing how little expectation there was of 'a' winning outcome, how much attention was devoted to the pleasure of the process.

I have already mentioned the political threat inherent in training rhetoricians in the techniques of appealing to the emotions of their audience: rabble-rousing demagoguery has always been used to incite action. The only defence against the manipulation of the listener's emotions was an alert ear trained to discriminate not only good from bad arguments, but successful from unsuccessful ploys. The best arguments used in a bad cause might be persuasive, but they ought not to succeed with someone educated. Bad arguments abound in early literature, and they are intended to be recognizable, as when Chaucer created Troilus' misleading inner debate on necessity and freewill. In addition, good readers should be able to recognize

good arguments based on faulty premises, such as the arguments of Despair
for the justification of suicide in *The Faerie Queene*, or the seductive rhetoric
of Milton's Satan. I shall look in greater detail in the next chapter at the
tendency of historians to ascribe such specious arguments to the villains of
the past, and to dramatize them as speeches. This is the point of Blake's
misreading of Milton. The interpretative culture, already in abeyance when
*Paradise Lost* was actually published, had changed so much that it would have
been difficult for Blake to recapture the rhetorical techniques with the full
weight of the irony with which Milton deployed them. Speech is not simply
– perhaps only very rarely – the spontaneous emotional outpouring of
character; a calculated speech may be a true representation of a character's
inner life – but equally the creation of inner life may be contingent upon the
quality and style of the arguments. If only because the *ethos* of Satan or
Despair was morally repugnant, readers would be on their guard against the
skilful *pathos* aroused by their speeches. Because the other fallen angels or
even the Red Crosse Knight succumbs to good rhetoric used in a bad cause,
we should be the more alert, the more resistant. Vittoria Accorambona's
self-defence in Webster's *The White Devil* reminds us that beauty introduces
an extra force: however seductive she is, she exemplifies bad ethos/good
rhetorician. These literary examples also remind us of the complexities that
can be created, of the ways that our sympathy is pulled simultaneously in
different directions: we may pity the speaker, or be seduced by her, but we
are meant to *think* and to resist.[52]

In addition to speeches about actions, either arguing for future courses or
defending past ones, there were 'demonstrative' speeches, originally referred
to as speeches of praise or blame, epideictic oratory.[53] In the Middle Ages,
this became a catch-all category: what was neither deliberative nor judicial
had to be epideictic. Saving the appearances of rhetorical theory encouraged
many medieval thinkers to twist the categories rather than question the
wisdom of ancient theoreticians. This helps to explain why lyric poetry was
categorized as epideictic: as it was clearly neither of the others, it had to be
demonstrative. Traditionally, funerals and festivals had provided the
occasions for displays of demonstrative oratory. Pericles' Funeral Oration,
like Lincoln's Gettysburg Address, which commemorates both the recent
dead and the values for which they died, are great examples of the kind. In
this kind of oration no strict adherence to the facts was required, nor did the
speaker have to limit himself to the person or persons who were his
ostensible subject, because the form of the speech invited digression,

expansion, and celebration of the fact that the speech was a celebration: the dead man's family, or country, or the audience listening to the praise, might equally come into the speech. Cicero's speech for Atticus, apparently a funeral oration, but too long ever to have been delivered, may have been written as a kind of literary restitution, since Cicero could not be present to make an actual speech. Once again the emotional effect is the goal, and the speaker's very heightening of loss might work as a kind of solace, emphasizing the significance of the dead. Such speeches used styles which called attention to the surface of the language of praise or blame.

Ector's panegyric of Lancelot is a short, simple, yet typical example. Malory invented the following, which has been laid out so that the rhythms will be clear:

> 'A, Launcelot!' he sayd,
> 'thou were hede of al Crysten knyghtes! And now I dare say,' sayd
>    syr Ector,
> 'thou sir Launcelot, there thou lyest,
> that thou were never matched of erthely knyghtes hande.
> And thou were the curtest knyght that ever bare shelde!
> And thou were the truest frende to thy lovar that ever bestrade hors,
> and thou were the trewest lover, of a synful man
>                             that ever loved woman,
> and thou were the kyndest man    that ever strake wyth swerde.
> And thou were the godelyest person
>                       that ever cam
>                             emonge prees of kyghtes,
> and thou was the mekest man and the jentyllest
>                             that ever ete in halle
>                             emonge ladyes,
> and thou were the sternest knyght to thy mortal foo
>                       that ever put spere in the reeste'.[54]

This is intense, and meant to be so, and it is expressed in the prose most suited to the style of mourning intensity that Malory could create. It is both social, in the virtues it celebrates, and rhetorical, in the way it celebrates them, and there is no reason to doubt that an *educated speaker*, inculcated with rhetorical habits of mind, might have spoken in just this way on this occasion. At the same time, Malory has invented the best speech he could for Ector, without worrying about creating in his readers' minds any assurance that Ector could have, woud have, had the educational background or the public experience to speak in this way. That is, particular character is less important than appropriate circumstance.

Not all demonstrative speeches were pitched at a high level of emotion, but they all derive coherence from an often unstated scheme of topics. An official speech of welcome was an epideictic category. Speeches to greet royal visitors survive in large numbers, and it helps to understand why mythical ancestors are hauled in, if one remembers that family, country, and teachers received praise according to known conventional patterns. Today, when school speech days are almost all that remains of such public events, it is hard to recreate the combination of seriousness and pleasure with which audiences responded to verbal displays. The formal, public style has almost entirely disappeared from our experience. When speeches lasted three hours there was scope for beginning with the ark. American Southern Baptist preachers (Martin Luther King, Jr and Jesse Jackson are famous examples) preserve this old-fashioned style, marked by organization in groups of three, by a variety of sound-play devices (paronomasia) including assonance and alliteration and the coincidence of rhythm with rhyme. In Britain, Enoch Powell was perhaps the last famous British politician to exploit the lessons of Cicero as a result of his own classical training.

Speeches were divided into identifiable sections, which graded the emotional stages of audience reaction. The number varies somewhat from handbook to handbook, though the outline is agreed. First comes, naturally enough, the introduction, called by the Greeks the proemium and by the Romans the exordium. Here the orator tries to capture the goodwill of his audience so that they will be well-disposed to the rest of the speech. If one remembers the oldest chestnut in advice to after-dinner speakers, 'begin with a joke', this may not seem strange. The idea, then, that a funny thing happened to me on the way to the forum is actually part of a recognized skill. So is 'unaccustomed as I am to public speaking', which is a ploy to make the audience sympathize with a nervous speaker. When Shakespeare's Anthony begins, 'Friends, Romans, countrymen, lend me your ears. I come to bury Caesar, not to praise him', his exordium cleverly claims that he is not going to do what his audience assume he must be (and in fact is) about to do: make an epideictic funeral oration. His denial is a means of ensuring close attention. Plutarch says only that Anthony made a speech; the rhetoric is Shakespeare's, an amplification of Plutarch's idea. Both Anthony and Brutus play on their 'ethos' in their speeches, that is, the moral integrity of the speaker. And of course assuming an air of moral integrity was one of the techniques – or tricks – of representation which would be inculcated in the orator both in the study of composition and of delivery (as referred to in the epigraph to this chapter). Brutus, who relies on the force of his arguments (which he therefore delivers in Shakespeare's version of the Attic, or plain, style), is defeated by Anthony's florid, exciting, 'Asiatic'-style appeals to the emotions of the crowd. The mob is carried away by insinuation, heavy irony, and what appears to be physical evidence: not just Caesar's corpse, but also his putative will.

The 'introduction' was followed by a narration. In judicial oratory this involved an exposition of the facts of the case. Here arises one of the curiosities of this whole system of careful codification, because sometimes the narration wasn't of facts at all, but skilfully calculated fictions, like Caesar's putative will. Rhetoricians repeatedly stress that the narration should be brief, clear, and that it should sound like the truth even when it isn't. The problem stems from the contradiction inherent in the textbook-writers' desire to stress the virtue of the orator, and to create an ideal handbook, while also taking account of the necessities of actual practice. Winning cases is the pleader's ambition. So the narration, *narratio*, might be a circumstantial account of what had happened, or an account which could be expected to move the audience to favour the client's cause. In effect, this loophole through which fictions crept permitted, even encouraged, a certain elasticity in descriptions of 'true' events. It might help to think of them as 'in the main true' events. This embroidery or embellishment of the truth will return again and again as a theme in subsequent chapters. In order to move the judge (or Lady, or Duke) to sympathize with one's case, the facts might have to be manipulated slightly. The pleader put a 'gloss' on the facts. This metaphor, which is taken from painting, was called 'colour': the colours of rhetoric here refer to the aspect or interpretation which the pleader put on the events. In the late first century Quintilian writes that damaging evidence should be suppressed, and that fictions are sometimes necessary when a case looks bad.[55] He reminds the budding pleader that a successful liar needs a good memory, and advises him on the best methods.[56] If it is necessary to create fictions, they should be both plausible and circumstantial, and should if possible fit closely with what *is* true, so that they cannot be disentangled. He stresses the importance of restricting inventions to things which cannot be checked and immediately disproved. Attributing words to the dead is a good ploy, and so is the attribution of words to someone living whose interests will be served by success in the case at hand, who will therefore have every reason to refrain from denying the invented speech. A risky, but often successful technique is to claim that one's opponent said something which he didn't say – think, says Quintilian, how suspicious his vociferous and affronted denials will look. But don't, he goes on, refer to commonly held superstitions – those have really lost their force. Finally, he warns against succumbing to the temptation to *over-dramatize* an account, because histrionics at an early stage may bring the whole performance into disrepute.

At this point in the speech a brief digression (IV.3) might be introduced on one of the topics appropriate to the case. By this is meant reflections on generally agreed subjects, like luxury or avarice or duty, so that the audience would relax into sympathy with the pleader and agreement with his point of view.[57] This is a direction to do the opposite of what modern analyses of good speaking and writing recommend; it is a reinforcement of 'stock responses' in order to lull thinking.[58]

If the narration was a claim to be a version of events, it needed the support of proof or confirmation, the next section of a well-ordered speech. Some handbooks say that this section should begin with one or more propositions (statements of what was done) followed by a list of propositions to be made and defended, in an outline of the topics to be treated in the rest of the speech. Important considerations in this section, though, include such unexpected topics as character assassination of the opponent (undermining his *ethos*), appealing to the unreliability of a witness's testimony, impugning its value because it was perhaps hearsay or obtained under torture or through self-interest. The vituperation expressed by controversialists like More and Tyndall comes under this heading. What may appear a lapse of taste reassumes its rhetorical place when one is able to supply the idea of attacking the opponent's *ethos*. At this point, too, it was appropriate to refer to any useful ideas of justice which transcended the sometimes irritating legal restrictions. The main method, however, was to argue by rhetorical syllogisms, from the known to the probable, by the enthymeme. It is different from the logical syllogism in several ways, of which the most obvious is its compression: 'Socrates must die' replaces the traditional syllogistic proof (All men are mortal. Socrates is a man. Therefore Socrates is mortal.). Or an enthymeme might be based on shared opinion, or even on a dubious premise. When an irate parent berates a child for staying out all night the shared opinion 'up to no good' is lurking in the background as a sort of dubious major premise: People who stay out all night are up to no good; this child stayed out all night; therefore . . . Clearly there are degrees of probability in all this, and the orator needed to be aware of them to make the best use of them. He also needed to be aware enough to recognize them and refute them when his opponent used them.[59] There is a strong sense throughout the handbooks that while strict logic is a virtue in forensic debate, it is not a necessity, and it may in any case confuse the jury. A well-chosen maxim could be far more valuable, especially given the ease with which an audience could be led to agree with weighty moral wisdom. These *sententiae*, as they were called, had several things in their favour. First, pithy sayings – in moderation – strike the audience and are remembered. Second, they impress upon the audience the grave and yet penetrating moral character of the speaker: his 'ethos' again. Third, they can be extended into enthymemes with ease. If, for example, Socrates is doomed to die (in the sense in which all men are mortal), a skilful orator can go on to suggest that Socrates will not knowingly break the gods' laws. This kind of exercise is clearly open to abuse. Milton's Satan, that model orator, uses these sections and tricks when persuading Eve to eat the apple: IX.549ff. (Proem), 571–612 (Narratio), 684–736 (Confutatio), 727–32 (Peroratio), with misused Sententiae at 654, 709–10 and descriptions of the orator's delivery at 665–76 and an epic simile at 631–42. Other arguments include parallel cases, often taken from history, or even fables (like Aesop's) if they lend themselves to the case at issue. And for those who find they lack a store of convenient examples, Valerius Maximus collected a large number, carefully categorized in order to provide an early example of the speaker's companion.[60]

If one had spoken thus far in support of the case, it would now be time to turn to specific refutations of the accusations. If this seems to come fairly late in the day, the reason is the necessity to create an unquestionable *ethos*, the orator's moral authority. By now the audience is assumed to be enlisted among his supporters. For the orator might need to argue from circumstances and probabilities. He might expand upon the character, or presumed character, of the defendant in order to argue that it would have been unlikely that this person would do that deed.

So when the end is in sight a rousing peroration would bring the auditors to a satisfactory emotional state, and the client would find himself acquitted. The constant appeal to the jury's feelings, and the stress on rousing feelings of sympathy for the client makes a marked contrast to any careful sifting the fact to get at the truth – except as a pose in its turn. The technical name for this arousal of emotion in the auditors is 'pathos', to be distinguished from the moral 'ethos' of the speaker. No 'unreliable narrators' are allowed in the rhetorical scheme; not to be convincing would be disastrous. Therefore, trainee orators – later preachers – had to learn not only to marshal arguments, but also how to make them either convincing or so moving that their audiences would think they were.

### THE EXERCISES OF RHETORICAL INVENTION

The problems of writing are different from those of analysis. Teachers (or handbooks) divided their discipline into five parts: invention, or the finding out of a subject; disposition, its arrangement; diction, its style; and then memory and delivery, which belong to the days when oral recitation was the goal. I shall be concerned with the first three, and primarily with the first, *inventio*. Even those medieval teachers who most suspected classical rhetoric nevertheless recognized that *ingenium*, a knack for thinking up arguments, was a universal art of discovery.

At the smallest scale, the unit of variation might be a single word. Cicero wrote of the necessity for *copia verborum*, and in the sixteenth century Erasmus used this phrase as part of the title of his best-selling textbook, *De Copia Verborum*: on the copiousness or multiplicity of words and things. This contrasts with modern educational instruction in writing, which does so much to foster originality of thought and expression. Even modern forms of translation tend to be exercises like the *précis*, a brief summary of a model passage in our own words, rather than anything which expands. While the ancients recognized that abbreviation was important, they stressed even more the ability to take advantage of opportunities to expand, to amplify, to correct and nuance an expression, to fill out by the use of synonyms and parallel phrases, whatever was implied – as I have just illustrated in this series of clauses. This *amplificatio* is one of the most characteristic features of medieval literature, if not the one that gives us most pleasure. In the successive versions of Geoffrey of Monmouth's Arthurian passage quoted above, *amplificatio* has been used to dramatize particular attitudes. It can be argued that what Chaucer did to his model poem, Boccaccio's *Il Filostrato*, was to amplify it. *Amplificatio* could be an end in itself; one reason for saying the same thing in many different ways is to make oneself aware of the many different ways there are for saying things. As a technique of repetition it is still used in polemical writing, where a series of examples appears to give greater force to an argument. Amplification can be achieved in any number of ways, by changing grammatical cases, or inserting dialogue, or adding details. An amplification might be invented, found, without presuming to represent anything more than an elegant expansion. The problems this raises for the truth content of writing which appeared to represent something which had actually happened will be the subject of the next two chapters. Here it may be worth anticipating far enough to say that the speeches of historical actors (such as the example of Cador and Gawain already cited) did not carry a claim to represent what had been said; rather, like so much of historical and biographical writing, texts represented arguments that might have been canvassed, clothed in the best words their writers could create. This general exercise of saying the same thing in many different ways could be predicated on almost any passage a student read. Not only did it create habitual acts of translation, it reinforced the assumption that *the same thing* was being said in many different ways, that is, that stylistic variation was a mere covering for *the* meaning.

It was the early Greek rhetorician Isocrates whose pedagogic efforts first formalized in the *progymnasmata*, the exercises of invention, the ways these habits could be taught. In the Middle Ages, of course, his work was not known directly, though handbooks of rhetoric repeated some of his ideas. The dozen graded exercises which follow may never have been taught in this sequence in any school even in Antiquity, but something along these lines will have been. The use of moral apophthegms and fables as the first exercise was traditional, as apparently were the habits of the most sophisticated writers who often returned to use them. Nevertheless, habits of writing and speaking cannot be isolated from reading and interpreting, annotating for present understanding and future imitation, and commented texts often called attention to good examples of one or another of the exercises.

The second exercise was called *narratio*. This name can make for difficulties, since *narratio* may mean 'narration' in the modern sense, but may in the context of a judicial oration also mean something which claims to be a statement of the facts of a case (see above, p. 60). Basic schoolroom practice recognized three kinds of narration. In addition to judicial narration, students practised historical narrations taken from events chronicled by pagan or Christian historians or poetical narrations which were pure inventions. The topics to be treated were the same in each kind of narration, and can be summarized as a list of 'circumstances' shared by writers from Cicero to Kipling, whose mnemonic verse appears in the *Just So Stories*:

> I keep six honest serving men
>   (They taught me all I knew);
> Their names are What and Why and When
>   and How and Where and Who.[61]

I shall look at some narrations in the next two chapters. The conjunction of history and amplification which appears almost accidental was to have major consequences on the choice of subjects for long compositions throughout the Middle Ages.

Third can the *chria*, a brief exposition of a wise saying attributed to a particular historical figure. The *chria* often appears as a brief appeal to authority. The formula for handling it was to begin by praising its author, to expound his wise saying and explain its circumstances. To amplify further a contrary example and a similar example might be added, with references to other opinions on the same subject. Examples were collected, and (once paper was cheap) kept in commonplace books. Bacon's essay, 'Of Boldness', begins with a *chria*:

It is a trivial grammar-school text, but yet worthy a wise man's consideration. Question was asked of Demosthenes, *what was the chief part of an orator?* he answered, *action*: what next? *action*: what next again? *action*. He said it that knew it best, and had by nature himself no advantage in that he commended. A strange thing, that that part of an orator which is but superficial, and rather the virtue of a player, should be placed so high above those other noble parts of invention, elocution, and the rest; nay, almost alone, as if it were all in all.

Bacon calls the reader's attention to what he is doing with a gesture as collusive as it is gracious which creates (by assuming it) a sense of a shared experience in which 'we' can all be reminded how basic his matter is. No orator had a higher reputation than the Greek Demosthenes, so his word would carry authority. Psychologically, this use of a 'reserve' of shared reference to school experience, to the texts everyone knows, something so universal and so simple as no longer to require analysis, has a strong confirming effect. Because we assent to the memory we are carried toward assent to the argument. The rest of the essay can build on a foundation of agreement because of the strength of the *chria* opening. Like the forensic speeches which built upon appeals to the audience's sympathy, both the fable and the *chria* function by a kind of collusion with their education and judgement. What 'we' knowledgeable readers share puts us on the speaker's or the narrator's side as soon as we sit back to enjoy the performance.

It may be helpful to think of the *chria* as a kind of topic sentence, a way of introducing a theme. As with many fables, one means of amplification is dialogue. Here is a fictional soliloquy, a kind of meditation which opens with a *chria* before going on to become the same kind of argument which is familiar from *Julius Caesar*: should a potential evil-doer be cut off before he can cause any of the mischief he promises? The very question reeks of the schoolroom.

Now (quoth he) I prove by experience, the saying of Sophocles to be true, that the man which hath many children shall never live without some mirth, nor die without some sorrow: for if they be vertuous, he shall have cause whereof to rejoyce, if vicious, wherefore to be sad, which saying I trye performed in my selfe, for as I have one childe which *delights* mee with her vertue, so I have another that *despights* mee with his vanitie, as the one by dutie brings me *joye*, so the other by disobedience breeds my *anoy*: yea, as the one is a comfort to my mynde, so the other is a fretting corasive to my heart: for what **gr**iefe is there more **gr**iping, what **p**aine more **p**inching, what **cr**osse more **c**ombersome, what **pl**ague more **p**ernitious, yea, what trouble can **t**orment me worse, then to see my sonne, mine heire, the inheritour of my Dukedom, which should be the **p**iller of my **p**arentage, to consume his time in **r**oysting and **r**yot, in **sp**ending and **sp**oiling, in **sw**earing and **sw**ashing, and in following wilfullye the **f**urie of his owne **fr**antike **f**ancie. Alasse, most miserable and lamentable case, would to God the destinies had decreed his death in the swadling clouts, or that the fates had prescribed his end in his infancy. Oh that the date of his birth had bene the day of his burial, or that by some sinister storme of fortune he had bene stifled on his mothers knees, so that his untimely death might have prevented my ensuing sorrowes, and his future calamities: for I see that *the young frie will alwaies prove old frogs*, that *the crooked twig will prove a crabbed tree*, that *the sower bud will never be sweete blossome*, how *that which is bredde by the bone will not easily out of the flesh*, that he which is carelesse in youth, will be less carefull in age, that where in prime of yeeres vice *raigneth*, there in ripe age vanitie *remaineth*. Why Clerophontes, if thou seest the sore, why doest thou not apply the salve, and if thous dost perceive the mischiefe, why doest not prevent it with medicine: *take away the cause and the effect faileth*: if Gwydonius be the cause of thy ruth, cut him off betimes, least he bring thee to ruine: *better hadst thou want a sonne than never want sorow*. Perhaps thou wilt suffer him so long till he fall sicke of the Father, and then he will not onely seke thy lands and living, but life and all, if thou prevent not his purpose: yea, and after thy death he will be through his lascivious lyfe the overthrow of thy house, the consumer of thy Dukedome, the wrack of thy common weale, and the verie man that shall bring the state of Metelyne, to mischiefe and miserie. Sith then thy sonne is such a sinke of sorrowes, in whose life lies hid a loathsome masse of wretched mishaps, cut him off as a gracelesse graft, unworthie to grow out of such a stock. Alasse Clerophontes, shalt thou be so unnatural as to seeke the spoile of thine owne childe, wilt thou be more savage then the brute beastes in committing such crueltie: no, alasse . . .[62]

No one would assume that this formal cogitation is meant to represent, to enact experience; it is not very much like thought. But, then, it is not meant to represent a process of pondering (like Molly Bloom's soliloquy) or even the idiosyncrasies of *this* father. It is, however, meant to convey emotion, and Clerophontes' anguish and self-reproaches once moved readers who were used to this kind of stylization. It is also meant to be read aloud, or at least read so that the inner ear hears the balanced clauses, even the rhyme. Some of the sound effects are marked by changes to bold type. Greene amplifies partly by variation and partly by interior monologue, where the father takes both sides of the argument. Modern readers who find this a distraction from the emotional experience which Duke Clerophontes is undergoing, used as we are to a different kind of economy, need to consider that for the duration of this set piece speech the elapsing time of the story halts.[63]

Both these examples use attributed sayings; mankind's store of proverbial wisdom also includes a vast stock of anonymous ones. In the fourth exercise, called *Sententia*, or, perhaps confusingly, in English, a 'sentence', of course one could not praise the author, but the other directions were similar to the *chria*. Both exercises represent appeals to the authority of collective moral guidance. Greene's sententiae are italicized. This kind of appeal is often suspect today, so that it is as well to remember that an apt quotation or proverb could have overwhelming force in a medieval or renaissance argument. On the other hand, there was a widely held view that the misapplication of such wisdom, or overdependence on proverbial lore was a fault, common, like similar over-use of fable, to simple people, but also to old men.[64]

Authors could exploit a range of reactions to the serious and satirical uses of sentences by creating levels of irony, and sometimes an author's apparently straightforward use of them may suggest ambiguities not about the sentences themselves, but about the character who speaks them. Being 'sick of the Father' is a bitter pun on the lesser illness, hysteria, which was called 'being sick of the Mother'. In Chaucer's *Troilus and Criseyde*, Pandarus' fondness for proverbs which support his view of events helps to characterize him as an almost pedagogic type, aware of and not overmuch

moved by the changeableness of life, yet that he uses so many proverbs also
suggests a certain literary as well as social vulgarity about him. Overuse is an
ironizing mechanism. Characters of the status or refinement of Troilus or
Criseyde seldom explore such quotations. Polonius poses a more difficult
problem of interpretation – like so much in *Hamlet*. The problems he
rehearses, for example, to Laertes, are individually unobjectionable, but
seem inappropriate in context, and there are too many of them, typifying in
a play which considers so many rhetorical styles, at least Polonius' constant
distraction from matter to art, and perhaps also suggesting that the once-
dependable adviser is now in his dotage. The context created by the whole
poem or play counts, too.

There is a fifth category even more general than the sentence, the
commonplace, which represents wisdom so universal as to be instantly
recognizable, like the badness of thieves or the value of courage. 'Locus
communis', a common place, is one of those spatial metaphors which
reminds us that medieval people thought of the world as interpretable in
ways that were analogous to reading.[65] The common places were thought of
as concretely *there* in the mind, locations of wisdom, of potential invention
('finding' 'in' 'a place'). There is an implication of familiarity. This kind of
appeal to 'what everybody knows' is characteristic, and particularly
important when one is trying to come to terms with the apparent credulity
of earlier times. To us, if a story too closely resembles a story we have heard
before, it is likely to be classed immediately as 'apocryphal', a folktale,
untrue. To audiences of medieval and renaissance Europe, repetition was, on
the contrary, likely to be taken as a sign of confirmation, because of a belief in
life's known and recognizable underlying patterns. That events had
happened before might be adduced as a proof that they were happening
again. The idea that events might be new and unique was a horror to a
society which knew (from the Bible and Christian eschatology) its
beginnings, its place, and its eventual end. Thus the nearer one comes to the
collectivity of wisdom and experience, the *more* convincing a story is likely
to have seemed, and even – or rather especially – coincidence revealed the
deliberate hand of God. This will be of particular importance in the next two
chapters.

Here is a historical speech invented by Thomas Gainsford in 1618 for King
Henry VII, who has just been informed of a plot to overthrow him:

At last he burst out, what my bosome friend? my Councellor? my *Chamberlaine*? then
I see there is no trust in men, nor as the *Psalmist* saith confidence in *Princes*: For as we

shal not want instruments to goe forward with what enterprise we please, as *David* had his *Ioab*: so shall we not lack enemies let them be neuer so carefull and desirous to fauour the least deseruer, but I may well now cry out, *Heu cadit in quenquam tantum scelus*! and with the kingly Prophet exclaime, It was not mine enemies abroad, but my companions, and such as eate at my table betraied me: What Sir *William Stanley?* he hath the gouernment of my Chamber, the charge and controlment of all that are next my person, the loue and fauour of our Court, and the very keyes of our treasurie. He made me a conquerour in the field, and by his hand I scourged tyrannie out of his Throne, therefore it is impossible, and I cannot belieue it.[66]

The same kind of rhetorical organization obtains here as in the outburst of Greene's purely fictional king. The mixture of *chria*, sentence, and commonplace stylizes the emotions which King Henry feels. Modern readers may be inclined to feel that eloquence sits ill with strong emotion: what *really* happens is that people splutter, unable to say what they feel. Eloquence might be thought to signal lack of sincerity. But these are criteria of realism, not the kind of stylization which medieval literature offers. King Henry speaks as a king should. He is also wrong: unlikely as it seems, Stanley has betrayed him.[67]

The *confirmatio* and *destructio*, two linked exercises, encouraged practice at proof and refutation, and these sixth and seventh exercises depend upon the use of the earlier ones. Similar formulae apply: the student begins by praising or maligning his source or opponent, then tells his story showing it to be credible or incredible, possible or impossible, like or unlike other known events, seemly or unseemly to be spoken of, profitable or unprofitable to have been done. Once again the speech is based upon arguing from *likelihood*, and the habit of thinking of writing as organizing an argument, the effects of which depend in part on the *ethos* of the speaker.

Demonstrative oratory was the goal towards which another pair of exercises was aimed: *encomium* or *panegyric*, that is, speeches of praise, or their opposite, dispraise or vituperation.[68] For these eighth and ninth exercises, speeches of blame were in fact much rarer than speeches of praise, for which rhetoric handbooks abound in possible subjects. A sample includes men, fish, birds, beasts, trees, stones, rivers, cities; arts and sciences; virtues like wisdom, courage, liberality. Appropriate topics for the praise of a man might begin with his nation, locality, ancestors, parents, and teachers before coming to his physical attributes, his acts, his wise sayings. I shall look at this in more detail in Chapter 3. The sophistication of such speeches can be seen in one of the great works of Erasmus, *The Praise of Folly*. This is the exercise which provided the opportunity for no-holds-barred all-stops-pulled-out bravura display; this is the exercise in which there was least obligation to restrict oneself to the truth. Anything that would excite admiration might be admissible. Recognizing this may help to explain the apparently odd insertion of extraneous material, or distracting digressions, or poetic licence to an astonishing degree. The implication is that the reader addressed – or at least the 'best' reader addressed – colludes in the pleasures of exercising style, recognizes technique, as it were. This is a simultaneous pleasure which coexists (as it coincides) with the content of the text, though part of the text's understood content is its mood. This 'understood' stylistic expression will be of particular importance in Chapter 4, where I shall look at attempts to translate it.

More subtle, perhaps, is the tenth exercise, *comparatio*, which weighs the merits of two things. Milton's paired poems, 'L'Allegro' and 'Il Penseroso' are a famous example of fine poetry transcending the trivia of the grammar school. The fashion for 'debate' poems, in which Spring argues that it is better than Winter, the Soul than the Body, Wine than Water, Winner (earning) than Waster (spending), sprang no doubt from this kind of exercise. Comparison may also extend to something more like what we might think of as simply *comparing*. Here is the beginning of a section of Sir Thomas Malory's *Morte Darthur*:

And thus hit passed on frome Candylmas untyll [after] Ester, that the moneth of May was com, whan every lusty harte begynnyth to blossom and to burgyne. For, lyke as trees and erbys burgenyth and florysshyth in May, in lyke wyse every lusty harte that ys ony maner of lover spryngith, burgenyth, buddyth, and florysshyth in lusty dedis. For hit gyvyth unto all lovers corrayge, that lusty moneth of May, in somthynge to constrayne hym to som maner of thynge more in that moneth than in ony other monethe, for dyverse causys: for than all erbys and treys renewyth a man and woman, and in lyke wyse lovers callyth to their mynde olde jantylnes and olde servyse, and many kynde dedes that was forgotyn by neclygence.

For, lyke as wynter rasure dothe allway arace and deface grene summer, so faryth hit by unstable love in man and woman, for in many persones there ys no stabylité: for [w]e may se all day, for a lytyll blaste of wyntres rasure, anone we shall deface and lay aparte trew love, for lytyll or nowght, that coste muche thynge. Thys ys no wysedom nother no stabylité, but hit ys fyeblenes of nature and grete disworshyp, whosomever usyth thys.

Therefore, lyke as May moneth flowryth and floryshyth in every mannes gardyne, so in lyke wyse lat every man of worshyp florysh hys herte in thys worlde . . .[69]

Some readers have assumed that the author (whoever he was) is here speaking in his own voice to condemn his contemporaries. Even if that be so, he speaks in a conventional gesture called 'complaint'; in any case it is of the foremost importance that readers be aware that the form in which this complaint is couched is the result of careful study of exercises such as the comparison. It is an argument by analogy, as the 'fors' and 'therefores' alert us. It moves from praise of a season to praise of the lovers of past times, and then specifically to the lovers at King Arthur's court. The stylishness of the prose may distract us from a certain speciousness both of analogy and application. Steadiness is no more demonstrated then than now. When, in addition, one remembers that Guinevere was not the sort of lover ever to be free of the body's demands, the inconsistency, even incongruity, of this introduction to the plot becomes apparent. Of course, some readers may argue that it was the strength of Malory's own feeling that welled up, and that the incongruity testifies to that strength. This would be to make the kind of psychological judgement about Malory that convinced Blake that the true poet, Milton, was of the devil's party. But given the regular inconsistency of medieval and renaissance narrative, and the emphasis upon local effects rather than subordination of all the details of a work to its plan, it is more likely that this address to the reader appears where it does for technical rather than personal emotional reasons. The desire to use a comparison, the perception that comparison makes a good section opening, may be the motives for its appearance here. Interpreting its content, what is compared and how, does not – at least in this case – reveal any more. Recognition of rhetorical games must not be taken as a formula for automatic interpretation, but a constant reminder of other cultures' different attitudes to the ways written expression could be stylized.

Recognition is a pleasure in itself, to the reader as well as to the writer who put things in the way that he did hoping for an understanding interpreter. To recur again to Bacon, *Of Marriage and the Single Life* is as graceful and knowing a comparison as the *chria* I have already considered. The intention, in Malory or Bacon, is to refer without really having to argue.[70]

An eleventh exercise is in theory a description, sometimes called an *ecphrasis*. Since description played an integral part in so many other exercises, some rhetoricians denied it a place of its own. Description of a city slid easily into either praise or blame of a city. It is not clear how 'neutral' a description could be. But many descriptions were not essentially matters of praise, blame, or comparison, and they afforded important set pieces at which writers could try their hands. I have already mentioned Virgil's storm at sea. In Julius Caesar Scaliger's *Poetics*, a Latin handbook to which Sir Philip Sidney was much indebted, much of Book v considers different treatments of great themes like Pestilences, Tempests, and other disasters, as well as less dignified subjects like lions, serpents, Amazons, and oaks.[71] Medieval handbooks devoted considerable space to the technique of *descriptio*, advising students to begin to describe a person with his head, and then to work systematically down to the feet (taking the middle with due circumspection). This visual sense, appealing to the eye of the imagination, takes precedence as well as physical point of view into account. A description of a garden should work up from flowers to trees to birds, not only because of where they are found, but also because, in this list of three, birds come highest in the ranks of creation. In the twelfth century, Matthew of Vendôme provided generations of medieval students with seven model descriptions of different persons: a church prelate, a prince, a clever orator, a cynic, and three types of women, virtuous, beautiful, and old.[72] This, too, instills and legitimates known character types, and while it emphasizes variation tends toward the restriction of variety, including Aristotle's category of consistent inconsistency. There was ample precedent for this restriction: Aristotle puts some 'types' in his *Rhetoric* (Book ii). Not only were there standard ways of describing; there were standard types to be described. Human nature was known. Individual idiosyncrasies hardly appear. The description of a person is a word painting, first of the outward physical appearance, then of the inner qualities. The *topos* which this established turned attention of a sort to what people looked like, to their stature, colouring, and clothes. But anyone who has tried this has recognized its limitations, as when one attempts to describe one friend to another (unacquainted with each other) accurately enough to facilitate a recognition in a crowded public place. We still rely upon the same broad outlines that formed the traditional *descriptio*: sex, age, height, weight, clothing, and especially the details of the head, from colour of hair and eyes and skin-type to those facial characteristics we can remember, hooked or snub nose, small or large mouth, protuberant teeth or none at all. On those occasions when we have to perform such a miracle we typically try to provide a prop: we specify the colour of a coat, carry a particular newspaper, or pin a green carnation to our left lapel. A reminder of how little description we actually require of a written narrative comes every time we see a film made of a book, and we discover, watching the film, or talking to our friends about the characters afterwards, how greatly our mental pictures have differed.

Nevertheless, however limited such descriptions may seem in practice, they could convey aspects of the inner person, the second part of the task of description. Bodily externals and choices about clothes may be conventional, but they are still fraught with meaning. Hair is a case in point. In western Europe red has always been a colour to arouse suspicion. One still hears the association of red hair and hot temper, which was originally due to views about the humours and excess of heat (where red is not just a metaphor for flame, but identifies the same quality). In medieval and renaissance writing red hair was an attribute of untrustworthy men; Judas was believed to have been a redhead – though which way around the association arose is now impossible to say. The high forehead of the medieval blonde beauty is well known. Hair could easily come to symbolize moral values, and in a culture in which cross-dressing was looked upon with horror, the Bible was invoked as the ultimate authority for hair-styles: men short, women long. A description of a male fashion for long hair often constitutes implicit moral criticism, an insinuation of effeminacy, with hints of vice and degeneracy. Criticism of new fashions may look as if the author thought them ridiculous, but the force of disapproval may amount to an accusation of immorality. The particularizing tendencies which are such a marked feature of the narrative poetry of exceptional twelfth-century authors like Chrétien de Troyes individuate the characters who speak them, but the characters remain types. As I shall show in Chapter 3, even biographers did not attempt to represent the gratuitous idiosyncrasies.

When schoolboys put speeches into the mouths of historical characters, they concentrated upon the arguments appropriate to a character of a known age and social status, in a particular situation. Contrary to our usual impression of amplification, there is something economical about this. By turning attention to the contents, sequence, and style of arguments, *all* we know about inner character comes in the specific category of the set speech. 'Personality' (in the eighteenth-century sense now normal) is subordinate to the character's creation of *ethos*. The *ethopoiea* or *mimesis* was meant to teach the creation of appropriate emotion. Hecuba on the fall of Troy was one of the common topics – once again we may think immediately of *Hamlet* and Shakespeare's games there with theatre rhetoric. When Hamlet asks the player to repeat the scene which so moves both player and prince, Shakespeare has many reasons for making it *Hecuba's* sense of loss; one of them is the very banality of the subject.[73] Such speeches need not be restricted to human beings: they could be attributed to cities, or trees, in which case the exercise was called a *prosopopeia*. There is an apparent paradox here, because we think that actual speech reveals character (in the same eighteenth-century sense that goes with the modern idea of personality), and assume that literary dialogue should do the same. When we listen to what people actually say, in addition to what they mean, we realize how far they reveal their innermost concerns by their choice of subject, types of comparison, preference for certain adjectives. Everyone has characteristic phrases. Literary speech, based as it was on ideas about *arguments*, had no need to imitate these idiosyncrasies, and it is important to beware of assuming that it was therefore inferior, and just waiting for a breakthrough which represented *progress*, as if there were a steady, laudable march towards mimetic realism in the history of western literary discourse. As Auerbach pointed out long ago, Petronius differentiated character by speech.[74] In the late Middle Ages we sometimes find dialogue which exploits personal idiosyncratic speech markers. But this is extraordinarily rare. Chaucer's Wife of Bath has a favourite adjective, 'jolly', and Hamlet repeats himself. Speech, literary dialogue, was – indeed still is – highly stylized, and for hundreds of years represented positions or arguments more than gratuitous characterization, though certainly character emerged, however contingently, as I shall show in the next two chapters.

It is a sign of the orientation towards argument that the most sophisticated exercises were those which considered abstractions. Twelfth and almost last, *thesis* is like the comparison, but considers issues which cannot be resolved, like a consideration of whether or not riches are the highest good, or the conflicting claims of the active versus the contemplative lives, or even – familiar theme – the arguments for or against marriage. One extra exercise, not likely to be popular in princely states, was the *legislatio*, supporting or opposing a law.

The emphasis on arguments expressed in oral delivery assumed speakers in special situations. While practice in the graded exercises encouraged writers to turn their compositions in ways which allowed them to take advantage of their training, the exercises themselves were never intended to be a comprehensive preparation for composition. They are small-scale schemes for imitation, and might be combined, parodied, or manipulated in many different ways or styles. To learn how to choose words and constructions appropriate to different styles the model exercises were of limited assistance except as models of how other writers had written. Students had to return to the analysis of actual texts, the same literary texts that formed the basis of their Latin education.[75]

In order to practice oratory or composition the student had to think about the 'clothing' of his speech, and from the beginning he would study the styles suitable for making the best impressions. In general, three levels of style were posited: high, middle, and low. In the abstract educational scheme there was no room to consider how oversimplified this is, how little attention it pays to the effects of variety, or how appropriate it might be to vernacular styles. It assumes analogy between a certain style and a certain social level of character and a particular type of plot; it takes it for granted that this concatenation is natural. Each was considered appropriate to different speakers and occasions, and once again the authority of Virgil's practice was invoked as the example and legitimation of how this was to be done. Description of what did happen became prescription of what ought to happen reinforced by analogies with other aspects of a writer's achievement. The aspiring poet was expected – and expected himself – to follow the course of Virgil's writing career and work his way up through the styles, from humble to grand. This could, of course, make the humblest work the sign of great ambition, staking a claim for the greater works to come. Virgil had begun with pastoral poetry, whose subject is ostensibly the life of shepherds. This associated the 'low style' with labouring men, wherever found, country, city, or at sea. They would use a vocabulary striking in its informality, simplicity, and restraint. There is a risk in this kind of poetry that the reader will think that the writer uses simple words and phrases because that is all he knows how to do, but it is important to remember that the 'low style' is a downward modulation, and may be just as artificial as any other register. After Virgil wrote his pastorals, the *Eclogues*, he produced his *Georgics*, which exemplified the 'middle style'. This was the means for describing the everyday activities of men of the middle ranks, and included the affairs of merchants, lawyers, or gentlemen. Comedy, interludes, and most love poetry used the 'middle style'. When the subject was the most notable deeds of the most important kings, princes, or gods, the appropriate forms would be hymns, epics, and tragedies, expressed in elevated or 'high style'. The Virgilian example is, of course, the *Aeneid*.

This kind of analysis assumes that there are 'pure' examples of the various styles, but of course there are not. A work of any length written all in one style would be boring. Theorists knew that, but beyond insisting that language at each level should be clear, exact, and appropriate, they found it hard to legislate. Some of their problems will recur in Chapter 4. What, in the end, the handbooks provided was a codification, with appropriate technical vocabulary, of the kinds of things we all do with words. And here, too, the attempts of teachers and textbook-writers to codify figurative language may appear self-defeating, with their long lists of kinds of tropes and schemes. Just as the idea of the three styles, each with its appropriate genres, restricted the kinds of composition and subject which seemed legitimate, so the concentration of the textbooks on figurative language encouraged would-be writers to demonstrate their mastery of the tricks of the trade, so that the exhortations to brevity and decorum disappeared under mountainous amplification. The notes to Spenser's own pastorals contain comments on the text of just this kind, because 'E.K.', the annotator, is keen to treat *The Shepheardes Calender* like a dignified classical text worthy of commentary. He points out rhetorical figures, like 'Stouping Phaebus) Is a periphrasis of the sunne setting' in the course of his gloss for March, or parts of an oration, as in April he identifies the beginning of a song as 'as it were an Exordium ad preparandos animos', expecting an audience learned enough to understand the range of his reference.[76]

E. K.'s annotations of the small-scale analysis of words and phrases explain why the vocabulary and register should call attention to themselves. By mixing intertextual reference to great Latin authors with low register composition, Spenser makes an ambitious bid for comparison with his classical predecessors. His creation of a literary dialect was contentious even at the time. This illustration of the end of the text of 'September' and the beginning of the explanatory gloss, indicates by its type face something of Spenser's pretensions. The use of archaizing type for the speeches of the Shepherds indicates their rusticity, while the use of humanist roman type for the explanatory notes demand the kind of attention from the reader that is appropriate to learned, commented texts. Two kinds of translation appear: from dialect into standard English (as far as one can speak of 'standard English' in 1579), and from English into Latin. This implies a reader who is learned in both Latin and the vernacular, who can appreciate, if not always recognize, allusions to earlier writers, and who is used to the habit of reading which isolates examples of clever tropes or schemes.

If the two major divisions of figurative language were the tropes and schemes, no satisfactory definitions or distinctions between them ever seem to have been agreed by medieval or by renaissance theorists. In the Middle Ages Bede was among those who encouraged the view that these were only appropriate to the High Style, but one may doubt the success which even his authority could impose. By the Renaissance figurative decoration was to be found everywhere. Tropes are words and phrases used in unusual ways.

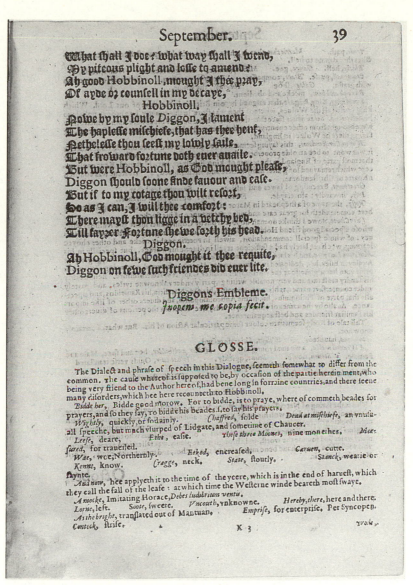

Plate 4   The final stanza of and the beginning of the Notes to 'September'
from Edmund Spenser, *The Shepheardes Calender* (London, 1579).

Some uses involve change of meaning; others are employed ornamentally for amplification. Schemes are unusual arrangements of thoughts, that is, concepts or emotions expressed in sentences. The distinction between the two types is very difficult to make, and impossible to maintain, as the confusion in handbooks indicates. Different authors reclassified long lists of up to two hundred named tropes and schemes in a constant attempt to get them into some kind of structurally satisfying order, an ambition doomed to failure. There was no single conclusive organic structure for their variety. This constantly directed attention towards demonstrating one's mastery of these figures of speech, the manner rather than the matter. As Chapter 4 will argue, the desire to imitate the grandeur of Latin led to the creation of 'high' items of vocabulary in order to make up the defects of the vernaculars, and encouraged the style called 'aureation' or the effects of the 'grands rhetoriqueurs' of sixteenth-century France. There were other reasons, too, for these manoeuvres, which included both stylistic and historical ambitions to make English *like* Latin, as supple, as subtle, and as – as it appeared to medieval readers and writers – as free of mutability through time.

Most of the rhetorical exercises I have described in this chapter were concerned to teach what kinds of compositions were to be created, what might, with reservations, be called the genres of oratory, and with the styles to be used to create them. While these genres do not really encompass the variety of genres of written expression, there was a theoretical investment in claiming that they did. Since most kinds of writing were neither to persuade someone to do something nor to defend them once they had done it, the third category, epideictic speeches, those of praise or blame, was stretched to cover everything else. Lyric poetry, to take an apparently extreme example, was still being forced into this category in the seventeenth century. This might be considered an instrumental categorization: what are the texts for? At the same time there were three categories which considered the relation of the *content* of the text to reality: *historia*, which recounts deeds actually done in the past (which I shall consider in detail in the next chapter), *argumentum*, the hypothetical case told as if it were historical, as in a law court, but not necessarily something which had happened, and *fabula*, non-verisimilar fiction which had never happened, could not have happened, and was narrated in ways that couldn't deceive anyone into thinking they could have done. Rhetoric manuals would instruct students in how to use these different categories; manuals for writing letters would deal with these and some others (asking for money or preferment might need to employ

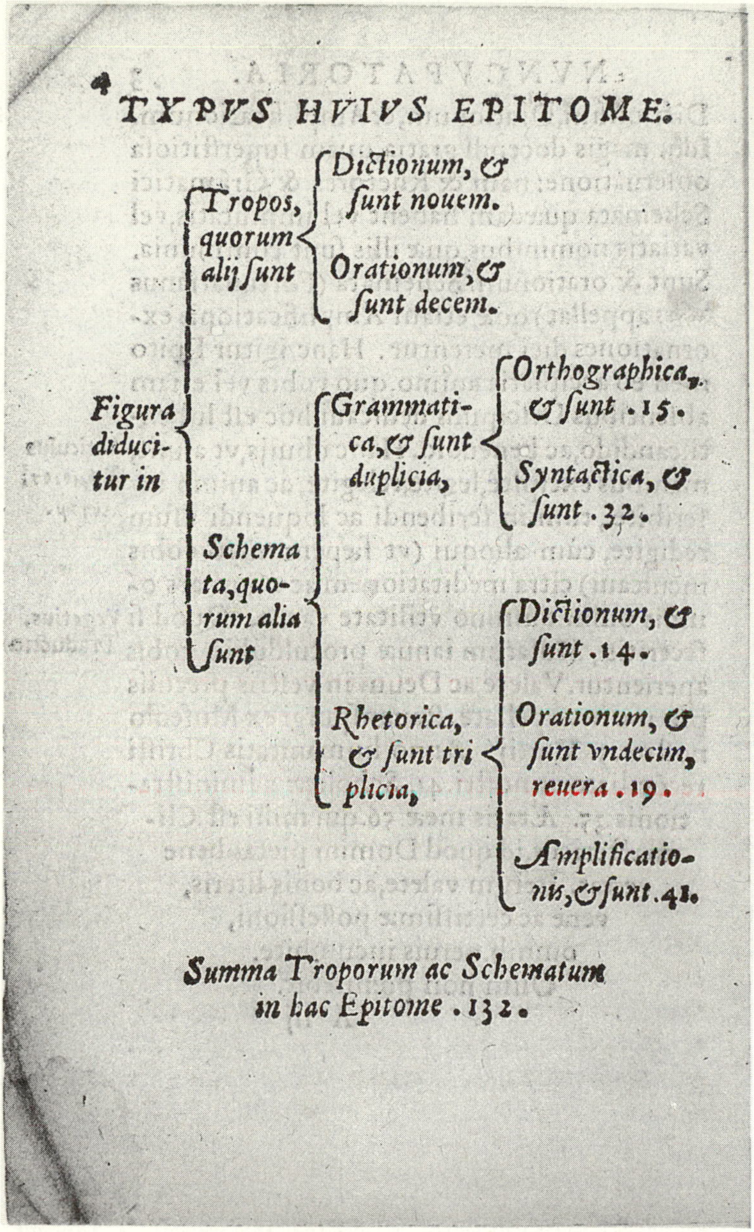

## TYPVS HVIVS EPITOME.

Figura diducitur in

- Tropos, quorum alij sunt
  - Dictionum, & sunt nouem.
  - Orationum, & sunt decem.
- Schemata, quorum alia sunt
  - Grammatica, & sunt duplicia,
    - Orthographica, & sunt .15.
    - Syntactica, & sunt .32.
  - Rhetorica, & sunt triplicia,
    - Dictionum, & sunt .14.
    - Orationum, & sunt vndecim, reuera .19.
    - Amplificationis, & sunt .41.

Summa Troporum ac Schematum
in hac Epitome .132.

Plate 5   A *divisio* of tropes and schemes from Johannes Susenbrotus, *Epitome troporum ac schematum et grammaticorum & Rhetorum, ad Autores tum prophanos tum sacros intelligendos non minus utilis quam necessaria* (London, 1562).

narrations, arguments, defences). Reading and writing, therefore, were organized under a general umbrella of rhetoric, in which categories are taught in order to be recognized and imitated, and in which the great texts of 'literature' are both the subject of lessons and the object of analysis. That is, Virgil is the great exemplar of the arts of rhetoric which students were trying to acquire, and their appreciation of rhetorical skill contributes to the pleasures of reading Virgil. These criteria were also applied to Christian texts, first to elevate them so that early Christians could claim that their inherited literature was on a par with the stylish achievements of the Pagans around them and then to reinforce the place of their literature in the education of the young.

As long as the different kinds of analysis are understood, problems need not arise: it is obvious that demonstrative oratory uses fables, and that fables may contain arguments between characters. A certain interpretative latitude, even uncertainty, is a necessity – as well as a pleasure. It is when demonstrative orations are invented for historical characters that recognition of the categories becomes important, and sometimes contradictory. Synonymy was a more complex business than might at first appear, because word of phrase might expand to scene, story, or history without raising questions of the *essential* meaning of the thing transformed. That is, with certain crucial exceptions, forms of expression might be thought of as 'trials', tentatives which 'clothed' something which could be expressed in other ways. It is as if the language of expression were a complex kind of sign to some inner reality.

Then much depends upon the status of the sign. Certain texts had particular claims to be the single best form of expression, where 'best' can imply something about perfection in terms of beauty (as with the great classical texts like Virgil's) or in terms of the precision of crucial vocabulary (the Bible, because it conveyed the word of God, or great philosophical writing, like Aristotle's). Since words are not static, like mathematical symbols, they have associations as well as references, and thus require interpretations which may be multiple and complex. Rhetorically trained readers learned to understand by recognizing just how to interpret particular kinds of text.

While it is clear that certain specific modern literary categories like 'novel' or 'essay' did not yet exist, the very category 'literature' raises difficulties. There was rhetorical organization of different kinds of writing for different purposes. Because of the flexibility of rhetorical transformations, 'history' was as literary a category as 'epic' or 'tragedy'; as for 'biography', it does not correspond to the writing of a life. The parlous relationship of composition to some kind of truth, some representation of reality, was further confused by the need to defend anything which did not redound to the teaching of moral wisdom. Even literature as the higher escapism needed protection. The claim that in some way serious writing signified wisdom and instruction to the experienced interpreter was its best justification through the Christian centuries, better and stronger than the instrumental argument that Virgil or Ovid would be treated as Egyptian gold. It isn't that fiction ceased to exist: people will tell stories, write poems, sing songs, whatever the legislation. It is that writing needed legitimation, and the habit of reading for a truth, or truths, that lay beyond the text, provided it. But it is not clear that there was a free-standing category, 'literature'; and 'poetry', which was something rhetoricians discussed, maintained uneasy relations with its associate, 'fiction'.[77] The rest of the book will consider the ways that readers learned to manipulate and to interpret the conventions in order to express and appreciate their truths. It may help to think of these hypothetical readers by analogy, as students who – in modern terms – have had a sophisticated musical education at school. Not only can they sight-read music, but they have an advanced theoretical training in harmony, experience of composition, including imitation of earlier styles, and a wide acquaintance with other people's music. That is, they are literate in Latin, know the categories and figures of speech of rhetoric, have based their own efforts at composing upon approved models of style, and have memorized a great deal. Now, just as musicians will hear differently from the rest of us, so our rhetorician will read differently. Whether or not they have attended classes in theories of composition, their attention to earlier masterpieces will have encouraged them to think in the terms set by those masterpieces. Musicians asked about some familiar piece of classical music, say the first movement of Beethoven's fifth symphony, may talk about its emotional power or its historical connection with Winston Churchill and V for victory, but they are at least as likely to describe the technicalities of its composition, from tonality to sonata form to themes and variations. That is, appreciation includes a great deal of what might be called technical recognition. (The techniques of sport, ballet, or painting invite the same kinds of discrimination, and participants and audiences enjoy the ability to verbalize in technical language.) Post-Romantic habits, which have become normal reactions in their turn, may lead to a dismissal of this apparently cerebral analysis of art as jargon, a dry study rather than a communion with Beethoven's stormy emotional self. Not only is this insulting to the musician, but it reveals a prejudice – and a foolishly anti-intellectual one – on our part. There is no reason to think that to know more is to feel less, nor ought we to assume that our elevation of feeling is the best way to approach any music. Beethoven intended to move, certainly, but this is no bar to hearing how he did it. Rhetoric, as a discipline, was intended to teach the means of moving and persuading. It was a codification of already existing practices in forms which could be taught. Even with the disappearance of the curriculum, its habits remained, and at any time the curriculum itself could be rediscovered, if only to be argued with, by medieval and renaissance scholars. It might be argued that nations get the education they deserve, or even that ignorance of history condemns us to an inability to repeat it. Just as it can be argued that without some knowledge of earlier symphonies and more private forms of music like the string quartet, we will have neither the genre background nor the contrasts we need to understand Beethoven's language, so it can be argued that without some learning we may fail to understand what medieval and renaissance writers were trying to tell us.

Rhetorically alert readers are in a position similar to the musician's. When they pick up a piece of writing or listen to a speech, sermon, or play, their eyes and ears are attuned to agreed expectations and technical recognition. This does not rule out transformation and surprise; on the contrary, it makes them possible. We, too, employ certain tacit general knowledge when we read, and our expectations of a novel are not those of a history book or a description of scientific method. Before the middle of the seventeenth century, when genre boundaries were still looser than they came later to be, other expectations, based upon the habits of mind I have been describing in this chapter, were applied. 'What kind of writing is this?' might elicit the answer 'encomium' before 'exciting' or even 'poor'. If 'encomium', the reader would know to look for extended praise; if 'blame' began to find its way into the speech he would be surprised, and would then need to ask if its appearance was deliberate. When the conventions are known, departures from them evoke questions and excitement: is the writer ignorant, does he know what he ought to be doing but has he lost control, is this a clever insertion which looks like a contradiction but will soon be resolved, is it a joke, is he deliberately breaking rules in order to do something unexpected, even new? The recognition of a clever exordium is no different from the musician's knowledge of variations on a theme, and the pleasures are similar ones. To be able to recognize and analyse is to listen better. The power of any work to move addresses the heart; the recognition of the means speaks in addition to the mind.

Rhetoric is not an answer; it is a label for a series of questions. Even in Antiquity there was argument as to whether or not Rhetoric constituted an art or craft, whether it had any content at all. As the collection of insights which enabled orators to learn to move and persuade audiences, it was defined against 'philosophy', and the hostility of philosophers to teachers whose first commitment was to technique rather than to content informs the Platonic dialogues, and lies at the root of reservations about teaching 'tricks'. Writers like Cicero or Quintilian could insist that the good orator would be a good man; this was not an answer to the commonly observed tendency of persuaders hidden or open to use whatever techniques are available to get people to do what they want them to do. Rhetoric named a curriculum, a set of handbooks, tendencies of style which concentrated on the means of moving and persuading (that is, speaking to the emotions of the reader or audience as much as, even instead of, the audience's reason), and even secular writing itself. Rhetoric meant many things, and many of its implications were pejorative. It implied both higher education, and a kind of specious attitude to the moral responsibility of governors of states who would habitually sacrifice truth to plausible persuasion. In so far as it was valued, it was something medieval writers sought; in so far as it was suspected, it remained something Christians should eschew. Both attitudes assume that there is something there inside, something prelinguistic or linguistic, which can be known, which words can advance or distort. This idea that words have a relation to a real thing (which may include words) which can be truly represented or ignominiously distorted encourages a view that there are true things which language describes, and that there are a variety of ways of making descriptions. These ways were taught in Antiquity, when schools of rhetoric were the avenue of higher education. But because so much classical writing assumes rhetorical techniques, because so much interpretation points out the techniques which students can recycle for their own writing or speaking, even when the educational system of the Greco-Roman world was lost, the texts and commentaries which conveyed much of it remained. Rhetorical habits of reading and writing assume a latitude of invention, of verbal variation, which is incommensurable not only with modern standards of representation of historical and biographical events, but also of the ways a text can claim to represent another text. The exercises of rhetorical invention offered a platform from which the aspiring writer could work, and because the exercises were widely known, they could be used without being labelled for the inventions they were. The routes by which these habits of mind reached the Middle Ages are many and complex. Schools texts, commentaries which pointed out the rhetorical achievements of their authors, and original compositions which attempted to emulate the techniques in those texts – all these were passive as well as active instructors. In isolating texts which appear to render the past intelligible by writing about events and their actors, histories and lives, I believe I have chosen examples which will be fruitful for readers of several different modern disciplines. There is nothing revolutionary about the introduction of scepticism in interpretation; revisionism is often a matter of seeing patterns.

Three areas of praise might be taken as examples of the incommensurability that makes the interpretation of medieval texts problematic. Medieval writers are often complimented when they appear to be classical, and reliable, and when they impress readers with their sincere and critical narrative voice. In the next three chapters I shall consider the ways that 'classical' implies an archaizing style interpreted and imitated from surviving model texts, sometimes with the help of handbooks of rhetoric, always with the mediation of commentaries; how 'reliable' may be a reaction to the creation of a literary style which convinces because it is plausible and consistent with known or accepted representations; and how the orator's *ethos*, or concentration on self-representation, impresses as trustworthiness because the analysis it 'speaks' of the world and its texts encourages an attitude of trust: medieval authors who appear to be critical are often excellent textual critics. The truths they tell, expressed in the terms of rhetorical invention, require interpretation in terms of that style – or those styles – of invention.

If this seems to imply nothing more complex than the good liar's need for a long memory, the problem it raises is the category 'liar'. In applying the analytical skills of literature to medieval texts which appear to claim to be telling true tales about the past, or conveying true equivalents to earlier or other texts, I am aware that I risk calling everything 'rhetorical' and 'literary'. It is a risk I feel bound to accept.

# 2

# THE MEANING OF THE PAST

'Yes, I am fond of history.'

'I wish I were too. I read it a little as a duty, but it tells me nothing that does not vex or weary me. The quarrels of popes and kings, with wars or pestilences, in every page; the men all so good for nothing, and hardly any women at all – it is very tiresome: and yet I often think it odd that it should be so dull, for a great deal of it must be invention. The speeches that are put into the heroes' mouths, their thoughts and designs – the chief of all this must be invention, and invention is what delights me in other books.'

'Historians, you think,' said Miss Tilney, 'are not happy in their flights of fancy. They display imagination without raising interest. I am fond of history – and am very well contented to take the false with the true. In the principal facts they have sources of intelligence in former histories and records, which may be as much depended on, I conclude, as any thing that does not actually pass under one's own observation; and as for the little embellishments you speak of, they are embellishments, and I read them as such. If a speech be well drawn up, I read it with pleasure, by whomsoever it may be made – and probably with much greater, if the production of Mr Hume or Mr Robertson, than if the genuine words of Caractacus, Agricola, or Alfred the Great.'

Catherine Morland and Eleanor Tilney discuss history in *Northanger Abbey*, Chapter 25.

Rhetoric and rhetorical education might have died – actively suppressed – and been replaced by some more narrowly religious education when Christianity became a power in Rome. But in the long years in which Christians lived with and finally converted their pagan contemporaries, education, like other aspects of civilization, retained its hold. Rhetoric had formed many, if not most, of those early Church Fathers who created the great corpus of Christian dogma and doctrinal texts, and Christian writers responded to their rhetorical training with ambivalence, but seldom with a desire to abandon it altogether. The unlearned, or those who rejected learning for complete self-abnegation, left no literary legacy; that was the gift of scholars like Augustine and Jerome, for both of whom classical literature and classical techniques kept their imaginative grip. Inertia and adaptation guaranteed that rhetorical texts and commentaries held a place and were among the means of preserving at least an ideal standard of models and a reservoir of methods for over a thousand years.

While it is therefore true to say that all historians had some exposure to rhetoric, it is also trivial, because where there was formal education it was based upon literary models. Attention to conventions, and to the *topoi*, the conventional segments, of history was encouraged by reading and interpreting texts about the past. This does not imply a univocal Middle Ages writing, automaton-like, a single kind of 'history'; it helps ask what controlled the latitude of invention manifested by the books identified as 'historical'. It traces habits and expectations of reference, and, with them, considerations of genre and style. To put it sympathetically, historials were praised for their ability to reduce the flux of the past to an ordered, patterned account which had a satisfactory overall shape. To Cicero (*De legibus* 1.i.5), Herodotus was both the father of history and the father of lies, and no one seems to have found this contradictory until Petrarch.[1] Though countless prefaces warn of the dangers and difficulties inherent in verisimilar presentation, no consequent texts avoid or solve them. Even to speak of 'history' as a genre is to introduce large-scale problems of definition. Like 'Rhetoric' itself, 'history' meant, and still means, a subject; it implied a style, the verisimilar, which might be carried over into other types of writing, fiction (pure or mixed), for example.[2] Plausibility or inconsistency offer no obvious means of verification or falsification; the reader who wanted or needed to make judgements about the truth or falsehood of a historical account had to rely in large part on literary grounds. It was almost impossible for untrue history to be falsified where there was no exterior criterion of verifiability beyond the memory and judgement, even the taste, of the individual reader. This chapter will consider how the medieval range of writing which claims to represent true events which actually happened in the past employs the literary techniques of organization and expression that were encouraged by exposure to rhetorical categories and habits. After looking at ideas of history, and their closeness to poetry or fiction, I shall look at a number of *topoi*, examples of set-piece historical inventions.

Historical examples formed part of the thesaurus of rhetorical exercises in the largest sense.[3] The past was the central subject, the one most worth writing about if one was to take a secular theme – or even if one was to use a secular theme to demonstrate God's hand in history. While there was an assumption that one of the things that distinguished historical from fictional examples was that they referred to events that had really happened, there was also recognition that, since the 'historical' and 'fictional' styles overlapped when the events they narrated were verisimilar, no foolproof method of distinguishing the one from the other could be established. Where historical events were adduced as examples of good or bad conduct this was less important than it might seem. Historical examples written in historical style were read as eloquent and elegant before they were judged to be true or false; historical 'content' (in so far as that was separable from historical presentation) referred to a complex combination of past events and the interpretation of those events which could be recognized and interpreted in accordance with rhetorically related habits of understanding. It might be as well to think of this as, 'On the assumption that something very like this might be thought to have happened, how are we to understand the events?' Particularly when 'events' came to be thought of as a method of interpreting God's purpose in guiding human history toward its eschatological conclusion, what the events signified went well beyond what they were. Admixtures of invention, elaboration, and embellishment were a method of stylization *in order to* make the past comprehensible. The past is plotted, and histories are what look like histories. In so far as history represented the past it made dramatized examples of something for somebody; as soon as it showed any 'literary' ambition it was implicated in styles and methods of interpretation which were the province of rhetoric. No doubt the good historian, like the good orator, was by definition a good man. But like the orator, the historian had reasons to move and persuade his audience, and the idea of the disinterested preservation of the past is part of the claim to a trustworthy *ethos*. Creating or avoiding a particular narrative voice is one of the historian's many choices; the use of annotation or commentary allowed multiple tones. There are many ways to trace this claim about medieval historiography: one method would exemplify it by its own chronologically arranged plot, another by selecting significant examples of the recognizable and interpretable *topoi* of historical invention.

This chapter attempts a preliminary gaze in both directions; the Middle Ages were not univocal, and medieval historians were not automata, so that tracing some of the ways they manipulated and modified their inheritance has explanatory force. While most examples will be taken from the late Middle Ages, it may be worth suggesting that although renaissance historiography – like other areas of ostensible reform – intended to return to the qualities demonstrated by classical histories, it was long in divesting itself of those medieval accretions through which it read its model authors. To consider how they read and interpreted means looking at the models they imitated with a rhetorically alert eye, and at their senses of genre and style. For the history of history is in part the story of the imitation of story: what *was* imitable. If there was no clear distinction between the core of truth and the expressive embellishments which turned perception into language, there were certainly patterns of classification which can be recovered. These differences in intention and assumption have sometimes lured modern readers into dismissing individual medieval and renaissance historians as 'primarily' writers of romance, as if there were two hard and fast categories.[4] Froissart springs at once to mind, and the men who followed his example throughout the late Middle Ages, like Olivier de la Marche and Georges Chastellain. Modern historians disapprove their embellished histories because they are unreliable on too many specific points, but we need to take their intentions and styles seriously. It would be foolish to belabour the difference in mentalités, but present-mindedness is always with us, and the desire to save the appearances, to rescue some medieval historians for empiricism, may tempt readers, who desperately want what a historian says to be 'true' in modern terms, to assume that he alone is an exception to the medieval rule. There are undoubtedly medieval historians whose attitudes to 'truth' and 'accuracy' overlap modern truth conditions, but that is not all they do. This dilemma already existed for medieval historians themselves. Sometimes they can be found writing as if they could recognize and extract certain fundamental truths from earlier accounts. But the idea that they could distinguish (in order to reject) embellishment is belied by their practice, in part because – whatever they say – they discriminate according to multiple criteria with competing and contradictory values. The same writer who dismisses a predecessor's unwarranted expansions will silently take them over before going on to invent his own. Where the desire to write well, that is, to create recognizably stylish narratives according to the canons of previous historians, conflicted with the limitations of pre-existing witness, literary ambition overrode other considerations.

Because the organizing ideas of composition grew from rhetorical models and analyses, from assumptions about *topoi* and how to manipulate them,

It's never quite clear where she's coming from — what she's arguing against — & it seems to shift a lot.

The meaning of the past                           89

what counted as history embraced a much wider spectrum of presentation than later came to be acceptable. It may be convenient to think of some medieval history as a kind of commentary on what was believed to have happened, where the writer is always expressing his own or someone else's views about the past, rather than attempting an objective record. Geoffrey of Monmouth, mocked by some of his contemporaries for his fictions, could be taken seriously by later writers like Ralph Diceto, Robert of Gloucester, Peter of Langtoft, Gervase of Canterbury, and the Abingdon Chronicler exactly because their assumptions about the style and content of true tales about the past were different from ours, more elastic in presentation and interpretation. They were neither stupid nor credulous, but considered that the historian's right of invention did not invalidate the truth of what he wrote. After the twelfth-century renaissance re-established contact with classical models of historical writing, and generally improved the training in rhetoric available in schools, historians became even more ambitious to emulate their models. Some historians show so much literary pretension that their narrative may be unusable today as primary sources for specific events. Some examples would be Ailred of Rievaulx's *Relatio de Standardo*, Jordan Fantosme's rhymed *Chronique*, or Ambroise's *Estoire*. When Robert Wace turned from the pre-history of Britain to celebrate the Normans in his *Roman de Rou*, he retained his method and style.[5] But even these highly fictionalized histories were used *as* histories by their successors, who were less well informed than we are, who had less access to other kinds of evidence than we do, and whose expectations of what historical narratives should be like varied so dramatically. Peter of Langtoft wrote in a highly embellished style, which was no bar to Robert Manning of Bourne, when he based his own history on Peter's. In turn Manning's history was one of the bases for the first English prose *Brut* – an account of Britain since its foundation by a legendary refugee from the fall of Troy. Even in annals or chronicles, bare and brief recitations of 'what happened', classical references and rhetorical methods of presentation call attention to the deeply literary organization of much early historical writing. The implications of rhetorical organization for modern historians who want to use these texts as evidence are manifold. Empiricism is a seventeenth-century coinage which began with new approaches to medicine and old attitudes to the law. When new standards of history arose, in different places at different times, they often involved different misreadings of classical models, which attributed to Herodotus or Thucydides views found among modern contemporaries.

'Facts' may appear to be disappearing over a literary horizon; they are at least becoming more problematic. A well-described and moving event may indeed represent a possible version; the difficulty for the modern historian lies in assessing it. That is, if elegance is no guarantee of truthfulness, it is no bar to it either. Suspicion can be taken too far, and not every writer was trying to deceive. It remains a puzzle that historians thought at the time to be superior models of the historical enterprise, like Bede or William of Malmesbury, were indeed brilliant writers who *also* recorded at least some of the time the events of the past in ways that seem analogous to our ideas of accuracy. Perhaps this gives weight to the otherwise perplexing view that the good orator will be a good man. Perhaps it is an instance of the ways that incommensurable cultures can nevertheless coincide, so that any medieval view of what seems to accord with 'accuracy' must be taken in its own context: what kind of representation, with what referrals? Bede and William, like John of Salisbury, were learned both in the classical traditions of rhetoric and in the model texts upon which classical rhetoricians drew; perhaps it is no more than that, needing historiographical precedents, they sought, and found, rhetorical texts that gave them what they required. Bede is the most ambivalent of the three, as well as the one prone to impute (in his exegetical writing, when trying to explain discrepancies between what Apostles ought to know and what they say in public) the kinds of forensic ploys to biblical actors which we also find him exploiting in his own historical writing. For modern historians there is as much need as there ever was for corroborating evidence: itineraries, accounts, archeological remains, witnesses of different kinds where literary ambition was unlikely to obtrude. On the other hand, of course, literary analysis may be extremely revealing about contemporary attitudes. There are gains as well as losses. No simple distinction between writers of history and writers of romance is sufficient to deal with the range of licensed invention which occurs throughout medieval and renaissance writing. Nor can chroniclers be safely excluded from the strictures of literary analysis because their entries were short. Nothing is too short to be fabricated, or to rejoice in embellishment.

Herodotus and Thucydides are likely to loom as the models upon whom ancient history was based. This was not, however, the view of writers who succeeded them. The kinds of ethnographic and other research which Herodotus attempted seemed to later historians methodologically impracticable.[6] In this they were right. In ages without documents, reliance on traditions of hearsay seemed to be the only memory of the past, and history sometimes appeared to be the record of what people believed had occurred. When documents did begin to appear, they brought with them intractable problems of forgery. The notorious 'Donation of Constantine' is a famous case in point.[7] Tools such as numismatics, archaeology, or the analysis of period style upon which modern historians depend had not yet been invented. Given this reliance upon hearsay it is no wonder that Herodotus founded no school, though later historians, like Herodotus, found that they had to repeat, if not rely upon, common report.[8] Nor was Thucydides much more successful in establishing a standard model. His attempt to solve Herodotus' problem of evidence had been to write about his own times, about events which he had witnessed himself, or events about which other living witnesses could be consulted. But if *The Peloponnesian Wars* established the model of how a historical subject should be selected, it did not regulate the practice of succeeding generations. Thucydides' idea of 'scientific' history did not 'take', though he made war (political history) the paramount subject and the reportorial middle style paramount. It is for style that Quintilian recommends both Greek masters whom he matches with Livy and Sallust respectively in a certain indication that his eye is not on strict veracity of content.[9] That the training of an orator should include the reading of history is itself indicative of the literary culture which dominated education. If the knowledge of history did nothing else, it established a reservoir of examples which orators were condemned to repeat; it is knowledge of a literature, not knowledge of the past. Pliny, too, discussed these questions in his letters to Titinius Capito (replying to a suggestion that he write history) and to Cornelius Tacitus. He put the historical style between the styles of oratory and poetry, and though he agreed that history ought to be true, he recognized that it is often distinguished by the ease and grace with which it treated themes larger than the particularities of its narrative.[10] But it was not the shape of the overall composition that inspired Quintilian's praise: rather, it was for specific local effects.

These local effects inspired the same kinds of emotional reactions that were considered in Chapter 1. From the point of view of the development of history as a discipline – and historians were self conscious – overt dramatization suggests a failure of intent here. That is, strict adherence to the truth of what happened was sacrificed to 'pathos'.[11] This shift in emphasis toward moving and persuading the audience turned history closer to other kinds of writing: tragedy and epic were the highest genres to which historians aspired, but fiction, 'poetry', especially of the kind now categorized as 'romance' also played a part in giving shape to a plot and in speculating about character.

HISTORICAL FICTIONS

The forms by which we recognize that a long narrative is meant as 'history' are readily identifiable. The medieval author announces a subject which is taken from the past, often the recent past. He begins at the beginning, recounts the political and military deeds of those men (occasionally, though only exceptionally, women) who influenced the course of events which were of importance to the city or state, describes anecdotal material which illuminates the effects of those men and events upon the city or state, and draws from this narrative lessons of individual or corporate behaviour.[12] (Those writers who concentrate on individuals rather than corporations may be distinguished as biographers, and will be dealt with in the next chapter.) The historians's style is for the most part the middle style, recognizably serious and verisimilar. In speeches it could rise to the heights of tragic declamation.

Yet verisimilitude is not the same as true reporting, nor need true reporting always be verisimilar. The right of invention is an important point, and this chapter will concern itself with what controlled invention, embellishment, and manipulation. The first justification is that historical representation – of a plausible situation, of likely as well as moving speeches, of exemplary characters of great and wicked men – both delights and instructs.[13] Unspecified invention was not limited to speeches, perhaps the most obvious place where it is to be found. The situation in which the speeches were made, with all its circumstantial detail, was equally open to literary modification according to the skill of the writer. Indeed, skill was in part measured by manipulation.

The defence of invention – where defence might be thought to be needed – comes through two claims which present themselves as moral. Since examples gain force when they are true, history may be said to be superior to poetry. Since true examples are more forceful than precepts alone (like the common-places of the rhetorical education), history may be said to be superior to moral philosophy. While neither of these claims was to go unchallenged, the poets and philosophers having rather a lot to say for themselves, they remained commonplaces of the arguments. This covering law that truth is *morally* superior to fiction and, concomitantly, the fear that fiction might be by its very nature corrupting, had appeared and reappeared in classical thought. Plato stressed the moral force of a fictional example which was *believed* to be true in Book III of his *Republic*, where his conclusion contradicts the basic premise. He wanted certain versions of the past (e.g. that no citizen ever quarrelled with another citizen) to be presented as a true report in order to influence behaviour. The implication of this kind of instrumental use of the past is that the report may be manipulated on moral grounds, and this remained acceptable practice. It makes the past something analogous to a text which can be represented, interpreted, and translated.

The inclusion of legendary preambles to the main matter of a history became an accepted convention because they were the place to introduce the themes of the stories to come. Herodotus recounts in his *Histories* numerous stories that were, in effect, what people told him they believed. That is, in his view the historian's task included the report of those beliefs about the past which influenced present behaviour. His *Histories* open with a generational plot: a series of legendary rapes and counter-rapes which (like the mythic cycles explored by Greek tragedians) explain by the very familiarity of their patterns the enmity between Greeks and Persians which led in his own time to the battles of Marathon and Salamis. The abduction of the young girl, Io, from the Greek city of Argos was followed by Greek raids first on Tyre whence they kidnapped the King's daughter, Europa, then on Colchis, whence Jason carried off Medea. These Greek outrages provoked Paris, son of King Priam of Troy, to abduct Helen from Greece to Troy, and that provoked the Trojan War. Herodotus reports these legends as the Persian view of how East–West enmity first began; he deliberately refrains from judging the truth or falsehood of the legends, or even commenting upon the ubiquity of *revenge* as a motive. If they were, in any case, too remote for his reach, they at least function as a literary introduction and focus themes to come.

Livy, whose history of Rome was a pre-eminent model for European writers from the late Middle Ages onwards, began with the fall of Troy, because one legend said that Rome had originally been founded by Aeneas, hat aristocratic Trojan refugee. Like his great Greek predecessor, Livy reflects on the legends and their place in his book, employing them while denying any responsibility for them, calling attention to what he holds at arm's length.

The traditions of what happened prior to the foundation of the City or whilst it was being built, are more fitted to adorn the creations of the poet than the authentic records of the historian, and I have no intention of establishing either their truth or their falsehood . . . But whatever opinions may be formed or criticisms passed upon these and similar traditions, I regard them as of small importance. The subjects to which I would ask each of my readers to devote his attention are these – the life and morals of the community; the men and qualities by which through domestic policy and foreign wars dominion was won and extended . . . There is this exceptionally beneficial and fruitful advantage to be derived from the study of the past, that you see, set in the clear light of historical truth, examples of every possible type. From these you may select for yourself and your country what to imitate, and also what being mischievous in its inception and disastrous in its issues, you are to avoid.[14]

Given that the point of history is to celebrate the past (with all that that implies about the latitude of the epideictic mode) and to provide examples of behaviour for the present, the details of traditional beliefs weighed lightly upon Herodotus of Livy or other classical historians. They were certainly weighed on a different scale from those events which had happened within living memory, where the historian's version might have to compete with several others. Despite Livy's strong assertion, poetry and history were not easily separable – perhaps the reason for the attempted firm distinction. Poetry had its own special prestige. What is initially more puzzling is why historical writing survived at all through ages when Christian education might have been thought to have eradicated anything but the example of aspiring to a heavenly future kingdom. Ambition is always with us, if not for ourselves or our families, then for the institutions with which we are associated, even for our gods. That Judaism was a historically oriented religion, in which an interpretation of the past was a proof of God manifesting Himself in time, provides part of the answer. But it is important to recall the high status of the historical accounts which survived as the classical heritage of poetry, and which formed the basis of classical education.[15] This never eradicated the problems raised by the existence of secular history, and many historians evince discomfort (which may in itself be a *topos* of perplexity) with the competing systems of values.

  Livy's retention of popular legendary stories (what hostile critics might call the fictions of poets) provided both a precedent and a justification for historians who followed him. Hundreds of years later, in what had once been an outpost of the Empire, the Christian historian, Bede, defined this method:

Should the reader discover any inaccuracies in what I have written, I humbly beg that he will not impute them to me, because, as the laws of history require, I have laboured honestly to transmit whatever I could ascertain from common report for the instruction of posterity.[16]

'Common report', essentially rumour, has never been thought to be an accurate source or a sceptical witness, and historians have always known this. Loathe to lose any remnant of evidence, loathe to relinquish a way of inserting non-authorized opinions which could be attributed to anonymous sources, medieval historians themselves argued about 'common report' and how it might be used. Even sceptical historians might accept that if oral traditions offered nothing else, they gave important testimony to what people had traditionally believed (which itself presented a topic for discussion, because such beliefs could be weighed and compared, where *comparing* might offer an opportunity to the rhetorically alert). An allegiance to truth never precluded the use of suspect material; nor did history exclude certain embellishments of that material. One embellishment might be an ostensible rejection of suspect material which, by its very existence, retained precisely what it pretended to discard. What kind of representation of what understanding for which audience are essential questions to ask when evaluating medieval and renaissance history. How far it is either any more than testimony to current opinion, or whether it can be trusted as a reliable account are questions which raise other issues. Most modern historians of the Middle Ages develop what they characterize as a 'feel' for when medieval historians can be trusted. Since the encouragement of some kind of intuitive sympathy was itself one of the rhetorician's goals, early warnings about *ethos* may help readers coming to medieval historians for the first time. The seductive experience of wanting what a favourite medieval historian says to be true sometimes to the detriment of one's better judgement continues to be part of the experience of many case-hardened researchers. By analysing individual *topoi* and situating them within a system of rhetorically manipulated reference, I hope to demonstrate how pervasive 'literary' habits of embellishment were, that 'realism' is a constantly shifting style which is constantly remade, not a guarantee of a true depiction, and that however convincing, charming, fresh, or intelligent an account, it may be no more (but no less) than a *plausible* construction which refers to known patterns of human character, behaviour, and event. The styles chosen by historians involve multiple reference: to the particular past narrated; to earlier models of writing history; to other, early literary models (like epics or fictions, or poems of many kinds); and to over-arching (or perhaps underpinning) eschatological ideas of human history. The next chapter will discuss the ways that Christianity expanded deeds done to include deeds suffered, and thus changed the meaning of heroism. The rest of this chapter looks at the implications of this freedom.

Rhetorical historians assumed a great latitude of invention, and went on doing so at least into the sixteenth century. Textbooks taught schoolboys to write speeches for historical agents. As Erasmus put it, describing the school exercise he called 'effictiones':

> To this class especially belongs the figure [dialogismos], that is, *serminocinatio*, the attribution to an individual of language in harmony with his age, birth, country, life, purpose, spirit, and behaviour. It is all right to compose speeches of this sort in history, for example; wherefore so many of the speeches of Thucydides, Sallust, and Livy are composed, as well as letters and apophthegms, and indeed, thoughts, as of the man talking with himself, although this is more common in the poets.[17]

This combination of direction plus reference to model texts will seem familiar from the *progymnasmata* described in the previous chapter, as will his remark that historians and poets use certain techniques in common. The description or dramatization of 'what happened' may represent 'what happened', but it may also be a sign of common report, of opinions about 'what happened', of 'what ought to have happened', or of what ought to have happened ought to have meant. The system of apparent referral refers also to systems of signs. The convention of unspecified invention, as Erasmus points out, was not limited to speeches, nor even to letters, apothegms, and thoughts. In this the historian was bound to be close to the poet (whichever of them was writing in verse), a conjunction which was repeatedly noticed. There is little comment on methods of interpretation that would distinguish the one from the other.[18] What truth was was not merely a jest for Pilate. It might be an understanding to which history pointed. Even when an author had no intention of slanting or distorting the past his plausible inventions might be the best way he could find to make his conception of it convincing. In the hands of a man who was trying to justify the present this could, and did, result in something which has for us the most unpleasant connotations: forgery and propaganda are two of the names by which we denote partisan accounts of the past. Yet if one remembers the orator's instructions to the speaker who is defending a client, the suppression of damaging evidence and the judicious use of fictions was enjoined upon him. In a court of law reliance on hearsay was suspect, but in a work of history hearsay might be all the evidence there was.[19] When documents did begin to appear they brought with them intractable problems, since the 'letters' included in any history, so far from having been written by the authors to whom they attributed, could be the inventions of the historian.

The *progymnasmata*, the rhetorical exercises of Chapter 1, suggest a rough guide to the kinds of scenes likeliest to turn up in medieval histories: speeches, especially exhortations before battles, arguments, defences of courses taken; descriptions of towns; and 'characters' of great men. It might be better to think of this the other way around: students of 'histories' would find specific instructions if they had access to rhetoric books. Since school exercises had often been derived from ostensibly historical texts, whether in prose or verse, histories made excellent models for orators – or historians. If the definitions of 'history' which Antiquity bequeathed to the Middle Ages seem to raise more problems than they resolve, that accurately reflects the uncertainties many writers felt – and exploited. Most rhetoricians use a phrase that can be traced back at least to Cicero: history is the record of deeds actually done in the past remote from our memory.[20] Cicero himself believed that the past could be – and should be – manipulated and embroidered in order to bring out important moral or exemplary points, and so did the writers who followed him.

It thus becomes important to know not only what classical texts were used as models by medieval and renaissance writers, but also to try to understand how those texts were read, or misread. An adequate assessment would require a large-scale historiographical study, but some indications can be made. One must always remember the importance of reconciling the pagan and Christian inheritance, and the long-lived belief that the Hebrew patriarchs and heroes had anticipated most pagan discoveries and adventures. There is a combination here of competitive emulation and sheer envious rivalry. Influential writers like Isidore of Seville, whose *Etymologiae* provided a basic authoritative encyclopedic guide to knowledge, continued to claim Moses as the first historian, followed by 'Dares' (the supposed author of a supposed history of the Trojan War), and only later Herodotus; sacred history preceded, but never finally displaced, secular models.[21] Roman writers Lucan, Livy, Sallust, and Suetonius joined the ranks of major authors, and after them such ostensible 'epitomizers' as the historian known as 'Justin'.[22] Important Latin histories were translated in the Middle Ages as *Li Fet des Romains*, the deeds of the Romans, and bound together with other, original French works in verse which created the impression of a continuous historical narrative from a beginning like the Foundation of Rome, or Creation, to contemporary times.[23]

If one thinks for a moment about this list, one author who stands out is 'Dares'. His book, purporting to be an eye-witness account of the Trojan

War from the Trojan point of view (unlike, that is, Homer), is concise to the point of crudity. It isn't a *history* at all in any modern sense, but it wasn't until the seventeenth-century edition of the text by Perizonius that there was a serious scholarly claim that it was less (or more) than it claimed to be.[24] Modern scholarship classifies the book as a late historical romance, a historical fiction which it occurred to someone to create, and to attribute to a character who appears in Homer as having been at Troy.[25] It was an influential book, and the various possible interpretations of its status led to other, apparently historical, books being based on it. It introduced a latitude, even an uncertainty, in its alternative version, which was fruitful for later authors, if only because it presupposes another point of view. If a historian's uncertainty principle might be suggested, conflicting evidence makes space for new interpretations. Whatever they say to the contrary, many historians love a vacuum. For the past was by no means exclusively the prerogative of the historian, however he interpreted his task. The epic poet and the tragedian had both extracted their subjects from 'deeds done in the past remote from our memories'. The poets' accounts of the past served as something very similar to history; for the Greeks before Herodotus Homer *was* history, but the kind of history written by poets. So, in medieval and renaissance Europe, were Lucan or numerous other verse-accounts. Poetic versions of the past might be assumed to convey a version, however partisan (like Homer, who was on the 'wrong' side), of what had happened. The 'Trojan' Dares provided a necessary corrective to the Greek Homer's version. Neither form nor style were necessarily dependable guides to truth; bad writing might be accurate, but so might the most elegant poetry be. Lucan's *Pharsalia*, which was intended as an epic poem to rival Virgil's *Aeneid*, benefitted from the dignity of its form, which gave a spurious validity to its content. Once it had been translated into French prose and amalgamated with Sallust to form *Li Fet des Romains*, its authority could hardly be impugned, but it was an authority with limits. The interpretation of a text in verse as unreliable tends to be an ex post facto reason brought in to reinforce other interpretative conclusions. The ostensibly superior accuracy of prose had become an accepted *topos* from which discussion began.[26] The extraction of historical matter from poetic manner was defensible on several grounds. The subjects of poets and historians had always been recognizably similar. The poet was allowed more latitude of embellishment than the historian especially when writing of the distant past; but for both kinds of writers embellishment stemmed from the same basis of reading and writing, and took advantage of the same techniques; latitude is a distinction of degree not kind. The historian of the distant past (sometimes difficult to distinguish from the poet) had more latitude than the historian of the recent past (although, as late as Drayton's attempt to versify history in his *Polyolbion*, the impulse to combine the two remained).[27] As the poet used history as his source, so might the careful historian extract the historical basis from the poet's fictional account. The association 'prose/accuracy' versus 'verse/fiction' is often unstated but present. The use of verse may indeed be an expression of ambition; but so, in a different ambition, may be the choice of prose.

The authors of the Anglo-Saxon Chronicle inserted verses that are usually classed as epic poetry into their historical narrative. In their eyes 'The Battle of Brunaburgh', whatever its shortcomings or problems as a source, was acceptable history.[28] Robert Wace amplified Latin sources for his history of the Dukes of Normandy. At the end of the Middle Ages we find a poem about Agincourt inserted into a history of the reign of Henry V; the writer began by transferring the poem into prose, but seems to have given that up, so that the verses are recognizably poetry.[29]

The known patterns of human character and behaviour referred to above are a particularly vexed issue, one which this chapter and the next will explore. Histories have actors, and the characters of great men were an area, like their speeches, which gave historians pause, both for thought and creation. Where they make their actors speak, they may be preparing a moral case against them, which they will summarize at some later point, or the speaking actors may be contingent to some abstract moral point. Each example may raise questions of many different kinds. Sometimes a preliminary decoding can take place. Consider the following simple sentence as an example of the complexities of representation and referral which may arise at any time. Matthew of Westminster, a thirteenth-century English chronicler, describes at one point a man's angry reaction to the news that his enemy has escaped from his power:

And when all this became known to the lord the emperor, he gnashed his teeth like a satyr and said, 'The wicked flees when no one pursues, and he who is conscious of guilt is afraid, though no one accuses him; I see plainly why he has fled: it is that he may meet the French and English, who are about to give him money'.[30]

It is not accidental that this passage reads like several quoted above in Chapter 1. The teeth-gnashing is one of the conventionalized expressions of anger, like biting the lips or shaking a fist, and signals the strength of the anger: he didn't just gnash his teeth, but he gnashed them like some frenzied, inhuman creature, a man succumbing to irrational passion. Medieval historians didn't see many goat-men; the 'satyr', like Geoffrey of Monmouth's use of 'Mars' quoted above, is a stylistic pretension. It is not a compliment, but a negative description. The emperor is represented as a man susceptible to irrational passion when crossed: bad ethos. This therefore provides a context for what he says. We may call such scenes 'acted out' or even 'dramatized' without introducing generic difficulties for ourselves because the legacy of 'tragic history' exploited the presentation of gesture and expression in texts of different kinds. This might be an entirely fictional emperor and it might be any man angry to the point of irrationality. When then Matthew attributes a generalization from the Bible, itself elegantly expressed in balanced *sententiae* which provide a commonly accepted analysis of human motive, there is not much difference between his angry emperor and the depiction of Henry VII's grief over Stanley quoted in the previous chapter.[31] The Bible dramatizes, too. Here the emperor's anger and suspicion are the point of Matthew's invention, a point which he can use both as characterization and explanation, because the behaviour – what we might call the paranoia – of angry and suspicious men is known and predictable. But so also is our recognition of the unmarked quotation, which, while it assimilates this instance to 'universal' perceptions of anger, simultaneously raises its importance without limiting our interpretation: in Matthew's scheme of styles the Emperor Frederick, though no hero, speaks in the high register appropriate to his status, even if, perhaps especially because, he misappropriates its resonance. That it is wildly implausible that a man in the heat of passion would quote such a *long* observation, even from the Bible, is neither here nor there. Matthew's presentation is dramatic and stylized, not *realistic*.

Matthew's entry for the year 1244 raises important, if smaller-scale, questions of historical genre, that is, of types of historical writing. There is an assumption that so-called 'chronicles' may contain less embellishment than ambitious, literarily organized 'histories' if only because the unit of entry, the year, is shorter – as if decoration were a kind of static. Matthew's book collects events of importance year by year, but many of the entries are long, long enough to be expressed with conscious artifice. There is an apparent relinquishing of any literary shaping in the large, architectonic sense: a year, not an event, shapes the work. Nevertheless, there is a semblance of plot, with England as its hero, on the largest scale, while at the small scale of scene the local effects are cunningly shaped. Chroniclers pride themselves on the strict brevity with which they record the past, and Matthew is typical in his insistence on these qualities when, at the end of his report on the battle of Lewes (1264) he interrupts his brief lament for the slain, which has been full of apostrophes:

Let a poet enumerate all the various occurrence of the day with more license or at greater length, and dwell upon the different kinds of death by which men fell, but brevity keeps us in by a much stricter law, and does not allow us to say how each thing happened, but only what took place.[32]

This *occupatio* demonstrates Matthew's awareness of other genres, and the decorum of the one in which he is writing. Even here, though, one is led to wonder about the elasticity of brevity's strict law. His final distinction, too, leaves considerable latitude. In some ways what distinguishes him is a matter of scale, of the size of the unit manipulated. More ambitious writers, who took reigns or crusades (i.e. delineated or boundaried events, with recognizable beginnings and ends) as their subjects, were much more expansive, and, if Gervase of Canterbury is to be believed, they distinguished themselves from chroniclers like Matthew, mere jotters down of unconnected events.[33] Historians aspired to literary unity. Yet, whether these writers about the past thought of themselves as historians or chroniclers, they used rhetorical embellishments.

The apparently obvious trap is the difficulty posed by plausible fictions: how could the historian be sure which parts of an epic were 'historical', which the inventions of the poet? The simple answer is that while plausibility and verisimilitude seemed to provide a basis for discrimination, in fact historians could seldom be sure. Yet there is a less obvious but no less problematic trap, which is how far their true/false distinction accords with ours: they say they adhere to the truth, but define 'the truth' with more latitude than we do, to include embellishment. Where legal claims depended upon an interpretation of past events, the precise nature of those events mattered, though even there interpretation intervened, as the disputes on either side of 1066 remind us. Where history represented a thematic story tracing exemplary deeds, it is not clear how much difference different reports made. Like the good orator's, the good historian's *ethos* posited his reliability. Criteria of plausibility and verisimilitude change, too. However much writers worried about the problem, it remained intractable – but they continued to extract what *seemed* historical from those earlier accounts of all kinds which were their only sources. Not only might a historian use what looked likely, he also used, suitably reinterpreted, unlikely looking material that he could find some way to rationalize. This may help to explain the constant reference to earlier authority: knowing the difficulty of vouching for the 'truth', authors could at least, or perhaps at most, vouch for each other. If not true, at least authorized (as Petrarch jokes in his famous letter to Boccaccio about his retelling of the Griselda story, which he took not from history, but from Boccaccio himself). The importance of jokes on the subject of truth and authority suggests that they were questions discussed and understood. If authorized, 'truth' might be secondary. An author might be quoted in order to introduce uncertainty. There is an inescapable but highly exploited interpretative circularity here which depends upon the varieties of authority which authorities had.

Methods of interpreting plausible reports by explaining them in rational or realistic terms were already habitual in Antiquity. One may think of it as reversing the direction of allegory: instead of making a symbol out of events, the historian would try to understand what events had encouraged poets to create a symbol. It is a process akin to translation.[34] One of the oldest examples is the assumption that many gods were in fact heroes or kings whose elevation was the result of stories told about them. Find the basis for their fame, explain it, and god returns to man once more. This analysis was traditionally ascribed to a Greek interpreter called Euhemerus – but there is not a lot of evidence for his actual existence, either. The implications are manifold. Not only does the idea of a 'euhemerized' Hercules enable the historian to employ the hero in his history of, say, Burgundy, but events, too, became grist for rationalization.[35] If Jason's quest for a golden fleece seemed hard to swallow, the fleece could be – and was – rationalized away. Some historians took it to represent the golden treasure of the Colchians from whom Jason stole it; for others, cruder perhaps, the fleece was a technological breakthrough in panning for gold. One held a sheepskin in a running stream, where it picked up gold dust, rather like a sieve. The absurdities of this method are obvious, but the impulse must be taken seriously. Whatever the extravagances of the explanations, the historians who invented them were trying, on meagre and misleading evidence, to understand what must have happened. Robert Graves exemplifies precisely this rationalizing tendency in both his historical fictions and his studies of myth. The assumption that a reader could prune away the poetical extravagances and reveal the underlying truth was both widespread and long-lived. One man's poetical extravagance may seem another man's gospel. Any incident or small-scale unit might be questioned without denying the validity of the whole. It seems clear that just as orators rethought their speeches for different audiences, so the audience to whom a work was addressed also made a difference to the latitude a historian might allow himself. A historical work written in the language of scholars for an audience of scholars might find itself submitted to stricter criteria than a rhymed vernacular narrative meant to amuse and instruct a comparatively ignorant nobility, for whom elegant Sallustian parallels would convey nothing. 'Stricter' itself introduces potentially anachronistic values, and one cannot draw lines simply according to language. By contrast to the attacks on Geoffrey of Monmouth's British history, Guido delle Colonne's thirteenth-century fabulous narrative of the history of Troy was widely accepted.[36] Both accounts are in Latin, full of rhetorical embellishments, inventions, and impossibilities; both were successful and often translated and adapted by vernacular historians.[37] No one knows Geoffrey's main sources, but Guido's are clear enough: in addition to the spurious historian, Dares, Guido used without acknowledgement the French *Roman de Troie* of the previous century, a versified expansion of Dares by Benoît de Ste.-Maure, a contemporary – perhaps a more successful one – of Robert Wace. Both these histories are accounts of the *very* long ago and far away, that other variable of permitted embellishment. Of necessity, there would be great gaps which the historian would endeavour to fill in. This would be the less true the more modern the events narrated.

For modern readers who wish to use these medieval and renaissance texts as primary sources this poses numerous problems. One needs not only to be able to recognize a variety of historical conventions in order to measure the extent and depth of authorial invention, but also to understand how the conventions are being used. With Matthew's angry emperor quoted above it is clear enough that the description tells us something that has to do, in literary terms, with character and motive. But *did* the pope flee because he was afraid of the emperor? Was he in the pay of the French and English? Did any of this happen? These questions are hard to answer; they require corroborative evidence itself untainted by influence, bias, or the same rhetorically conceived method of presentation. Money talks, and though accounts can be padded, they may well provide that useful corroboration. Perhaps we can only say that there was discord between the temporal and spiritual powers. The temptation to realize the potential of any dramatic scene proved practically irresistible to most medieval and renaissance writers; the more learned, the more widely read in historical writing, the likelier they were to embellish the bare bones of historical report. Their schooling and their reading had encouraged just this. Nor should we blame medieval and renaissance historians for dramatizing or embellishing their accounts of the past. In terms of their understanding of the organization of good writing, the clear light of historical truth meant a rhetorical presentation of what was believed to have happened. Or, a plausible narration of what was likely to have happened – which could mean the attribution of speeches or deeds to 'villains' of the whole story or period who were perhaps not *actually* present at the scene or scenes described. This implies, too, that characterization may precede events. That is, the assignment of roles may be due to a prior judgement about who was or might have been or might later have become an evil figure, a corrupt servant, an untrustworthy councillor. Richard III's hump, the outward manifestation of his inward evil, is an invention now too well-known to belabour, but that it is one example of a widespread habit is worth remarking. This offers, along the way, an explanation of the use of invented letters and even forged documents: in presenting the truth, historians understood themselves to be obliged not only to repair the gaps in the record due to the mischance of fortune, but to embody their conception of the past.

Perhaps one should refer to a hierarchy of pasts. For authors dealing in 'ancient' history gaps were inevitable, and eye-witnesses impossible. The question of European origins and of moral example provided by the glorious deeds of forebears justified what they were doing. The same rhetorically inspired conventions supplied them with ideas, models, and examples not only of how to write, but of what to write – that discipline of finding the 'places' which the schoolboy's habit was to expand. We can schematize the kinds of criteria that I have been suggesting are part of a rhetorical mode of writing history. In order to understand how much embellishment a reader is likely to find in a historical work one needs first to ask a limited question about what kind of history it is: e.g. annal, chronicle, or unitary history dealing with precisely defined events, then to match it both to similar and to related works to consider possible literary affiliations – though this smacks of a counsel of perfection. As this may appear to contradict something suggested above, I shall develop this in a moment. What audience is the work intended for, and what can we expect from this about style, extent of embellishment, selection of material? Latin-writing historians often reveal their sources and models by their style, imitation, and actual quotation of classical historians. Guido delle Colonne is one of several authors to make explicit reference to a range of classical texts. Those of us who read in translation are dependent upon scholarly notes, but even in translation it is often still possible to recognize a set theme when it appears, even if we do not hear allusion or quotation. Each new work was a potential addition to the tissue of 'prior' writings. Each might offer reinterpretations of conventional representations, modifying the conventions subtly as they reworked them. An excess of scepticism can only increase a reader's caution when trying to decide whether things reported were actually things done.

## EXERCISING HISTORICAL INVENTION

In a writing society in which humility was (at least ostensibly) a paramount virtue, historians were unlikely to push themselves forward. They tended to justify their undertakings in several ways: in a general sense they agreed that it is important to avoid idleness (and writing is an acceptable action) and that they were obeying a command (so that personal ambition has nothing to do with what moved them), or even – though this came late – that they were interested in the study of the past or the establishment of institutions, interests, given the otherworldly emphasis of a great part of medieval culture, which needed some defending. Reference to earlier secular texts which do just this act as one kind of defence via appeal to precedent. It may be also that they claimed to have witnessed events, or to have had access to witnesses, or to have possessed important sources. During the Middle Ages, when there was a tension-producing divide between the great actors of political deeds and men who could write, historians were almost without exception in religious orders and defenders of religion's institutions. The value of ambition might well depend upon the writer's point of view, so that local saint, monastic house, generous magnate or king might find praised what in rival saint, monastic house, or hostile aristocrat was unacceptable.[38] Interest in secular writing was a marked curiosity. Even Dante did not choose to write the prose history of his times, but something complex, more ambitious, and more precious, which does not scruple to use the historical style for revenge.

The double distance of historian from his subject and from the assured generic ambition of literary accomplishment led writers to insist that they wrote under correction, that is, that they did not set themselves up as *authorities*, but submitted to the judgement of their readers a tentative account, written in poor style because they were – whether they were or not – rude, untaught fellows entirely lacking in eloquence. This is, of course, the humility *topos*, but it is worth remarking that the aspiration on which it focusses is high rhetorical style. Concomitantly, they did not claim the high textual status for their prose that accrued to, say, Livy's. Even when they *were* eyewitnesses they seldom seem to have expected close *textual* attention.

An author like Philippe de Commynes may *claim* eye-witness status, and that he tells the truth and nothing but the truth, but he embellishes what he saw in order to point his moral lessons, as his description of the death of Louis XI shows.[39] His claims to innovate by avoiding panegyric resemble Anthony's denial in *Julius Caesar* that he will praise the dead; Commynes is led to internal inconsistency when faced with the drama of the deathbed scene, and although his dying king can barely speak he is nevertheless full of wise discourses upon government and the duty of the prince. As to the most general justification of writing about the past – important in a society which pretended to be above ambition, to despise the world and the flesh – there are a series of moral defences, which came slowly to be common coin. First, it is right to remember the deeds of one's forebears; they present the current generation with models of how to act, or of how *not* to act; and they remind their readers of the vicissitudes of fortune and the stoicism and faith necessary to deal with the turnings of Fortune's Wheel. It is this idea of the past as a *moral* example which constantly legitimated the embellishing or moulding of earlier accounts, and encouraged the conception of the past as a source of actual moral exempla which ultimately justified the study of secular history. That is, writers tended to *say* that there were certain acceptable ways of interpreting written history which justified writing it. The shock created by Macchiavelli came partly from his refusal to follow this traditional pretence. Yet even he could not bring the reign of poetic justice to an end.

In its way, history asserted continuity, not least as a repository of rights and privileges, very like the law whose servant it might be, since the precedent of ancestral deeds (in both senses) might be used to argue for or justify current claims to rank, land, liberty, or, that great intangible, prestige.[40] This is not the same as recording, or finding out, exactly what happened in the past. While its extreme form might be described as developing plot as argument, there is almost always an element of the justifying or explicative story about historical narrative. In the fifteenth century, the apparent nonsense of working Hercules into the Duke of Burgundy's family tree was an attempt to elevate the integrity of his family and their holdings through a claim to supra-princely antiquity; this was a step in an argument which might be thought to 'restore' (that is, claim by invention) its status as a principality rather than a dukedom. 'Let us now praise famous men' had biblical as well as classical force behind it, and the Dukes of Burgundy assimilated Gideon, too, to their banner. One sign of an author's allegiance may be a reference to those earlier authors in whose footsteps he claimed to be following. Nicholas Trevet (who is explicit about the manipulations of style and historical fiction) began his 'Annals' with a reference to Sallust; John of Salisbury alluded to the biblical books of *Chronicles*.[41] These are not only justifications for an activity, but cues to what we may expect to find, cues to literary expectations and to the style in which the history is presented. The more learned and ambitious the writer, the likelier he is to organize his writing according to convention. Knowing the conventions is incumbent upon his readers, and a feel for style may reveal the author's attitude.

To his well-beloved lord Robert, son of King Henry and Earl of Gloucester, William the librarian of Malmesbury sends the wish that he may triumph in heaven when he has ended his victories on earth. Most of the achievements of your father of illustrious memory I have not failed to set down, both in the fifth book of the deeds of the kings and in the three little books to which I have given the name of Chronicles.

Now Your Highness's mind desires the transmission to posterity of those things that by a very wonderful dispensation of God, have befallen in England in recent times: indeed a very noble desire and like everything in you. For what is more to the advantage of virtue or more conducive to justice than learning the divine gentleness to the good and vengeance upon traitors? Further, what is pleasanter than consigning to historical records [monimentis tradere litterarum] the deeds of brave men, that following their examples the others may cast off cowardice and arm themselves to defend their country?[42]

This introduction tells us of an almost panglossian plot to come, in which God manifests himself in history, and good triumphs in the end. That William sees his work as 'pleasant' (the original is 'iocundius') suggests literary stylishness, with an eye to the form of the story. And indeed his attributions of motive confirm the suggestions of the prologue.

Of the exercises discussed in Chapter 1, certain were eminently useful to historians, and might turn up at any appropriate point. These *topoi* are a category of rhetorical organization, individual 'topics' which people recognized as being discrete subjects for treatment. The style of treatment could vary, depending on the register of language being used (high or low style), the place of the *topos* in a larger work, the kind of work in which it was being used. It is repetition which makes *topoi*: as soon as writers become aware that they are repeating a unit which has appeared before, their interpretation becomes self-conscious, because it expects readers to compare it to another. Such units can be recognized across genre boundaries, and it is important to remember that this recognition and comparison was part of the pleasure of reading. There is something inescapably intertextual in this kind of reading, when the alert interpreter is constantly on the lookout for what it is he is supposed to be reminded of, and in which texts he has seen it before. This intertextual recognition distracts from any concentration upon the distinct truth or falsehood of an account and encourages attention to the style of the dramatization. Spotting the scheme, trope, or *topos* could be an end in itself, but need not be. It does, however, introduce an extra mimesis: of other books, other representations, as well as of a possible past. It is a kind of deferral.[43]

Set pieces, units, topoi, whatever one calls them, they may even have begun with a new description of something which had happened. The dangers of crossing a river are real dangers; writing about those dangers becomes a literary *topos* when the writer has one eye on the ways other men have dealt with them. The better educated, the more steeped in Latin literature an author was, the more certain it would be that rhetorical ways of reading and writing had been inculcated in him from an early age, and the likelier he would be to write with an ambition to emulate his Latin predecessors. The implications of this, if drawn to their logical conclusion, suggest that the more sophisticated the historian in terms of his literary education and the breadth of his reading, the less reliable – in modern terms – his narrative might be. He would constantly transform the material at his disposal according to the habits of rhetorical reworking he had learned. This does not mean that because an account is well-written it lies, distorts, or misrepresents the past, but it warns against thinking stylistic or architectonic skill (or lack of skill) guarantees truth. Narratives must be tested against sources of other kinds, which point at least to the historian's attitude to past events. It is time to turn from precept to example, by looking at some set pieces that are typically found in historical works. The point of identifying these *topoi* is not to discredit them, for that would be to return to a modern empirically based true/false test; it is to suggest the beginnings of a flexible critical analysis. I take the following examples to be common and important, but indicative rather than exhaustive. While they may derive from a specific classical source, they undergo intermittent modification, especially in the hands of talented writers.

The set piece description of a place was one of the categories of *descriptio* which all schoolboys practised. Fortifications, forests, or rivers constantly appear, though they seem to have been lower in descriptive status than, say, descriptions of cities. The Angevin historian 'William FitzStephen', spent several pages on London, its buildings, cookhouse, countryside, inhabitants, schools (one can almost feel his teacher's list of topics cranking away) before getting down to the business of describing the events which led to the death of Thomas Becket.[44] William quoted Horace, Virgil, Ovid, Persius, and Geoffrey of Monmouth in the course of his description, which involves his ambition for his subject and his book. The more of a metropolis London is, the more important its events. Ralph Diceto expatiates upon the beauties of the ancient city of Angers as part of his annal entry for A. D. 1150.[45] He attends to the city walls, its buildings, inhabitants, its wealth of saints and religious houses; he calls attention to the rivers which run through it, the Loire and the Mayenne, and to its famous bridges, on which small workshops had been erected. As William mentioned London's cookhouse, so Ralph emphasizes the cookery of beef and ducks in Aquitaine. Both authors are including the customs of the inhabitants as part of the description of a city, and there is no need to posit local patriotism as the main reason for its existence. Such descriptions could be turned to satire, as in Richard of Devizes' criticism of London, which he puts into the mouth of a French Jew (thus, given the anti-Semitism of the age, creating an equivocal speaker, whose *ethos*, moral trustworthiness, is questionable):

When you reach England, if you come to London, pass through it quickly, for I do not at all like that city. All sorts of men crowd together there from every country under the heavens. Each race brings its own vices and its own customs to the city. No-one lives in it without falling into some sort of crime. Every quarter of it abounds in grave obscenities. The greater a rascal a man is, the better a man is he accounted . . . whatever evil or malicious thing that can be found in any part of the world, you will find in that one city. Do not associate with the crowds of pimps; do not mingle with the throngs in eating-houses; avoid dice and gambling, the theatre and the tavern. You will meet with more braggarts there than in all France; the number of parasites is infinite. Actors, jesters, smooth-skinned lads, moors, flatterers, pretty boys, effeminates, pederasts, singing and dancing girls, quacks, belly-dancers, sorceresses, extortioners, night-wanderers, magicians, mimes, buffoons: all this tribe fill all the houses.[46]

This is clearly a conglomerate description, which owes something to Horace on Rome, a city which is likely to have been much better supplied with the iniquities Richard lists than was medieval London. This is *not* evidence for the existence of theatres, for example; they are part and parcel of the list of vices. That many historical descriptions contain similar lists is one signal that the author has his eye on a model: here a moral warning against bad companions.

The position, as well as the tone, of a description of a place, with its normal adjuncts of praise or blame, may tell us something. Sometimes it forms part of the geographical background to events (often an early section in a history).[47] It may be somewhere visited, even a key scene of action, thus there to tell us something about what kind of person moved in what ways for what reasons. In Lucan's *Pharsalia* the description of a place sometimes led to another insertion, a story explaining how the place acquired its name.[48] This kind of learned digression continued to be popular: 'Nennius' included legends about place names, sometimes legends which contradicted each other.[49] So did Geoffrey of Monmouth, and after him Orderic Vitalis.[50] It is difficult, often impossible, to tell whether the historian is reporting local belief (Bede's true law of history) with or without his own embellishments, or when he is making a story up altogether. Yet we must ask, because, in a society which thought of words as real indicators of real realities, and of the physical world as being interpretable in the way that a book is interpretable, names of places, legends associated with places, might be a guide to events and the way those events were meant to be understood. In addition, there was another kind of encouragement to digressive descriptions (one more purely literary): they gave pleasure to the reader for themselves, and for the change of pace they provided. While a description *may* offer a true report of what something looked like, it is as well not to assume that it does without corroboration, like archeological remains, even a map to confirm that hills or rivers really are where the author says they are should always be sought.[51]

The rhetorical exercises of *suasoria*, the throes of a difficult decision, and *controversia*, the defence of a course already taken, were adapted for innumerable speeches. Since arguments require speakers, the historian may also find himself choosing whose mouth to put them into, whether or not a historical speaker was present, and the choice of speaker may be a key to the historian's view of events and their actors. The more vexed the issue, the more emphatic the accounts, as the histories of the Norman Conquest or the deposition of Richard II exemplify.[52] Where the exploitation of traditional exercises reaches its apogee is in the pages of Froissart, who, as much as any medieval historian, illustrates the distance from our conceptions of writing about the past. He habitually took advantage of the licence to dramatize. One scene, justly famous, concerns an incident when the Duke of Brittany tricked Olivier de Clisson, Constable of France, into his power, had him imprisoned, and prepared to have him executed against all the laws of war, hospitality, and custom of his time. The Duke finally spared Clisson's life after a long night of indecision during which the Lord de la Vale dissuaded him from this illegal and dishonourable act. Here is one exchange, quoted from the translation of Lord Berners.

when this lorde de la Vale herde the dukes strayte commaundement to put hym to dethe, he kneled downe before hym, lyftynge up his handes sore wepynge, and sayd,

'Syr, for Goddes sake take mercy: advyse you, shewe not your cruelte agaynst the constable; he hath deserved no dethe; syr, of your grace that it may please you to shewe me the cause of your dyspleasure agaynst hym. And, Syr, I swere unto you ony trespace that he hath done, he shall make you such amendes with his body and goodes, or elles I for hym, as ye yourselfe shall demande or judge; syr, remembre you howe in your yongth ye ii. were companyons togyder, and brought up bothe in one house with the duke of Lancastre, who was soo gentyll a prynce that there was none lyke hym; also, syr, remembre howe before his peas was made with the Frensshe kynge alwayes he truely served you; he ayded you to recover your herytage; ye have alwayes founde in hym good comforte and counsayle: yf ye be now moved or enformed agaynste hym otherwyse then reason sholde requyre, yet he hathe not deserved dethe.'

'Syr de la Vale,' sayd the duke, 'Let me have my wyll: for Olyver of Clysson hath soo often tymes dyspleased me, and nowe is the houre come that I maye shewe hym my dyspleasure: wherfore departe you hens and let me shewe my cruelte, for I wyll he shall dye.'

'A, syr,' sayd the lorde de la Vale, 'refrayne your evyll wyll, and moderate your courage, and regarde to reason: for yf ye put hym to deth there was never prynce soo dyshonoured as ye shall be; there shall not be in Bretayne knyght nor squyer, cyte nor castell, nor good towne, nor noo man but he shall hate you to the dethe, and do that they can to dysynheryte you; nor the kyng of England, nor hys counsayle, shall gyve you no thanke therfore. Syr, wyl you lese yourselfe for the dethe of one man; syr, tourne your ymagynacyon, for this thought is noo thynge worth but dyshonourable, that ye shoulde cause suche an honourable knyght as Sir Olyvere of Clysson is, to dye, comynge unto you at your owne desyre.'[53]

This is typical of Froissart's technique: the dramatic opening is as visual as it can be, the Lord de la Vale physically in the position of a petitioner; then

Froissart presents a series of arguments: Clysson is innocent; if he is not
innocent compensation is better than execution; you have known each other
since boyhood and he has always served you well, so that even if he has done
something evil he does not deserve to die (i.e. it is a commonplace that we do
not murder the friends of our childhood); because you are very angry ('evil
will' and 'courage' have to do with passion and what is happening in the
heart) it is hard to be reasonable; it would be dishonourable to break the laws
of hospitality, and the dishonour will set everyone against you. These
arguments in turn tacitly refer to the rhetorician's list in Chapter 1, which
contains directives to argue that something might be wrong to speak of or
wrong to do. Dramatized as the arguments are, it is easy to think of them as
speeches conceived to reveal the psychology of the speakers. If we think of
'characterization' this way around, that is, arguments stemming from the
personality of the speaker, we will have difficulties with the inconsistency of
Froissart's presentation. If, however, we think of 'character' as something
which may emerge contingently from a series of arguments presented as
consistent with the age and status of the speaker, we will be better able to
interpret Froissart's historical strategy, which lead him to use *convenient*
speakers. Froissart is here dramatizing, rhetorically, and with all his skill, the
events of a night in which arguments may – but may not – have been
canvassed.[54] We do not know who was present, or who spoke in what ways;
these are the inventions of a good writer. Other sources, such as itineraries,
would have to be compared to Froissart to check. In this story, the Duke of
Brittany was dissuaded from murder. When historians innovate, by
adapting the methods of one mode of writing to what we think of as
another, the search for influences may resemble a hunt for culprits. Froissart
exploited the techniques of poetry as he understood them; this has been held
against him. But it is equally the case that the conventions of *psychomachia*, of
inner debate and the exploration of the emotional life that were appropriate
to invented fictions were *well* appropriated to the study of historical actors,
and encouraged the analyses of motive as well as action. In all this it is
important to remember that 'success' is literary, and style is a high priority;
what we might call 'accuracy' is a contingent quality of Froissart's
presentation.

Froissart's success was unprecedented. His history was translated not only
into English, but into the universal language of Latin, accepted by
subsequent historians all over Europe not only as true report, but as a model
of how to write history, within the bounds of rhetoric, for vernacular

imitators. Here is a case of successful innovation affecting a genre. The re-invention, or rediscovery, of dramatic, even tragic, history invigorated Froissart's imitators. If he accomplished nothing else, he confirmed a fashion for secular history.

I have already mentioned the way commentary could be used to create the impression of dialogue from outside the narrative. Froissart extended the use of dialogue within it beyond the dramatic presentation of arguments and defences. He used conversation as an alternative to the narrator's voice, to carry events forward. Consider the following four examples. He used dialogue, attributed not to a single speaker, but to a group, to dramatize current opinions.[55] So, just before the arguments of the Lord de la Vale, he tells his readers that many knights in the vicinity blamed the Duke of Brittany, and 'quotes' (that is, creates) their phrases of condemnation. He is particularly prone to attribute group dialogue to citizens of towns where discussions of policy and alliance take place: Ghent, Vigo, and Portugal are all places where anonymous men give dramatized utterance to what Froissart wishes to establish as widely held opinions. This is a way of providing himself with authority for what he wants to write without having to take it upon himself as his own judgement or opinion of what people thought. Bede had recorded common report; Froissart dramatized it. There is an unspoken social snobbery, too, about his creation of the opinions held by citizens, that is, non-noblemen. Two of his well-known mob scenes contrast a group speaker with someone bravely confronting them: Jan van Artevelde stands up to a mob which is accusing him of crimes against them, and the young King Richard II confronts a mob of peasants outside London and persuades them to return home, breaking the revolt of 1381. Obviously oratory could and did affect events. Froissart used dialogue to anticipate future policy; sometimes it is more speculative. His characters articulate their intentions, whether or not it seems likely that they would have told people who could, in turn, have told the historian, what their ideas were. There are none of the hedges used by modern writers, who label speculation: 'it is believed that the Count of Foix thought . . .' or 'the Duke of Brittany must have wondered . . .'[56] Sometimes Froissart used speeches to summarize a narrative which was to come, so that the reader could keep the plan of action clear before Froissart began the confusing details of, for example, a battle. Even if some readers came to believe that they were reading transcripts of what historical speakers had said on any occasion – and it is hard to imagine that many such naive readers existed in a culture informed by rhetorical habits of mind – it would have mattered little as long as the moral points were made. Characters, after all, could be created backwards – as when someone known to have been a traitor at the end provided a convenient mouthpiece for disloyal speeches at the beginning of a narrative. Students had described persons and qualities of men of different kinds, and historians capitalized on these skills, expanding the thesaurus of types. Physical descriptions tend to be sparing in detail; some may be true, most are organized according to the rules of the manuals. When Bede gives a short description of the missionary, Paulinus, he may be giving the first English historian's description of what a man looked like:

tall, slightly stooped, hair black, face thin, nose slender aquiline; at the same time his appearance was both venerable and awe-inspiring.[57]

But this is so unspecific we must wonder if models of venerable and awe-inspiring men did not help to mould this description. Paulinus may well have had an aquiline nose, but how many dignified words for nose shapes had Bede at his disposal for use in this context? The slight stoop looks suspiciously as though it belongs to the description of an aged counsellor who goes right back to Aristotle.[58] Interpretation may depend upon recognizing the 'moral' qualities implied by the physical description. This, in turn, implies a method of characterization to which we need to be alert; character is representative by its reference to a tradition of exemplary types.

The insertion of invented letters, of which Bede also provides examples, may owe something to training in rhetoric, and specifically to the training in writing letters, the *ars dictaminis* that was part of the course of study which prepared boys to serve their rulers as a nascent civil service. And once letters had found their way into as important a history as Bede's, they were safe as models for other historians. That many letters and documents copied into histories represent correspondence actually sent or charters actually issued is no bar to many of them being embellishments of the originals, imaginative reconstructions of what the originals must have said, or wholly invented forgeries representing what someone thought ought to have been written. Students who were exposed to 'form letters' as part of their training internalized strict conventions that could be summarized, as in Plate 6, and distributed as models for all occasions. The commented lists, which look like something between a flow-chart and a menu (take one from column a and one from column b), insist upon a basic method of composition. It is testimony to the importance historians accorded to maintaining the

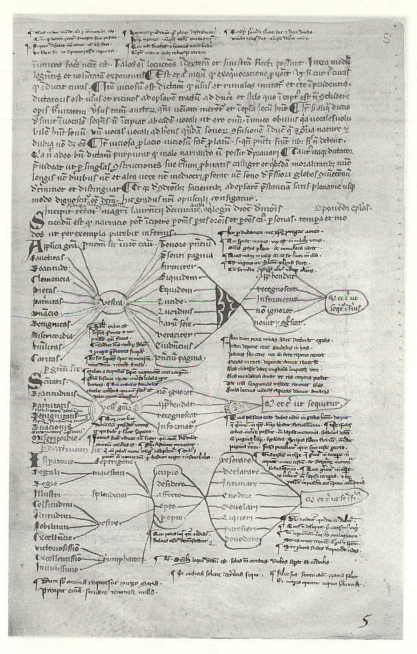

Plate 6    A page from the *Summa Dictaminis* of Laurentius de Civitate Austriae, from Add. 3312, a fourteenth-century manuscript in the University Library, Cambridge.

narrative flow – a purely literary consideration – of their works that some of them relegated documentary and epistolary evidence to appendices. Formal, literary, generic considerations shaped the form, style and content of history and were shaped in turn by histories that found favour. Just as an indication of the way in which any study of medieval writing leads one across modern genre lines, it is well worth recalling the existence of letters which were themselves history: the correspondence between the twelfth-century couple, Abelard and Heloise. In the thirteenth century Jean de Meun, most famous for his original continuation of *Le Roman de la Rose*, took the time to translate the Latin letters into French prose. What made these letters candidates for translation? 'Letters' were certainly a category of literary production: Seneca's *Essays* take the form of letters to a named, but perhaps hypothetical, correspondent. The mystical treatise, *The Cloud of Unknowing*, is also cast as letters. Letters written by the Church Fathers were familiar enough and go back to the New Testament. Certainly the letters were written with literary self-consciousness, full of references both correspondents would recognize.

'Letters' are a fairly discrete category, since their form alone, with its opening salutation and epistolary conventions, makes them recognizable. The contribution of epic poetry to historical writing is harder to see at a glance. It encouraged the dramatized presentation of events. The importance of Virgil is so well known as hardly to need mentioning; because everyone knew so much of his work by heart, allusions could be, and were, made constantly, analogously to the way modern English speakers have absorbed Shakespeare as part of our common system of reference. I have already mentioned Lucan, whose *Pharsalia* took as its subject the struggles between Julius Caesar and Pompey the Great which convulsed and finally destroyed the Roman Republic. Because Lucan took for his subject events of the recent rather than the remote past his poem had more claim than Virgil had to reliability as a historical record. The *Pharsalia* is a highly rhetorical confection which includes along the way several set pieces of epic tradition which Lucan helped to transfer to other kinds of historical writing. I have already mentioned his inset stories to explain place names. In addition, to name only three, Lucan provided models for the catalogue of participants in a battle (ultimately this can be traced right back to Homer's enumeration of the ships which came to Troy), the terrors of a storm at sea, and the detailed, even exultant, description of the horrors of death in battle (this, too, is something with which Homer filled the *Iliad*). The prestige of Latin models never failed, however the view of how they were to be interpreted changed.

It should be clear that I am *not* arguing that every medieval historian who used these *topoi* derived them from close study of Lucan, though in fact many did. Lucan's use and development of these *topoi* was part of the long process by which the dramatized style of writing Epic and the dramatized style of writing History merged in late Antiquity, so that certain scenes could be, and were, used by writers of either genre. Their imitations and manipulations might take into account any recent success, the way Froissart's dramatized history set the fashion for the vernacular histories which followed.

One set piece of which Lucan was fond is the lurid description of atrocities committed by enemies not only on soldiers but also on non-combatant populations. While everyone would accept that men do terrible things to each other, and to women and children, when war releases civilization's normal inhibitions, literary convention took a hand in determining the reports of exactly what was done. In part, speaking in terms of moral lessons to be extracted from literature, one measure of precisely how vile the wicked are is the atrocities which can be attributed to them. If classical precedents suggest that mutilation is the worst thing, then mutilation will become a matter of course. Then, just as a wise man had to be *wiser* than Solon or Solomon (depending on your tradition), so atrocities had to be more horrible than those committed by the malefactors described by the author before last. Here we need to recognize not only the use of models, and the need to avoid mere repetition by going one better – in this case, of course, one worse – than the model, but also the tendency of a culture to use what it considers the most unthinkable (paradoxical as that is) horrors as characteristic deeds of its enemies. One consistently finds that the ultimate mark of savagery is cannibalism, followed closely by incest (and the extension of these vices to, for example, witches, should not go unremarked). In wartime the violation of women is a normal accusation; thus the rape of *nuns* is worse because they are a special category, higher because vowed to God and more helpless because of their vows of stability. One sometimes finds soldiers accused of cutting open pregnant women (as in the anarchy during the reign of Stephen). These atrocities are not signs of mental imbalance in the historian, but his mark of the wickedness of those who perpetrated such deeds – a dramatization of their *ethos*. *The Peterborough Chronicle* describes tortures inflicted by 'evil men' to emphasize the breakdown of order in England during the reign of King Stephen (in the entry for 1137).[59] When one discovers similar descriptions in the *Liber Eliensis*, the *Historia Ecclesiae Dunhelmensis*, William of Malmesbury's *Historia Novella*, and the *Gesta*

*Stephani*, it is time to wonder whether the horrors described really were widespread, or if perhaps historians were enumerating examples of what could be assumed to happen in a period of anarchy. That is, the reports may indicate a literary convention about what constitutes utter lawlessness rather than an accurate report of what happened. Atrocity reports and allusions to tortures are, in fact, two related *topoi* which share common features. Related to these accounts is the *topos* of the mutilated corpse which can only be recognized by a known mark, especially a scar. While the *Odyssey* immediately leaps to mind, reality may have had a hand to play as well.[60] Torture (enduring it or inflicting it on Christian martyrs) is often a constitutive feature of hagiography. The attribution of vice to a king and his court is often expressed in terms of fashion: long hair or excessive concern with clothing may signal degeneracy, effeminacy, or homosexuality. The court of William Rufus is a traditional site of such offences.[61] Where reality intersects with *topos* interpretation becomes a difficult matter indeed: as with Richard III's putative murder of his nephews.

Deaths in general were a favoured occasion for amplification. The deaths of monarchs were a natural opportunity for historians to expatiate upon common experience, as well as to reflect upon reigns, even characters (of which more in the next chapter). I have already mentioned in passing the kinds of laments which battles (especially defeats) stimulated in, for example, Old English, where it is only now beginning to become clear how much 'bardic' poetry is also learned, and learned in classical rhetoric. When Suetonius made Augustus meet death standing up, or attributed to Nero the last words, 'What an artist perishes', he was indicating something about their (different) ideas of themselves as rulers. The deaths attributed to Bede, to Ailred (which Walter Daniel modelled on the death of Bede), or of William the Marshal are all exempla of correct passing.[62] They make a place for prophecy, which is also a narrative device, anticipating the plot. To do this authors have to keep their dying characters conscious: it is remarkable how infrequent coma, or dying in one's sleep, seem to have been. The Croyland Chronicler uses brief references to Roman history to contextualize his dying King Richard III (s.v. Old Style 1484). Philippe de Commynes' dying Louis XI, who has needed Commynes near him because Commynes is the only person who can understand what he is trying to say, becomes alert enough to make wise speeches at the historian's need. The internal contradictions include a story which Commynes may have found in Suetonius' description of the death of Tiberius. In the English tradition, the death of Henry IV assumes a special status because Shakespeare dramatized it. Yet there cannot have been eyewitnesses to the scene; indeed, the story originates with Monstrelet, for whom it is a way of indicating the guilt felt by the usurping king, and thus of criticizing the English monarchy.[63] From Monstrelet it found its way into Hall's Chronicle, from which Holinshed adapted it before Shakespeare gave a more sympatheic rendering in 2 Henry IV.

The deaths could be followed by laments, the planctus which was a part of medieval poetry (an example of which was discussed in Chapter 1, above, after the death of King Arthur). The Commendatio Lamentabilis of John of London mourns the death of Edward I, comparing him to Brutus the Trojan, Alexander the Great, and his famous English predecessors. John celebrates the values he thought Edward embodied, and puts his celebration of those values into panegyric.[64] It was Edward's status as a conqueror which most moved John.

A large proportion of most medieval and renaissance histories was devoted to warfare – the sport of kings – and especially to the deeds of great men during battle. War is a repetitious business, and it is scarcely surprising to find similarities between battles. The succession of lances broken, of swords thrust, of gallantry and suffering, offered traditional rhetorical opportunities to the historians who wished to glorify particular men. Even Homer's Iliad sometimes seems too well provided with descriptions of exactly how men died; medieval and renaissance historians added to the catalogue. Occasionally reality must have lent a hand, as when the blind King of Bohemia insisted upon actively participating in a battle: Froissart gives a splendid description of the king's men tying his reins to theirs, riding out to certain death together, and of the bodies being found after the battle, with the dead king's loyal men dead around him, with the horses' harnesses still knotted together.[65]

More commonly found battle-oriented set pieces may be distinguished: one exemplifies oratorical bravura display, the other is a further case of narrative used to indicate moral position. These are the speech before the battle, which I referred to in Chapter 1, and the behaviour of opposing armies on the night before a major battle. It is clear enough that generals did address their troops before engagements, though one must wonder just how far the unamplified sound of their voices carried, or how often records were kept of what they said. For the historian this speech was a special invitation to display his talents. The leader's oratory could exemplify his relation to his men and to his cause, his courage, his reasons for fighting. This extract from a

much longer poem gives the following classicizing speech to Harold before
Hastings:

> Aduocat ipse duces, comites, terreque potentes;
>    Verbis, ut fertur, talibus alloquitur:
> 'Milicie pars summa mee, magnatibus orta,
>    Solus non bello uincere cui pudor est,
> Nothica quos misit per te superauimus hostes,
>    Et per te nostrum strauimus equiuocum . . .
> Nutriuit proprio matris quem lacte papilla.
>    Tu mihi presidium, murus, et auxilium,
> Audisti nostrum quod gens Normannica regnum
>    Intrauit; predans, pauperat, exspoliat.
> Hoc Willemus [agit], qui te sibi subdere querit.
>    Nomen habet magnum; cor tamen est pauidum;
> Est uafer et cupidus nimiumque superciliosus;
>    Nec nouit pacem nec retinere fidem.
> Si possit leuiter, molitur tollere nostra,
>    Set Deus omnipotens non erit hoc paciens.
> Quantus erit luctus, quantus dolor et pudor ingens,
>    Regni quanta lues, quam tenebrosa dies,
> Si quod querit habet, si regni sceptra tenebit!
>    Hoc omnes fugiant uiuere qui cupiunt.'

He himself summoned to him the captain, the lords and great men of the land, and is
said to have addressed them in such words as these: 'Leaders of my army, sprung from
great forebears, to whom the only shame is not to conquer in war: Through you we
have overthrown the enemies that Norway sent, and through you we have laid low
our namesake . . . [and] him whom [our] mother's breast nourished with its own
milk. My guard, my help, and my defence, you have heard that the Normans have
entered our kingdom, plundering, robbing, and despoiling! William does this,
because he seeks to subject you to himself. He has a great name, but a queasy stomach!
He is cunning and avaricious and arrogant beyond measure; he knows neither peace
nor how to keep faith. He is striving to seize what is ours, if he can do it easily. But this
Almighty God will not suffer! How great will be the grief, how great the anguish and
how mighty the shame, what ruin for the kingdom, how dark a day, if William gain
what he seeks – if he shall wield the sceptre of the realm! May all shun this who wish
to live!'[66]

I have already mentioned Henry V before Agincourt. Here is an
anonymous chronicler inventing a speech of encouragement for the English
king:

Syres and ffelowes, the ʒondere mayné thenke to lett us of owre way, and thei wil nat
come to us, lete every man preve hym silfe a good man this day, and avant baneres, in
the best tyme of the yere, for as I am trew kynge and knyght, for me this day schalle
never Inglond rawnsome pay; erste many a wyght man schall leve is weddes, for here
erste to deth I wil be dyght, and therfore, lordynges, for the love of swete Jesu, helpe
mayntene Inglondes ryght this day. Allso archers, to yow I praye, no fote that ʒe fle
away, erste be we alle beten in this felde. And thenke be Englysshemen that never
wold fle at no batelle, for aʒenste one of us thowthe there be tene, thenke Criste wil
help us in owre ryght.[67]

It is perhaps more obvious in this clumsy and self-contradictory speech
than in a better-written one that this is a conventional concoction – after all,
one of the skills rhetoricians sought was to make things not only moving but
freshly so. The large number of rhyme-words suggests that some of the
clumsiness may result from an attempt to adapt prose from poetry. One
might dare to extract from this only the circumstance that the English forces
were outnumbered, and that they depended upon their bowmen. These are
the basis of speeches in several accounts of the battle. In the *Gesta Henrici
Quinti* the king is made to say

By the God in Heaven upon whose grace I have relied and in whom is my firm hope
of victory, I would not, even if I could, have a single man more than I do. For these I
have with me are God's people, whom He deigns to let me have at this time. Do you
not believe . . . that the Almighty, with these His humble few, is able to overcome
the opposing arrogance of the French who boast of their great number and their own
strength?[68]

Holinshed combines this remark about numbers with the same concerns
as the anonymous chronicler, making his Henry say

I would not wish a man more here than I have, we are indeed in comparison to the
enemies but a few, but if God of his clemencie doo favour us, and our just cause, as I
trust he will, we shall speed well inough. But let no man ascribe victorie to our owne
strength and might, but onelie to Gods assistance to whome I have no doubt we shall
worthilie have cause to give thanks therefore. And if so be that for our offenses sake
we shall be delivered into the hands of our enimies, the lesse number we do, the less
damage shall the realme of England susteine . . .[69]

Shakespeare combined the thoughts expressed in the different versions for
his long speech at the beginning of *Henry V* IV.iii in a masterly rhetorical
presentation:

If we are mark'd to die, we are enow
To do our country loss; and if to live,
The fewer men, the greater share of honour.
God's will! I pray thee, wish not one man more.
By Jove, I am not covetous for gold,
Nor care I who doth feed upon my cost;
It earns me not if men my garments wear;
Such outward things dwell not in my desires:
But if it be a sin to covet honour,
I am the most offending soul alive.
No, faith, my coz, wish not a man from England:
God's peace! I would not lose so great an honour
As one man more, methinks, would share from me,
For the best hope I have. O do not wish one more!
Rather proclaim it, Westmoreland, through my host,
That he which hath no stomach to this fight,
Let him depart; his passport shall be made,
And crowns for convoy put into his purse:
We would not die in that man's company
That fears his fellowship to die with us.
This day is call'd the feast of Crispian:
He that outlives this day, and comes safe home,
Will stand a tip-toe when this day is named,
And rouse him at the name of Crispian.
He that shall see this day, and live old age,
Will yearly on the vigil feast his neighbours,
And say, 'Tomorrow is Saint Crispian':
Then will he strip his sleeve and show his scars,
And say, 'These wounds I had on Crispin's day.'
Old men forget; yet all shall be forgot,
But he'll remember with advantages
What feats he did that day. Then shall our names,
Familiar in his mouth as household words,
Harry the king, Bedford and Exeter,
Warwick and Talbot, Salisbury and Gloucester,
Be in their flowing cups freshly remember'd.
This story shall the good man teach his son;
And Crispin Crispian shall ne'er go by,
From this day to the ending of the world,
But we in it shall be remembered;
We few, we happy few, we band of brothers;

For he to-day that sheds his blood with me
Shall be my brother; be he ne'er so vile
This day shall gentle his condition:
And gentlemen in England now a-bed
Shall think themselves accurs'd they were not here
And hold their manhoods cheap whiles any speak
That fought with us upon Saint Crispin's day.

(IV.iii.20–67)

As a speech that rouses the pride of the army by *emphasizing* the fact that they are outnumbered, this is hard to better. Its sources have been traced right back to Tacitus' *Germania*, and to Xenophon's *Anabasis* before that, so old is this set piece. In effect, historians who wrote about the Agincourt campaign built up a picture of Henry's piety, courage, and good management that Shakespeare was among many to celebrate. Shakespeare is also exceptionally fine on Henry's calculating ruthlessness. The King's actual words at any moment are invented to illustrate the arguments necessary to the situation; in Shakespeare's hands they also illuminate his *ethos*, part of which is his rhetorical skill. Queen Elizabeth's famous speech at Tilbury is another example, and an example of the necessary adaptation of a *topos*, since a woman could not lead troops. She may indeed have said that she only had the body of a weak and feeble woman, but that she had the heart of a king, but there is no evidence beyond the letter which reports it that the speech was actually made.

Not only can such an exemplary demonstration be made of one man, it can also be made for a group. This tendency to choose *topoi* for exemplary purposes rather than strict representation can be seen in historians' descriptions of opposing armies on the night before a major engagement. There is a familiar example in Shakespeare's *Henry V*. While the French are drinking and enduring the boasts of the Dauphin, the English king makes the rounds of his army, deep in serious reflection upon his responsibilities for them. This gives the victorious side a kind of moral superiority to the vanquished. Readers of the French historian Enguerrand de Monstrelet will find this same *topos* used for the night before Agincourt – but with the moral balance reversed. In Monstrelet's version the French spent the night in prayer while the English played trumpets.[70] (The French are none the less defeated in Monstrelet – there were limits to what a historian could manipulate.) Froissart uses this convention in his narrative of the night before the battle of Crécy. His contrast is slightly more balanced and certainly more subtle than

Shakespeare's popular and exaggerated dramatization for Agincourt: the English king kept his men well-ordered at Crécy, while

The lordes and knyghtes of France came nat to the assemble togyder in good order, for some came before and some came after, in such hast and yvell order, that one of them dyd trouble another.[71]

The literary manipulation that these historians are using is a kind of moral commentary; responsibility for what happens in a battle is in part due to the spiritual preparedness as well as the outward behaviour of the combatants – at least in books. For Shakespeare and Froissart the English deserve their victories; for Monstrelet English behaviour is just one more sign of the perfidy of those sometime conquerors whose sins made it just that they should, in the end, have been expelled from France. France, of course, was being tried by a patient deity.

The 'historical' becomes a mode of writing which covers a broad spectrum of attitudes to recording the past. An extreme view would take the incommensurability of the rhetorical organization of history with the modern expectations of how history is to be written as a claim that it is impossible to use early histories in the ways that modern historians wish to use them. It would reduce modern historians to figures like their medieval predecessors, trying to disentangle what was 'historical' from basically poetic, fictional creations. It would turn medieval history into an extended plot. It is probably unnecessary to go this far, but constant scepticism remains crucial. Making an account convincing is a literary art; it may coincide with what happened, but it may not. An underlying assumption may remain that the extremely fictionalized history, like the twelfth-century French *romans antique*, can be recognized as different in kind as well as in degree from reports closer to the time of writing. I shall return to the idea of historical fiction in Chapter 5.[72] Let the reader beware. It has been the argument of this chapter that a knowledge of rhetorical ways of reading and writing enable modern readers to think of a range of medieval methods of presentation as part of a coherent system of reference; it has been the polemic of the chapter that approaching history in this literary way is not just an aid to, it is a necessity of, interpretation. The next chapter will continue this analysis, looking at the writing of lives.

# 3

# LET US NOW PRAISE FAMOUS
# MEN

Our passions are therefore more strongly moved, in proportion as we can more readily adopt the pains or pleasure proposed to our minds, by recognizing them as our own, or considering them as naturally incident to our state of life. For, not only every man has, in the mighty mass of the world, great numbers in the same condition with himself, to whom his mistakes and miscarriages, escapes and expedients, would be of immediate and apparent use; but there is such a uniformity in the state of man, considered apart from adventitious and separable decorations and disguises, that there is scarce any possibility of good or ill, but is common to human kind. A great part of the time of those who are placed at the greatest distance by fortune, or by temper, must unavoidably pass in the same manner, and though, when the claims of nature are satisfied, caprice, and vanity, and accident, begin to produce discriminations and peculiarities, yet the eye is not very heedful or quick, which cannot discover the same causes still terminating their influence in the same effects, though sometimes accelerated, sometimes retarded, or perplexed by multiplied combinations. We are all prompted by the same motives, all deceived by the same fallacies, all animated by hope, obstructed by danger, entangled by desire, and seduced by pleasure.

Samuel Johnson, *Rambler*, Saturday, 13 October 1750

### ENCOMIASTIC LIVES

Dr Johnson rested his argument for the superior moral appeal of biography as against history on the reader's emotional and imaginative identification with the protagonist. For Johnson, the biographer's art was to reproduce the sense of the unique individual striving with the general circumstances of life. The failure of most previous biographers to convey the particularities of a man and the texture of his life was his chief charge against them: 'But biography has often been allotted to writers who seem very little acquainted with the nature of their [subject's] talk, or very negligent about the performance. They rarely afford any other account than might be collected from publick papers, but imagine themselves writing a life when they exhibit a chronological series of actions, or preferments; and so little regard for the manners or behaviour of their heroes, that more knowledge may be gained of a man's real character, by a short conversation with one of his servants, than from a formal and studied narrative, begun with his pedigree, and ended with his funeral'. This stress on empathy, as we would now call it, on feeling with the character we read about (or see represented on the stage: this same theory is central to Johnson's views about why Shakespeare moves us), however different his superficial circumstances may be from our own, is at the heart of Johnson's analysis of 'affect' or, as it was called by rhetoricians, *pathos*. What Johnson's considered prose entirely fails to convey is how far this – now widely held – view of the biographer's task rests on Johnson's own innovations as a biographer. It was Johnson's *Lives of the English Poets* which established biography as we now know it. Modern arguments about biography ultimately stem from Johnson's view that the purpose of the Life is to convey a strong sense of the humanity of the subject; whether or not that is possible within the strict confines of historical truth has occupied every biographer whose task has been to convey his understanding of character and motive, to capture the unique idiosyncrasies which made his subject *this* person and no other. Johnson's impatience with earlier lives is the measure of his own intense curiosity about the thoughts, reflections, and reactions of other men to the vagaries of human experience. His belief that human nature is everywhere the same issues in the apparent paradox that the very multiplicity which the biographer records will be grist to the individual reader's *recognition*, and to his meditations on his own singular experience – a moral exemplary view not far removed from that which prescribed the study of past societies in order to avoid their mistakes that is the 'immediate and apparent use'. If one starts from a Johnsonian view of biography, earlier periods must seem deficient in the extreme. Though morally useful, perhaps they contain *no* biography worthy the name.[1]

Yet there is no shortage of texts about individual historical actors in medieval and renaissance writing. Great men illuminate the study of history. Great deeds require great doers, and the report of their actions usually includes some sense that it was a particular man who built or burned, who organized or destroyed, whose holiness or whose wickedness impressed the men around him as worthy of record, for good or ill. Yet however much particular men, and, occasionally, rarely, particular women, occupied the minds and pens of historians, histories did not provide readers either enough of the deeds of their lives or analyses of their characters. In fact, although the 'character' of the great man was a *topos* of historical writing, very few medieval or renaissance works about the past can be said to concern themselves with character for its own sake, with that detailed exploration of gratuitous idiosyncrasies which develops the sense of human uniqueness. Such works are almost non-existent, and character, in the modern sense, emerges only contingently and almost by accident in the course of other kinds of writing than the directly historical or biographical.[2] It was part of the argument of Chapter 2 that often what *looks* like material inserted in order to illuminate character turns out to be organized according to ideas of argument and illustration, and that few writers worried about the inconsistencies to which arbitrary assignment of those speeches might lead. The same tendency to write about conventional, topical, episodes when reporting events encouraged writers to subsume historical actors into recognizable character-types who experience well-known stages of life. Whether one is reading a history of the life and reign of someone so important that his status and actions serve to organize a narrative of large-scale events, or a free-standing commemoration of an exceptional man, similar conventions determined what was worth recording and how the record was to be preserved for posterity. Chapter 2 explored some of the *topoi* of historical writing. In this chapter a more chronological approach is appropriate, both because the development of writing about lives and characters is less well known, and because an analysis of that development will counteract any sense that the *topoi* and categories described were necessarily static. The patterns on which life-writers modelled their work come not only from rhetorical practice through the works of classical writers, but also that practice as modified by the early Church Fathers whose hagiographers attempted to replace pagan heroes with the glorious witness of the saints. The adaptations of *encomium* by religious writers may go some way to answering the question of the ostensible hostility to rhetoric in the cloister, for the lives of saints were an important route for transmitting the models of writing well, i.e., according to traditional, rhetorical, models, within the putative rejection of the world. The idea of *encomium*, whose conventions were considered in Chapter 1, lies behind both the secular and the sacred traditions, and rhetorical transformations of the encomiastic *topoi* inform the composition of Lives.

Any expectation that writers were interested in the study of 'personality' must be discarded at once. When medieval writers narrated the lives of famous men they purported to record their deeds and sayings, sometimes including a physical description, even more rarely an analysis of *mores*, of which more below. Not only did the composition of lives follow patterns, but the lives themselves were often, in hagiography almost exclusively, *signs* of something. The life of a person through time, like history, or the natural world, could be interpreted like a book. That is, incidents were included (or invented) because they belonged to a pattern, because they signified something quite specific about the status, the symbolic being, of their subject. As with many of the *topoi* mentioned in the previous chapter, circumstantial narratives may be included because they fulfil expectations rather than because they are true. 'Biography' may be taken to include the story of a man's life from ancestors and antenatal portents to his death and posthumous miracles, or a more strait and narrow description of the deeds of his reign, where regnal years provide a unifying principle. There are other texts which can tell us something about the possibility of this kind of analysis in medieval society, which I shall consider briefly at the end of this chapter. One question which lurks in wait for us is the problem about whether or not earlier societies 'saw' what we see, interpreted human experience in terms we would understand, suffered and enjoyed what we do, if not always in the same ways. Importing our own motives into past societies can bring serious misinterpretation in its wake. Castigating those societies for not feeling what we feel, not writing as we write, imports a 'developmental' view of the history of writing which judges in terms of leaps of realism, and elevates a few unusual texts as the only 'true' biographies in an age dominated by stale and stifling conventions. Rhetorically adept writers striving to embody moral qualities in human experience created and sustained 'an ethical poetic' which exemplified the values to which they subscribed.[3] They were not 'failing' to write what we might have preferred them to have written. If the measure of their achievement has now to be recovered by careful scholarship in support of the historical imagination, that is not a condemnation.

Chapter 1 described the rhetorical exercise *encomium* as a composition which praised a person, place, thing, or quality. Here *encomium* is the praise of a person. In Antiquity such speeches were often made as part of a funeral, where the memory of the dead man was celebrated. Anthony's speech over Caesar, as I pointed out earlier, is exactly the oration in praise of the dead man which Anthony begins by disclaiming, and it is addressed to the emotions of its audience, the mob, not to their careful judgement. Sometimes the funeral panegyric was recorded; it seems likely that Tacitus wrote one for his father-in-law, Agricola, because he had been unable to make the traditional oration at the appropriate time.[4] *Agricola* takes the form of an *encomium*, but its length exceeds anything that might actually have been delivered — a case where the pretence of oral delivery to an assumed audience enabled the writer to expand what had hitherto been restricted, moving oral to written creation. Such oratorical pretence has appeared before: Cicero's *Pro Milone* looks like the speech of defence that was given, but other evidence tells us that it was never delivered.[5] Funeral orations were unlike judicial or deliberative oratory, because there was no element of persuasion to a course of action, no decision to be taken or defended; funeral orations belonged to the *epideictic* branch of rhetoric, speeches made to celebrate. The listeners were meant to receive pleasure from oratorical display: the speaker appealed directly to their emotions. He was not on oath, and his duty to the memory of the dead man encouraged decoration and invention for the sake of the occasion.

Aphthonius gives a scheme which the student could use to organize an *encomium* of a person:

I. Prologue

II. Race
   A. Nationality
   B. Native City
   C. Ancestors
   D. Parents

III. Education
   A. Pursuits
   B. Art
   C. Laws

IV. Achievements
   A. Of Soul
      1. Manliness
      2. Judgement
   B. Of Body

       1. Beauty

       2. Speed

       3. Strength

    c. Of Fortune

       1. Power

       2. Wealth

       3. Friends

   v. Comparison

   vi. Epilogue[6]

This scheme, or a variant of it, continued to be used for generations, and could be extended or adapted for other uses. In early editions of Chaucer the apparently biographical introduction followed just such an organization.

And later the speeches of welcome performed so often before Queen Elizabeth followed similar patterns. When once one has grasped that the ruler was greeted by an oratorical display which honoured her (the representative of the monarchy) by honouring her (the particular monarch), the apparent gross flattery of the *encomium* reassumes its proper proportion, because the display can be understood as a celebration of virtue; though directed to a particular woman, it is meant as an example of praise to ruler and country. From time to time orators, carried away by the form of the *encomium*, disregarded the tact required in tailoring the content, and found themselves confronting a displeased monarch. In theory the queen was less the subject than the occasion for display; in practice orators were often well-advised to stick to general topics rather than to risk clear and specific application to their sovereign's life. That *encomium* is closely related to – and could be easily confounded with – historical modes of writing, is clear enough. Ancient historians were aware of the danger, and Polybius among others often contrasts his own history with less scrupulous examples by insisting that it is impartial, unbiassed, and free of that concern with praise and blame which marks oratorical display.[8] When Philippe de Commynes insists with similar vehemence that *his* account of his king's reign will be free of the blemishes which concern with panegyrical history brings with it one may wonder what he has been studying. In *encomium* the celebration of virtue comes first, so that the facts of a man's life are mentioned only to illustrate the points at issue. Yet it is clear nevertheless that an *encomium* might

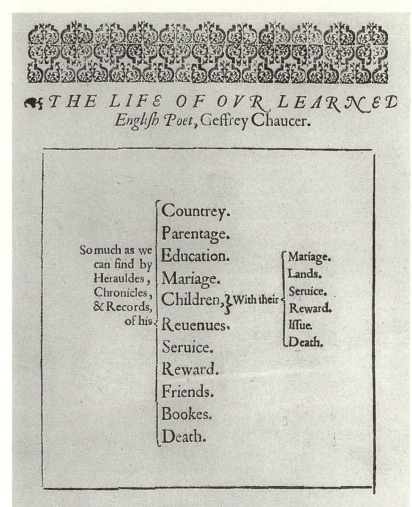

Plate 7    The *divisio* which precedes Thomas Speght's Life of Chaucer in his
edition of the *Workes* (London, 1598).[7]

function as a free-standing story of a life, or might appear as a biographical essay inset in a longer historical work. It might be organized by chronology or by rhetorical *dispositio*, topics. Therefore a modern reader needs to be on guard when something seems to be recounted as a true report of a life: apparent facts may not be facts at all, and the overall narrative may follow the exposition of virtue (or vice) that is the author's expressed or tacit purpose.

A late and somewhat unusual example, Boccaccio's *encomium* of Dante, invites consideration of what such compositions might include. Boccaccio's Life of Dante is less a biography in modern terms than a stick with which to beat fourteenth-century readers, an *encomium* deliberately conceived to advance its subject's fame and the prestige of poets.[9] That it is organized on a rhetorical model is apparent from the first chapter, in which Boccaccio outlines his plan. He begins with a *chria* from Solon, the ancient Greek lawgiver, which stresses that his subject is virtue. Then there is an *exclamatio*, an address from the text to the reader, outside its narrative scope, against Florence, the city from which both poets came, for banishing Dante; this leads to a reason for writing, since the creation of the Life can go some way to making amends. This is a new reason in an old position. Of course, Boccaccio apologizes for his weakness as an author and for the humility of his style, as every good rhetorician did. He proposes to treat first of Dante's life and habits before discussing his works (here books take the place of deeds). This is recognizably a *dispositio*, intended as an organizing preface.

Chapter 2 also begins with the city of Florence, first – briefly – with Dante's remote ancestors before coming to his parents. Boccaccio tells us that Dante's mother had the traditional prophetic dream while pregnant with him. Boccaccio uses an *occupatio*, an explicit reference to a *topos* he intends to omit, to inform us that he will spare us any recital of the infant poet's promise of future greatness. Chapters 3 and 4 recount Dante's private and public lives, first the meeting with Beatrice and his marriage to and separation from his wife, and then his seduction into public affairs despite what he knew of the vagaries of Fortune. Each of these chapters concludes with general reflections, commonplaces which situate the particularities of this life within general experience. For readers interested only in those particularities these chapters are most frustrating, because they tell us practically nothing. But once one has remembered that in *encomium* events are subservient to the demonstration of virtue, Boccaccio's method becomes clear. So two more 'chronological narrative' chapters are succeeded by another general diatribe against the ingratitude of the Florentines, who sent Dante into exile. There is no detailed analysis of the civil disorders, the rivalry between Guelphs and Ghibellines which were the cause of that exile; not here. But there are balanced reflections on timeless abstractions: Women, Ambition, Ingratitude. Chapter 8 gives a summary account of Dante's physical appearance and habits (*mores*), but again Boccaccio is schematic enough that one can hardly tell if what he says bore any relation to what Dante was like. Three of his *topoi* are so suspiciously standard that one might find them in any hagiography: there are paragraphs on Dante's height and colouring (which tell us something about his 'humour'), his moderation in food and drink (which tells us that he kept his passions under control), and his love of study. Three of them are unusual, and have to do with *Boccaccio's* claims for the dignity of his subject and the status of the poet: Dante's dedication to love (as a subject for poetry), his intelligence and memory, and his desire for Fame. These are all secular virtues, and required defending. After three more chapters of general interest (on Poetry, Theology, and the Laureation of Poets, i.e. the public recognition of their fame, and thus the public acceptance that poets convey honour upon the city in which they live), Boccaccio tells us something of Dante's shortcomings: he was haughty. His subject is a secular man, not a saint, and therefore shortcomings are to be expected. That the particular shortcoming is the reverse of the saintly virtue, humility, may not be accidental. For the first time, in this section, something that Dante said is quoted (or invented). Then follow four chapters on Dante's works, though with little attention to their content (which, of course, commentaries supplied) before Boccaccio concludes with his *peroratio*: it has been briefly shown, besides certain other matters by way of digression, what were the origins, studies, the life, habits and works of that glorious man and illustrious poet. Briefly indeed, and after seventy pages (in the modern edition) we are not much better informed about Dante the man than we were when we started. Those individual traits which have seemed, since Dr Johnson so elegantly espoused their cause, of the essence in capturing the indefinable uniqueness of a man, may have appeared to pre-modern writers (if they thought of such things at all) as engaging anecdotal material which would, if included, lower the register of their work as well as distract the reader from its purpose. That Dante exemplified virtues which mattered to Boccaccio – also, after all, a learned poet keen to raise the status of his ambition – manifests itself throughout his 'oration in praise of Dante'. This organization on the model of an oral form, an *oration*, is a classicizing claim. But by Boccaccio's day such a claim occurs in a Christian context, and the *topoi* evoke the prestige of saintly achievement. For this a retrospect is necessary, a backward view which never forgets that with societal change, as well as the multiplication of texts, medieval readers regarded classical works through accretions which reinterpreted them. This is not to canonize Dante, but to suggest that there are secular aspirations which may teach as well as the religious life. The idea of a life as an example of something is crucial to any understanding of the ways men wrote about other men. The literary representation of a life represents the life's meaning; it, too, can be read and interpreted.

Lives exemplified abstract virtues and vices; men and women embodied qualities. We may think of them as being like Imlac's definition of poetry in *Rasselas*, chapter 10: 'The business of a poet, said Imlac, is to examine, not the individual, but the species; . . . he does not number the streaks of the tulip, or describe the different shades of verdure of the forest.' This is, of course, not Johnson himself speaking, but his sober philosopher, who represents none the less a venerable tradition of critical thought, which can be found growing in fourteenth-century Florence. What is striking in Boccaccio's generalizing approach to his *writing about* Dante is not the approach alone, which I shall consider in greater detail below, but that he should have made the claim that a vernacular Italian poet is worthy of extended treatment. Boccaccio was an enthusiastic and energetic writer of lives; two volumes of his Latin *exempla* survive (and will be discussed below). *This* free-standing *encomium* has a special place in his work. It is not only classicizing in its form and style, but in its claim for its protagonist. Boccaccio's praise elevates Dante into the company of saints and kings. Yet one could not know this were one unfamiliar with the conventions of life writing with which Boccaccio grew up.

The models for writing lives might be purely rhetorical, as for any *encomium*. But manuals of rhetoric did not provide the same exemplary force as those texts which presented actual lives to emulating writers. That is, it is all very well to look at books which prescribe rules, but the real force is in the analysis of earlier examples, which give much richer and much more complex models for imitation, because they are particular and serious. Medieval and renaissance authors learned equally from classical and traditional texts, both secular and sacred; their habits of reading meant that they did not come fresh to any texts, but that they interpreted according to the practice they had acquired when young. The same Roman writers who represented the height of achievement as historians also provided models of how to write about the lives of famous men. Sallust used Jugurtha and Catiline as the pegs on which to hang his histories of the events in which they were major figures.[10] Suetonius showed how one might deal with both a reign and a life in his sequence of biographies of the Caesars.[11] His so-called 'anecdotal method' established the illustrative story as worthy of the dignity of serious genres but did nothing to establish that the story should be *vero* as well as *ben trovato*. If these two authors came to be as important to medieval life writers as they were to medieval historians, it was in part because of the success of their earliest, late-classical, imitators. By a process of adaptation, Christian writers legitimated the use of classical patterns (the sort of directive one could extract from a rhetoric manual) for their own heroes; like Augustine's arguments for Egyptian gold. In the late fourth century Sulpicius Severus used Sallust among his chief models when writing his life of St Martin of Tours (Tacitus, too, was among his favoured authors) and St Jerome has Suetonius' example in mind for his own *De Viris Illustribus*.[12] The prestige of these two early Christian writers established the legitimacy of classical rhetorical models: one could copy the Christian adaptation, or, with earlier adaptations in mind, go to the pagan works direct. Whenever there was a 'revival' of learning this latter method became popular, not only for the astringent view that getting one's classicism direct was a superior way of going about things, but also because unassailably virtuous and pious Christian writers had already shown that this was the way. This will be of importance later in this chapter in the movement from sacred to secular life writing.

Christian religious communities were bookish. Freestanding biography received its greatest impetus from the monastic habit of reading the lives of saints at mealtimes. The discipline which insisted that the religious listen instead of talk encouraged, however contingently, the ordinary impulse to take pleasure from stories: mealtimes were not times for listening to sermons, or any other kind of 'difficult' text, but for the relaxing, and yet instructive, kind of reading which is remarkably close to fiction enjoyed for its own sake. The need for large numbers of these exemplary narratives for cloister audiences encouraged both the constant updating and adaptation of existing ones and original compositions. And what was sauce for the monastic goose was equally stimulating to the lay gander. Biography became a habit before it became a discipline, and its conventions spilled over into other kinds of writing. It began in serious Saints Lives.

In Antiquity the subjects who inspired biographical writing were usually men of exceptional political importance. Stories of a more or less apocryphal kind about heroes, which are familiar from folklore collections, were succeeded by tales of great deeds and anecdotes illustrating the strength and wisdom of leaders. Sometimes folklore and historical report become indistinguishable, as with the variety of Lives of Alexander, who, already the subject of romantic imaginings even while he was still alive, remained an absorbing biographical subject for centuries.[13] Other famous examples of extravagant fictional biographies go right back to fifth-century Athens, where Xenophon was not above concocting a kind of pedagogical thriller which pretended to be the story of the Persian, Cyrus.[14] Both Xenophon and Plato invented versions of a wise man to celebrate their friend Socrates, though as their Greek compositions were little known in the West until late in the Renaissance I shall not pursue their influence except to remark that the example of Socrates – neither hero nor king – legitimated other biographies of writers and sages, many of which were concocted from hints extracted from these early writings.[15] The idea that a wise man was as worthy a model of imitation as an active politician or warrior was clearly one that was of paramount importance to Christian writers, whose subjects often demonstrated their special status by rejecting the very world which so absorbed their pagan rivals. Nevertheless, since the *topoi* remained conventional, if not static, the change in content shows a reactionary interpretation, taking the same values or ideas but asserting their opposite to be the true case. Making heroes of saints was a special challenge to the earliest Christian hagiographers, who adapted Roman political *virtus* to a kind of supernatural strength. From this early point, *virtus* was on the way to becoming virtue.

Secular and religious lives share many themes – not just those, such as the moments of passage in any human life – of which beginnings and ends are among the most obvious. Although the 'birth' *topos* may not begin the Life, its inclusion in one of a number of forms was to be expected; the hero's birth was typically preceded by difficulties: a prohibition of marriage, a secret love, long years of barrenness before the arrival of a special child.[16] The hero's mother often experienced a threatening or promising dream or vision during her pregnancy: Dante's mother comes in a long line which includes St Columban's mother dreaming of a rising sun, Christina of Markyate's mother receiving a visit from a white dove which came from a nearby monastery (doves can be read as 'love' and white is the colour worn by virgins dedicated to Christ, so that the bird is an analogue of her daughter),

St Thomas of Canterbury's mother dreaming that all the water from the Thames ran through her, as Hecuba once anticipated Paris as fire or Virgil's mother dreamt of laurels; the labour itself might be specially marked by difficulty.[17] Many heroes have to survive dire threats upon arrival: their mothers die alone in the forest and they are suckled by wild animals (fierce carnivores seem to be preferred to gentle herbivores) wicked relatives or powerful rulers seek their lives. Exposure to water or wilderness is not unusual. But despite all these initial setbacks the hero demonstrates unmistakeable promise of his future greatness and grows up to become exceptionally wise, or powerful, or even wicked. Like the preface to a history, the unit which describes the birth may function as a thematic introduction. Its style may be high, but it may also be low, as in many folktales. It is folklore tradition which lies behind many of the inventions of the Apocryphal Gospels, those enormously popular tales which supply the narrative of the childhood of Jesus which escaped Mark, Matthew, Luke, and John.[18]

As the Gospel narratives repeated motifs found elsewhere in the world's holy stories, so they also fulfilled prophecies and promises from older sacred texts. In their turn they provided models for holy living and holy dying. In a secular context one speaks of life mirroring art. Bede's St Cuthbert behaves in ways that are illuminated by reference to the Bible; Christina of Markyate's biographer makes her speak in biblical quotations and allusions; St Francis was one of many to seek to imitate the life of Christ.[19] Interpretation begins with recognition, and recognition is a matter of knowing texts.

The mixture of styles, of types of narrative, is a reminder that rhetorically well-formed, seriously written lives were not the only model for medieval biographers – and that it is always important to look outside the genre one is studying in the search for imported material and styles. Some traditional stories that found their way into the conventions of writing lives include the special distinction of the hero's parents: the father is often a king, sometimes a god, frequently disguised or absent, leaving the son maximum room for growth without the threat of the older powerful male. Rumours that Alexander was not the son of Philip of Macedon but of the Egyptian deity Ammon began early; obviously the need to provide a superhuman explanation for super-human deeds is part of the momentum behind this. Great men are not like us, for the perfectly good reason that they are not us, but touched by the divine.

MODELS OF SANCTITY

There is no typical saint's life any more than there is a typical history, and in this case the manuals are silent. As I did in Chapter 2, I shall proceed by looking at conventions in the hope of being able to provide enough key examples to enable readers to recognize the kinds of intentions, references, and unspoken assumptions that may lie behind a biographical narrative, and which are the first step before one can begin to ask how these conventions are being used. There are no strict genre boundaries, and use of one style in a narrative ostensibly of another kind may constitute a claim to sanctity. Here again the problem of ambition arises for the narrator. What might be called the conventions of holiness are also recognizable in narratives which are not concerned with saints as their subjects: King Charles I of England is one of a long line of monarchs whose biographers canonized them by stealth. 'Stealth' depends upon the idea of a normative sequence of events through which holiness manifested itself, and some generalizations can safely be made about biographies of holy men; as they were related to *encomium* their authors were not on oath, and as they dealt not with doctrine but with example, their authors had great freedom to make their narratives emotionally satisfying stimulants to imitation. As always, the most ambitious writers, trained or aspiring rhetoricians, went back to famous classical texts for direct inspiration. Where the new text attempts to claim sanctity a slightly different attitude is required of the narrator from texts about known saints. If sanctity is to be recognized by certain human characteristics (resistance to normal human experiences like sexuality, hunger and thirst, and secular ambition) as well as certain events (bodily manifestations such as stigmata, acts of endurance – particularly fasting or resistance to pain) apparently beyond normal human capacity, healing the sick, power over natural forces, prophecy, or even unusual influence over other people, then these are the 'obvious' components of a narrative whose hero or heroine is meant to be recognizable – without question or doubt – as one of the elect of God. That is, the story itself compels this recognition by a kind of matter-of-factness about wonderful, even awesome, events, about which the narrator must maintain a pose of apparent neutrality before the evidence. The addition of new miracles or the rehearsal of a well-known holy life put the narrator in a slightly more comfortable position, because 'authority' for the life was already established. The narrator addresses a reader who can be moved and persuaded by the story of saintly life to awe and imitation; that is, there is an expectation that the reception of the Life will be a reaction to a 'biography as praise'. And the encomiast is in the malleable position, for a writer, of not being on oath about what he claims is true. If this seems paradoxical, even confused, it is because it is both, but it is a position about which medieval writers argued; it is not something they reconciled. At different points they say opposing things.

The anonymous author who wrote the partisan account now known as the *Encomium Emmae Reginae* began his work with an acknowledgement that 'when in writing the deeds of any one man one inserts a fictitious element, either in error, or, as is often the case, for the sake of ornament, the hearer assuredly regards facts as fictions when he has ascertained the introduction of so much as one lie' – in effect an *enthymeme* arguing that no one who knows the risk of losing credibility would insert a fiction.[20] This functions as a rhetorical ploy: having attempted to establish an *ethos* of veracity, the author inserts elaborate imitations of and explicit references to the usual figures: Virgil, Lucan, and Sallust. A general allegiance to the truth is no bar to good writing; as we saw in the previous chapter, the ambitious writer embodied his vision of events and persons in his narrative with all the skill at his command: not embellishment, but false embellishment, was to be condemned. The successful writer achieved an art that hid art, that subordinated his style to the effects he meant to convey. For most writers, elaboration, 'fictitious elements', were only clearly wrong when they became a distraction; if they broke the reader's (or listener's) concentration on the narrative they were a certain sign of failure. If the generalizations in prefaces seldom give more than an indication of the theoretical goals to which writers thought they ought to be seen to be subscribing, occasionally they give some evidence for the ways historians and biographers discriminated among the authors and texts they used, as the genres in which they wrote. Usually, however, imitations are tacit, inviting readers to recognize (and appreciate) manipulations stylish or daring – or slavish – reproductions. In multiplying examples, to enlarge the field through which hypotheses can be tested, the more imitated, the more canonical, a particular text, the more useful it becomes. Bede is one author whose work acquired unquestioned authority for his successors; among the most famous, influential, and intelligent of these is William of Malmesbury, whose own position likewise became authoritative. And here once more the coincidence of stylish writing and some kind of commitment to a recognizable (if not modern) accuracy raises its head, like the belief that the good orator will be a good man.

That the outline of events through which could be expressed the sanctity of the subject, as well as models of character and, sometimes, physical description have much in common with the familiar formulae of *encomium* may now seem startling only in its obviousness. Concomitantly, of course, it means that no particular description, debate, or action need be true; it may be included to symbolize the status of the subject, or indicate by its sense of appropriateness, how the text is to be interpreted. The sum of deeds was not always enough to convey a sense of the *character* of the subject, although they manifested his virtue, so that they created a sense of the ways in which he exemplified certain abstract values, like constancy, holiness, courage, etc. 'Sayings', also to be found in classical panegyrics, cater more to a sense of a possible unique individual – nevertheless they, too, may be invented, copied or adapted in order to indicate what *type* of person the subject was. Modern readers, used to 'matching' their experience of actual living persons to literary descriptions in order to hypothesize about what the literary character was like, as if the text were a guide to a possible person, are most likely to overinterpret when dealing with speech, which, as we have seen, may not be meant as a psychologically mimetic stylization at all, but as the statement of a case, or an argument. The style of the case or argument may be uppermost on the writer's mind, not only for the sake of his own ambition as a writer, but as a way of celebrating in the most moving and persuasive language the saintly achievements, the deeds, of his hero. Major changes of order, or of style, so far from creating an original contribution to a developing literary genre, threatened to discredit the text at issue, by distracting attention from the claim being made onto the apparent illegitimacy of the narrative, or the ignorance of the writers. Yet careful assimilation of other exercises might contribute successfully to the new Life: the familiar units of description, comparison, the *chria*, commonplace and sentence. These habits of formal rhetorical organization, and their emphasis of 'finished' and dignified style of reported speech, militate against the recording of the informal, the spontaneous, the characteristic utterance, the unique.

From the earliest days of Christian hagiographical writing, authors were in effect competing with the classical literature which had preceded theirs. This led to the establishment of their own set of 'canonical' literary texts; among the most influential is the Life of St Martin by Sulpicius Severus, who was a contemporary of Augustine and Jerome, and, like them, part of that late-fourth-century attempt to use pagan literary forms in the service of Christianity.[21] The importance of the *Vita Martini* justifies detailed explication of its shape and content. Like Augustine, Sulpicius came from an

outpost of the Empire, and, like both Augustine and Jerome, he had received
a traditional education and was a trained rhetorician. He was an ambitious
imitator of classical texts and styles, though without the talent of either of his
greater contemporaries. He filled his *Vita Martini* with allusions to pagan
writers, chief among whom was Sallust. If the choice for classical
biographers had been that between hero and sage, Sulpicius tried to
amalgamate those categories by creating a figure whose sanctity would
show him to be both. The Roman 'virtues' – concerned with the exercise of
political power – were transformed in his pages into a demonstration of
supernatural power manifested in the saint's ability to perform miracles.
Martin is opposed on the one hand to Socrates, that supreme figure of earthly
wisdom, and on the other to Hector, greatest of the defenders of Troy.
Martin's 'character' is a demonstration of an unwavering *ethos* manifested
from earliest infancy as constancy in the service of God. That which is true
and permanent in the saint is only slowly revealed as his life passes and can be
read, recognized, and interpreted. Character is absolute and unchanging.
Revelation of that character as time passes is what history provides. The inset
narrations which exemplify Martin's saintliness all illustrate this perfectly
embodied holiness. It is not something Martin learns, acquires, or perfects; it
is a gift of God's grace demonstrating itself as a spur to ordinary men and
women. Martin came, not from the class which controlled politics in Rome,
but from a family bound by Imperial law to supply the emperor with
soldiers, therefore a humbler social status than the usual secular hero. This, of
course, reinforces the emphasis on humility that was so important in the
early years of Christianity; the upward mobility, as it might be described,
which Martin enjoyed came as a result of the recognition of his personal
qualities, and not a part of his inheritance. The implicit lessons of the text
include exhortations to aspire although they also include the contradictory
message that God's grace alone is the source of the strength which called
attention to his saint.[22] There is a plot in which the true self is revealed by
means of the vicissitudes which the text narrates. Virtue may not be
rewarded until after terrible martyrdom, but in happier cases (and the
contradiction this implies should not go unremarked) recognition and status
may be showered upon the truly holy. This schema thus enshrines precisely
those values it pretends to deny. The narrator's point of view may also cause
difficulties when there is a shortage of witnesses (either because none
survived martyrdom or because the reward has to be assumed as subsequent
to the martyrdom).

The structure of the *Vita Martini* adapts the *encomium* while encompassing both the New Testament model (particularly the Acts of the Apostles) and the traditions of classical literary biography. Although it is the work of the saint's younger contemporary, one who met his subject (or at least claimed to), it is stylized according to Sulpicius' literary ambitions. While its tone suggests an artless simplicity, its construction reveals a careful mind at work, and there are numerous reminiscences of classical authors. Indeed, in his second chapter Sulpicius gives us clues to his intention. After a preliminary justification of his own involvement in the act of writing, despite the (formulaic) rudeness of his style, he argues that the memory of great men and their deeds is not intrinsically worthy of preservation. Only if the reader is incited to follow the way of true wisdom, to become a soldier of Christ, is literary activity justified. This is a reply to the *topos* which argued that remembering the deeds of the great was worthwhile in itself, justifying both the exercise of memory and the fame of great men. Sulpicius' self-justification is that essential rhetorical ambition to move and persuade, in this case to capture the imagination of the reader and turn him or her to God. This, after all, is the first *carrière ouverte aux talents*. Some of the striking force of this story comes precisely from Martin's rise. His story will include acts typical of the saint, but without any pretension to completeness, both because Martin himself was too modest to make everything known and because Sulpicius hesitates to overwhelm his readers – the kind of address which creates a modest collusion between author and audience. Now this preface, by stressing the inadequacy and incompleteness of the narrative, and especially by its assumptions of pattern and typicality, accepts and encourages additions and decorative expansions by subsequent writers, for whom the *Vita Martini* was both matter and matter-for-transformation, like those endless Caesars crossing their Rubicons in generations of classrooms.

Sulpicius uses a tripartite plan through which Martin's constancy and supernatural powers appear. While the different sections are unequal in length, they are nevertheless balanced against each other. After the preface the first section describes Martin's early life, in which his future promise becomes clear (chapters 2–11). First, Martin's birthplace and parentage are briefly mentioned: as his father was a soldier, of low status, and a pagan, he can hardly be a subject for extended praise, but 'ancestors' has appeared. Martin's early desire to serve God was frustrated by the edict that made soldiers of soldiers' sons. Though he found himself serving in the Imperial army, he served God as far as he could, and stood a model of gentle dedication despite his circumstances (chapter 2). Note that there is no analysis of the organization or duties of the army, that is, no background. Only one example of Martin's early piety is given: the famous incident of the division of his cloak with a beggar. In order to resign from the army Martin had to make a public profession of his faith, and in order to show that it was faith and not cowardice that impelled him, he offered to go into battle unarmed. This movement from private to public creates a kind of literary climax which Sulpicius then repeats. With Martin's profession accepted, he graduates to opposing pagans, heretics, and Satan himself. He preaches, cures, and casts out devils; not only are these gifts tacit references to Christ's promises of power to his followers, but they are explicitly recognized within the narrative by Martin's patron, Hilary of Poitiers, who acts within the story as a commentator of high status who tells us how to interpret what we read about the hero. Public recognition of Martin's holiness culminates in his election to a bishopric. In effect, the first third of the *Vita Martini* is a *curriculum vitae*, full of exciting actions, and empty of any explanation of Martin's rise beyond the grace of God. The hero's *ethos* which has emerged and been suitably recognized (and rewarded) is further illustrated in the second part by the narrator's *ethos*.

While the first section was more or less chronological, the second deals with the twenty-six years of Martin's episcopate as one unit. One might think of this section as corresponding to the Sallustian or Suetonian *divisio* which demonstrates virtues under successive topic headings. Like the divisions of Martin's early life, there is a campaign against pagan worship in Gaul, generously illustrated with miracles that demonstrate Martin's special power. Secondly, there is Martin's gift to cure and exorcise. Thirdly, there is direct confrontation with Satan (chapters 20–24). Once again, the miraculous occurrences are far from being an arbitrary collection of events: they progress, neither chronologically nor in terms of Martin's power, but according to the rank of the virtues themselves. The temptations to false worship are first Caesar, then a false image of Christ; so also Satan begins by tempting Martin to despair before taxing him with more interior mystical assaults. The idea of tests of increasing difficulty is as old as the first fairy story; no one would claim that Sulpicius invented either the challenges or the form in which they were expressed. His crucial importance is that he helped to establish a Christian genre, in which the saint and his actions exemplify his significance as a manifestation of divine power on earth. Along the way, of course, they establish a special kind of adventure story, acceptable to centuries of pious readers otherwise nervous of the lure of fiction.

Recognizing the tacit principles of organization enables readers to understand and interpret, though it does not control their interpretation. Once again, literal truth is not the key criterion.

The recital of Martin's career and 'virtus' is followed by a third, but shorter, section: three final chapters which describe his 'character' and *mores*, his habits. As with Boccaccio's Dante, any expectation that Sulpicius has 'caught' Martin the man will be disappointed. He has selected examples that typify: Martin the bishop, the ascetic, the saint. Sulpicius explains that having heard of Martin's faith, life, and spiritual power (*virtus*), he wished to meet him, *so as* to write his life, as if he were aware of the increased status given to the eye-witness historian. It allows him to make his text, and to make claims for its truth and exemplary value. It moved even Gibbon to praise. Much of what Sulpicius included in his life of Martin must have come from what other people told him, that is, from common report. He does not present his journey to see the saint as a unique opportunity for research, and it seems to have resulted in very little additional material for the Life. The first-hand experience of Martin's holiness does provide the reader with an added legitimation, and makes Sulpicius himself an authority for what he reports. Martin's spiritual power struck Sulpicius with great force; he recognized the saint's *ethos*. Martin's graciousness to his visitor, his humility, is exemplified in his invitation to Sulpicius to eat with him. In a culture which showed marks of status and respect by segregating people at table Sulpicius would have expected to eat among other visitors rather than with the Bishop. Martin's invitation is meant to suggest that although the soldier's son now found himself enthroned, he had not lost his humility, and cared only enough for the outward marks of respect. The conversation on this occasion was of the obligation to leave the world and follow God (which is the point of the whole narrative, and which may therefore be the point of including or inventing this conversation); Sulpicius reports Martin's seriousness, learning, understanding of Scripture, but he neither describes the exact topics that the saint expounded nor any of the words that were so affecting (chapter 25). This is a double opportunity lost: we hear neither the wisdom of the saint nor in his wisdom the rhetorical skill of the author. His last two chapters (26–7) are a straightforward paean to the holy man's spiritual qualities. There is no description of his physical appearance.

Succeeding Christian writers were thus supplied with a model composition in which the *encomium* of sanctity was a moral example appropriate to the needs of the community. The record of the holy man's *vita et virtutes* was also a success story. The important thing to remember is perhaps that this composition provided authority for the biographical enterprise itself: life, deeds, and character could be celebrated by following the model. Or, using this model's own adaptations of classical historians and biographers, a combination could be created according to the needs – and ambitions – of the individual writer. Sulpicius' tacit attitudes to evidence of different kinds also provided his imitators with the same kinds of distinctions they would find in historians of all kinds: the authority figure, the eye-witness, the satisfactions of pattern, and the concerns with style.

This Life was often copied and illustrated. It was also expanded, translated into prose and verse, and used as pious teaching model. Paulinus of Perigueux turned Sulpicius Severus' prose into Latin verse in the fifth century, as did Fortunatus in the sixth and Marbod of Rennes in the twelfth.[23] Gregory of Tours wrote about Martin's miracles (because of course they continued, as testimony to the power of the saint's relics and the prestige of the place which housed them) and they were collected in four books.[24] One finds Martin's story, in one form or another, in all the European vernaculars: one of the Blickling Homilies adapts Sulpicius for its Anglo-Saxon audience, and in the thirteenth century a canon of St Martin de Tours translated Sulpicius' prose into French octosyllabic couplets.[25] Just as the destruction of Troy provided its own inexhaustible subject for practising Laments, from the poems of medieval students to the self-consciously old-fashioned speech which Hamlet could still find full of emotional power, so the life of St Martin appears wherever piety strove to prove – or improve – its rhetorical accomplishments.

While Sulpicius Severus provided both a model of how to structure a *Vita* as well as what topics to treat within it, other early Christian writers also contributed detailed descriptions, *ecphrases*, that could be inserted in the relevant places. Sidonius Apollinaris was a useful source.[26] He begins, unusually, with a physical description before going on to narrate the way the Emperor Theodoric spends his days (his *mores*). Here a secular model is created for subsequent biographers. Not only do historians like Reginald of Durham and Peter of Blois follow the order of Sidonius' topics, as impressive a writer as Einhard himself adapts the physical details for his own picture of Charlemagne, who appears with Theodoric's round head.[27] When secular figures again began to be possible subjects for biography, the models that were available were not just the classical historians mentioned above in Chapter 2, but that classical and late-classical tradition as modified by generations of hagiographical writing. As early Christian writers had striven to assimilate their saints to pre-existing models of civic or literary *virtus*, so subsequent writers reversed the process to dignify their secular subjects. One may wonder when characteristics actually belonged to the subject of a Life, since they may be included because the author thought them appropriate to the type his protagonist exemplified. If being just a little taller than the average was the 'correct' height for a king or hero, if it was traditional for him to ride a wilder horse or pull a heavier bow, then the alert biographer will assign him the necessary attributes. Conversely, divergence from the accepted pattern, including the omission of topics one could reasonably expect to find, may be implicit moral criticism rather than part of accurate observation.[28]

As a model for a free-standing *encomium* the *Vita Martini* also proved useful to writers developing claims for their own subjects. Among the descendants of Sulpicius' Life are two tenth-century Latin Lives by authors resident at the Ottonian court: the *Vita Mahthildis*, which celebrates the wife of Henry the Fowler, and a Life of her son Archbishop Bruno of Cologne by Ruotger.[29] The former reminds us that the model could be adapted for a saint of the other sex. What is important is that it is written as a panegyric, praise of the progenitrix of the royal family; that is, so far from being the tale of the ascetic life and a bishopric, the outline of the success story of the soldier's son could be transformed by use of its structure and topics as a model for a woman whose fame seems to rest on her social status and successful production of children. Archbishop Bruno was her younger son; like his mother, he was instrumental in furthering the political ambitions of their family. In addition to aiding his brother, Otto I, to govern the Holy Roman Empire, he also consolidated power by reforming his diocese. Yet Ruotger's Life stresses Bruno's pious desire to be united with God; Ruotger's combination of Bruno's position and his fervent (but discreet) asceticism claims him for the communion of the saints. He shows Bruno's fortitude and self-discipline. In both these biographies the panegyric elevates but does nothing to illuminate, the character of their subjects.

The authors adapt significant models in rewriting them; they do not use them as suggestions of different ways in which their subjects might be described. To depart from the method might attract accusations of ineptitude, even – where the subject was active in the world – risking accusations of inappropriate ambition, both for the subject and for the author. They have no genre ambitions which might lead them to extend or modify. They are compilers, not observers, but they are by no means unsophisticated. Their apparently pious aims in effect glorify the Ottonian royal family. The justification for the biographical enterprise is derived from the celebration of holy men and women, but the net effect is to move that tradition back toward the recording of politically significant people. Like Boccaccio's *encomium* of Dante, the existence of a rhetorically ambitious Life stakes a claim for its subject, and whatever its subject exemplified. I shall return to this.

Hagiographical writing was by no means always of a high standard. Mechanical celebrations of holiness by endless squads of indifferent stylists (whose enthusiasm abused the most generous interpretation of acceptable latitude of embellishment) have earned medieval saints' lives considerable contempt. Most writers in most times and places do not stand out, and it would be foolish to expect most early lives to repay rereading, just because they have survived a long time. Most pious lives were written to a recipe for a purpose. An extreme example of pious patchwork can be found in the Life of St Vincent Madelgarius: the preface combines the prologue to the life of St Ermin, a dash of Sulpicius Severus, and the opening of the life of St Patroclus by Gregory of Tours. The section on his birth and childhood is copied from the Lives of Saints Ermin, Waldetrudis, Aldegund, with a marriage out of the Vita Leobardi by Gregory of Tours. His deeds come from Gregory, too, this time from the Lives of Saints Martius and Quintinianus. His miracles are St Bavo's and St Martin's.[30]

Reginald of Canterbury is quite explicit about the method. In his own *Vita Sancti Malchi* he 'advises his readers to compare his story with Jerome's. Where the two agree, he says, the reader meets with history; where the two disagree, the reader is to believe Jerome, not Reginald. If I ran across a good story anywhere, says Reginald, I included it, for *all things are common in the communion of the saints*. Since Malchus was just, saintly, loved by Christ, full of the very essence of righteousness, I do not deviate from the truth, no matter what miracles I ascribe to Malchus, even though they were manifested in some other saint.'[31] Why, we might wish to ask, did Reginald then rewrite a life which existed from the hand of Jerome himself? Had Jerome's Latin become too difficult? Or was his text in some way too short? Is this a case of authorial ambition, in which we see a desire to emulate the achievements of the earlier text? In the earliest life of St Gregory the Great, the anonymous Monk of Whitby insists that even if the miracles he describes didn't happen, they are true anyway. That is, the subject manifests God's work. The logical conclusion of this is unlimited invention, and a hagiography that bears no relation to anything that ever happened.[32] Though these are extremes, they represent widespread attitudes: in the genre of holy *encomium* events are less true or false than signs of the subject's holy *ethos* and of God's abundant grace. As they seldom comment on each other's practice, their attitudes must be deduced; stupidity, incapacity, and misunderstanding must be allowed for, as must the desire to sneak something in under the cover of a 'safe' convention.

As with the practice of historians, the more popular the audience, the greater the latitude of invention. Some saints' lives seem to blur the edges of the genre and enter the territory of the kind of fiction categorized as 'romance'. Today the Middle English poem 'Sir Gowther' is classified as romance because it is recognizably a fictionalized saint's life with adventures that are more secular than we have come to expect. In a period with no independent concept of 'literature', pious authors adapted popular adventures to appeal to the piety of lay audiences, without worrying about whether or not they were transgressing critical categories. No doubt there were some among them who deliberately prepared adventure stories which would convey a 'higher' message than the usual run of giant-killing, who were adapting the conventions of fiction in order to preach by stealth. The story of the two great friends Amis and Amiloun gave rise to two self-sacrificing saints of the same names. Another writer celebrated his local saint, Vidian, with events adapted from the adventures of the epic hero, Vivian, nephew of William of Orange, originally recounted in the *Enfances Vivien* and *Aliscans*, two *chansons de geste*.[33] Clearly fictional stories about pious heroes and heroines who suffered remarkable adventures without losing their faith celebrated divine power on earth by preserving God's favoured figures through miraculous intervention. There are Apocryphal Romances, like the pseudo-Clementine *Recognitiones* or the *Acts of Paul and Thecla* that seem neither one thing nor another. The point at which free-standing biography becomes free-standing fiction is harder to define than to recognize, and how much medieval and renaissance readers varied in their reactions it is very hard to say. Rhetorical embellishment of lives which claim to be true, look true, were written by contemporaries, even eye-witnesses, raise problems in an acute form. In a society which recognized the difference between the historical and the fictional as critical categories of narrative, individual writers were more willing to agree that the distinction existed than to identify which kind of narration any particular *unit of narration* represented.

This indeterminacy enabled writers to circumvent prohibitions and inhibitions of many kinds.

The likely truth content in the *Life of Christina of Markyate* raises just such problems.[34] The manuscript lacks several folios at the beginning and end, so none of the prefatory or concluding material which may once have accompanied it – and which is so useful a place to begin interpreting the author's intention – remains. It is a copy of a life written in Latin prose in the mid twelfth century by someone who represents himself as having known Christina, and who was probably a monk of St Albans. There is corroborating evidence that Christina was a real person; after her death a cult was established and there were moves to have her canonized. A book survives which probably belonged to her: she was educated enough to want a Psalter which contains both Anglo-Norman French and Latin.[35] At the time the Life was written, however, although Christina's exceptional holiness was recognized, she was not officially regarded as a saint. This might suggest that a writer wanting to support her candidature for official saintly status would have every reason to interpret her life in the terms which belonged to biographies of holy men and women. The extant Life is basically a chronological sequence which depends upon Christina's own reminiscences: it is unusually *autobiographical*, though there is a strong sense of the monastic narrator, who comments upon the action from time to time. There is little formal *divisio* into abstract categories, though once one of Christina's spiritual gifts (precognition) is mentioned examples of it are multiplied. What makes this Life so striking is its verisimilitude and unmistakable literary realism.

The narrative follows Christina's memories from her point of view, and contains many of those 'mistakes and miscarriages' which Johnson took to embody true biography. But they are suspiciously like the mistakes and miscarriages of invented story. As a small child Christina, whose baptismal name was appropriately Theodora (she changed it later to elude recognition), vowed to live celibate in the service of God, and fought for years against her family and the church hierarchy to be allowed to follow her vocation. Christina's most pressing concern was to preserve her virginity, that almost magical attribute which would qualify her soul for a special place in heaven. As so often, the ostensible religious concern tells us as much about secular values as the ones it purports to support: Christina's adventures seem to arise from her exceptional beauty. As a young girl she claims to have escaped the advances of Ranulph Flambard (King Henry I's chancellor, who early acquired a reputation for storybook wickedness, and who attracted a number of folklore stories to illustrate it) by means of an equivocation: tricked into finding herself alone with him in his chamber she pretended to accede to his desire but insisted upon bolting the door. She says that he made her swear that if he let her go of her she would only bolt the door. She kept her oath but shot the bolt from the outside, thus locking him in. This is so like a fabliau incident that it is hard to credit: even if they had been alone, even if there were no servants within call, even if the door had bolts on both sides, it is highly unlikely that a suspicious man would have let go of the young girl. He would surely either have kept a grip on her or have bolted the door himself. Later, Christina says, having in a moment of weakness agreed to a betrothal, she managed to talk her husband out of consummating their marriage by recounting to him the story of the married celibacy of Saints Cecilia and Valerian. On a third occasion she hid from pursuers ostensibly intent upon deflowering her then and there by climbing up behind a tapestry on the wall of her own bedchamber; though someone actually grasped her foot through the hangings he did not realize what he had in his hand. A certain scepticism seems called for, but there is no evidence outside the narrative. Some of the 'realistic' touches may well be based on what actually happened, but they may – like the fabliaux – be stylizations 'down', recounting, in low style, tricks of deception and escape. Much of the narrative depends upon repetition of and allusion to other narratives, but whether it was Christina reading her own experience in the light of the Bible or her author assimilating her story to more authoritative ones cannot be resolved. Sometimes the narrator anticipates his audience's criticism of Christina's behaviour: having decided to escape from her family to take shelter with a recluse who was willing to hide her, Christina put on men's clothes (a shocking immodesty) and rode away. The incident is told with dramatic skill, and includes suspense when her accomplice is delayed, and a moment of peril when the sleeve of her new clothes protrudes from the sleeve of her gown and she has to invent an explanation on the spot. In the moment before mounting her horse she hesitates, embarrassed to ride astride. Whether or not any of this happened, the description (or invention) of her inner life is extraordinary. So is the perceptive comment of the narrator that Christina's zeal to live the religious life resembled her family's refusal to agree, and that the family was united in the trait of stubbornness. We may ask how it is that the narrator has achieved such vividness; the answer is something to do with his ability to dramatize and create suspense.

There is no simple explanation which will help to account for the unusual features of the Life; indeed, describing those features builds some of the problems into the analysis, like Chinese boxes. First, it is both intertextual and mimetic. But before readers could recognize it as a piece of writing which is shaped by reference to the conventions of earlier texts, as well as containing explicit reference to them, both Christina and her reporter must have seen her own life according to the experience of other women known through their reading. She tried, in her life, to imitate, not *art*, but the way of perfection offered by historical, sacred report. The written *Life* is thus a literary construct which attempts to convey a true report of something modelled on other literary constructs. Second, the 'other literary constructs' upon which it is modelled *as a piece of writing* are not just other religious narratives. The dramatized anecdotes are the work of an author who was well-read in secular literature, and it may be possible for some future readers to identify his sources, even to the point of finding that he has adapted adventures from known texts. Third, his amalgam also includes direct reflection upon the traits of character shown by people with whom he was acquainted, mediated by his experience of human behaviour, amounting to an inexplicit collusion with the potential reader, from whom he expects recognition of, and agreement with, his analysis – so that he is assuming that his literary picture conveys a sense of a *person* who can be interpreted by other persons in ways that he intends. All of this makes it an exceptional text for the period.

It is possible that the *Life of Christina of Markyate* was intended as a first step in a process of canonization, and that its chronological arrangement marks an early stage in that process, but while that would account for its existence it would do little to explain the style of its content.[36] It may be that there was a debate at the time it was written over the status of unwitnessed vows; certainly a great deal turns on whether or not the young Theodora/Christina bound herself by her unexpressed oath to enter the religious life; there may also be some legal implication about the age at which such vows could be made, given the opposition of the family. The concern with virginity was of overriding concern to a woman, but Christina's adventures read like a Greek romance, with its exaggerated perils, and she clearly goes on being desirable despite her mortifications and illnesses. All of these are speculations which put us, as readers, in the traditional position of analysts who have nothing to go on in making an assessment about the truth of the narrative beyond the narrative itself, and thus far suspicion has been awakened only when plausibility (reference to life as we know it) and inter-textuality (imitation of other books) suggest that we should question the assertions of the narrator. Did *she* invent the stories which her reporter transcribed? Some of the narrative is embellished enough to raise the suspicion that it was invented, but it is impossible to say which parts, how much, or by whom. It is so well narrated that we are constantly invited to believe: the epitome of the rhetorician's success. Perhaps we can say no more than that the author, whoever he was, made a coherent story about an unusual woman, whose success in dedicating herself to God was worth preserving in order to inspire others to do likewise. To complete the literary ironies it must be recorded that if that is what he intended he seems to have been unsuccessful: the text as we have it looks like a copy of his original, but once again there is no evidence of its having been known to other medieval readers or writers. And this is another reminder that 'literary realism' is a possibility at any time or place.[37] It is hard, given our retrospective judgements about literary realism as an improvement, not to feel that medieval biography is a perpetual incitement to invent the wheel.

If we turn to a writer whose works were much studied, and about whose influence there is no doubt, we can see many of these same processes. In the case of Bede there are particularly clear examples of genre-related manipulations, since there is one matter which he treated three times, in different ways. Each of Bede's Lives of St Cuthbert is in a different genre, and awareness of them goes some way to explaining why they take the forms they do.[38] In Bede's great *Ecclesiastical History*, which recounts the story of the English Church, and God's manifestations of his plans through history, Bede tells how 'King Egfrid, ignoring the advice of his friends and particularly of Cuthbert, of blessed memory, who had recently been made bishop, rashly led an army to ravage the province of the Picts.'[39] That is, the story is the king's story, as is appropriate to history, in which Cuthbert makes an appearance as an apparently minor (but not contingent) figure. The king was killed during his Pictish campaign, thus exemplifying God's speedy punishment of the unrighteous, while demonstrating Cuthbert's judgement (and therefore his *virtus* in the sense of spiritual power). There is nothing exceptional about this kind of historical writing as moral example. But at the end of this section Bede inserts, out of strict chronological position, a summary life of St Cuthbert.[40] Three chapters narrate Cuthbert's life and work, especially as a successful preacher. As this is inset biography in a larger history, Bede is careful to name other men who were influential at the time, and also to describe something of the customs of the English in the late seventh century. This is the kind of straightforward historical narrative which has earned Bede his high reputation for organization and observation. Then, however, follow three chapters on Cuthbert's cult and miracles: Bede explains that he includes these instances of the saint's power to heal because they have come to his attention since the completion of his earlier book (not hitherto mentioned) on Cuthbert's life. They are addenda to a pre-existing *Vita*, which he expects his reader to know. If we turn to that *encomium*, genre distinctions emerge.

Bede's prose *Life of St Cuthbert* is based on an earlier anonymous *Life*, and uses the form established by Sulpicius Severus.[41] Bede is familiar with the genre: he begins with a *chria* from the prophet Jeremiah, and treats of Cuthbert's early days as 'praise of his boyhood', in which the familiar promises of greatness appear. The chronological account of his life and works contains the miracles (his deeds), so that the earlier tripartite division disappears. So, too, instead of a final section on character and habits, Bede interpolates numerous speeches which illustrate Cuthbert's piety, forebearance, and even humour. The ascription of the writer's own words to his subject is by now a familiar rhetorical convention; Bede, who was the author of the elegant dramatization of the debates at Whitby over the dating of Easter, makes Cuthbert speak not only in formal addresses, but also in conversation, which begins to create a sense of what the man was like, though Bede does not include any physical description. Given the requirements of holy *encomium*, the *Life* includes material which make the biographer look more credulous than the careful observer of the *Ecclesiastical History* – but of course *credulousness* is not at issue here at all. *Encomium* has wider latitude for inclusion and embellishment than does history; Bede is a good writer, not an inconsistent man. In an age where revised editions are possible, the discovery of new material is handled by republishing. But Bede could not rewrite and reissue his biography when parchment was scarce and books were duplicated by copying them out by hand. His solution was straightforward, but requires a modern reader to be alert. He adds to the *life* in the course of the *history* because more information had come to his attention. If he had instead rewritten the biography the miracles which seem out of place in the later work would have formed a consistent part of a freestanding biography. They belong to the more symbolic genre and not – in rhetorical terms – to the historical narrative of the English church and people. Yet, given the over-riding concerns of Bede's work, and his desire to

educate, preach, and teach, the literary sacrifice is minor. It is also well
marked. In effect, Bede signals the change of genre at the end of Book Four
when he digresses from the main line of historical narrative in order to
include his new information. Chapters 26 and 27 are part of that historical
sequence; at the beginning of chapter 28 Bede mentions his earlier
composition in order to indicate the additions that he is about to make.
Narrator 'speaks' directly to reader in a kind of *dispositio*, and lest, in the
course of the final few chapters (28–32) the reader should forget that he is
reading a kind of *digressio*, Bede reappears with a quiet reminder at the end of
chapter 30:

> The miracles of healing that take place from time to time at the tomb bear witness to
> Cuthbert's holiness, and I have recorded some instances in my book on his life. And
> in this present history I have included further examples that have recently come to
> my knowledge.

There is another reminder in the following chapter (31), as if Bede were
worried that the reader might have missed it the first time. The recognition
that there is a literary change at issue here resolves Bede's apparent
inconsistency at the same time as it implies awareness of genre. Bede may
himself have felt that his chapters on Cuthbert did not really belong in the
*Ecclesiastical History*, since they stretch the conventions of what was
acceptable, but that mixtures of genres was a small price to pay in order to
complete and preserve his record of Cuthbert's witness to the glory of God.
Setting the digression at the end of one of his larger divisions, and marking it
as material additional to another book was the best solution to a difficult
problem. Rhetorical ambitions were subordinate to religious ones.

   Bede's own concern with good writing included a pedagogic ambition to
teach rhetoric to his pupils, and to teach the skills of rhetoric via a morally
inspiring model he wrote a third version of the Life of Cuthbert, a metrical
Life to be used as part of the school curriculum, since the holy matter is used
like a musical theme on which to write variations. By writing an
emphatically English as well as a sound Christian model for his students Bede
avoided the difficulty that arose every time style and the figures of speech
were dissociated from their content. The metrical Life, of course, created a
model for other verse lives. Alcuin and the anonymous author of the *Song of
Arthulwulf* were among those to contribute to this tradition.[42] As biography
approaches poetry it claims greater license of elaboration. Later, when such
compositions moved into the vernaculars, where they were intended for a

less well educated audience, their embellishments pushed them to – even beyond – the limits of what might by modern standards count as a true report of the subject's life and deeds, and they become hagiographic romances. That is, although the poetic biography can tell us about attitudes, without the corroboration of other kinds of sources it cannot be relied upon as a source for deeds and it can never be relied upon as a source for words. Bede also reminds us that the practice was modified whenever successful new texts were written. His successors recognized his superiority in most genres and sincerely flattered him.[43]

Felix of Crowland was one of the first to press Bede's St Cuthbert into service for a new hagiography. In his *Life of St Guthlac* he acknowledges Bede's eloquence by repeating many of his phrases and sentences in a new context.[44] In so far as *Guthlac* imitates *Cuthbert* Felix legitimates his own composition. Incidents in Bede's narrative continued to reappear: mortification of the flesh is one of the *topoi* of the saint's life, and Bede reported that Cuthbert's self-discipline included immersing his body in the sea in order to subdue desire. When Walter Daniel has Ailred repeat the technique in a Life which is in many other ways modelled on Bede's, one may wonder if total bodily immersion has become symbolic.[45] Then, when the Becket biographers, who had some understandable difficulties with their stubborn and unsaintly subject, relate that the Archbishop, too, used the cold water cure, suspicion is a natural reaction.[46] Literary repetition is required: the claim that Becket behaved in unusual ways but that he was *nevertheless* a saint is too hard for most of the writers about him. They report the immersion as a claim to his devout attempts to subdue his unruly flesh, so it is a sign of their view of his intention. Contingently, this implies that the inner man may wish something which we can know and understand, but which he himself cannot accomplish; that is, the possibility of a literary distinction between inner life and outer becomes feasible. It also suggests that within living memory there may have been constraints upon what an author might attribute to his subject. Even allowing for differences in genre and normative standards for permissible invention, there remain those authors who say one thing and do another. It is hardly likely, in the end, that a medieval or renaissance author will call attention to fictional embellishment of an apparently factual account, however aware, even proud, of its existence he might be. Attesting the truth of the account which is to follow became as much a part of the author's preface as his apology for his rude, humble, and unpolished style; his acquaintance with his subject (which led the plodding Anglo-Saxon hagiographer, Willibald, to explain that he only knew his subject, Boniface, 'indirectly', i.e. only through report or, to put it another way, not at all). Yet even Boniface's disclaimer suggests the transparency of these rhetorical transformations. Reality was visible through them, even if clouded.[47]

William of Malmesbury's rhetorical and generic sensitivity and discrimination appears throughout his own hagiography, the *Life of Wulfstan*.[48] This is one of two biographies of saints by William; the other, a Life of St Dunstan, survives only as rewritten by Dunstan's monks at Glastonbury, so that it is difficult to reconstruct how much is William's. The *Life of Wulfstan* is divided into the traditional three parts, preceded by a dedicatory letter and prologue, like Sulpicius' *Martin*. There are sections on Wulfstan's early life, his miracles, and his habits and conversation (though there are few speeches – William gives the 'gist' of what the saint said). In best rhetorical style William claims to eschew rhetoric, and he refers several times to the temptation (into which other writers fall through excess of zeal) to embellish, and how unnecessary embellishment is, given the worthiness of his subject, as for example in this almost Wittgensteinian address to the reader:

if one desires to expatiate as an orator to his audience on all the blessings that happy day brought to Worcester which first saw Wulfstan a monk, he would find his powers unequal to his purpose. What the tongue cannot utter let the mind strive to ponder.[49]

And, criticizing his predecessor in his most stylish prose,

I have left out some fine words and phrases which Coleman borrowed from the Acts of other saints, and in his blind devotion inserted . . . When the truth is high enough, the man who tries to raise it with fine words loses his labour. When he is trying to praise he dishonours and diminishes: for it seems as if he cannot trust his own story, but must needs borrow help from another.[50]

Here we see a highly educated twelfth-century monk using his rhetorical skill to analyse and correct its own habits: the inexpressibility *topos*, the identification of rhetoric with oratory, despite centuries of texts for *reading*, the historian's dedication to the truth of his representation, and the ostensible deference to the authority of a perceived and interpretable life-narrative. Ostensible, since William's own stories, the anecdotes he includes to exemplify Wulfstan's holiness, may well have been invented for the purpose. As ever, one needs to consider each of them on their individual merits, as best one can, with an eye to the secular values and ambitions they admit. When William says that as a boy Wulfstan excelled at village sports he illustrates Wulfstan's double triumph, both his excellence and his humility, since he overcomes the temptation to worldly success that pride in his skill offered. This is the same paradoxical reinforcement of secular values that appeared in the emphasis on Christina's continued desirability. That is, writers stress that their protagonists were deliberately sacrificing something that was within their grasp; they were not failures retreating from a world in which they could not win. However much being good at games has come to seem a *topos* of English writing, it is unusual in the Middle Ages, and the less likely an example is to be merely traditional, the more we may be inclined to credit it. There are, however, traditional temptations as well, like the saint's resisting a townswoman's sexual advances (so, like Christina, Wulfstan was attractive). Sex is always with us, and there is no reason why, just because something similar once happened to Joseph in Egypt, it should not have happened to Wulfstan in England. Some stories may have been traditionally told about this saint (that is, accepted as true by the people, and therefore, according to Bede's 'true law of history', worthy of record and perpetuation), some may be original to William. They are all of the same genus, panegyrical or encomiastic exempla. While in the *Life of Dunstan* William characteristically objected (though his revisers allowed them to stand) to the invented conversations in the earlier Life by Osbern, he was willing to present the words of both his saints, as of his secular subjects, when it was convenient to him to report speech. It is a good guess, too, that the revisers would have included such traditionally vindicated additions as speech when they amplified. (William of Malmesbury was not alone in his objection to Osbern; Eadmer, the biographer of Anselm, made the same complaint.)[51] In the end there is no more reason to think William's stories and conversations literally true than to believe his anecdotes in his secular *Gesta Regum*.[52] The same talented and well-read writer is responsible throughout, and his allegiance to the truth co-exists with his allegiance to good writing. Like Bede, on whom William consciously and explicitly modelled his histories, William was concerned to make his view of the past and its actors as vivid as possible. His hagiographical *encomia* had, for him, the added virtue of being a way of praising the Anglo-Saxon past in a period of Norman ascendancy, when the old saints were being discredited by the reforming zeal and the cultural pride of Norman piety. I shall return to William's vivid biography below.

That there was a concern with accurate testimony – and not only within the bounds of the rhetorically embellished text – is clear. Canonization depended on it, though, as with the biographies of Beckett, strict accuracy was sometimes sacrificed to the good of the cause. It is as well always to remember that deliberate slanting or forgery were time-honoured options. It is only, after all, where the author is claiming that what he writes is strictly true that a well-written embellishment can pass for convincing. It is equally clear that, mediated through layers of rhetorical invention or stylish presentation, 'accuracy' takes on a different meaning as part of a different culture. Even when Inquisitors 'transcribed' what witnesses said, they translated from the vernacular into Latin. What other changes they must have made must be familiar to anyone who has seen actual speech transcribed. How much manipulation took place it may never be possible to determine. Pious motives, and their belief that they were only writing what 'ought' to have happened, or rewriting an earlier text as the author himself would have wanted it rewritten, if only he had had access to the information the transcriber had, saved them from thinking of themselves as liars or forgers.[53]

### EXERCISING BIOGRAPHICAL INVENTION

The serious hagiographical tradition which stems from Sulpicius Severus was, of course, not the only line of Life writing, however pre-eminent it was. Historical and biographical conventions are similar. They shared a rhetorical basis, so that whatever the larger outlines, the same *topoi* appeared: the *descriptio* of persons and places; the *encomium* of individual, city, or abstraction; the style of writing speeches, documents, letters, and defences; the habit of appealing to received wisdom. Nevertheless, as early as the Carolingian period, such was the hegemony of monastic book production that turning hagiographical habits towards secular biography was a real challenge. Einhard's *Life of Charlemagne* seems to have come into being almost by accident, as if the biographer, struck by the *virtus* of his subject, strove to assimilate a royal life to the saintly by means of the classical models at his disposal. Like Bede, Einhard was an exceptionally well-read, intelligent innovator. Einhard's innovations are the result of creative synthesis. His success is his own. He used classical models when they suited him, as part of his own design. Now it may be that it is sheer coincidence that Charlemagne indeed had a head shaped just like Theodoric's. It is, however, more likely that Einhard, studying the attributes that his model ascribed to *his* Emperor, deliberately copied them to ensure that his own hero would appear unmistakably imperial and Roman. Since a good part of Einhard's intention was to justify Charlemagne's claim to be not only Roman Emperor restored, but *Christian* as well, it is easy to see why he should have been scrupulous in the creation of his image – if less scrupulous in his preservation of what a later age might consider to be the truth. A later age might also find it tempting to class Einhard's project as propaganda, and therefore work to be discounted, but this would be anachronistically strenuous. Einhard believed in his vision of Charlemagne and created it according to his ability as a rhetorician following the best models: his use of Suetonius has long been recognized. The combination of historical events and the description of the Emperor became typical not only of free-standing secular biography, but also of many inset biographies. The testimony to that success is the number of writers who imitated – well or badly – Einhard's *Life* and the existence of over eighty manuscripts of the work is evidence of its continued popularity with those who wanted, for whatever reasons, to read it. By showing how to make use of Suetonius, Einhard opened the way for blame as well as praise.

Einhard's preface makes such claims as must now seem familiar, although in his case it does actually seem to be true that he was the eye-witness of Charlemagne's court that he claims to be. There are letters and documents which corroborate his claim. But his book is far from being the memoirs of a courtier whose forty years in the service of his prince form the subject of his book. The *Vita Caroli* is a rhetorical production, written some time between the years 814 and 821, by a sophisticated and ambitious writer who also wrote Letters; a conventional piece of hagiography, *De Translatione et miraculis sanctorum suorum Marcellini et Petri*; and a composition on the Cross, *Libellus de adoranda Cruce*, dedicated to his friend and fellow-author Lupus of Ferrières. This dedication tells us about Einhard's picture of himself and what he thought he was doing, as Lupus is another of those classicizing writers of the Carolingian Renaissance who created that informed readership to which Einhard could address a new kind of book in the confidence that his recapitulation of Latin style and scholarship would be recognized and appreciated.[54]

The form of Einhard's *Life of Charlemagne* is Suetonian, and Suetonian from reading Suetonius, not as modified and adapted from the Sulpician tradition.[55] It is cogently and clearly organized, though not much more than a sketch, as no single section is very long; it does not approach the kind of disquisition on virtues that Boccaccio wrote in his *encomium* on Dante. The treatment of Charlemagne is laudatory, like a saint's life; there is nothing of

Charlemagne's relations with his brother, whom he dispossessed, or of his treatment of his first wife or his daughters, and nothing of the discreditable events of his Bavarian War, all potential topics in the Suetonian pattern. Einhard was creating a legitimating Imperial biography, a new pattern for the west. His Life begins with a section on Charlemagne's ancestors, and tells how his father, Pepin, came to be king of the Franks. At Pepin's death Charlemagne and his brother Carloman succeeded, and when after two years Carloman died (by disease, as Einhard is careful to make clear), Charlemagne reigned alone. Einhard acknowledges the expectation that there should be a section on the king's boyhood and education, but substitutes an *occupatio*, explaining that he omits these topics because no written evidence survives and the eye-witnesses have all died. This is probably due to a desire to get on to the events of the reign, his real subject. He gives a *divisio* of the sections he intends to include: Charlemagne's deeds and habits, subdivided into his *res gestae* at home and abroad, followed by his domestic *studia* and *mores*, the administration of his kingdom, and finally his death. The section on 'foreign wars' allows him to describe, in good historical fashion (complete with rhetorical flourishes) the Saxons whom Charles had only defeated with some difficulty. He goes on to list Charlemagne's treaties (with some exaggeration of the readiness of foreign potentates to offer friendship to the Frankish king) and then his *opera*: his works of building like the Church at Aachen, the bridge over the Rhine, the palaces, the fleet and coastal fortifications. All of this is carefully signposted, as if Einhard had analysed and listed Suetonius' topics, and filled in under each heading.

It is when Einhard moves, in chapter 18, to Charlemagne's domestic life that Suetonius' influence becomes most striking, since much of the content transforms units from the Lives of Augustus and, to a lesser extent, Tiberius. The physical description, probably adapted from Sidonius Apollinaris' later Emperor, shows how extensive Einhard's researches were. What Einhard's translators have often represented as his description of Charlemagne's character is, in Einhard's terms, a consideration of his *animi dotes* and *constantia*. These are difficult terms, for which there are no English equivalents, and refer to concepts quite unlike modern notions of character. Einhard seems to mean that Charlemagne was (like a saint) firm, steadfast in those gifts of the spirit, those 'essences' of the inner man, which made it possible for him to persevere in prosperity and adversity. There are very few examples which would illustrate Charlemagne's *ethos*; most of this section is a description, of a most carefully selected kind, copied from the Latin models. Like Augustus, Charlemagne kept his children around him, and always travelled with them. Records and charters of the time show that this is not true; Einhard must have thought it was appropriate, and certainly it goes some way to suggesting a sentimental rather than a political reason why Charlemagne's daughters remained with him. Charles's affection for his children also gives Einhard the opportunity to describe a human weakness in Charlemagne, who wept when one of them died, as he wept when he heard that Pope Hadrian I, whom he counted as a friend, had died. In the first case Einhard describes Charlemagne's inability to bear adversity with patience as a limit upon his magnanimity, that essential quality of a ruler; the second is an occasion to point out the strength of his friendship. Einhard returns to magnanimity when he stresses the quality of court hospitality to foreign visitors, which Charlemagne made a point of, because it was important to his fame. The description of Charlemagne's daily life is as problematic as the rest. Einhard says that Charlemagne enjoyed swimming for exercise; as far as literary models go, this is unusual (Charles swam for the pleasure of it, not at all as an exercise in sexual continence). Are we meant to compare this bodily immersion to the discipline Bede described, or is it perhaps included because it is true? There is no answer in the text, beyond plausibility and likelihood. It is plausible and likely that, as Einhard writes, he made a point of wearing Frankish national dress, and was not pretentious in his tastes, yet we must allow that the description of dress is there to assert both his sense of rank and his indifference to ostentatious riches. In terms of Suetonian topics, Einhard covers physical description, leisure, clothing, food and drink (Charles, too, exhibits moderation in eating and drinking, but always had difficulty fasting – this is a king not a saint), and sleep (moderation here suggests that the king was never slothful). When Einhard praises Charlemagne's eloquence and his knowledge of foreign languages one may have one's doubts; the encouragement of learning is, however, well-attested from other sources. Charles's own attempts to learn to read and write are, of course, famous (though that does not make them true). Einhard then moves on to his piety and care for the Church, his concern for his country's laws and for the calendar. Like so much of the rest, this section is short and list-like, and tells us little about the man. There is, for example, though it must be a familiar omission by now, nothing of his conversation, though Einhard spent years at court and must often have heard his eloquent emperor speak. It is not clear what such speech would have been useful as an example of, and that may be why it is omitted.

Einhard ends with the Emperor's death, then the portents which preceded it, the obsequies, epitaph, and a copy of the will. The schematic model which this provided could be, and was, imitated at various lengths. The physical description, in particular, was put to use by other writers, such as Notker, for his own anecdotal life of the Emperor; and Thegan for his life of Louis the Pious; and the anonymous monk of Caen who used Einhard's phrases to describe the death of William the Conqueror as did Asser for the *Life of Alfred*.[56] Once Einhard had established the outline of the secular biography, an organizing schema, others could add illustrative anecdotes, that most Suetonian trait.

Describing some of the *topoi* of history in the previous chapter, I postponed the discussion of 'the character of a great man'. If we move forward in time, and across the genre line from free-standing biography back to history, and biography inset within it, many of these elements can be seen in the work of William of Malmesbury, the twelfth-century historian and hagiographer whose saints' lives we have already considered. As the traditions of Bede's Cuthbert and Sulpicius' Martin lie behind William's Anglo-Saxon heroic saints, so Bede's *Ecclesiastical History* and Suetonius' *Caesars* can be discerned as models for William's Norman kings.[57] Writing at much greater length than Einhard, William includes illustrative anecdotes, speeches, and all the examples which make his work lively – if not necessarily true. The paired lives of William Rufus and Henry I are strikingly Suetonian. The divisions are clear, although implicit. Both lives are divided into eight sections. William Rufus's life is structured at birth, the settlement with his brother which led to his own accession to the English throne, his wars, his private life, his acts *against* God, the church, and his subjects, then a description of his person. Henry's life is similar: early years, accession, internal wars, external wars, *mores*, description of his person, his *opera* (mainly buildings), and family. It also includes two digressions which concern general topics of the day which tie secular concerns to those of the church: investitures and noble ecclesiastics. The lives of the two brothers are meant to contrast. In William of Malmesbury's judgement the elder was a bad man and a bad king, whose immorality was held in check as long as the saintly Lanfranc lived, but whose wickedness approached tyranny once the Archbishop was dead (sections 312–13). William's literary powers were considerable, and the picture of vice he drew persuasive, but if one looks carefully its conventionality is clear. He used ideas about clothing and fashion to great effect: at William Rufus's court men grew their hair long and became too interested in what they wore; this is because they were homosexuals, vicious and effeminate. If one turns from this diatribe to the praise of Henry I, one finds that by contrast Henry is described as a model of chastity. Records inform us of about nineteen of Henry's illegitimate children, and William mentions several of them in passing, so it seems likely that Henry's chastity is posited as an appropriate virtue and a contrast to his brother. While it is true that there are no records of illegitimate children for William Rufus, there is no confirming record of homosexuality either, and it may well be that the historian borrowed 'vices' from the Roman court in order to symbolize his disapproval of the English king. Certainly the section devoted to the growth of vice in William Rufus after the death of Lanfranc is carefully composed, even elegant. The very spontaneity of the anecdotes may arouse suspicion. One of the continuing criticisms of William Rufus is his rapacity, especially towards the church's lands and property. Since a king is supposed to be magnanimous, William's behaviour is doubly disgraceful. One of the best-known anecdotes concerns an incident with the court chamberlain, who brought the king a pair of shoes worth only a few marks. William, reacting angrily to his servant's purchase, complained that kings didn't wear cheap shoes, and sent the man out in search of a more expensive pair. The servant's revenge was first to buy an even cheaper pair of shoes than the offending pair, and then to tell the king that they were more expensive. Further, cheating his master in this way became a habit, and an important source of revenue. The story is unlikely, if only because such deceit would be too dangerous for a servant to risk. It is there to illustrate the king's misplaced sense of values, his offences against magnanimity. It is focussed on clothes to be of a piece with the rest of the criticism of the reign. The apparent consistency, or coherence, of William Rufus's 'character' is a creation of the historian's ethical analysis. Anecdote is the method.

The use and treatment of anecdotes reminds us once again that diverse models may coincide in any new work, and that the *ways* they are used are not to be explained or predicted from their place of derivation; it is difficult to tell if the anecdote about William Rufus's shoes was intended to be funny. It seems unlikely, not only because the narrative is about a king, and the decorum to be expected of such a subject suggests more dignity (that is, serious satire is acceptable, jokes are probably not), but also because most serious writing at this level is homogeneous in effect. This is *not* the case in twelfth-century romances, though, and it is therefore possible that it was not the case in contemporary history. It is one of the characteristics of folklore traditions that stories are invented and repeated to epitomize ethical types and recurring situations. Once an outline was organized, the insertion of extra material followed naturally. Notker's 'anecdotal' biography of Charlemagne, following Einhard's schematic one, illustrates just this tendency. So does Joinville's *Life of St Louis*.[58]

As more and more secular histories were written, with their concentration on and celebration of, non-religious, non-saintly historical agents, they provided, almost by inertia, secular models of concomitant importance. A certain defensiveness continues to appear in their prefaces, since there is a (sometimes, but not always) tacit assumption that properly speaking, men ought to despise the world and its ambitions, for the sake of the hereafter. But the strength of worldly ambition and the power of power continued to exert their charm, and the argument that it was *right* to remember the great deeds of the past remained a standard invocation. Hagiographies, however skilfully adapted, proved inadequate as models for the complexities of life in the world. Their plot is too simple. As annals and chronicles were supplemented by ambitious narrative histories, from the twelfth century onwards, kings and their reigns remained the most convenient organizing principle. It became common for histories to contain inset biographical sections, and, conversely, for works that seem to announce themselves as biographies to treat a reign as a whole. It would be a mistake to place too much stress on the distinction between inset and free-standing biography; it is a convenience. Nor is there a simple line of descent which will distinguish kinds or styles of biography. Each text requires analysis on its merits – or demerits. Richer's tenth-century history of France is full of highly rhetorical biographical material modelled on classical historians, while William of Poitier's biography of William the Conqueror is replete with material on the reign.[59] Both writers stylize their historical actors in order to embody in them the virtues (and vices) suitable to their age, sex, status, and role. Because these roles now involved more complex moral judgements than was the case in hagiography, or in the compressed entries of earlier, annalistic writing, new models impressed themselves upon ambitious writers. From antiquity both Suetonius and Sallust presented abundant and various vice. Ambition, treachery, and tyranny fill their pages. In the Middle Ages the epic writers, the creators of dozens of *chansons de geste*, added to the stock as writers of history. One of the most profound models of historical analysis, already mentioned above in Chapter 1, is the view, enshrined in Sallust and Lucan, that national success encourages turpitude, which weakens and leaves open to defeat once 'virile' societies: a 'decline and fall' theory of enormous popularity, appealing, as it does, to that dual streak of asceticism and misogyny which is so emphatically male-oriented. Virgil, at the heart of education, pervades educated writing, with his sense of public life and national destiny; the role of women is either monstrous regiments of temptresses or providers of more soldiers.

Christianity had, of course, its own models of history. Roman writers were not the only models for creating villainy. Although the historical books of the Bible could be useful for comparison, they were not very analytical about the behaviour of individuals, and were weak on motivation and cause. When Tacitus was rediscovered, his tragical dramas, with all the suspense of which he was master, proved irresistible, as the work of More and Hayward, and even Clarendon, shows.[60] Sallust's Catiline and Jugurtha reappear throughout medieval and renaissance historical writing: Richer used Catiline's speech for his own Otto II, and adapted Sallust's exchanges for some of his own conversations, such as those of Louis IV.[61] William of Poitiers managed to tailor his own comparisons to Julius Caesar to make his description of William the Conqueror straightforward, and William of Malmesbury's William Rufus is at one point so 'close' to the dark side of Julius Caesar that William is constrained to insist that history repeats itself.[62] Well-read historians like Orderic Vitalis pointed out the imitations of their predecessors, but that did not stop them from making imitations of their own.[63] The traditions of the nine worthies, three each from biblical, classical, and vernacular history, remind us that history itself provides a system of references. The vernacular sagas or *chansons de geste* were rich in examples of ambition, treachery, envy, revenge, and Ganelon is as useful a comparison as Judas. Raoul de Cambrai is a fictional villain who is the protagonist of the eponymous *chanson de geste* which recounts his ever-more-wicked deeds. He burns nuns to death inside their convent, including members of his family. When Robert of Avesbury castigates John of France he accuses him of sexual incontinence with secular women, with religious, and with members of his family.[64] Eadric Streona was a figure around whom stories of villainy collected, and he boasted of killing his overlord.[65]

Certain roles are conventional: good kings are wise and just; they maintain good laws in their own country and conquer where they have rights. They establish the succession, exhibit magnanimity, and support the church. By contrast, tyrants abuse this same power. Herod provided a conventional model tyrant in the Christian tradition, both for kings and for the persecuting magistrates who appear throughout the acts of the martyrs and the inventions of hagiographers. If Herod came also to symbolize dramatic crudity, he was no less potent for that, and the angry rant when the tyrant loses his temper remained a useful model. The Roman model is more subtle. The political characteristics of the tyrant were part of men's thinking about power, the role of kings, and formed part of a more general political discourse, if only because the problem of the Republic would not go away. Tyrants abused their roles by excess, perverting the values they ought to have espoused. Injustice replaces the ruler's commitments to maintain the law, avarice replaces magnanimity, and so forth. Private vices can be equally conventional. Above all, tyranny brings duplicity with it. This is of crucial importance in societies dependent upon loyalty, upon men keeping their word. In the absence of clear-cut laws or constitutions, and where there are no police and little by way of armies, only men's obedience to that ideal kept anarchy at bay. Often anarchy was not kept at bay. The association of duplicity with court life is venerable and widespread. 'Duplicity' appears in Skelton's *Bouge of Court* as 'Harvey Hafter', the smiler with the knife beneath the cloak; More's Richard III is the epitome of the type.[66] Because the duplicitous man is disloyal himself, he also anticipates betrayal from everyone around him, so he is suspicious, by turns ingratiating and bullying, prone to lose his temper, and tortured by insomnia and bad dreams. Tyrants are as much a type as any of the other *topoi* we have considered, and we need to be alert to the use of a recognizable description as an accusation of tyranny. It may seem to reveal a knowledge of motive, but the limited nature of the motivation will be clear to anyone who has read any of these descriptions. 'Tyranny' seems to be its own explanation.

Much of this chapter has been concerned with saints and kings, but it must be remembered that it began with a poet. New subjects may be legitimated by old models, creating new ones in their turn. The manipulation of *topoi* need not be a sterile or automatic exercise, and the search in different genres for new models may be a creative response to recalcitrant material. Boccaccio's praise of Dante is a claim which elevates Dante to a dignity hitherto reserved for saints or rulers. By contrast, Boccaccio's short lives of famous, or notorious, men and women exist to exemplify the instability of worldly fortune. But from the beginnings of his so-called 'de casibus' tradition grew another line of descent, a group of discrete secular lives which could be used as illustrations of political views as well. Their existence alone called attention to them as important, worthy of preservation, a compendium of models. Translated, and expanded, first by Laurent de Premierfait into French and then by John Lydgate into English, they were imitated in the series of poems known as the *Mirror for Magistrates*, published in its first, shortest, edition in 1559. This is a vernacular, poetic, amplification of earlier histories which the authors (it is a group compilation) have found elsewhere. The quality of the best of the contributions to the collection, such as the 'Induction' and 'Complaint of Henry Duke of Buckingham', by Thomas Sackville, is high; Sackville used the rhyme royal stanza of Chaucer and his imitators, and pressed Dante and Virgil into service as well for his own tragical historical poem. Once again we are reminded of the essentially literary nature of much biographical and historical writing, and of the disjunctions between literary success and either empirical truth or causal analysis. Authors saw their characters in terms of abstractions, abstractions both of qualities and of human types. For Thomas More, translating the *Life of Picus*, the point of the text was the question where 'true nobility' was to be found; Pico exemplifies the argument that it is behaviour rather than birth which made a man worthy of imitation. Like so many writers, More expects his reader to recognize the argument to which his example is directed. The 'De Casibus' collections which heaped up examples of disappointed ambition were ostensibly presented as warnings, perhaps for rhetorical amplification in schools, but their effect must, paradoxically, have been to enshrine the histories of the striving.

If the tendency of this chapter has been to suggest that there are no reliable biographies (in any modern sense) before the seventeenth century, that the texts which purport to tell us of the lives of real men and women in fact tell us almost nothing, or at least nothing that can be used by modern historians who come to these texts with their own purposes, is there anywhere we can look for the description and analysis of human experience throughout the hundreds of years of the Middle Ages and Renaissance? There do exist a few works which seem recognizably biographical in Johnson's sense, that is, concerned with the personalities, the inner lives, the mental and emotional experiences of historical men and women. Nor is it anachronistic to ask if some writers perceived human experience in terms different from the major forms of written expression; cultures are not homogeneous, not insulated from the effects of trade, travel, conquest, or the changes which come with time, even with reading books. It is another activity.

Accident must never be underestimated as a fact of literary life. Nor is literary history likely to be a straightforward matter of descent lines. Collateral relations are always potentially as *enabling* for writers as direct ancestors because they suggest alternatives and combinations.[67] One of the oddities of medieval literature is that exchange of letters between two learned and serious correspondents, which begins by commenting on a text, moves into the interpretation of biography and autobiography, and then becomes something more formal, more akin to the quasi-public letter-writing we know from the *ars dictaminis* and the correspondence of other literate, Latinate friends. There exist numbers of what we might describe as courtly clerical exchange between a 'directing' mentor, who is both pedagogue and priest to a witty but essentially humble female respondent. There is, however, only one where they have been man and wife.

Peter Abelard's contributions to logic, philosophy, and their place in the study of religion are undoubtedly of the kind which radically altered the approaches to and understanding of those subjects, however little his own books remained set texts of university study. In terms of biographical writing as an attempt to understand the particularity of human experience, Abelard innovates despite himself. In his *Historia Calamitatum* the events of his own life are selected and presented as analogous to a text, the correct interpretation of which reveals the demonstration of God's grace at every step to correct and chastise his beloved, exceptional sinner. Abelard uses the genre of the familiar letter like a homily, an exposition of a scriptural text in a conversational mode, then popular among preachers and writers alike. Looking back, he assimilates his personal history to abstract categories such as pride and God's providence: this is a polarity in which the wilful soul opposes itself to Grace. In a way, perhaps, Abelard may have had the Old Testament stories of King David at the back of his mind; he, Abelard, is the sole protagonist, the only sufferer in this divine comedy. What was is subsumed in what was meant: the history of Abelard's misfortunes becomes readable only in retrospect as a series of symbolic events in which the hand of God can be discerned, guiding and directing an elemental drama of pride, fall, and redemption. As there is only one voice, one narrator, and that the voice of a master rhetorician, it is convincing: confident and coherent, Abelard moves and persuades. The *Historia*, couched as a letter of exemplary instruction, carries no evidence of an intended recipient. Whether or not there was one, the *Historia* was treated as 'published', copied and circulated publicly, and it seems that Heloise read it without it having been Abelard's intention to send it to her. The addition of her voice modifes the impression of his, and it gives us unusual evidence of reading and interpreting against the rhetorical conventions of the presentation. It seems clear that Heloise was angered by the 'letter'. Her intervention appears to have come after a period of twelve years (unless twelve is meant to signify something symbolic) during which she had no contact with her husband, and during which she had struggled to live with – although she could not acquire from her own conviction – the vocation he had thrust upon her after he was castrated. The intensity of emotion, the particularity of her descriptions and the force of her analysis are unique.[68] Heloise covers the ground Abelard has traversed, from her point of view, that is, as a person in her own right, not a contingency in Abelard's scheme of personal salvation, and she attributes motive, however obliquely. Her concern for what was, in all its exactitude and passion, is clear and compelling, and it demands that the reader (who, it must be remembered, is at least in the first instance Abelard himself) is challenged to deny her account and analysis if he dare. Heloise's ability to recall and embody the characters and motives of the actors in their drama is the more moving for the comparative superficiality of Abelard's – differently intended – account. One of the arguments, indeed, for the authenticity of the letters is how much better Heloise comes out of them than does Abelard; a judgement extremely unlikely from a forger, given the misogyny of the period. By restoring the human messiness of their life together she defies his attempt to make literature of it, that is, a coherent salvation narrative; at the same time, she uses all the rhetorical skills at her command to increase the pathos of her own description.

There is carefully calculated *dispositio*, with all the stylistic and rhythmic effects Heloise had learned from years of study. Her writing is meant to be *heard*, full, as it is, of carefully balanced rhythms. If she objects to Abelard's manipulation of his 'life' as a salvation narrative, she herself exploits to the full a combination of the familiar letter and the Ovidian plea. She brings herself into the action, and by stressing Abelard's jealousy and lack of trust in her, adds layers of complexity to his version. While it is true that Heloise seems more humane to modern readers than Abelard does, once again we must remind ourselves that this is because of the values we bring to the letters now: we praise Heloise's grasp of reality as she experienced it, and as she conveys its force to Abelard. She uses rhetoric, knowing that whatever Abelard's reaction to the content might be, he will be intrigued by, admiring of, her expression.[69] It appears as if Abelard – tactless as this is – was trying to construct a *consolatio*, making his life an *exemplum*; he was not writing his autobiography nor an Augustinian confession. And even here we need to remind ourselves of the manifold differences which distance their culture from ours. Heloise and Abelard subscribed to the same ethical imperatives; he achieved them in some measure. She did not. We treasure her for her failure but must be wary of condemning him for his success, spiritual blackmailer though he be. In a way that is both serious and intriguing, Heloise's reaction suggests that different possibilities of interpretation existed for her as a reader, and Abelard's rebuke insists that she 'misread' his text. In accepting his criticism she also accepted that hers was the inferior way of understanding their past, though she could only aspire to strive to transcend it, to read it symbolically, as he now did. She obeyed his injunction, ceased to write to him about that personal past, and turned to the matters which concerned them both as shepherds of souls. But she did not destroy what she had written. The first passionate commitment to what was survives, born of its odd circumstances, attesting to such an exceptional ability to see, to understand, to express, that we must regret that she wrote nothing else. The rhetorical elegance of her Latin style, and the tendency of both correspondents to allude to classical and Christian writers, is a final reminder of their training and of the conventions of their literary culture: to express the highest planes of emotion, the highest style is the best medium.

It seems, however, that strong emotions sometimes distorted even the loose genre boundaries of medieval literary culture. We might wish to think of the new book as referring to an older one, or an older tradition of books, while, because of the pressure of emotion, the urgency, of the 'new' writer, something different appears. Guibert of Nogent's 'autobiographical' writing stands as an example of this peculiarly intertextual creation. Guibert was a twelfth-century Abbot of a small monastery in northern France, a historian, an exegete, and the author of a work he called *De Vita Sua sive monodiarum suarum libri tres*.[70] The earlier author who stands behind Guibert's book is Augustine: Guibert begins with the beginning of the great *Confessions*: 'confiteor', then, like Augustine, gives us a kind of spiritual autobiography in which his mother looms large. It is the intertextuality of the references to the mothers which makes Guibert's suspect. How far Augustine's description of Monica lies behind Guibert's description of his mother is impossible to say; it has always to be considered, too, that Monica *as subject* legitimated Guibert's desire to write about the figure who obsessed him.

This sense of one life as an analogy of another one can be found throughout the writings of the late-medieval mystics, whose ostensible concern with their own inner experience includes wide-ranging reference to earlier, similar writing. There are reasons for this which are purely self-defence: particularly in the case of women mystics, the self-aggrandizement which came with the claim to exceptional experience, exceptional gifts, could lead to accusations of heterodoxy, and all the punishments which society used to enforce conformity, of which confinement might be the least onerous. The same kind of interpretation which Christina of Markyate used to legitimate her experience can be seen in the *Book of Margery Kempe*. Making her book recognizably like the books by or about earlier mystics is a way of claiming her own legitimacy; the repetition of their experience – as in the Lives of the Saints – is a method of insisting upon its truth and authenticity. Its very roughness may be the kind of literary ploy which exploits *sermo humilis*, simple language for a 'simple' woman; the refusal to make an elegant, coherent 'story' another way of making it all seem true. That is, reference back to 'romance' would discredit Margery in one direction as surely as reference back to hagiography would discredit her in another. Her book is a collection of instances, of anecdotes, which follow the patterns of her reading in the lives of holy women, but there is no overall architectonic sense beyond the chronology of her life. There could be no section of *mores* or *opera* without conveying some kind of claim to exemplary status.

Not all intertextual reference was to historical or biographical texts, and in the fifteenth century we find authors writing about themselves in new ways. Christine de Pizan creates a narrator-figure for herself on the model of earlier practice, but with the striking innovation that comes with the use of *her* life: that is, female autobiography. It is important to remember how far bringing the details of her difficulties forward constituted a cue to her patrons that she needed help.[71] Whereas the author as narrator had been a feature of fourteenth-century court poetry, in Petrarch and Boccaccio, Machaut, Chaucer and Gower, the narrating voice, sometimes straightforward, sometimes equivocal, was a creation for the sake of the fiction, building a commentary into the text by the addition of an apparently privileged voice from 'outside' it. The case of Hoccleve introduces something new: his references are mainly to Chaucer, and he seems to be expanding the Chaucerian narrator. In so doing, he describes his life as a civil servant, and includes a long section in his *La Male Regle* on his mental state.[72] Anecdotes, too, where they undergo rhetorical amplification, begin to aspire to some kind of literary status, as with the erotic encounter called *De Duobus*

*Amantibus* or *Euryalus and Lucrece* (1444) of Aeneas Sylvius Piccolomini. Conversely, it is possible to find authors writing about themselves under the cover of an apparently conventional fiction, what, in a later age, we call fictionalized autobiography. *Les Angoisses Douleurueuses qui procedent de l'amour* of 'Helisenne de Crenne' begins with a section in which the emotions of the writer seem to spill over from the force of her own suffering.[73]

Unusual mental states may be a way of circumventing literary convention, at least to some extent. If what Hoccleve suffered from was something like the state we describe as 'depression', we are moving towards the curious position that something about the discovery or at least the legitimization of the inner life as a literary subject may be contingent upon an excess of human misery, perceived as a medical condition. The examples which survive are so rare that it would be foolish to generalize, but from time to time we find self-examination preserved in writing. Sorrow was a spur which drove some writers – and artists – among them Otloh and Opicinus de Canistris.[74] The ratiocination displayed in Montaigne's series of *Essays* revivified the old Senecan and Plutarchian genre, the moral essay, and made it a central literary form.[75] At the end of the period with which this book is concerned, two famous and influential studies of depression appeared; Timothy Bright's *Treatise* (1586) and Robert Burton's great *Anatomy of Melancholy*.[76]

The more books, the more complexity, of course. In writing about the history of a genre some reference has to be made to contrasting genres, against which definitions may be made. I have referred to the drift toward fiction in the saint's life, and of the use of history as a 'cover' for other kinds of narrative. Philosophy, too, is a potential source of change for other kinds of writing where the arguments are embodied, or enspeeched, in contending figures in the Dialogue. Clearly, where speakers are exchanging arguments, there is, necessarily, the creation of *ethos* for each speaker, and with *ethos* comes an impression – sometimes tenuous – of character. One of the most striking, because most rhetorically prepared for, of their successes is their skill at moving and persuading their audiences, and along lines which were complex, secular, and led to questioning the simpler truths upon which 'morally' inspired writing was based. Good kings and holy men exemplify safe uses of writing which are easy to interpret and hard to misuse.

Throughout this chapter one of the difficulties has been to find terms which would accurately convey medieval ideas without carrying with them a cargo of anachronistic expectations, while never losing sight of modern preoccupations. A description of the past is always predicated upon the present. I have tried to distinguish historical actors (men and women who really lived, however unreliable the surviving evidence as testimony about the details of their lives) from literary ones, and to be clear and explicit about 'characterization' and the analysis of motive as an activity distinct from creating 'characters' who do things and feel emotions. How clumsily and inadequately I have described the complexity of the past I am only too well aware, and this is by no means meant as a humility *topos*. The problems of analysing the descriptions of persons are notoriously difficult, and the source of some of the most basic disagreements among historians and literary critics when dealing with the texts of these remote periods. I have tried to paint a picture by peopling it with examples of texts which readers can study for themselves. I have tried to be explicit about the central argument of this chapter: that people were seen as instances of unchanging types.

One of the courses one must take is to look at the vocabulary available to medieval and renaissance writers for the analysis of what people were like, though this involves a historical and philological analysis of the most difficult kind. Words and phrases which are apparently metaphorical may reveal underlying assumptions about the world which determine the questions by determining how they shall be put. The first thing that strikes one is the consistency and limitations of that vocabulary across the European vernaculars and the Latin which was the language of learning and philosophy, and the source for much of the vocabulary of analysis. A few words do service for a wide range of ideas, and depend for their coherence upon an implicit, but potent, metaphorical relation to the language used for the analysis of inanimate objects found in nature, objects like wood, water, stones, or metal, the penultimate *things* of the universe of human experience. The most real, perhaps the only real reality, which existed in the mind of God, was the ultimate source, and was thought to be beyond language, pre-existent. An unquestioned Platonism thus pervaded the discussion: inanimate objects were considered to have an *essence*, an essential nature which could be identified, and which directed, and limited, the uses to which the objects could be put. This is crucially a language of desire: not gravity (which had not yet been perceived) but the desire of objects to come to rest accounted for their falling to the ground. Desire is to be understood as the energy directed towards the *telos*, the moral goal or end for which things exist. While it may seem trivial to call attention to the essential wetness of water or the heaviness of lead, these fundamental characteristics mattered not only as what was taken for granted about them but also attributed moral values to them. The whole universe appeared to exist in a series of moral rank hierarchies. The idea that a person possesses, is, or is defined by, a stable, identifiable *ethos*, belongs to the same world of discourse which searches for the complexion, disposition, or nature of the physical world. In the brief analysis which follows I shall restrict myself to English, but examples could be multiplied from the other languages of western Europe.

The word 'character' itself presents an initial difficulty.[77] In modern English we often use it to indicate the sum of idiosyncrasies, habit, style, and moral qualities (but not physical attributes, age, or intelligence) which make a person (sometimes group or nation) uniquely, and recognizably, this and no other. We may use it to suggest eccentricity ('what a character!') or criticism ('a weak character'). Another common use, which can be confusing in literary analysis, indicates an actor or agent in a literary work (the characters of a 'plot', the persons of the action). It can be confusing when we wish to discuss the characters of characters, but for the most part we are clear enough in context what is meant. These current meanings are themselves metaphoric extensions of the word's origin as 'a distinguishing mark'. We preserve this now restricted usage when we identify letters, runes, or ideograms ('Chinese characters'). The medieval and renaissance uses of 'character' are closer to this etymological meaning, distinguishing mark, than they are to the modern ones. While medieval and renaissance 'characters' may be said to have 'characters', they rarely exhibit gratuitous idiosyncrasy, either in action or in habits of speech. The vocabulary of symbolic gestures which indicate characters' inner states is itself highly conventional, and fairly restricted: among them biting the lip to show anger, throwing the arms into the air to indicate a desire for revenge, and changing colour. Hamlet's famous tic of repeating himself ('thrift, Horatio, thrift', 'words, words, words', 'except my life, except my life, except my life') is practically unheard of earlier. Where the word 'character' itself makes one of its rare appearances, it is usually reserved for stable imprints, either in metal or in men. The rediscovery of the sketches of Theophrastus were a powerful force for change; this discovery and imitation belongs to the very end of our period, and is one of the boundary markers between premodern conceptions and modern ones. Yet even these sketches are not individuals in our sense; they are ethical characters, recognizable types, who are what they are, once for always. They are not described in action or over time, and they do not change.

Two words, both derived from Latin, were used to describe the type of imprint which men displayed: 'disposition' and 'complexion'. The former, while related to the rhetorical *dispositio*, the arrangement of the part of a speech, probably derives from astrological thinking about planetary positions and the ways that the relative situations of different heavenly bodies affect or influence events. 'Complexion' is related to this conceptual framework by the strong analogies which bound analysis of the heavenly bodies to descriptions of earthly objects (the vocabulary for astrology and alchemy). Both 'disposition' and 'complexion' were used to express nature or constitution, and thus might describe innate qualities or cast of mind, more like our use of 'will' than like our use of 'inclination'. These are in theory permanent psychological essences, the result of a balance or arrangement of factors that might be analysed further as part of the theory of humours, or the Stoic theory of the passions, like love or longing. But because balance, in the nature of things, is unstable, and because the external world changes, these terms could also be used to allow for change. There is little by way of explicit analysis of how these states could be contradictory, but every acceptance that they were. That is, the same words might be employed to indicate either a permanent characteristic or a temporary condition. The reader is dependent upon the context. 'High complexion' is as likely to mean a red face in a physiological description as it is to describe a noble nature in a psychological one. Indeed, there may be no distinction between physiology and psychology. People changed, as premodern writers knew perfectly well. Because their system of description was essentially static (rather than progressive, in our sense of supplying a series of reasons to satisfy our expectation that people are different at different periods of their lives for causes that extend beyond the different stages of life itself), their vocabulary restricted them to series of abstract categories.

'Nature' and the allied word, 'kind', are used with a similar combination of specificity and freedom. Their tendency is to address what is permanent and essential to people as types of humanity, and it is their sense of grasping a fundamental which ties this vocabulary together to make a coherent – if sometimes apparently contradictory – psychology. This modern term for the study of personality was not, of course, coined until the seventeenth century. The sense that human nature is, however puzzling to witnesses at the time or after, *known*, is one of the apparent assumptions of premodern culture. It is among the achievements of, for example, Montaigne, to make humanity mysterious. A complex typology existed, based on age, sex, status, balance of inner qualities, virtues, and vices, as we saw in Chapter 1, but – as so often in the Middle Ages – no one brought together a *Summa* of psychology; the nearest thing is the constant focus on the will, corrupt since the Fall. The force of the examples enshrined in the manuals cannot be underestimated. For this chapter, where we have considered exemplary figures like saints or secular princes, the medieval examples are of paramount importance because there were no such examples in Athens or Rome when classical manuals were being prepared. Here we have another reminder that literary models do change as society changes. The *ethos* of a saint is fundamentally stable, and medieval authors disclosed virtues according to a pattern in order to celebrate them and to provide an example for ordinary men and women. Recalcitrant figures like Thomas Becket could be forced onto the Procrustean bed of mortification, humility, and conventional holiness, or could be made to refer to standards they could only appreciate from a distance, like Margery Kempe, whose married status effectively kept her in the world. This emphasis on the permanent *ethos* of a life goes some way to explaining attitudes to children in medieval writing: they are the father of the man.

Any rhetorical manual will give the impression that the *descriptio* of a person, either as incidental 'observations' of externals, or as a summary of the person's life, deeds, and habits, recounted at some appropriate position in a narrative in accordance with the schemes for biographical writing, was a combination of units which conveyed an *ethos*. Bad kings, for example, demonstrated the vices that inverted the virtues they ought to have displayed: dis-loyalty, in-justice, un-lawful sexuality, avarice rather than magnanimity. Yet it would be a mistake to take as an accurate description of medieval writing the recommendations of the handbooks. In theory characters embodied, acted out, abstract vices, virtues, and passions; in practice writers made them change. One source of dynamism in the apparently static model can be traced to Aristotle's codification of the ages of man: at different times of life different emotions held sway, and the lust of youth yielded to the avarice of age. Humility, however often it was perceived as a gift of God to the virtuous, might be sought and achieved through just those exercises in mortification ascribed to saints like Becket. Authors were perfectly capable of discerning the holiness of the private man under the necessary and appropriate pomp of the public office: Thomas More's hair shirt under his chancellor's robes is a famous historical example, however much the devotions of St Louis or St Margaret of Scotland may belong to the expectations of their biographers. What we do not find is much description of the process of change; this seems to have been the purview, and the achievement, of certain rare poets like Chrétien, who shows characters learning something, or the *Gawain*-poet, who shows them obstinately refusing to. Gradual revelation, realizing and understanding, is not one of the literary effects much sought. It is among the most spectacular achievements of Elizabethan drama.

Another source for character change comes from temptation to sin or, later, from the Stoic theory of the passions. Character shades into motive. Even what seem to be straightforward embodiments of sin − ire, lust, avarice, sloth, or envy − may be set in motion by pride, and the temptations to pride by worldly fortune. This may be another reason why writers set their plots in courts, then made their characters leave: motion makes for change. Two of the most important motives were revenge and, though it came late, ambition. So, too, kinship loyalty was a constant and natural spring of action, most likely to appear where the actors have families concerned with the riches and status of this world, and how much of them they can acquire. Overall, there is an impression of coarse grain: a little 'explanation' goes a long way. We have found, in the last two chapters, that authors typically attribute deeds to their agents in accordance with their pre-existing views of the agent's *ethos*. That is, what characters do or say, and what other characters say about them, stems from the author's evaluation, and not necessarily from what they really said or did. The more ambitious, in the literary sense, the author, the better educated, the more capable of assimilating his subject to the conventions of his art, the less dependable his narrative may be as a source of what his subject did. The author of *Le Traison et Mort de Richard II* wrote a moral tale useless to the modern historian, but enormously popular, as a moral tale, among his contemporaries.[78] Froissart is another notorious case where speeches are attributed to characters who may not *in fact* have been present on the occasion described, but who became *appropriate* speakers of the speech which is convenient to the action at that time. A 'bad' character may appear and reappear to mouth 'bad' actions, but equally, an author may use a character inconsistently and without much concern for 'characterization', as a convenient speaker. No history can be relied upon without external checks from itineraries, rolls, charters, or archeological remains. History and biography may be unreliable, too, as guides to what historical figures were like; they may tell us only what historians thought they symbolized.

By implication, the reader's interpretation, the effort to assimilate the evidence of the text to a consistent human type, constitutes one of the fundamental illusions of literary creation. Stylization occurs at many levels, and requires astringent attention. When modern readers bring anachronistic expectations to pre-modern characters, the risk of over-personalization increases in proportion to our ignorance of literary conventions and psychological assumptions. It will be objected that 'creative' literature escapes rhetorical categorization because it is based, profoundly, upon observation of how people behave in the world. Expression is almost always literary, and impression is not far behind. All historical writing was creative, and there was no separate and independent category called 'literature'; there was 'poetry', fiction, but good examples of it were bound by the same categories as any verbal expression. Good writing might be true or not true; it was still rhetorical. The exemplary and the allegorical depend upon categories of interpretation which were inculcated at school: the habit of expecting meanings beyond the literal one.

Medieval and renaissance readers recognized themselves and their human situations – but unlike Johnson's understanding of self and situation with which this chapter began, these tended to be moral or ethical perceptions rather than psychological or social ones. Discovery of an abstract, permanent essence is not the same as consistent personality fuelled by instincts, drives, or the complex and 'over-determined' psychological dynamics we take for granted now. These last are concepts which belong to different, incommensurable worlds. To represent those perceptions they exploited the training in writing and interpretation which their rhetorical education had given them. The units of composition could be amplified or exchanged, transformed in any number of ways, yet still claim to represent the essentials of a historical narrative or a life. At this point we might pursue the innovations of fiction, but let us turn, instead, to another idea where rhetoric might be thought to control transformations of language. The next chapter looks at translation as an aspect of rhetorical interpretation and rewriting.

# 4

# TRAITOR TRANSLATOR

For of necessity, when we speak what is true, i.e. speak what we know, there is born from the knowledge itself which the memory retains, a word that is altogether of the same kind as the knowledge from which it is born. For the thought that is formed by the thing which we know, is the word which we speak in the heart: which word is neither Greek nor Latin, nor of any tongue. But when it is needful to convey this to the knowledge of those to whom we speak, then some sign is assumed whereby to signify it . . . But whereas we exhibit these and the like bodily signs either to ears or eyes of persons present to whom we speak, letters have been invented that we might be able to converse also with the absent; but these are signs of words, as words themselves are signs in our conversation of those things which we think.

St Augustine, *De Trinitate*, XV.10.19

## REFERENCE AND REPRESENTATION

The title of this chapter is a translation. The proverbial Italian original, 'traduttore, traditore', might also be rendered 'the translator is a betrayer', or, 'to translate is to betray'. Both renderings add those little words which are how English indicates grammatical relationships, while keeping the word order of the original language, but at a heavy cost in style, that simultaneous perception not only of what is meant, but also of something about the feeling with which it is expressed. By increasing the number of words we lose both rhyme and rhythmic repetition, and make an ordinary proposition out of an epigram. That pithy, forceful impression created by a rhythmically parallel pair of words has evaporated. The excitement of the small sound change has disppeared. We might still claim that the meaning, what is understood, remains. Even in that case we should wish to allow that more is understood than can be represented by a prose paraphrase. Though more sophisticated than Cato's distichs, stylistically speaking 'traduttore traditore' shares their effect. And what this opening paragraph is doing, as you read, is just the kind of commentary which was the habitual method of literary analysis as we have studied it in the previous chapters: translation, elucidation (to invent another epigram).*

Thus far we have looked at the ways experiences of rhetoric (including model texts which exemplified rhetorical precepts) encouraged readers and writers to believe that the same thing could be expressed in different styles or narrative units without significantly altering the representation of the thing itself. The tensions between correspondence to events which had actually, verifiably, occurred and a sophisticated convention of signs for their depiction reveals certain contradictions between what authors say they do, and what they do in practice. At the simplest level, 'truth' means something at least as much like 'exemplary' or 'representative' as it does 'what really happened so far as it can be ascertained'. 'Evidence' can be moral rather than actual. 'Accuracy' is one of a number of competing values and may be variously defined. Imaginative and fictional writing can be presented as true when it exemplifies eternal verities of human (and supra-human) activity. This insistence that certain conventionally expressed fictions were true was reinforced by the medieval and renaissance anxiety about 'lying', broadly defined, and the accompanying fear that the beautiful lies of literature might be a complete waste of an adult's time, as well as conducive to immorality. I have looked at interpretation as a method of deciphering conventional stylizations of character and event, and at the limits of such convention, in order to interpret expression, as well as to consider how change and innovation occurred. Literary success has been a key criterion, defined largely as the recognition and desire to emulate and imitate of succeeding writers; thus there has been a need for circulation in order for something to be deemed successful. And the success of key writers such as Bede, William of Malmesbury, or Boccaccio, or Froissart, has been a triumph of literary expression which *coincided* with some kind of allegiance to a convincing, verisimilar, historical account which probably bore a close relationship to what they believed to have occurred.

This chapter considers translation practice.[1] As in the previous chapters, the discussion of individual examples rests upon the premiss that readers and writers thought that the particular expression they were reading referred to

---

* And what this footnote does is introduce an annotating commentary on a text which *already* contained a gloss within it marked by the convention of parenthesis (brackets). And the use of a bracketed (or parenthetic) synonym is a reminder that the readers of this book will come from more than one dialect area, and areas which use different words for the same thing.

an underlying meaning which they could grasp by interpreting what lay before them. Interpreting meant both translation and glossing for elucidation, either in the original language or into another. Just as 'historical writing' rested upon conventions which enabled the cognizant and alert reader to understand what was indicated by a speech or description, rather than upon our expectation of 'facts' which can be externally verified, so translation was often a matter of amalgamating various forms of elucidation. Both text *and* translation represented a prelinguistic reality.[2] The status of their representations varied in important ways. This is not to deny for a moment that at least some medieval and renaissance translators understood demands for literal rendering, for familiar kinds of accuracy; it is a reminder that any such translator, as any reader or writer, depends upon the idea of types of reference, which includes an audience-based decision about how the translation will be used: is it an accompaniment to or a substitution for the original one? This is perhaps a simple, but not a trivial, point. In shifting attention from the translation as an independent text (a text which attempts to represent an equivalent for the original in another language, and which can be read continuously) to the intertextual relationships between translation, source text or texts, and the translation and other works in the same (target) language, I am trying to suggest more process than product. The best representation would be a verbal equivalent of the real thing to be expressed; one explanation of the greatness of Homer, or Virgil, or the Bible, is that in those texts language finds or achieves a triumph of correspondence: it makes the otherwise arbitrary choice of particular words or phrases inevitable expression. Such texts are few. In the next chapter I will consider the point at which translations themselves began to attract the attention hitherto focussed on their originals, texts in their own right with some verbal authority. In this chapter I will look at how dynamic the relations between the original, the translation, and the prelinguistic reality represented by the original might have been thought to be. That is, both the original and the translation may refer to the same things, so that a translation of a translation could claim to represent the first text, or even what *it* represented. Beginning from the idea that all translations refer in one way or another to their source text, or texts, the following translation schema might be erected:

## Accompaniment translations

1.  Interlinear translation (glossing).
2.  Literal translation (small scale asyntactic accuracy).
3.  Commentary, e.g. Latin/Latin or Latin/vernacular.

Any of these accompaniment translations might form the basis for

## Substitution translations

4.  Equivalent translation (small-scale verbal correspondence).
5.  Edited translations (substitution or excision to bring a source text into line with the expectations of what would have been written had the author had access to the knowledge which the translator had *or* to the social or cultural expectations of the translator's contemporaries, e.g. Pope's excision of Homer's vulgarities).
6.  Redaction translation (of an amalgamation of several texts).

At the point at which any of these transformations resulted in a text in the new language (or later register of the same language, to allow for modernization) which could claim the status of a text to be read in its own right we might begin to discern

## Replacement translations

7.  Fluent-text translation which would differ from the first six categories because, however much it continued to refer to the original, source, text, it had become independent. The most important instance would be certain kinds of Bible translation, but some fictions also belong in this category.
8.  Narrative-paraphrase translations (as an extension of 7) which, as fluent texts, rehearse the plot-contents, or some embellishment of the plot, of a prior text or texts.
9.  Alternative representations which, like fluent-text translation, continued to refer to the original text(s) and/or their matter, but changed medium. (Either 7 or 8 could be heavily redacted.)

These nine types overlap. They are not meant to be exclusive, nor do they suggest either a historical process, since different kinds of translation continue to be made at different times, or within a single work, neither are they a trajectory of quality. The usefulness, or otherwise, of different kinds of translation, must be calculated in accordance with the use to which the translation was to be put, so that no confusion of quality arises because a paraphrase of a biblical story retold in accordance with vernacular poetic expectations appears to be 'inaccurate' as a close verbal equivalent of the original. This suggests that there are other calculations to be made which intersect this scheme, which have to do with the audience for which the translation was intended. More liberties were taken for less educated readers or listeners, and there was little thought that 'accuracy' was being 'sacrificed'.

How many ways of referring did they exploit? No one would want to argue that there is one thing, and one only, which 'is' translation, or that one language had the same status either as any other language, or as its own earlier forms (e.g. medieval Latin never had the prestige of classical Latin). The 'language' of highest status was described by Augustine as being neither Greek nor Latin, but the carrier of thought in the mind of God, something humanity might sometimes experience as direct perception or understanding without words, an experience which is prior to the transference that becomes verbal articulation.[3] The original universal human language spoken before Babel was thought to have been as close to this direct perception, this preverbal nonlingual language, as mankind has ever known. By extending arguments of priority, it came to seem obvious that the older the language the closer it must be to pre–Babel expression, and thus also the more likely to hold mysteries impossible to put into words. Hypothesized languages, such as 'ancient Chaldean' might claim to hide, through symbols, secrets known to the ancients but since lost. Hermetic writing is full of such assumptions. This implies that the modern languages – the vernaculars – are inferior, lacking the lexical and syntactic complexity of earlier languages as represented by their written registers.

The problem of vocabulary, particularly for abstractions, often perceived as a *lack*, a fault, or a flaw, focussed an area of argument about the target languages. Making up missing words could lead to the use of the 'closest' pre-existing word, to redefinition, to new coinage from the available roots of the target language; adaptation (from straight borrowing) to manipulation of the source-language word by morphological transformation according to the rules of the target language; or a combination, often by the use of doublets, two words in the translation to represent one in the original.[4] The creation of 'translationese' might not only be deliberate, but be thought a virtue because it improved the style and resources of the target language. While the skill and imagination of the translator cannot be disregarded, the 'quality' of the original counted, too, because some vocabulary is 'crucial' in ways that other vocabulary is not. God's Being involves this kind of crucial lexis; Roman ranks, though equally problematic in many ways, do not. Words such as senator (or denarius) are not crucial vocabulary in the sense of the importance of what is conveyed to the beliefs of readers. Translators were often multi-lingual, and aware of choices and precedents in other languages than their own. Not only could they turn for resources to more than one language, their positions changed with time, not only vis-à-vis the development of their own vernacular, but in terms of translation inertia, whereby methods and traditional equivalences might come to seem right even when they had once been thought to be wrong. Prefaces, too, have their conventions. A fifteenth-century translator had more choice in some areas than his eleventh-century predecessor but less in others where earlier choices had come to seem binding.

Different kinds of texts invited different kinds of attention. Sacred texts thus created serious challenges for reading and interpretation simply on account of their age and singularity. Scientific and philosophical treatises (often not categories which their authors would have distinguished) posed similar, if less pressing, problems. If a disagreement over an interpretation of Aristotle was unlikely to carry with it the severe, and unpleasant, penalties which sometimes resulted from disagreements over sacred writings, there were, nevertheless, complex concepts to be understood. Language use that we think of as literature inspired translations, adaptations, and imitations of overlapping kinds. As we shall see, many activities could be thought of as 'translation', from interlineation to paraphrase, from amplification to redaction. Once established, habits of effective paraphrase could be extended to other kinds of texts.[5] Once there were enough 'secular' texts to warrant 'redaction' (the translation of edited or combined texts) we find methods of paraphrase, extension, and adaptation growing more and more widespread. And, in turn, the ambition to emulate successful style grew once again, as it had done in Rome centuries before. There were and continued to be temptations to make the Bible the paradigm case. It is certainly a special case, but it is not one which determined how every other kind of text would always be read, interpreted, or transformed. When the Bible was divided into distinctiones, glossed and commentated, it was being treated like a classical literary text. Priority in this method belongs to key poems like Homer's or Virgil's; it is a matter of chronology and the tendencies of rhetorical education. The habit of subjecting first order texts to second order discussion was established long before there was a Bible, and treating the Bible like the *Iliad* was a natural reaction by people who 'knew' how to treat texts. So in discussion of translation most of the same topics arise, but any discussion must keep constantly in view the medieval certainty that the word of Aristotle could not begin to be commensurate with the word of God. Not even the word of Cicero ever mounted that high.

The Bible's pre-eminence might suggest that it would be the obvious text with which to start. The collection of canonical books (itself a problem, since even after arguments about which books should be considered canonical were finally settled, there remained important texts on the periphery, not just the Apocrypha, but even more doubtful pseudo-Gospels like *The Gospel of Nicodemus*) which represented the word of God, or the interpretation of that Word, as revealed to divinely inspired men who had enshrined it in writing in the great languages of Antiquity, Hebrew and Greek. The Bible is an inescapably 'referring' text, as are the translations made of it. This reference backward to earlier texts in different languages and representation beyond to a reality perceived but not necessarily articulated has been one of the continuing themes of this book. Literary works seemed to be verbal artifacts which referred to something (a history, a life, an idea, even a style); their expressions were distinguished from the things represented. The achievement of 'composition' makes the expression seem to be the inevitable way of moving and persuading. In secular work we would classify this kind of success as aesthetic beauty, rhetorical force, or some kind of truth to life. The Bible, at the height of sacred work, is the most exact, congruent, felicitous, and true expression of the perfection that is the word of God, even where God is imitating his own earlier styles. This makes it literally inevitable in every sense. It also lends urgency to the need to reconcile the parallel narratives, where different writers give different accounts. The meaning or meanings of these biblical books presented inexhaustible possibilities for interpretation, for restating in different words; like the books considered in Chapter 1, biblical texts came with commentaries, not only surrounding them, but independently, in books about the canonical books by the Fathers of the Church, whose interpretations, in turn, posed problems of translation and interpretation. Whether it was licit to apply these techniques to other compositions occupied medieval interpreters for whom the 'discovery' or attribution of secret wisdom could provide a much-needed defence of imaginative literature. Because many translations and commentaries precede the Bible, so that the Bible came to be treated with all the dignity already afforded important texts, it will be appropriate to precede a discussion of the Bible with a discussion of one of the translators who appeared to articulate the principles of translation.

### THE CONVENTIONAL WISDOM OF TRANSLATORS

Discussions of translation survive from the time of Cicero and the principal problems which concerned him also concerned Augustine and Jerome, whose arguments about translating the Bible became the central discussions for the Christian Middle Ages; the topics around which their disagreements revolved are still the ones which occupy translators and theoreticians of translation. These have above all appeared to be predicated upon questions of accuracy: whether or not the translations under discussion are or are not accurate reproductions of their originals, and what, in any case, would constitute measures of accuracy, with lexical, grammatical, and syntactic equivalence leading the field. With this assumption comes the view that the translation is itself a text worthy of consideration, a fluent equivalent of the original (schema 5 or 7). There is an unstated presupposition about textuality here with which medieval translators did not necessarily agree – but they did not discuss it either. The question has traditionally been posed, since Cicero, as a choice between word-for-word and sense-for-sense correspondence as if all translations reproduced their originals in adequate, exact substitutions. This might be thought of as a tendency to accentuate verbal expression at the expense of the things or ideas the words represent, or, conversely, to convey the ideas (the 'sentence') without overmuch regard for the style in which the original expressed them. One still finds modern translators making this distinction, as if style were not always implicated in meaning.[6] This early dichotomy pre-empted other kinds of discussion.

Accuracy often turns on scale. This concern with the size of the unit to be translated arose in Antiquity, where we first find this distinction between word-for-word and sense-for sense translation. It is to be found scattered through Cicero's writing, when translation is at issue. 'Scattered' gives a good sense of Cicero's method, or lack of one; like so many of a busy politician's opinions, Cicero's ideas about translating vary with the context, something taken insufficient account of by his successors, who were prone to enlist him on their side of an argument without much attempt to analyse the circumstances in which a favoured quotation occurred. Since it was to the authority of Cicero that the great late-classical Church Fathers all appealed, Ciceronian catch-phrases recurred for centuries as the headings of arguments over accuracy of translation, or what look like such arguments. Cicero was concerned with that end of all oratory – to move and persuade his audiences, and he saw his writing as a representation of that aural experience. The attractions of the pagan orator were further increased when his views about translation were compared to the apparently opposing views of medieval Jewish translators, whose insistence upon literalism was notorious, and notoriously seductive to certain biblical exegetes.[7] Cicero never found himself trying to translate a holy text, and even in his discussions of Stoic philosophy (as in the Fourth Tusculan) he managed to deal pragmatically with technical vocabulary, by using the equivalent Latin word, by defining what he meant by the nearest Latin word, or by Latinizing a Greek word. It must be repeated that any attempt to sketch his views must stress their pragmatism, their frequent contingency to other subjects, and therefore their lack of all-encompassing coherence.

In the preface to Cicero's translation of two opposing speeches of the great Greek orators Demosthenes and Aeschines, which is all that survives of the work known as *De optimo genere oratorum*, he insisted that his translation was composed *eloquently*, by a translator known for his own success as an orator, for the instruction of those who wished to learn the best manner of speaking (schema 7). Since, to be eloquent, a speech must move its audience, Cicero made the arousal of equivalent emotion in his Latin readership his prime concern, since eliciting that response is the essence of a good oration. He stressed his imitation of the Greek orators' intentions vis-à-vis their original auditors, and contrasted orations with history, using Thucydides as his example of excellence in style for another function.

For I have translated the most illustrious orations of the two most eloquent of the Attic orators, spoken in opposition to one another: Aeschines and Demosthenes. And I have not translated them as a literal interpreter, but as an orator giving the same ideas in the same form and mould as it were, in words conformable to our manners; in doing which I did not consider it necessary to give word for word, but I have preserved the character and energy of the language throughout. For I did not consider that my duty was to render to the reader the precise number of words, but rather to give him all their weight. And this labour of mine will have this result, that by it our countrymen may understand what to require of those who wish to be accounted Attic speakers, and that they may recall them to, as it were, an acknowledged standard of excellence.[8]

The key phrases, *fides interpres* and *verbum pro verbo*, recur for hundreds of years to support the argument that claims that the less literal (on the small, lexical, scale) a translation is the more faithful it can be to the spirit of the original. The arguments come in terms of the difficulties of creating equivalences, equivalent representations of the words, the speech in context, the effects it was supposed to arouse in its audience; it does not consider the translation as known to be referring constantly to someone else's speech, that is, as a second-order and derivative 'text' which is always supposed to keep the original before us. The authority of the original, Attic model of excellence allows Cicero to present his own version of it without claiming to present his *own* words as such an authority – though no doubt that is more or less what he had in mind. But he also had in mind the debates he inherited about the *best* translation, as if there were such a thing, and only one, at that. The *true interpreter* acquired a bad name, as if strict faithfulness were a fault of mechanically minded artisans rather than the artistry of translators who truly understand. It seems as if what Cicero meant was to make a disclaimer about inaccuracies accepted for the sake of the effect he wanted to make on a Roman audience: first century reception theory. He could be quoted on either side of arguments about literalism and accuracy, and he was – out of context. Reference to the word-for-word/sense-for-sense debate became in its turn the major *topos* of translators' prefaces, a heading for discussions of accuracy, even if only an indication of direction.

Sometimes these debates sound like the optimist and the pessimist arguing about whether the same glass of water should be described as half full or half empty (the translator thinks it half full; the critic of his translation is resolute that it is half empty). This is because the reproduction of a text in another language remains unattainable and irresistible. As long as people want to read something written in a language they cannot understand, as long as writers wish to emulate or incorporate in their own language the achievements of another one, there will be attempts to recreate written texts. As with the historical or biographical motifs already considered, discussions of translation, too, raise topics which may appear because they are conventional rather than because they are there to be analysed. In these discussions, as in the prefaces to many medieval and renaissance translations, the inherited argument about 'accuracy' is paramount. But the conventions may be deployed in order to signal something about the kind of text being translated, or how the new work is to be interpreted in its turn; the translator may be trying to protect or advertise himself, or simply to deflect criticism. An anonymous fifteenth-century rhymed translation of the French *Mélusine* ends with verses that are part disclaimer, part apology:

> As ny as metre can conclude sentence,
> Cereatly by rew in it have I go.
> Nerehande stafe by staf, by gret diligence,
> Sauyng þat I most metre apply to;
> The wourdes mene, and sett here and ther so,
> Like as of latin ho-so will fourge uers;
> Wourdes most he change sondry & diuerse,

Whilom þat be-fore put, And sette behynd,
And oft that at end gretth best before;
So oft trauersing the langage we shall fynd
Be it latyn, frensh or our tonge to-bore.
Ho it metre well, so do moste euermore,
Be it in balede, uers, Rime or prose,
He most torn and wend, metrely to close.

And so haue I done after my simplesse,
Preseruing, I trust, mater and sentence
Vnwemmed, vnhurt, for any excesse,
Or by meusing don by violence.
Warded and kepte haue to intelligens,
That will vnderstande And knowin may be
In our moder tonge, spoken in contre.[9]

Because no theoretical discussion of translation could ever begin by considering the range of tolerable inaccuracy, that is, of its limits, or what might control the compromises necessary in all translation practice, the history of these discussions remained bound by agreed assumptions which disguised certain important issues which only appear contingently if at all.[10] Yet translators were aware of the kinds of changes that could be, and were, made. Although Lydgate, that most prolix of fifteenth-century Chaucerians, claimed no authority for himself, and was far from suggesting that he himself took liberties with his texts (although he constantly amplified what he translated) he knew – and explicitly approved – other translators' manipulations. When translating Laurent de Premierfait's translation of Boccaccio's *De Casibus*, he prefaced his work with a defence of Laurent's practice, which was also, tacitly, his own:

In his [Laurent's] prologe affermyng off resoun,
Artificere hauyng exercise
May chaunge and turne bi good discrecioun
Shappis, formys, and newli hem deuyse,
Make and vnmake in many sondry wyse,
As potteres, which to that craft entende,
Breke and renewe ther vesselis to a-mende.

Thus men off crafft may off due riht,
That been inuentiff & han experience,

Fantasien in ther inward sigt
Deuises newe thoruh ther excellence;
Expert maistres han therto licence
Fro good to bettir for to chaunge a thyng,
And semblabli these clerkis in writyng,

Thyng that was maad of auctours hem beforn,
Thei may off new fynde and fantasie,
Out of old chaff trie out ful cleene corn,
Make it more fressh and lusti to the eie,
Ther subtil witt and ther labour applie,
With ther colours agreable off hewe,
Make olde thynges for to seeme newe.

Afforn prouydid that no presumpcioun
In ther chaungyng haue noon auctorite,
And that meeknesse haue dominacioun,
Fals Envie that she not present be;
But that ther ground with parfit charite
Conueied be to ther auantage,
Trewli rootid a-mid of ther corage.[11]

Despite this apparent awareness of Laurent's amplifications, Lydgate refers to Boccaccio's original as if Laurent's intermediary work were merely a window through which he had direct access to the Latin text.

Two of these tacit topics are of particular importance: first, how does the translation refer to the original and, second, does the target text have its own integrity, that is, was it meant to be read as a text in its own right (schema 7 and 8)? The variables abound: what kind of text is what kind of writer translating for what audience for what purpose? Lydgate's Princes were exercises in praise and blame that gave vernacular readers *exempla* of behaviour taken from the historical past; the combination of *encomium* and the vernacular may have encouraged great latitude of manipulation. How many languages are involved and of what kinds? How distant is the syntactic, grammatical, and lexical 'fit' between (or among) them? How close are the correspondences between the cultures? Is there a status difference between the languages? Or a long lapse of time between original and translation? How skilful is the translator: how good is his command of the languages he is reading and writing, how comprehensive his understanding of the original text, how patient, or ambitious, or sensitive a craftsman is he, and what are his criteria? Many translators gloss in the text, sometimes correcting information or adding it, as Caxton did in this typical addition to his translation of Raoul Lefèvre's 'history' of Jason:

Thus endeth myn Auctor his prologe. And how wel that hit is sayd afore this prologe that Eson was sone to Cacus, yet Bochace saith in the *Genelagye of Goddes* that he was sone to Erictheus, the xxix sone of Jupiter, as ye may see more playnly in the xiii book of the *Genelagye of Goddes*, the xxiii chapytre.[12]

Ineptitude must be allowed for. Translations were made by the medieval version of the hack. Medieval forgeries, too, masquerade as translation, as do new compositions. Translators who beg and borrow also steal.

The period with which this book is concerned is bounded by the great Bible translations of Jerome and the Authorized Version; it contains Wycliffe's and Luther's. From the controversies which surrounded them arose much (but not all) of medieval and renaissance theory of translation, and ultimately of language itself. Even before Babel, the mind of God had once revealed itself to the mind of men. While scholars argued over *which* language God had used, they were in no doubt that it was a language of words, not a direct experience of perception. And although they referred to this language of the heart that was neither Greek nor Latin, the priority, superiority, and concomitant prestige of the ancient languages led to a prejudice (often unexamined) that Greek or Latin or Hebrew were as close as men could come to the unitary tongue.[13] After Babel, even the three great languages of antiquity would be treated differently at different times. The great Bible translator, Jerome, treated the Greek Fathers with more freedom, more artistry, than he did the Sacred Page, as his readers noticed at the time. Style – the integrity of the translation as a *readable*, even a beautiful, representation of its Greek and Hebrew models – was a concern, but only one of many; the integrity of the new text was subordinate to other concerns.

SACRED WISDOM

Because the Bible represented the Word of God as dictated by God, even word-order might be crucial to correct understanding. This posed a challenge for which 'style' is too narrow a word: given the impossibility of translating this most difficult of texts, perhaps the 'best' Bible translation would be one which represented, by grammatical misordering in the target language, the sequence in which the original words appeared.[14] Perhaps the 'best' translation would be, not a translation in the usual sense at all, but an interlinear gloss, a grammar-free guide to the original (schema 1). The visual relationship of gloss to text represents the most basic kind of accompaniment translation. This implies that the translation is an interpretation dependent upon the source text, and not in any way to be considered a new and independent text, not even a 'text' at all; it introduces the ideas of simultaneity, and of 'voices' in dialogue. That is, there is an odd but potent imitation of a commenting voice, explicating small-scale (viz., word) units as they are read aloud in some kind of studying group. Reference is, must be, immediate; it is impossible to 'lose' the original in the translation. One cannot read continuously, but must constantly look back and forth. The illustration of Ascensius' Virgil, or of the commented Bibles in Chapter 1 remind us of this habitually interrupted reading.

The discipline of interpretation was acquired as early as the first reading of a fable, often by interpreting pagan poetry, as I argued in Chapter 1. A reader's first duty might be thought to begin by understanding the literal meaning of the words; but even in the early years, when Christian readers might be supposed to have been multilingual, this was difficult, since not only had they to be readers of Greek and Latin, but also of Hebrew – not a language many Roman citizens cultivated. And even though many of the books now called the New Testament were written in simple language by men who were not highly trained rhetoricians, these apparently humble expressions conveyed, simultaneously, numerous different meanings. They themselves referred to earlier canonical texts – often in order to maintain that traditional prophecies were being fulfilled – but also to assert by their archaic or Hebraizing style a claim to be taken as consonant with sacred depictions and therefore sacred in their turn. God's message, his Word, was *clothed* in simplicity: in the status Jesus chose for his Incarnation, the language he spoke, the disciples he spoke it to. But the message was not simple. Even at the time, he spoke in riddles, and his followers lost no time in increasing the difficulty of the texts which attached themselves to his legend. The contradictions or inconsistencies of the Gospel accounts were rich for potential interpreters; with the passage of time even the details of botanical names could be a source of discussion and speculation. The cultural references of early first-century Palestine were soon lost, first assimilated to what a sophisticated Roman literary scholar could understand, and then, with the collapse of the Roman imperium, maintained by traditions of exegesis. The synonymy involved in explaining meaning is already a kind of translation. Writing a single word over a single word of text became more and more challenging. Some scholars were to go so far as to deny that the apparent literal meaning of the words on the scroll before them were there to convey what they seemed to say; that is, they might see them *only* as a sign, not as meaning something which, perhaps, they could no longer interpret. The more systematized that interpretation according to agreed allegorical levels became, the less likely scholars were to question the literal meaning of the text. Indeed, for Christian exegetes literal-mindedness became a patronizing description of the limited way in which Jewish Bible interpreters read. This in turn meant that the literal could be the dangerous reading, because it was a style of interpretation associated with infidels. For commentators who wanted to use the work of Rashi, the greatest of the Jewish literalists, this made the closest translation the riskiest.[15]

Knowledge of and familiarity with the Bible changed over time, until its difficulties meant that most of the people who read it were learned. At first, no one could forget that the Latin Bible was a translation, and that large parts of it were translation of translation. Nor was the text stable: even if copyists of Jerome's Latin texts (written at different times of his life for different purposes and with different standards, from originals of different authority and quality, at speed or at leisure), had reproduced his work accurately (and textual transmission was no more reliable for Jerome than for anyone else), Jerome's translation never drove out of circulation the so-called *Vetus Latina*, which he had meant his own to replace. When Jerome's translation first appeared some of his innovations caused near-riot in the congregations where they were introduced. His younger contemporary, Augustine, wrote to him in vigorous terms of his own reservations about particular choices in the translation.[16] For these rhetorically trained leaders were divided by their different allegiances to audience and to text. As the Empire disintegrated, with a speed and completeness which neither Augustine nor Jerome could have anticipated, and the Latin-speaking West forgot its bilingual culture, reference to the original texts diminished while the inertia of familiarity did not. Even the wealthier, less disrupted, Greek-speaking East was itself at one or more linguistic removes from the biblical originals in Hebrew or Aramaic. Spoken Greek and Latin continued to develop, and so did their written registers. There were no dictionaries; though some readers noticed that language changes, they had no way of ascertaining what particular individual words meant at specific historical moments. For all their rhetorical training to avoid solecisms and barbarisms (or ambition to write well in a clear style), scholars faced with vernaculars less rich in formal registers adapted vocabulary, grammar, and syntax to accommodate the concepts they needed to translate, as had Cicero before them. One man's neologism is another's barbarism. In the absence of histories of literature, bibliographies, even chronological lists, readers and translators had no check on context, so that even the most sensitive ones, most alert to the ways that words change their meanings depending upon their circumstances, could seldom compare similar uses. Even when they could compare usage within a text, they were without the resources of comparison to known contemporary texts that would illuminate the range of possible uses. The tendency of medieval scholars to take words and phrases out of context is easier to understand when we consider how little 'context' was available. It is not as if there was a recognized semantic field at the edges of which inventive, poetic uses could stretch meaning through metaphor and metonymy; all uses were potentially symbolic. This increased the tendency to assert that this word meant that meaning, whether or not that meaning was appropriate, or even likely. Words as counters of representation might always refer to any of their possible referents. This was also underwritten by the assumption that words represented real things; to a degree all medieval writers were Realists. The tendency to quote phrases out of context, to allegorize them in order to support some quite remote argument is too well-known to require description. But it is important to remember that new interpretations, if they could be argued with some ingenuity, were considered as discoveries encoded forever in the text, awaiting a generation alert enough to find them. That is, translation, too, bears the burden of history.

For a text-centred religion to find itself dependent upon a radically unstable version of its holy book posed profound threats. The authority for the biblical originals could not have been higher: they were the word of God uttered through divinely inspired men. The solution lay to hand. Already in the Jewish community in Alexandria translation had become necessary as Greek replaced Hebrew as its spoken language. The translation which they accepted as standard, *The Septuagint*, that is, the translation of The Seventy, came with legendary justification. Seventy scholars, so the story went, had been set to translating the Bible (the books now called The Old Testament), independently, and without consultation. When the task was completed and their translations compared (some said after seventy days), they were found to agree at all points, i.e. word for word. This congruence was obviously miraculous, given the low probability of translators all making the same choices throughout a long and difficult text, and proved that the Seventy were themselves instances of God's inspiration working through them. Thus the idea of divinely inspired translation, with its own special status, entered the history of translation. However the status of Jerome's translation might be tempered by the continued existence of the *Vetus Latina* and the criticisms of Augustine, its claim to be the result of an inspired saint encouraged readers to treat it as something not very far away from the word of God. Even mistakes might have been deliberate – not on Jerome's part, but on God's. The magic of difficulty does not fade. Nor does the double message: first, a translation is always a choice of possibilities which, second, always refer to a single original. The translation indicates, even if accompanying commentary defines. This in turn encourages the survival of as many translations and glosses as will aid understanding. But Jerome's Vulgate acquired a special status which justified treating it as a text whose individual word-choices could be analysed as authoritative in the same way as the original – even though translation must be imperfect. It is the first translation to assume authoritative status as a text whose individual words had the same claim to interpretability as its original.

Jerome's translation is *not* identical with the text now known as the Vulgate. Throughout the Middle Ages the choice of readings invited thought and argument, though seldom doubt. For Bede or Abelard textual uncertainty could be a way around apparent contradiction. It was not, however, something that could be wished away. Until the great work of Alcuin of York in the ninth century there was no one standard Latin Bible text; standardized chapter and verse divisions came late.[17] Breaking long texts into visually bracketed paragraphs was an important convenience for readers who could otherwise only with difficulty find the lines they sought. Standard glosses, i.e. textual, literal, and metaphoric explanations, were the achievement of the great efflorescence of scholarship now called the twelfth-century renaissance. The *Glossa Ordinaria*, which collected the interpretative wisdom of the great Bible commentators, began with Anselm of Laon in the early years of the twelfth century.[18] Even then, however, few individual readings remained beyond question: the paradoxical position was that the *whole* Bible was clearly divinely inspired, but scholars might take issue with any particular expression. Respect for the *sacra pagina* and the traditions of commentary meant that doubts were likely to be expressed in the most tactful terms; readings or interpretations were not 'wrong' but 'various' or 'disputed'. It was easier to multiply interpretations, that is, to find new meanings in this inexhaustible text, than to pare unlikely ones away. Indeed, 'unlikely' itself suggests modern assumptions about interpretation that medieval commentators seldom shared. Any new interpretation was implicated in the tradition of interpretation; it could not be a final nor an exhaustive reading. The first endless analysis was interpreting the Bible.

Bible commentary took its conventions from the study of classical literary texts. Like Virgil, who referred to Homer, the New Testament books looked back to the Old, as the Old now seemed to look forward to the New. Like commentary on classical texts, interlinear translation or interpretation must be an accompaniment (schema 1 and 2), not a substitution, as it would be useless, indeed, incomprehensible nonsense, were it divorced from the original; it is equally obvious that this kind of accompaniment is intended for readers at least acquainted with both languages.[19] Glosses usually appeared with the text, though they could, and sometimes did, appear separately, keyed by lemmata. This exercise of constant reference keeps the reader thinking in two languages (or two historical registers of one language) concurrently. But gloss did not remain segregated, and this had implications for translation. The penetration of the gloss into text as translation can be illustrated from an apparently trivial example of Latin commentary on a weed in one of the parables, where the interpretation of the story influences the translation of a plant name. In the parable which is now called 'the wheat and the tares' (*Matthew XIII*), Jesus tells of a man who planted wheat in his field. But his enemy came during the night and sowed the seeds of another, undesirable, crop. The name of the plant to which the farmer objects became, because of its special, botanical, name, impossible to identify, and commentators expended learned reference trying to agree a Latin equivalent for the Greek name of a weed first perhaps named in Aramaic. Identification depends upon one's interpretation of the parable: most late-classical exegetes believed that the point was that it was almost impossible to distinguish the two plants (not the modern understanding), that the parable was about the difficulties of separating true Christians from hypocrites. On this interpretation the weed had to be something which looked like wheat, and commentators suggested wheat-like plants. Jerome calls it 'lolium' and Augustine 'avena' or 'lolium'; later Rabanus Maurus quotes Isidore of Seville on the problem, referring to Virgil's *Georgics* (1.154): 'Avena, lolium, zizania, quam poetae semper infelix lolium dicunt', which reminds us that poetry was as important as botany in the minds of those two rhetorically trained Church Fathers.[20]

Botanical speculation may seem trivial, but I quote it for more than its value as an illustration of the complexities involved in even the interpretation of a noun. First, it reveals the 'poetic' habit of interpretation, familiar from commentaries on Virgil, as well as Psalms. Second, it reminds us that the commonly used distinction between word-for-word and sense-for-sense obscures other factors which may equally come into play. Third, this happens to be a *locus classicus* of biblical hermeneutics, an example that anyone studying the traditional commentaries would come across. Translation is commentary is interpretation. The point is that the false is indistinguishable from the true: there is another *locus classicus* of interpretation of concern to readers of Chaucer, who invented a famous fake authority whom he called 'Lollius'. Accident? Or the sort of learned pun he could expect his *learned* readers to recognize, one that would do no harm to those left out of the joke. A possibility, if no more.[21]

Later I shall consider more substantial effects on translation, where words, phrases, even whole sentences from a gloss are incorporated as part of the translated text without distinction. Even without these difficulties, the range of choices open to the translator often depended upon an interpretation of the meaning of a unit much larger than a single word or even a phrase. The meaning of a whole parable or event had to be taken into account. In terms of scale, this might be described differently from the usual 'word' or 'sense' distinction, because the word-for-word selection is controlled by the interpretation of an entire narrative unit.

To turn to the opposite case, it may be that the replacement of the original word with a single and exact lexical equivalent is possible, but that the result is a poor translation. One of the traditional examples of this problem is naming coins. In the incident where Jesus, faced with the problem of whether or not to pay tax to the Romans, confounds his questioners by telling them to 'render unto Caesar the things that are Caesar's' (in the words of the Authorized Version), the Gospel writers specified a particular coin. Here commentators and translators agree that it is not the name or even the correct monetary value of the coin but its function as 'the coin of tribute' which must be rendered. Yet the sum of money it represented was bound to make a difference to the reader, whose views of whether it was a lot or a little would be affected by the equivalent coin chosen. Here the coin stands for something; it is on the way to being a symbol, though in *this* occurrence it is not a symbol yet. If, however, another author used it elsewhere, with reference to this occurrence, there would be no question that it had become symbolic.[22]

Both of these interpretative hazards might be extended. Sometimes, because of the status or importance of a particular story, an allegorical interpretation became so widely recognized as to become one of the meanings of the word, as if the word could not occur without its metaphoric associations, and a thing was always symbolic. The apparent concreteness of place names might seem to make translation fairly straightforward even if the location of the place was forgotten. The flight of the Israelites from Egypt was traditionally interpreted as the retreat of the enlightened soul from the world: the fleshpots of Egypt for which the exiles yearned was only an interpretative step away from temptations of the flesh. So common was this identification that any trained reader would habitually supply 'the world' as a possible meaning for 'Egypt'. Less succinct, more arbitrary, but equally typical in method, is an exegesis of Gregory the Great on I Samuel XIII.19–20, where the Philistines (a word whose own metaphorical trans-formations mean that a modern reader may need the reminder that in this context at this time it meant inhabitants of Philistia) forbid the Israelites to have smiths, for fear that the smiths will turn ploughshares into swords. Gregory expounded as follows: the Israelites only possess divine literature; the smiths stand for writers of secular literature, without whom the Israelites cannot be victorious. The Philistines are demons who try to prevent the acquisition of secular learning. When Gregory interprets 'Philistine' as 'demon' he believes that he is *recognizing* something which really exists, not inventing a story which corresponds to a kind of template given by the original.[23] The Sacred Page was believed to contain coded information which would tell the learned exegete real truths about the real world, like a scientific treatise, not like a hypothesis. As far as Gregory was concerned, he was decoding, recognizing, not inventing an interpretation for the sake of special pleading. How, it may be asked, does this happen, how does the gloss become part of the meaning? A trivial answer is that sometimes copyists and translators put what had been a gloss into the main body of the new text. This was likelier to happen with secular than sacred texts, but it certainly happened to all kinds of texts from time to time. Or they might choose between variant readings on the authority of a gloss. In the sixteenth century Thomas Wyatt's English translation of the seven Penitential Psalms shows the results of his studies of continental Latin texts and expositions.[24]

A more important answer lies in those habits of reading considered throughout this book. Any word, phrase, or story might refer to something other than what it appeared to represent. One might be tempted to observe that if such apparently straightforward cases raised problems of such complexity, the challenges posed by words with doctrinal implications would have been practically insuperable. In practice, the Bible was thought to be interpreted at several allegorical *levels*, which meant that a spatial metaphor was used to categorize different kinds or type of symbolic equivalence in a way which introduced a hierarchy of significance, thus encouraging multiple translation, until not only place names, but even the commonest of nouns might signify insuperable complexities, too. 'Signify' indicates a kind of reference which we are prone to classify as 'metaphor', that is, something which happens in the imagination, a likeness which we perceive, almost a game of ingenuity, something which is our own invention. But for hundreds of years that perception was considered to be not a human creation at all, but recognition of the universe as its maker intended it to be comprehended. That metaphors were real and 'deeper' legitimated the idea of *progressive* interpretations of increased mystery, which reached toward that prelinguistic truth which was neither Greek nor Latin, but represented the thought of God. Aquinas opens his great collection of religious commentary and analysis, the *Summa Theologica*, with a discussion of exactly this problem: 'words signify the things understood, for we express by words what we understand'.[25] Aquinas seems to have considered the Bible to be a special case, where words are signs of things which are, in their turn, signs of something further (1.1.10). This sentence was often quoted, and often quoted out of context, to suggest that the Bible is only special by being a paradigm case, and that all writing is potentially allegorical in this same many layered way.

Metaphor, of course, is the way we would classify most of the interpretations that allegorizing translators and commentators supplied. That is what *translatio* meant in Latin. (The classical Latin term for 'translate' is 'transferro' or 'verto' – our English 'to turn' is, straightforwardly, a translation of 'verto'.)[26] Where we would separate translation (finding an equivalent word or phrase in a different language) from interpretation (explaining the sense in the same or another language), earlier practice saw the activities as part of one spectrum. The basic opposition in translation practice saw the activities as part of one spectrum. The basic opposition in translation practice, that between word-for-word and sense-for-sense, parallels the distinction between 'the matter' and 'the sentence' (in French 'matière' and 'sens') which separated the surface narrative or subject from its kernel of meaning, theme, or 'moral'. That the distinction is itself often expressed in spatial metaphors, similitudes to clothing, or to exteriors and interiors, suggests a belief in a 'real' meaning separable from linguistic expression, and basically unaffected by the variety of possible articulations of it. The distinction between 'wheat' and 'chaff' which recent so-called Patristic criticism has made so familiar distinguishes a hierarchy of realities that denigrates the outer or surface or literal for the sake of the moral message which it veils. Of course that very stress on the distracting, even deceiving, nature of the apparent narrative emphasizes its power. In *De Casu Diaboli* Anselm makes his Magister express this view to his Student at the end of his first chapter: 'But we shouldn't so much cling to inappropriate words which conceal the truth, as we should seek to discover the genuine truth which is hidden under the many types of expression.' For Anselm the surface expression, the style or texture of the language, has much less importance than that prelinguistic core of truth which it indicates. The status of their representations varied in important ways. This is not for a moment to deny that a man like Anselm had literary sensitivity; it is to recognize the context of the dialogue, in which a Master is trying to educate a Student in methods of reading.[27]

Even in periods when there was widespread acknowledgement of bilingual culture we can find assessments, or at least acknowledgements, of the irrational power of the primacy of one or another of the languages. This insistence upon reference to the Latin text is sometimes argued in terms of the emotional force which the right word, the Latin word, could inspire, like this advice to the young Charles VI of France which Philippe de Mézières put into the mouth of 'Queen Truth' (la royne Verite)

Insofar as you can, read the books [of the Bible] in Latin, and be certain that you will enjoy reading in Latin, that stories or instruction will please your heart more than half a dozen stories in French. For Holy Scripture, written and dictated by the Saints in Latin, and afterwards translated into French, does not give the same substance to readers as streams as from the source itself . . . For there are in Holy Scripture certain, even many, Latin words which pierce the heart with great devotion in the reading, which, translated into French, are without spice and taste in the vernacular.[28]

This is also a reminder, even a warning, that no vernacular translation can be a substitute for the original. Fluent and graceful translation was certainly possible; but it was dangerous, because it removed the reminders that the substitute text was a means not an end. Philippe's promise of delight is also an attempt to protect. That emotional argument which Philippe de Mézières used to entice his pupil into studying the Bible in Latin in order to experience the immediacy of its emotional power can be found elsewhere.

When Montaigne discusses the issue, almost in passing, he locates these feelings through one of those metaphors of *layers* to which these chapters have so often called attention:

Original qualities are not abolished, they are covered, hidden. Latin is part of my nature, I understand it better than French; but for forty years I have never used it to speak or to write, except when I have fallen, two or three times in my life, into extreme or sudden emotion, for example, seeing my father, in good health, fall on me in a faint, my gut reaction has always been to burst out with my first words in Latin.[29]

Two factors must be remarked. First, the language of education and of great literature retains emotional priority. Second, there is a mental analogy here to the spatial metaphor which links 'depth' to 'importance', so that Latin's emotional 'centrality' in Montaigne's emotional experience reinforces its great status. Latin's comparative richness was the despair of vernacular writers who found themselves in the position of Cicero centuries before. There is a great distance, however, between the view that a good translator can emulate his model, absorb its qualities, and in so doing actually improve his own language to the point where it rivals its predecessor (Cicero's confident ambition), and the more modest judgement of most medieval writers that Latin's prestige was unchallengeable because of the imperfections of the modern vernaculars with their lack of regulation, their paucity of vocabulary, their constant change.[30] Not only did attitudes to Latin affect writers, so did attitudes to their own vernaculars, which changed with the passage of time and the increase in confidence that those vernaculars were not only adequate but great mediums for expression. This confidence must almost always be retrospective, based on the existence of great vernacular texts (perhaps the writers of Golden Age Latin thought their literary predecessors *had* written great texts in Latin). Accuracy for its own sake had less value than did making a new text which would convey the subtleties of the original. We begin to see evidence of revision. No one labours to make a text worse, so we may ask in what ways rewriting improved. The commonest criterion seems to be clarity, but there is also evidence of change for style, particularly in vernacular history translation.

The spatial metaphors were and continued to be important. Understanding takes many forms, of which the paradigm is often a spontaneous and apparently simultaneous moment of realization or recognition, when we feel that everything suddenly slots into place and we understand at last, truly and completely, and for the first time. This is a powerful experience, and frequently involves an act of naming which realigns or reorganizes previous observations (and moments of understanding). Even such moments, however, come after many others, and it is this process of coming to an understanding which is often ignored, or abandoned, once we have had it. When texts are treated as puzzles to be decoded, as if they stood for an answer, reading appears to be the search for equivalence. Both the 'answer' and the 'process' views of interpretation were common among medieval and renaissance readers, depending not least upon what kinds of texts they were reading. Any text which involves comparison (in the rhetorical sense) or arguments might implicate the audience in an assumption that the positions would inspire discussion — and not perhaps discussion that would issue in a resolution. That is, texts might be thought to be embedded in an oral culture of talking about them.

It is the most obvious of observations to say that words are not mathematical counters with a single agreed meaning, that languages function associatively, so that meanings themselves are part of processes of sequence, juxtaposition, and habitual use (or the transgression of any of these). Translation attempts to find and sometimes create coincidence between two dynamic systems (this is also why they date so quickly). It appears to be unavoidable that translators first agree on the impossibility of their task then insist that it could be done better by pointing out infelicities of particular word or phrase choices.

When Augustine, Jerome, and Rufinus argue about their own and each other's translation of Divine Scripture or the Greek Fathers, their mutual accusations cover the ground from inaccuracy to paraphrase, and stem from different habits of mind which themselves define approaches to translation which remain current. Active rhetoricians (politicians, lawyers, teachers, bishops who had habitually to preach) tended to be audience-centred: Augustine insisted upon the need for biblical translations that could be understood and used by his congregations, whose familiarity with older, traditional liturgical translations complicated matters further with an understandable recalcitrance towards innovations in the sacred texts they had used from childhood. Recent reactions to the changes introduced after Vatican II or by revisions in the Anglican liturgy did not rise to the heights of stoning the priest who attempted to introduce the new text, which Augustine reports in one of his complaints to Jerome, but they evidenced the same conservative habits, and remind us how strong is the belief of post-Antique culture that the words of sacred texts – larger than simple charms – are in some way magical, that they are instruments of power that must not be tampered with. By contrast, the rhetorically trained and scholarly (but socially withdrawn) Jerome, in any case a far better scholar than his ambitious (and aggressive) younger colleague, leaned toward devotion to the *original* text, i.e. the Hebrew from which the Septuagint had originally come; he was preparing texts for study which, if they finished as replacements, were certainly intended, in so far as possible, to accompany their originals. An acceptable compromise was annotation (introduction of a commenting voice whose language and authority might differ from that of the primary text) to explain the problems as they arose. But commentary, however basic, neither solves nor circumvents the basic difficulties. They knew that. Both men, of course, vastly underestimated the speed with which ancient norms of general level of cultural attainment were collapsing. Soon the assumption that culture was bilingual would be reduced to so much less than a living memory that in the Latin-speaking West Jerome's translation might appear to promise to be the Word itself, rather than one translation of the Word. The subservient 'voice' acquired the authority of a primary text. One way of thinking about the shifting authority of these 'voices' and texts which move from primary, or 'original' to secondary, or commentary, or translation status might be to imagine the latter group of texts (like Jerome's Bible translation) as a pane of glass which can be looked at as well as through. In addition, of course, it is as well to remember that the status and understanding of texts varies at different historical moments. In late-classical antiquity Jerome's style may have seemed simple to the point of clumsiness. By Bede's day it had risen to the heights of eloquence, not only because of its status, but because of historic changes in Latin and by comparison to the writing of Bede's immediate precursors and contemporaries.

If the Bible is all the word of God, although mediated by human amanuenses, it ought to follow that no one part be more or less privileged than any other part. In practice, however, certain parts of the Bible, parts that were especially familiar because of their place, for example, in the liturgy, became the subject of continuous interpretation and the first candidates for translation. In the course of the twelfth century, with the growth of scholastic commentary, the institutional development of schools in which prestige and advancement depended upon mastery of certain set texts, one by one the biblical books came under the creative attention of commentators. These two stories, of 'professional' commentary and of vernacular translation, intertwine, because the difficulty of biblical Latin necessitated commentated translation if the significance of the 'plain' text was to be understood. Nor must we forget the scholarly pressure to define terms, to discover exact ways of expressing new and complex abstractions, which made scholastic Latin the precise instrument it became. Once again Cicero could be called as a witness: in *De finibus* and in his *Fourth Tusculan* he discusses (briefly and in passing) and then exemplifies the use and adaptation of Greek words for philosophical discussion in Latin.[31] He points out that the Greeks enjoy the advantage of the innovator: simply by their priority they pre-empt the vocabulary of complex analysis. He also mentions (again, in passing and without considering the basic issue of commensurability) his choices for translating words for the emotions, both where the Latin seems equivalent to the Greek and where it does not. In turn, Christian Latin inherited these Greek 'calques', and added to them those Hebrew words such as 'Amen', 'Hosanna', and 'Selah' which were so special as to resist translation altogether. In addition to these lexical items, the Latin Bible absorbed lengthier calques where an apparent oddity in the Greek represents a Hebraism, which is justified by its stylistic relation to the Old Testament narrative, that is, by copying the phrasing of the earlier prophecies, the New Testament writers could claim, in part by the style they chose, that the prophecies were being fulfilled, for example in the expression which we translate 'And it came to pass' at the beginning of a sentence. As long as a culture is bilingual, or at least aware of the vocabulary and structure of another literary language, recognizable words or phrases from the source language can be imitated as a stylistic device which refers to another language's literature and ways of doing things.[32] If it is the case that translations were meant to carry reminders to their readers that they were translations, perhaps unusual vocabulary or word-order were instrumental in creating constant strangeness.

In practice it was the Psalter which focussed the problems of translation; because it was part of daily worship, because it was recognized to be a collection of hymns, because it was an extractable part of the Bible which lay as well as religious worshippers used, we find it translated early and often. Bilingual texts exist in French and Latin which instruct the worshipper in correct behaviour (both physical and mental discipline) during the daily rituals of worship, by framing the Latin of the liturgy in a French account of the correct way to experience it. Here we see an example of *diglossia*, where

Latin has greater prestige than French. It may be worth reminding ourselves that worship continued to be focussed upon the Latin text, however little understood by the worshipper. In English we find 'substitute' metrical psalms from an early date, but it was an 'accompaniment' translation (schema 2 and 3) which had widespread circulation (both among the orthodox and the so-called Lollards, who interpolated their own commentary into it). This early fourteenth-century translation of the Psalms was a striking case of reference back to the original; the reader is never for a moment allowed to lose sight of the fact that the English *translates*. It practically grapples with the Latin to which it is addressed. According to a verse prologue which was added to the work, it was originally written by Richard Rolle for a woman, Margaret Kirkby, but a glance at Rolle's own prose prologue reveals that he was well aware that it would be recopied for the use of many different readers.[33] Most of this prologue, or *accessus*, is condensed from Latin introductions to commentaries on the Psalter, particularly Peter Lombard's, but the end contains a brief, compact, address to the reader, which is also a kind of defence of Rolle's effort.

The matere of this boke is Crist & his spouse, that is, haly kyrke, or ilk ryghtwise mannys saule. The entent is to confourme men that ere filyd in Adam til Crist in newnes of lyf. The maner of lare is swilke: umstunt he spekis of Crist in his godhed, umstunt in his manhed, umstunt in that at he oises the voice of his servauntes. Alswa he spekis of haly kyrke in thre maners: umwhile in the person of perfite men, somtyme of unperfite men, som tyme of ill men, whilk er in halikyrke by body noght by thoght, by name noght by ded, in noumbire noght in merit. In this werke I seke na straunge Ynglis, bot lyghtest and comonest, and swilk that is mast lyke til the Latyn, swa that thai that knawes noght Latyn by the Ynglis may com til mony Latyn wordis. In the translacioun I folow the lettere als mykyll as I may, and thare I fynd na propire Ynglis I folow the wit of the worde, swa that thai that sall red it thaim thare noght dred errynge. In expounynge I fologh haly doctours, for it may come in some envyous man hand that knawes nought what he sould say, that will say that I wist noght what I sayd, and swa doe harme til him and til othere if he dispise the werke that is profytabile for him and othere.[34]

Here we find Rolle first introducing the subject and why we should read it: both what its overarching intention is to us (to move and persuade us to righteousness) and what its particular method is (following learned example of exposition). The translation is meant as an accompaniment, to bring readers to the Latin. Rolle stresses the humility necessary to his readers, because he knows the risk of misunderstanding that his work may encourage among the ignorant. But the work, in best rhetorical terms, is nevertheless profitable to be done.

What in effect Rolle has done is to assemble a bilingual Psalter with English Commentary, so that the devout, but unlearned, reader (not imagined as a female reader, nor as a collection of female readers, as will be obvious from the pronouns) can meditate upon the Latin, sentence by sentence. The opening sentence of Psalm 1 elicits a commentary of almost two pages, of which this is the beginning:

**Beatus vir qui non abijt in consilio impiorum: & in via peccatorum non stetit, & in cathedra pestilencie non sedit.**
In this psalme first he spekis of Crist and of his folouers, bloundisand til us, hightand blisfulhed til rightwisemen; sithen he spekis of vengaunce of wickedmen, that thai dred pyne sen thai will noght luf joy. He bygynnes at the goed man & says
Blisful man the whilk oway ȝed noght in the counsaile of wicked and in the way of synful stode noght & in the chaiere of pestilens he noght sate.
He is blisful til whaim all thynge comes that he covaites, or that has all that he will & will nathynge that is ill, and as Saynt Austyne sais, fife thynge falles til blysfulhed . . . (p. 5)

Notice that what we might want to call the translation of the verse comes after a short introduction instructing us in how to interpret; the commentary begins with an exposition of the first word (schema 3). After this, it should be said, Rolle's habit is to give the Latin verse and then, immediately, the closest lexical-equivalent English translation that he can, before giving the allegorical exposition (schema 4). The English *words* represent the sequence of Latin *words* in order to indicate the template from which interpretation arises. Lexical equivalence is a stage, an indication of small units which represent both the Latin and what the Latin represented (an adaptation of schema 2). Judgements about accuracy or inaccuracy are incomplete without the expansions which follow. It is part of a process of translation-and-interpretation which always refers back to the original. One other example may serve as an illustration of textual variation. In what we now number as the twenty-third Psalm (but which in Rolle's numbering, following Jerome, is Psalm 22), the opening of which is familiarly rendered 'The Lord is my shepherd', the medieval Latin text reads 'regit' where the Hebrew, which omits the verb 'to be', gives a word which means 'my shepherd',

**Dominius regit me & nichil michi deerit: in loco pascue ibi me collocauit**
Lord governs me and nathynge sall me want; in sted of pasture thare he me sett.

The voice of a rightwisman: *Lord* Crist is my kynge, and forthi *na thynge sall me want*, that is, in him I sall be sikere and suffisaunt, for I hope in him gastly goed and endles. And he ledis me *in sted of pasture*, that is, in undirstandynge of his word, and delite in his luf, where I am sikere to be fild. *Thare*, in that *sted, he set me* to be norist til perfeccioun. (p. 85)

Once again, the commentary takes a word or a phrase at a time, which I have once again tried to indicate by using distinctive type faces. This kind of translation is compressed, as commentaries tend to be, so that the reader has to recognize that 'The voice of a rightwisman' identifies the 'voice' of the poem, what we might today call the 'persona', the imaginary speaker, here an unspecified righteous man, and that the translation is partly repeated, inset into an expansive (relatively) interpretation. Using different type faces is one way of conveying the break-up of the line – in certain intriguing ways the best analogy is with modern poetry, from T. S. Eliot to John Berryman, where the reader has to acquire an alertness to which voice is speaking now. This is reader-oriented translation, which never forgets the emotional impact the text should be enabled to make – though Cicero would have been horrified by the sentiments, he would have recognized the intention to address the audience's emotions. Translation and commentary are methods of indirection which will let *direction* out.[35]

Accompaniment translation is not meant to be read easily, as a flowing sequence, but to be the means of meditation, of constant reference to the Latin. An exhaustive commentary would attend to units of different sizes, and would move back and forth between them: a single word, as here, a word as it appears in a phrase, or as it is used at other places in the Bible, or the phrase as *it* appears elsewhere. This process might be described as radial reading: turning the pages, referring backwards and forwards, constantly rereading and meditating. It is a kind of mental 'scrolling'. In that way, far from being a *substitute* for the original or any kind of literarily ambitious English creation, its success as a medium for contemplation depends upon the choppiness of its effect, the constant interruption which prevents the reader from carrying on. The English is not 'bad', but certainly not fluent or graceful – this is important, because a tribute to the sacredness and difficulty of the Sacred Page. It is not meant to be read as a uniform prose sequence which is conveying information, or narration, at speed; it is better to think of it as a sequence of voices. What I called earlier the 'integrity' of the language of translation is not an issue. It is glass to be looked through, not at, never to be studied as of interest in its own right. It is dynamic, but it is not a 'text'.

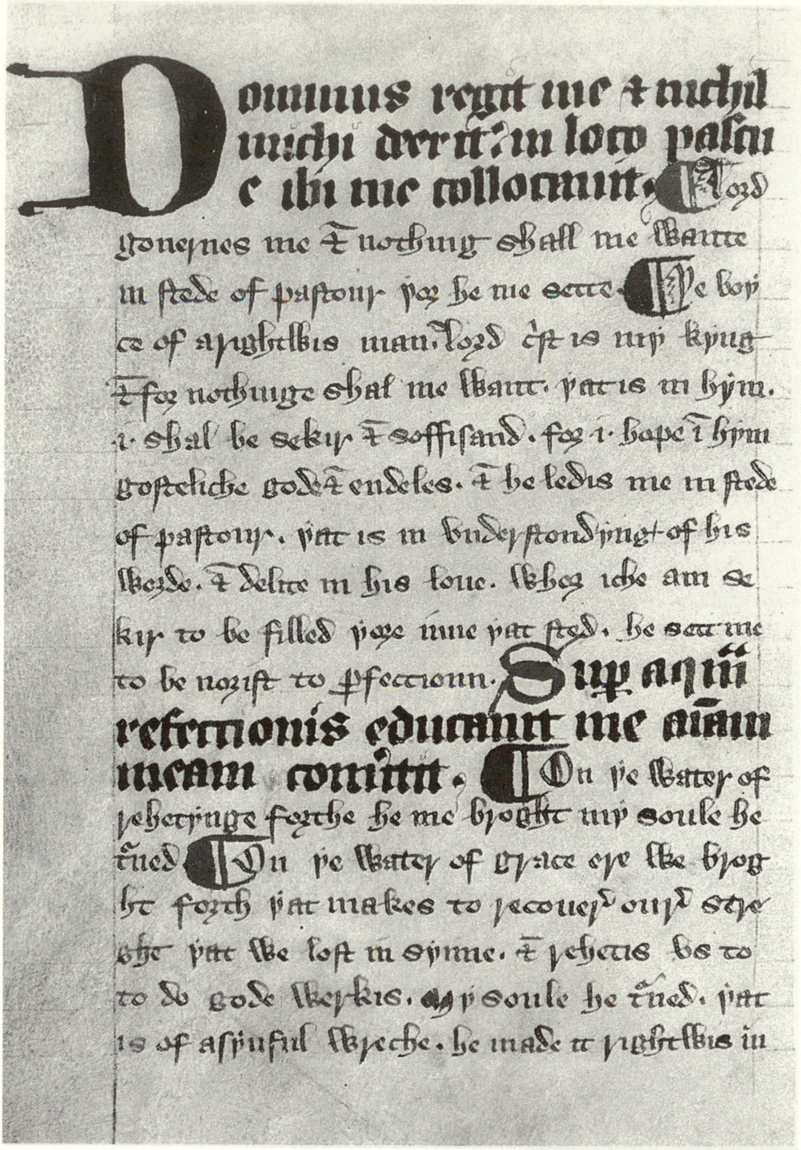

Plate 8   The opening verses of the Twenty-third Psalm in Rolle's Translation and Commentary. The rubrications in the original are red, emphasizing the different sections, which are lettered in slightly different scripts.

## WORDS AND DEEDS

But not all readers could be referred to the Latin.[36] For audiences limited to or more comfortable in the vernacular another approach might be necessary. Anglo-Saxon translators, for example, sometimes treated the plot or story as a unit larger than words or phrases and translated *that*. This appears as a kind of narrative paraphrase (schema 8), often expressed in the style of vernacular poetry. All the rhetorical exercises which treat of expansion come into play when narrative-paraphrase translation converts the original plot into something referring-but-not-equivalent in the vernacular. In addition, amplifications include the introduction of new characters and incidents, often subordinated to some abstract scheme of reference, like Shakespearean subplots, which 'refer' while they exemplify. One important check upon this kind of paraphrase is that new adventures for known characters are always fitted into chronological periods for which nothing is recorded, like the Harrowing of Hell or the Apocryphal gospels which invent the childhood of Christ. 'New' characters are controlled by the same historical conventions we considered in earlier chapters. Since it is clear that no woman could go through labour unattended by another woman, the midwife who delivered the Virgin of the infant Christ is an obvious necessity of the story. Narrative-paraphrasal 'translation' could exploit such resources, and extended the already capacious category of translation by increasing in practice (without explicitly extending in theory) the latitude of addition.

Peter Comestor's mid-twelfth-century *Historia Scholastica* was narrative-paraphrase of sacred 'history' in sequential Latin prose, and it provided a text, as it were at one remove from the holiness and linguistic difficulty of Sacred Writ itself, on which, or from which, translators could work. Peter's nickname refers with respect to his having *digested* the Bible. His paraphrase was supplemented by the *Aurora* of Peter of Riga, and vernacular translators used both works as bases for verse paraphrases of biblical material.[37] Jehan Malkaraume inserted the tale of Pyramus and Thisbe into his Bible paraphrase at the end of the story of Susanna and the Elders.[38] The *Ormulum* is another versified paraphrase, though one which had no currency. Almost two dozen more limited poetic paraphrases survive from eleventh and twelfth-century Germany, including two celebrating the exploits of Judith.[39] Anglo-Saxon poets recreated the stories of Genesis, Exodus, and Judith for vernacular audiences, and Middle English is rich in other such similar exercises in telling the story, paraphrasing the 'narrative matter' at a literal level, without being either a word-for-word *or* a sense-for-sense translation. Poems like *Genesis A* or the late Middle English alliterative *Susannah* (today usually classed as part of the *Apocrypha* but in the Middle Ages contained in the *Book of Daniel*) reveal the limitations of the simple dichotomies accompaniment/substitution or word-for-word/sense-for-sense translation. They incline from 'substitution' to 'replacement', but only in the limited sense that they are addressed to an audience for whom the Latin original was probably out of reach; they tend to follow the order of events as given in the original, but they are not close enough to it at any verbal level (that inescapable metaphor of layers again) to be considered simply as translating either word or sense. To complicate matters further, those medieval vernacular poems often translate both from the biblical books and from their accompanying commentaries, so that it would require both an alert and a scholarly reader to disentangle the sources of the vernacular composition, precisely the reader to whom the translation is not addressed. These new texts might be categorized as redaction-translation (schema 6), amalgamations directed at an audience for whom neither accompaniment nor substitution is really an adequate description, because they could never be in a position to study the Sacred Page directly (with an accompaniment translation beside them). And what they were *translating* was not in any simple sense words. Nor did this restrict the vernacular-bound audience to the sacred plot alone.

While an audience of unlearned listeners could not supply immediate recognition of the commentary traditions of understanding, or be expected to grapple with the multilayered mysteries of the allegorical interpretations, neither allegory nor symbol were alien to them, and a great many meanings were probably much more accessible than we might predict – Mak, in the Wakefield Master's play, *Secunda Pastorum*, the *Processus Prophetorum*, and the devotional lyrics were all sources which both exploited and transmitted multiple interpretation. Among the motives for recreating biblical stories as vernacular poems was a desire on the part of religious writers to provide a substitute for poems of war, or love, or any of those wordly ambitions which distracted lay men and women from God. The purpose of and audience for the story-telling justified accommodations to the style of vernacular fiction. The pleasures of interpretation were a crucial part of the pleasure of the text; that is, authors could direct interpretation and expect the direction to be recognized – though no one would want to claim that direction was in every case a successful restriction. The author of *Pearl, Patience*, and *Cleanness*, in fourteenth-century England, was a masterful poet who integrated biblical substance into his poetry, which is didactic without tears. Misunderstanding – that is, misinterpretation represented *within* the text by uncomprehending characters – elevates the interpretative status of the reader. Internal misreading is an encouragement to correction by the implied, external, reader. Nor should medieval vernacular drama be left out of account. Change of language, change of medium, adaptation to an unlearned audience's expectations – nevertheless the *matter* of the Bible stories or the lives of saints remains, and remains the prominent thing (schema 9). Events are prelinguistic. It is only when we recount them that we turn them into language, which can be clothed in many guises. The new representation offers acts, visual and verbal, for interpretation.

What is striking about a great deal of medieval writing is how often new texts avoid aspirations to be verbally authoritative, even when the details of expression offer themselves for interpretation. When the Middle English poet wrote about his dream-vision of a lost Pearl, both his choice of medium (dreams remain famously interpretable texts) and his symbol invite speculation. It is not just that we recognize the 'Pearl' as a traditional symbol (like the coin of tribute, this symbol works by reference to a well-known biblical text, the 'pearl of great price' which in turn stands for salvation itself). The context of the dream vision in which, because the Dreamer appears not to be responsible for his experience, the narrator disclaims authority for his fiction, since dreams and visions were well known to be interior manifestations of exterior forces, in fact implies a greater authority than any individual poet could claim, by presenting the text as a locus of interpretation: what was seen and what happened are enigmas to be understood by the intelligent and knowledgeable reader.[40] Both Will Langland and Julian of Norwich represent themselves as humble seekers after truth, recipients of coded messages which their waking selves (and their readers) can interpret into clear. Dream visions, journeys to the Other- or Under-world (like the Latin poem of St Patrick's Purgatory which Marie de France translated), abdicate responsibility. The author can say what he (or she – this visionary literature is a haven of safety for women, for whom responsibility and authority posed special problems) likes while disclaiming responsibility for having invented it. 'It' is something *seen*, so that writing about it is already an act of interpretation and translation from the visual to the verbal (schema 9). This is another reminder that we must reverse our ordinary views about the priority of language. It would not be absurd to read the old chestnut about pictures being poor men's books backwards to remind ourselves that books are learned men's pictures; language cannot achieve the instantaneous simultaneity of visual or aural perception. Texts may be second order redactions. The fascinating case of dreams arises here, because dreams are – as both visual and verbal experiences – *like* texts. That they were involuntary and sometimes 'sent' might convey the authority to interpret them as if they were texts. They could be spurs to faith, to action, or to contemplation, without being themselves intended for detailed study, word by word. For the large number of people who could not read Latin, would never be able to read Latin, lay piety included an awakening of the emotions toward God in order to stimulate them to work toward their own salvation. The *gist* was enough, because the integrity of the sacred narrative would guarantee its message through the most humble words.

It may seem that the English Mystery Plays of the late fourteenth or fifteenth centuries which, after all, only use translation of the words of the Bible from time to time, and usually depend at most on paraphrase, go beyond whatever boundary the idea of translation erects. And so, in important ways, they do: they do not appear to offer extended vernacular equivalents for the Latin words of an original *text*. But it was still possible to argue that staged representation was a way of articulating things which had happened, deeds done, words spoken, all of which had a reality which language and dramatic gesture imitated and conveyed, for the most important *res gesta* of all, the historic arrival of mankind's salvation (schema 9). When Mak hides a stolen lamb in a cradle and pretends that his wife has just given birth, the Second Shepherds' Play makes a complex visual pun which assumes that the audience understands perfectly well that the shepherds of the Gospel story visited the Lamb of God. Even the relatively ignorant can enjoy the joke. 'Fluency and grace' imply a concentration upon the style of the new, the translated, text. In some large-scale way the matter may be preserved despite the translator's inattention to the details of the manner. But in remaking the story in a new medium (and this refers to plot and character) medieval writers were uneasy about whether or not they were creating an authoritative text, one whose own words carry the weight of interpretability. Are the words value free when it is the plot, the matter, the history or life which they express? The invented characters become metaphors for the message to be illustrated. They neither pretend to be accurate representations of the past nor elicit interpretation as factually true any more than do the expansions or speeches of the characters in historical writing. This kind of translation paraphrases and amalgamates events without implying that the words in which it does so correspond to the original. This is neither a substitute nor an accompaniment text in the sense in which Jerome's or Augustine's translations were; nor does it pretend to be a representation of 'a' text at all. That would imply that the lay (or uneducated) audience had the capacity to read (and interpret) the difficult originals, which it had not. This is audience-based translation, telling what there is without representing its words.

If the drama suggests the most *distant* kind of translation, the problem remains that medieval writers or audiences might crave that impossible feat of *close* reference, vernacular translations lexically equivalent to the Latin, fluent enough to appear to be a substitute and not an accompaniment, but none the less constantly referring by means of glosses, *accessus*, and notes. The great vernacular translations all grow out of rich translation cultures permeated by multi-lingual awareness, inheriting written styles that allowed for extensions into what comes to be seen as peculiar, even unique, archaizing, artificial literary registers capable of sustaining the necessary strangeness which preserves the sense of a referring translation. Manipulation of the vernaculars was deliberate and added famous resources of lexis and syntax, not contingently, but as part of the translators' perception of the remedies necessary to make lower status languages approach Greek and Latin. English arguments about 'ink horn' additions to lexis (like the debates in France over the 'grands rhetoriqueurs') are a sixteenth-century phenomenon which displaces anxieties about incipient nationalism onto language. To have reached the point where defence and illustration of the vernacular are part of the day's debate, language-culture must progress through long periods of experimentation, accretion, and amalgamation. Controversies about lexis, viewed as controversies about competition either with the ancients or with other national groups, depend upon a measure of retrospect and a certain confidence in what has already been achieved.

Throughout the Middle Ages, while the Bible and sacred history were the most important category of original texts to be interpreted, other kinds of ancient texts raised similar problems for the evolving vernaculars. What the language of an ancient text represents could raise complex problems of referral, especially if it was itself a translation. Just as the Bible was a translation (and in some places a translation of a translation), so equally were many of the philosophical texts to which the interests of vernacular audiences turned from the early years of the thirteenth century onward. While there is a clear distinction, in theory, between the crucial vocabulary of a sacred text and the vocabulary of moral philosophy, there is still a profound need for precision. Latin had been the language of theological commentary and speculation for centuries, and had developed under the impetus of medieval scholarship. The translations of Greek and Arabic texts which so fertilized the schools brought calques from those languages into medieval Latin; words as familiar as 'algebra' are successful adaptations from Arabic. Like theology, philosophy requires a specialized vocabulary; we find translators – indeed, we found Cicero – importing words from their original texts into their translations when the target language did not seem to provide an acceptable synonym. Transliteration of Greek into Latin set an important precedent, enlarging the vocabulary first of Latin then of the European vernaculars, but it remained a contentious issue. No one ever claimed that the exact, and exacting, language of scholastic disputation was elegant. Yet it served its function and served it well, and the rejection of it by Renaissance humanists as part of their own archaizing and purifying campaign over the style of Latin they were to employ struck an important blow against Latinitas itself. Latin had been an evolving language, and over several hundred years, and under pressure to develop new ways of dealing with new concepts, changes from classical Latin had resulted in a rich medium that could be universally understood. It provided a centralizing and regularizing standard. Medieval translators frequently bemoan the difficulty of their originals; the challenge of classical Latin was often further complicated by the unreliability of the textual tradition, by ambiguities in terminology, or by specialist jargons. It is also likely that the reflections we read on the difficulty of certain texts constituted claim, justification, and excuse.

Fourteenth-century rulers such as Charles V of France or Robert the Wise of Naples ordered translations of texts which might be categorized as broadly political, that is, both moral instruction and advice to princes, for their non-Latinate court readers, just as Charlemagne or Alfred had done centuries before. Demands for vernacular versions of Latin texts appear wherever court culture creates a class of potential readers who need – or want – knowledge enshrined in the traditions of Antiquity; for their various reasons, courts recreate, or perhaps give additional impetus to, the conversation with the classical past which increase the number of readings and interpretations of its texts. In this perpetual confrontation with Antiquity there are no terms of surrender. War, government, law, and history (all subjects which stimulate, or are stimulated by, worldly ambition) were absorbing subjects for readers – and not just secular readers – for whom power and prestige could be matters of learning, especially when the learning was presented as an expensive object, a luxury book. Commissioning translations became one of the marks of munificence for princes. The attitudes of the men from whom the works were commissioned varied; most of them had been formed by learned habits of reading and explicating. When they found themselves translating for an unlearned, but not unsophisticated, audience, they often amalgamated several texts in order to create a *readable* replacement text which could nevertheless bear some kind of comparison to the original (schema 6). This is the moment when pretensions to style move forward, and translators express a new kind of uneasiness. The prefaces which repeat *topoi* about the need for accuracy begin to show signs of sacrificing that accuracy to the need to create a new text, or perhaps the desire to emulate the old one in the new language. In this way they begin to move in directions not dissimilar from adaptation of biblical material.[41] But new composition, in the sense of new genres, new poems, new *texts*, was not an immediate result.

Nicole Oresme was one of many translators to remark his own adaptation of foreign terms in his new work, as for example the astrological terms which abound in his own translation of his own Latin essay, *Le Livre des Divinacions*. This is a reminder of the many reasons besides sacredness which might inhibit translation. Oresme addressed a scholarly audience first, when denouncing astrological divination, but the obvious importance of the subject to non-Latinate readers led him to rewrite his book; its technical and restricted subject led to a steady literalism. Yet we may ask why he translated this way when the original was his own. More's *Richard III* raises similar questions. Technical books raise slightly different ones (on the one hand they may be addressed to a 'professionalized' group for whom either Latin or a specialist jargon is known, on the other the information conveyed may not require sentence structures of a complex kind). The Galenic tradition of medical writing, the codes and commentaries of Roman Law, as well as many kinds of scientific writing were originally addressed to people for whom Latin was the ordinary language of their work. Even when translations exist it is sometimes difficult to know how widely they were used, or even known. In the course of the thirteenth century Justinian's *Institutes, Digest*, and *Code* were all translated into French, the first of these into verse by Richard d'Ennebault about 1280. More research is required before the status and use of such a translation will be clear.[42]

Just as with the study of the Bible, the closed world of an educated language invited accusations that the learned were maintaining a closed shop in order to prevent the non-Latinate reader from benefitting from knowledge which might aid him, or even enable him to do without such learned mediators as priests, doctors, or lawyers. This created a complex kind of aggression, which had as much to do with the power symbolized by the use of Latin as with the use itself. As late as the seventeenth century when Culpeper translated his *Herbal* for vernacular English readers, and after several centuries of vernacular writing, his preface has an air of committed monopoly-breaking.[43] Lighter in tone, but no less serious in intent, are Ben Jonson's plays upon the obfuscations open to alchemists or lawyers – or rather, pseudo-alchemists and -lawyers – in *The Alchemist* and *Epicoene*. Even *Volpone* has its scene of medical mumbo-jumbo. Latin could be perceived as the language of social control or the means of deceit, translation as the method of freedom which provided access to information and learning for plain men. The archaeology of knowledge is matched by geological strata of language.

Further, and despite the ostensible achievements of Renaissance trans-lators of either the Bible or Aristotle, there is inertia in translation history. Many translations which were claimed to be new were in fact based upon previous versions (the roots of the King James Bible translation lie in the late fourteenth century); versions which were dismissed as inadequate no doubt came to seem more impressive under the pressure of searching for alternative solutions to difficult problems. The respect which a new translator comes to feel for a once-despised, earlier, inadequate version also leads to a kind of piety which preserves for the sake of preserving, or by a kind of psychological process of familiarization, by a respect for the authority of writers now dead. What once seemed a barbarism comes to seem acceptable, even the word always used for the thing or concept. Innovation for its own sake is as hard-won a concept as preservation for its own sake later came to seem. This has, of course, important intellectual defences. Enshrining chronological stratification in the literature of a language is an important impulse in preserving its range of style and reference; that is, the witness of the past, in an evolving language, actually works to preserve understanding of texts which are rapidly dating. It also has the often-remarked effect of keeping the translation clearly a translation, because as current language use changes, the archaic style of the translation has an otherness that works as a reminder. Thus, despite the ostensible criticism of later translators, there remained an unmistakeable continuity from thirteenth- to seventeenth-century versions of Aristotle, just as surely as successive Bibles retained an increasingly archaic vernacular. Certain Humanist editions of Aristotle preserved scholastic translations as parallel texts, as, in a way, commentaries not quite synchronized to the newly printed originals. Even scholars from the East, who spoke modern Greek, were dependent upon 'bad' Latin translations sometimes several hundred years old. So the Aristotle commentaries of Aquinas continued to be quoted and praised despite the assurance that the text of Aristotle on which they were based was corrupt.

Arabic translations of Aristotle included versions with quite different amounts of commentary, some of it included in the text. When in the thirteenth century William of Moerbeke turned his prodigious energies to translating Aristotle, he attempted the word-for-word method which would preserve everything in his model, but 'everything' included interpolated glosses.[44] This method of small-unit lexical equivalence which was meant to represent as precisely as possible, by manipulation of Latin itself, the verbal and syntactic expression of Aristotle's philosophy, modified the Latin which was then used as the medium of discussion. This is important, not only for an understanding of scholastic innovations, but also as a precedent for attitudes to vernacular translation. The preservation of calques may represent not only a method of reminding readers that they are reading a translation, but also a bid for stability, by attaching the translation to older, and therefore honourable, methods of expression. We are used to thinking about 'aureation' (or doublets) as a fashion, but the use of Latinate vocabulary was more than an attempt to heighten register; it was also a means of attaching the vernacular to the timeless qualities of the classical languages. 'Method' itself is a transliteration of Greek, and one opposed by many humanist translators as unacceptable.[45] Translators no doubt had many ambitions for their vernaculars as part of their cultural identification. In the absence of an available synonym, transfer by adaptation is an enriching solution. It should also come with a reminder that words come in phrases, and that the use of a word often implies consequences at a larger unit level. The enrichment and the establishment of new literary languages increased as time passed, so that writers in English feel that English has a special relationship with French (but no longer any relationship with Norse). Nicole Oresme's justifying preface to his version of Aristotle's *Ethics* begins with a reflection upon Latin's evident superiority:

Priscian dit en ung petit livre que il fist des metres de Terence, que de tous les langaiges du monde latin est le plus abille pour mieulx exprimer et plus noblement son intencison . . . et comme il soit ainsi que latin est a present plus parfait et plus habondant langaige que francois, par plus forte raison l'en ne pourroit translater proprement tout latin en francois, sicomme entre ennombrables exemples peult apparoir de ceste proposition, *homo est animal* . . . parquoy je doy estre excuse en partie se je ne parle en cest matiere si proprement, si clerement, si aornement comment il fust mestier.[46]

Nor is this remarkably different from his careful defence of biblical translation.[47] While with less contentious texts, written with less crucial vocabularies, there is more stress on the challenge of turning difficult Latin into vernacular versions which will read fluently, some were still presented as scholarly texts actually intended to make a choppy impression. Jacques Bouchant's Seneca is preceded by reflections on the moralist's pithiness.[48] These are difficult texts which require study and meditation.

The rational arguments for regarding Latin as superior to any of the modern vernaculars depended upon traditions of complex syntactic organization and extensive abstract vocabulary which combined to create powerfully expressive resources for the well-read reader. Of course, what he had been reading varied, and no one would want to argue that a diet of Aquinas would be the best preparation for reading classical Latin poetry, or that a medieval scholar used to working in a highly devolved lingua franca Latin would have easy access to the vocabulary of, say, Terence. Nevertheless, the passage of centuries and the constant use and expansion of Latin literature gave writers in the language an undeniable certainty about the variety of registers that might be available to them; Latin had *actually* what the European vernaculars seemed still only to promise *potentially*. Latin was hard; its difficulties posed problems which were by no means simply an opportunity for conventional translator's modesty.

Prefaces can often tell us a great deal more about the book they precede than we might expect, given the conventionality of so many of their elements. That essential early distinction between the word-for-word and sense-for-sense translation combines in certain cases with the need to create a replacement text for a non-scholarly audience which may well also require additional explanations and require them in a language insufficiently endowed with the vocabulary to make subtle distinctions (schema 5 and 7). Much depends, too, upon the calibre of the translator. Men like Nicole Oresme or Jean de Meun are not only capable, but articulate about what they are doing. Jean's translation of Boethius' *De Consolatione Philosophiae* is a striking example. He provides an *accessus* to his text, explaining what it is,

who wrote it, and why we should read it. The whole is preceded by an
address to the king:

A ta royal majesté, tres noble prince, par la grace de Dieu roy des Francois, Phelippe le
Quart, je Jehan de Meun qui jadis ou Rommant de la Rose, puis que Jalousie ot mis
en prison Bel Acueil, enseignai la maniere du chastel prendre et de la rose cueillir et
translatay de latin en francois le livre Vegece de Chevalerie et le livre des Merveilles
de Hyrlande et la Vie et les Epistre Pierres Abaelart et Heloys sa fame et le livre Aered
de Esperituelle Amitié, envoie ore Boece de Consolacion que j'ai translaté de latin en
francois. Ja soit ce que tu entendes bien le latin, mais toutevois est de moult plus legiers
a entendre le francois que le latin. Et por ce que tu me deis – lequel je tieng pour
commandement – que je preisse plainement la sentence de l'aucteur sens trop ensuivre
les paroles du latin, je l'ai fait a mon petit pooir si comme ta debonnaireté le me
commanda. Or pri touz ceulz qui cest livre verront, s'il leur semble en aucuns lieus
que je me soie trop eslongniés des paroles de l'aucteur n'i met ou aucune fois mains,
que ils le me pardoingnent. Car se je eusse espons mot a mot le latin par le francois, li
livres en fust trop occurs aus gens lais et li clers, neis moiennement letré, ne peussent
pas legierement entendre le latin par le francois.⁴⁹

Here we have a text which seems to be intended both as a Replacement Text
and also as an Accompaniment. Close attention to the translation shows that
it includes elucidation and commentary wherever obscurity threatens. The
difficulty of the Latin legitimated that, and not surprisingly, Chaucer
depended upon Jean when making a translation in his turn. I considered this
briefly above when looking at style. Nor is Jean's practice significantly
different in his translation of the Letters of Abelard and Heloise, though if
there ever was a preface to that work it has not survived. Jean is capable of
suiting his register in French to Eloise's Latin, achieving that fidelity which is
not literal in the strict sense, but manages to convey non-semantic elements
of the original, both emotional and stylistic. He glosses in the text wherever
he finds a need to elucidate its references – and given the erudition of the
writers, for whom allusion was a constant pleasure, the need arose
frequently.⁵⁰

   But this is to run ahead, beyond the problem of texts which might be
categorized as marked by the demands of crucial vocabulary. It is, however,
an instructive reminder of the complexities of the issues. A single, articulate
writer of exceptional learning might be expected to vary his practice with
the type of text, but it is not clear that he distinguishes types of text into
modern categories. What can be said is that the medieval translations of
Boethius are remarkable for the number and variety of their interpolations.⁵¹

It seems plausible to hypothesize that the needs of the secular audience were more important than the kind of word-for-word restriction that marked interlinear accompaniment texts. While some distance from the original would not hamper the reader who was comparing translation and original (schema 1–3), and using the translation as a means of meditating upon the Latin, perhaps even as a kind of commentary upon it, any syntax-wrenching complexity or obscurity of vocabulary would make the translation unreadable for the audience at which it was directed. Concomitantly, translators seem to have distinguished the kind of original they were translating, reserving the strictest adherence to syntax and vocabulary to the most sacred originals where the vernacular was to accompany, not to replace. Yet any attempt to generalize founders on the variety of practice, not only of different translators, but of single translators at different times, confronting different texts, for different audiences. It is easy to assume that Marie de France allowed herself great latitude in her Fables, since they recreate traditional Aesopic material. We might ask the usual question another way, why should she have adhered as closely as she did to her models for the *Espurgatoire St Patrice* or the *Vie Ste. Audree* (if she is the Marie who translated it)? That is, why do we find 'accuracy' where we need not expect it? Why, in cultures which emphasized the importance of learning by heart, do we find such inaccuracy in quotation made – it seems clear – from memory? While there may be no single, simple answer, it may be possible to describe the latitude of interpretation.

Many of these issues can be studied in the prefaces of Caxton's philosophical editions. When Caxton printed Chaucer's translation of Boethius' *Consolation of Philosophy*, he knew that Chaucer had used Jean de Meung's French version, with its interpolated glosses. His gestures include praise of Chaucer for developing the English literary language.

And for as moche as the stile of it is hard and difficile to be understonde of simple persones, therfor the worshipful fader and first foundeur and enbelissher of ornate eloquence in our Englisshe, I mene Maister Geffrey Chaucer, hath translated this sayd werke oute of Latyn into oure usual and moder tonge, folowyng the Latyn as neygh as is possible to be understande. Wherein in myne oppynyon he hath deservid a perpetuell lawde and thanke of al this noble royame of Englond, and in especiall of them that shall rede and understande it. For in the sayd boke they may see what this transitorie and mutable worlde is and wherto every mann livyng in hit ought to entende. Thenne for as moche as this sayd boke so translated is rare and not spred ne knowen, as it is digne and worthy, for the erudicion and lernyng of suche as ben ignoraunt and not knowyng of it, atte requeste of a singuler frende and gossib of myne I, William Caxton, have done my devuoir and payne t'enprynte it in fourme as is hereafore made, in hopyng that it shall prouffite moche peple to the wele and helth of theire soules and for to lerne to have and kepe the better pacience in adversitees. And furthermore I desire and require you that of your charite ye wold praye for the soule of the sayd worshipful mann, Geffrey Chaucer, first translatour of this sayde boke into Englisshe and enbelissher in making the sayd langage ornate and fayr, whiche shal endure perpetuelly and therfore he ought eternelly to be remembrid.[52]

His claim for the English version of Cicero's *De senectute* lies in its solution of difficulties for his audience, the kind of publisher's blurb which says that the translation actually improves while preserving the original.

. . . prayeng to take this reducyng pacyently and submyttyng me to the amendyng and correction of the reder and understonder that is disposed to rede or have ony contemplacion in th'ystoryes of this book whiche were drawen and compyled out of the bookes of th'auncyent phylosophers of Grece, as in th'orygynal text of *Tullii: De Senectute* in Latyne is specyfyced compendyously, whiche is in maner harde the text. But this book reduced in Englyssh tongue is more ample expowned and more swetter to the reder, kepyng the juste sentence of the Latyn.[53]

The expansions necessitated by translating the text *and* its accompanying commentary are justified by the view that the translation represents the full meaning of the discussion as generations of readers understood it. Equivalent translation (schema 4) may attempt a kind of completion, translating both text and gloss. Some modern readers may hear a slight defensiveness in Caxton's tone, as he justifies his 'sweet' Cicero. The question of whether or not the glosses count as part of the text to be translated arises as well in certain vernacular texts.

Clearly some innovating authors, of whom Dante might be the most famous, intended their work to assume the status of great texts to be read allegorically; where the intention is embodied in the text there are cues to tell the reader what to expect, how to read. The vexed question of how many vernacular authors wrote glosses to accompany their texts is only now being explored in detail.[54] Dante's ambition – adapting the dream vision journey to the underworld for a great vernacular poem – brings us at last to the category of 'literature' and the translation of Latin or vernacular texts. Once again the question arises of what kinds of work for what kinds of audience by which translators. Translation already has a long history. It is important to remember how bilingual, even multilingual, medieval and renaissance culture were, and how imbued with the continuing history of Latin culture, not just the culture of Antiquity, but the evolving Latinity which included medieval Latin historiography, hagiography, philosophical and scientific writing, as well as poetry. Oresme is not alone in taking Latin as a model of imitation and growth which European vernaculars came to repeat, almost, as it were, knowing the way. It had not been necessary, in Classical Rome, for Catullus or Virgil to make direct translations of Greek poetry, because they belonged to an audience that read Greek. Nevertheless, both poets, by imitating Greek achievements in lyric and epic, and by adapting Greek metres and forms, instantiate more than the aspirations of individual poets. They are an early example of a kind of linguistic nationalism: Greek and Hellenistic culture possessed something which Latin writers wanted for their own language, something which, if they could provide it, would immortalize them as Greek poets had immortalized themselves by their earlier achievement. Their borrowings and imitations were in effect intended to make good a lack they perceived. There is a confident competitiveness about their success that still arouses wonder, despite, perhaps because of, the occasional defective line, the awkwardness as Catullus tries to bend the natural cadences of Latin to fit his Greek ideal, neologisms to supply a want in Latin vocabulary. The relationship between Greek and Latin was not static, and seemed different depending upon the subject treated, the time of composition, or the individual competence and confidence of Latin writers.[55] In the course of the hundred years around the change of era a sequence of fine writers raised the 'status' of Latin literature to the point where Latin-speaking readers could feel on a par with the older, Greek-speaking, culture. Their representatives had reacted to the desire for the Greek literary achievement by emulation, and had succeeded. This assumes a self-conscious awareness of a category 'literature', that register of written language in which the texture or style is regarded as important for its own sake. The words call attention to themselves in more than purely semantic ways: style (the 'how' expressed) must be taken into account however apparently inseparable from content (the 'what' described), but this doubleness (words and what they represent) carried no sacred overtones. Translation and imitation were methods of creating verbal culture for writers uninhibited by the Christian ambivalence toward non-sacred, non-religious writing. 'Literature' was not only possible, it was central.

The very existence of such a category was problematic in societies ostensibly dedicated to the pursuit of salvation, not such worldly goals as fiction. With rhetorical education the means of training literate readers and writers, some form of literary awareness was built into every serious student's intellectual formation, however much the apparent religious beliefs of its context appeared to deny that. Story-telling is always with us, and the poetry which was its highest expression loomed – however problematically – over education. It may have been vilified, since it not only dealt with those essential human experiences which it was the Christian's duty to despise and transcend, but it dealt with those undeniably central events beautifully, distracting its readers from their otherworldly business and encouraging them at least to go and write likewise. For all the religious writing of the Middle Ages, it is the secular, questing, questioning texts which survive to move and persuade their readers, works in which love, ambition, character and motive contradict the known goods of contemplation, self-abnegation, and humility. That the language of human desire is the most intense metaphor available to even the most rigorously religious writers opens the window, as so often, to just those kinds of writing against which the door was barred. Justifying the study of classical poetry and history, in so far as these were even perceived as radically different categories, occupied the authors of countless prefaces, caught as they were in the need to defend what they were doing. This does not mean that we should wrench the meaning of their texts to some obvious, simple, and straightforward religious interpretation, as was popular a generation ago, but that we should recognize that they were caught in a web of irresolvable arguments. Those for literature as a good-in-itself came hard, and they came late. In the meantime, throughout the Middle Ages, the presentation of the commented text which had been the achievement of late-classical scholarship, provided the model for Christian texts. That is, many scholarly texts looked so similar as to provide visual cues towards interpretation. The glossed Bible imitates the glossed Virgil. The glossed Justinian presents itself as a difficult text for study. The glossed presentation of Spenser's *Shepheardes Calender* is a vernacular example of a kind of 'aspiring' text, 'packaged' as it is by typeface-cues. It demands treatment as a classical text-to-be-interpreted. Translations of Chaucer, Henryson, and Milton into Latin suggest similar linguistic-nationalist claims.[56]

The text-and-commentary which established itself as such an important part of Hellenistic and Roman scholarship may seem at best an unfortunate necessity to enable late-comers or apprentice readers to read ancient and difficult texts, at worst an invitation to unhindered antiquarian nostalgia

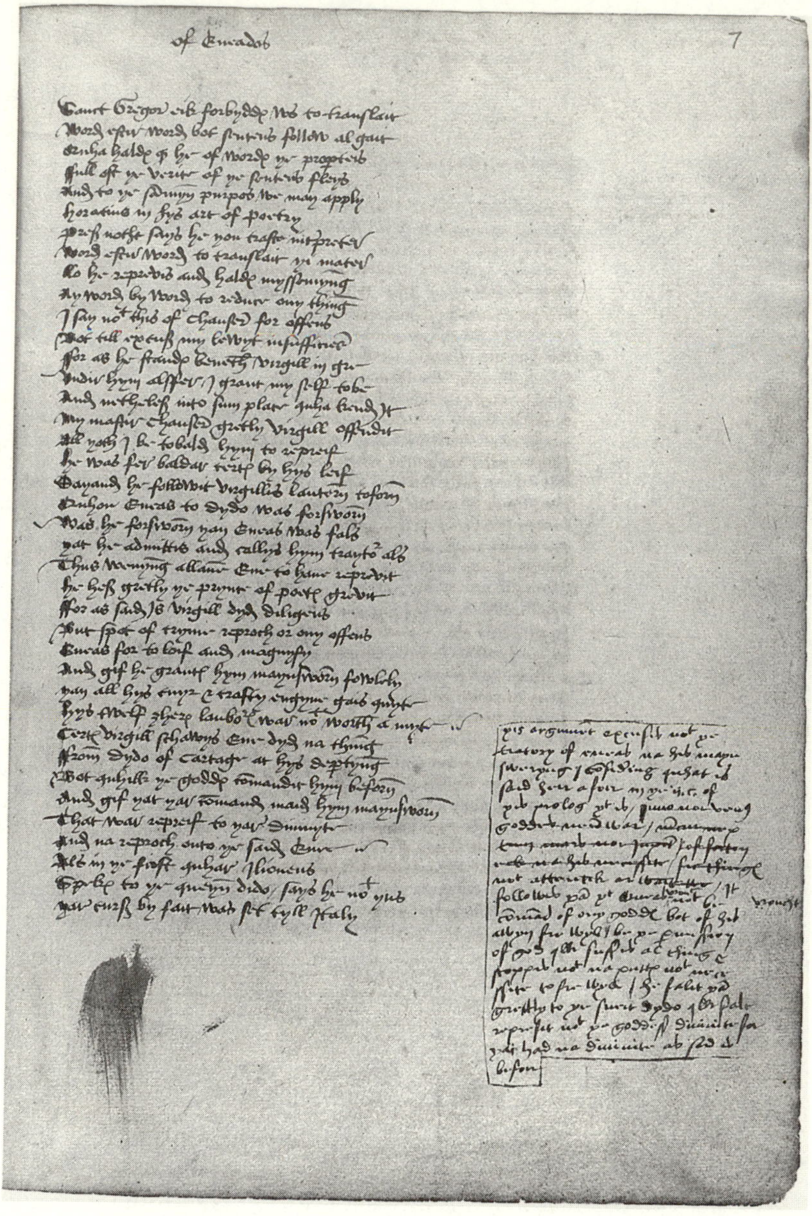

Plate 9    An extract from the Introduction to Douglas's *Aeneid*, with a fragment
of his accompanying commentary. He is taking issue with Chaucer's
interpretation.

which erects such barriers of apparent scholarship that in fine the original work becomes impossible to read through the thick aggregation which surrounds it. Yet, as we have seen, the multivocal commentary provided scope for scholars dedicated to educating their sometimes solitary students to share the complexities of their experience. The multiplication of meanings itself created a parallel experience. In the course of the high and late Middle Ages the variety of texts which attracted the attention of scholars form a testimony to their love of the classical past, their desire that – however incapable they might be of emulating its achievements – as little as possible might be lost.

Practice anticipated theory. Translations were commissioned in increasing numbers. The range of translation activities, from the accompaniments of interlinear glossing and commentary and the substitute text of accurate verbal correspondence (schema 1–3), to the replacement translation of single or conflated original texts (schema 4–6), to paraphrase and adaptation (schema 7–9) can be traced throughout the Middle Ages in many kinds of non-sacred writing. Emulative envy seems to be a feature of what we term 'renaissances', whether of the court of Charlemagne, Robert of Anjou, Philippe le Bon, the Medici or the Tudors. Just as a concern to read and understand classical writers marks a period of increased intellectual activity, so does a concern with the status of vernacular. The passion which such discussions arouses is itself marked by a strong linguistic nationalism, powerful and irrational, whose metaphors correspond in turn to patterns of kinship, so that the force of the phrase 'mother tongue' is revealed by the word which expresses it. This commitment to making Latin writing available to a secular audience appears regularly in prefaces to translations from the classics into the European vernaculars. As we have seen, the mere appearance of a subject in a preface is not in itself a guarantee that the subject will be treated seriously in what follows, but here the justification of the activity – writing itself, especially non-religious writing – inspired the adaptation of earlier defences of translations and of translation practice. Saying that a figure of authority had requested it was not only a way of circumventing accusations of time-wasting, or ambition, it was also a recommendation to potential readers, as dedications later became in early printed books. It is possible that such prefaces were a means of indicating the kind of audience for which the new translation was intended, perhaps distinguishing scholarly works (with special demands) from those intended for a secular readership. And, of course, new works could *pose* as translations, as Geoffrey of Monmouth's did. This implies first, that non-professional readers wanted access to texts which might profit them (especially texts of military strategy or political thought); second, that although such readers were comparatively uneducated, they were nevertheless adequate to the demands of the texts; third, that non-religious books were in demand.

'Translationese' may itself be a referring register, that is, medieval translators may have deliberately developed (especially for their substitute translation, schema 4–6) a style which constantly reminded the reader of its reference to another language. Or they may have been driven to create a kind of compromise register because they found themselves of necessity absorbing calques of word and phrase to supply lacks in their own languages. Certainly the difficulties of finding, or creating, equivalent styles occupies many translators' prefaces. The earlier the translator the more defensive he is likely to be, because he thinks he is doing something exceptional.[57] Nicole Oresme deals with what might be thought of as a question of snobbery when he writes, 'sont pluseurs gens de langue francoise qui sont de grant entendement et de excellent engin et qui n'entendent pas souffisanment latin . . .' (there are many French-speaking men of great understanding and excellent intelligence who do not sufficiently understand Latin); or there is Raoul des Presles, addressing Charles V at the opening of his translation of Augustine's *City of God*, using the standard rhetorical defences that an action (in this case the translation itself) is useful and profitable to be done, 'Vous avez fait translater plusieurs livres, tant pour plaire a vous, comme pour profitez a vos subgéz . . . Vous avez voulu estre translaté de latin en francois, pour le profit et utilité de vostre roiaume . . .' (You have had many books translated, as much to please yourself as to profit your subjects . . . You have wanted [them] to be translated from Latin into French for the profit and usefulness of your subjects); Christine de Pizan gave Charles particular credit for these commissions in her *Livre des Faits*, written after his death.[58] Caxton hides behind friends, nobles, and countrymen.

It has been the history of modern studies of medieval translation to begin by considering their accuracy (in effect their lack of it), and to attempt to explain the apparent 'mistakes' in translation practice which characterize them. This began with the strictures of Etienne Dolet in the mid-sixteenth century.[59] It is in the first place dangerous to treat the Middle Ages as a monolith, in which all translators shared the same views about and competence in their activity. Their disagreements are numerous, and instructive, and increase both with the passage of time (and increase in translation activity) and the variety of texts translated. The range from interlineation to paraphrase was repeated in technical, scientific, and philosophical texts. While the change in kind from 'holy' to 'crucial' vocabulary ought in principle to be absolute, in practice the claims of the vocabulary, syntax, and word order to exact, one-for-one, same order representation, were often a matter of degree.

Texts which might be categorized as historical pose all these problems, and the range of vernacular originals which represent themselves as translations of Latin texts illustrate the same categories that I have already considered. That is, there are commentaries, which appear on the same page as the Latin text (Livy may be taken as one example), like so many of the books with which we have been concerned. There are small-unit-equivalent prose translations of single texts, which follow their originals phrase by phrase wherever possible including distortion of current target-language syntax (and allowing, as always, for anachronistic substitutions for Roman offices), there are amalgamations of a number of Latin originals in order to create a chronologically coherent narrative of ancient history (the so-called *Histoire ancienne jusqu'à César* and *Li Fait des Romains* are two of the best known of these), and there are what amount to new narratives loosely based upon classical originals. The *Romans antique: Eneas, L'Histoire de Thebes*, and Benoît's *Roman de Troie* belong in this last category. The history of the history of Troy can be taken as a supreme illustration since the fall of Troy was thought to be the beginning of European history, and a secular benchmark for subsequent chronology. From the twelfth century, too, the Trojan war became the subject of fictional expansion at French and Anglo-Norman courts, and the subsequent life of these texts, via the adaptations of Guido delle Colonne and Giovanni Boccaccio, inspired English poetry for centuries.

At the point at which we find ourselves arguing over whether to categorize Benoît's poem as 'translation' or 'adaptation', it becomes clear that in the Middle Ages the lines of distinction may have been differently or more variously drawn. Benoît used the matter of the 'histories' of Dares and Dictys as a kind of armature on which he hung expansions taken from other texts or of his own devising; *Le Roman de Troie* is thus as much like Peter Comestor's *Historia Scholastica* as it is like *Eneas*, the preceding *roman antique*. What justified his free treatment of the Latin was surely the audience for whom he was writing; it is also with works like this that we see new and newly literary texts emerging. Whether Benoît knew what he was doing, of course, we shall never know. His work was in its turn adapted, turned into prose and readapted, translated into different European vernaculars, for about two hundred years. For the most part, the audiences for his poem, or its progeny, were secular ones. But it is worth remarking that there were objections to Benoît's claim to be translating the ostensible eye-witness who had travelled to Troy to support Priam, and whose 'history', a late-classical historical romance, was often copied, and was taken at face value. Twice in the thirteenth century translations of Dares so close as to look like probable accompaniment texts were made. Jean de Flixecourt prefaced his version of 1262 with the reflection that the exigencies of rhyme may help explain Benoît's expansions:

Pour che que li roumans de Troies rime continet molt de coses que on ne treuve mie ens u latin, car chis quie fist ne peust autrement belement avoir trouvee se rime, je, Jehans de Fliccicourt, translatai sans rime l'estoire des Troiens et de Troies du latin en roumans mot a mot ensi comme je le trouvai en un des livres du libraire Monseigneur Saint Pierre de Corbie . . .[60]

The claim to translate *mot a mot* assimilates this work to the kind of accompaniment text which helped readers to deal with the difficulties of Latin. There is no claim to be making a 'literary' text which takes the liberties of a 'sense for sense' translation in order to please the non-Latinate reader. But nor is there any humble excuse for Jean's inability to translate closely. He does the job he set out to do. Jean's practice is enough like Benoît's to allow the possibility of adaptation. He occasionally remarks that expansions might be made from what can be read elsewhere than in the particular book he is writing. The other version does not indulge itself even that far.

Even positing a hard and fast divide between secular, vernacular audiences and scholarly Latin ones can raise difficulties. It happens that Benoît's poem also inspired a translation back into the learned language, by one of the members of Robert of Sicily's court. Guido delle Colonne, a judge of Messina, had written verse in the vernacular, but his prose adaptation of Benoît was in Latin. Benoît's poem formed the base for Guido's prose in much the same way that Dares had formed the source for the *Roman de Troie*. Guido's moral reflections may have seemed more elevated, more serious, than his vernacular source, but they were no more accurate as a representation of what Benoît wrote than Benoît was of Dares. Guido's critical vocabulary is an excellent indicator of his method. Modern readers, approaching Guido as a putative writer of romance, have found his authorial voice pompous and interfering, and he has been accused of plagiarizing, but in Guido's terms he is a translator who adapts a translation of Dares, and who is therefore correct in identifying his own translation as 'of Dares', however supplemented it may be by learned additions and reflections. That his version was the one most regularly relied upon by translators back into the European vernaculars is striking testimony to his success.[61] The vernacular versions represented themselves as translations of history: by contemporary standards they are, however supplemented or interpolated they may seem today. The correction of a text was anybody's concern, and what one needs to ask is what controlled the corrections. That is the point at which the translator's attitudes to his original, his audience, and his own work must be taken into account. The views engendered by a broadly rhetorical culture or education supported the practices of distinguishing what should be retained or expanded from what should be omitted on grounds of probability or utility, and of referring to the original author when in fact the actual text being studied was a translation of that author. This latter habit seems to have been reinforced by the scholarly practice of not referring to living commentators by name (and not just when one was disagreeing with them). At the same time we must not lose sight of the sheer difference made by competence, not simply of the two languages involved, but in the ability to versify or control prose.

The range of translations that I have so far looked at in this chapter raise questions of relationships to originals that are defined as relations of dependence. From the visually dependent (interlineation or gloss or marginal commentary) accompaniment translation intended for side-by-side use with the original, the new languages propose a voice in dialogue (this must, of course, include modern Latin side-by-side with classical texts). Lexical and stylistic manipulations constantly remind the reader of the status of the base text being read. Even when translated texts assume a role as substitutes they do not seem to impose themselves as texts whose actual words invite study, that is they do not presume to 'authority', to the status of being elucidatable. This tentativeness is more pronounced when the translations are themselves based upon translations; although the translators claim to represent original works, their freedom to transform the verbal unit seems potentially greater. Re-presentation in terms of conventional manipulation allows for changes, or regularly observed kinds, to be made across such apparent generic categories as historical or biographical writing (non-inspired, non-crucial-vocabulary), or romance.

There is also a perpetual tension for translators between their perception of the source meaning and the resources of the target language. Any choice excludes other possibilities. Traditional theories of word-for-word vs. sense-for-sense translation are bound to obscure some of the problems raised by the size of the unit to be translated, since size is not simply a matter of counting in words or phrases. Nor do they consider what registers exist in the target language at the time that the translation is made, or whether, at that time, the target language is provided with a history of its own which allows for reference back into archaizing registers, so that the target language itself contains resources for coinage and expression. In addition, since the time of Etienne Dolet, who first listed the prerequisites for good translation, certain expectations about the integrity of the target language have been taken for granted. There is a traditional insistence that the register of the translation must, while corresponding to the meaning and style of the original, remain nevertheless entirely consistent with the habitual expressions of the target language. This evades certain attitudes at particular historical periods toward the status of the source language and desires to augment the vocabulary or increase the syntactic potential of the target language; that is, some translators deliberately attempted to use their translations to modify the target language. Aureation, ink-horn terms, and the periodic style exemplify this tendency, and may indicate a desire to make the vernaculars as apparently timeless as Latin. Thus, the idea that a translation should be colloquial enough to avoid 'translationese' is false in two directions. First, the target language is almost always restricted from using those of its own resources which would alert the reader to its own unique characteristics. This is most striking in terms of slang, fashion, or modishness, but should also take into account aspects of social organization, geography, flora or fauna, or any of the material areas of life which would introduce either anachronism or impossible correspondence. Second, some amount of 'translationese' is of the first necessity if aspects of style (calques of lexical or phrasal equivalence, obsolete terms) are not to be lost altogether. Archaic or innovatory representations must be found or coined in order to preserve the 'referring' function of translation. The assumption that readers expect a translation to read like a primary text in their own language is a mistake; they do not.

# 5

# TEXTS AND PRE-TEXTS

## INVENTION AND REPRESENTATION

Thus far I have considered some of the varieties of medieval narrative transformation and translation, and what legitimated and controlled medieval writers' claims that their new versions were the same as, or elegant variations upon, a prior authority. These transformations have often involved a double reference: the words have represented events (or agents, or ideas) while also representing the words of some prior text or texts. That is, either the order of being prior to any verbal expression *or* the earlier words as words could be alluded to, manipulated, or transformed. In both cases, the representations discussed have depended upon certain conventional kinds of expression, *topoi* which, while apparently describing something which had happened, what someone was like, speeches that were made, could be interpreted by knowledgeable readers as conveying opinion about the status of what was represented. Categories of representation, particularly the range of historical categories for 'deeds done in the past', exploited fictional embellishments in recognizably patterned ways which make categories such as 'history' and 'fiction' less separable than they later came to seem. Medieval writers worried about the fictions contained within historical narratives, as they worried about accurate representation in their translations, but they never resolved their ambivalent and often contradictory beliefs.

They worried equally about the status of their work: did the new text demand, or might it be susceptible to, the kinds of attention to its language and its claim to be true manifested by the original text or texts? This derivativeness, this ambiguity about the text-status of the transformation, translation, or new composition, is an outstanding feature of many medieval narratives. The authority for their truth lies elsewhere. Or, at least, it appears to. The deference of narrators and translators to some prior work, some 'pre-text', is the last of the vexed categories which I shall consider. The very deference which appears tentative and humble, in practice allowed authors to exploit a rich narrative uncertainty and to create a space within which they could manipulate their true tales about the past. The conventions of narration, description, and dialogue, of argument and representation, implicated them in complex series of displacements, by which they could represent and refer without needing to assume the responsibility for their work which later came to seem necessary. Not only did intertextual reference create a dynamic relationship between present and prior texts; the addition of marginal glossing, the suggestion of a parallel narrative, changes of book-hand or type face, all contributed to the creation of dialogic commentary upon the text, sometimes questioning, sometimes supporting, but always intervening.

Medieval histories and lives are susceptible to the techniques of literary analysis, not only in so far as any text or *topos* might imitate some classical or medieval model, but also in small-scale habits of expression, which I have classed as rhetorical. Indeed, they must be so susceptible, in order to be understood. Especially where 'realistic' depiction may tempt readers to mistake plausibility for a reliable, factual, account, some sense of the tentativeness, the hypothetical nature of the narration, is a necessity. A convincing text may be a literary success, a triumph of consistency, plausibility, and style, the triumphant creation of a gifted narrator's good *ethos* rather than an exact and accurate depiction in terms consistent with the professional expectations of modern historians. The objective order of being, prior to any linguistic expression, had to be mediated by language even in those cases of direct perception open only to mystics, who could rise above verbal expression only until they wished to convey it. Being precedes text, is prior to linguistic interpretation, but verbal expression is text's only method of communication. Saying 'what happened' means 'saying'. Saying means voice, and it means order and sequence. The search for simultaneity is bound to be frustrated as long as readers can only absorb one thing at a time. Even the existence of marginal commentary or the constant interruption of certain kinds of translation cannot transcend that limitation. Banal as it is to remind oneself that words are not mathematical symbols with restricted and agreed meanings, it remains necessary. Where there is linguistic represent-ation there is room for more than one interpretation. But more than one expression could represent the same prior order of being, in − as I hope I have shown − a different level of style, or a manipulation of the kinds of things that happen in war or to saints, or by change of language by translation. Precisely in that slippage between the event and the expression of it lay the writer's

room for manoeuvre, for creation. Representation must always be an
approximation, and the authority for that representation – or those
representations – varies, too. Between the pre-text and text falls the shadow
of narrative indeterminacy.

Only biblical expression – and only, ultimately, in its original languages –
could claim complete coincidence between true event and true representation, and, as I have argued, although there could be no question about
biblical authority, its difficulties, both in terms of its textual transmission and
the mysteries its verbal texture hid, made it susceptible of multiple analysis in
ways not entirely unique. Indeed, even here the evidence of medieval
quotation, with its constant approximation and inaccuracy, suggests that
there was less care for exact replication than theory might predict. After all,
widespread misquotation of the Bible cannot be attributed simply to
widespread bad memory. The coincidence between representation and
expression in great poetry, or great history, could only be felicitous (rather
than holy), a medieval version of the best words in the best order. Human
representations of truth could not be guaranteed. The verbal expression of,
for example, Virgil, gave the *Aeneid* a different, but related, kind of status.
While it had its own *text*-authority, there could be, and were, large questions
about the truth or falsehood which lay behind Virgil's representation, and
commentators gave reasons why Virgil chose the manipulations he did. For
plots, events, historical agents, and oral traditions all carried some kind of
authority, though exactly what that authority implied was seldom directly
addressed, if only because it led to accusations that Virgil lied.

One way of dealing with these difficulties was to approach them
obliquely, to reckon upon the variety of certain possible presentations, and
thus to claim that they could be used in one of a number of different ways. As
matter for interpretation they may, but in essential ways need not, be exact
and accurate accounts of deeds actually done in the past. Aeneas (or Jason, or
Alexander the Great) and the legends – or history – which surrounded him,
could be interpreted and represented in many different styles, 'historically',
or 'biographically', in poetry or prose, as examples of how to behave (or of
what behaviour to avoid), as pretences for practice speeches, as allegory or
images for wisdom – or folly.[1] Each representation was free (within limits) to
choose among a variety of early poems and prose accounts which gave quite
different testimony to Aeneas, his deeds, and how they could be interpreted.
Indeed, so different were the versions that there was no way they could be
reconciled, no way that the pre-text could be recovered; yet the assumption

that something, and something readable, ought to have been recoverable, underlay many medieval treatments of the legends. Despite the variety of methods of interpretation which lay to hand, none of them would unlock the secret of precise correspondence to the deeds and motives of the Aeneas who once lived. And the more poets who treated of Aeneas, the greater the latitude for poetic embellishment seemed to become. Whatever the representation, medieval writers assumed reference to a known – if seldom explicitly analysed – 'Aeneas'.

The *Aeneid* was a *historical* poem, which referred to prior events, to things which had happened before the text was conceived. At the same time, in Virgil's conception of a historical *poem*, he interpreted the pre-text to embody the multiple reference of his inventions and communicate his own ideas of Rome and its destiny through Homer and *his* destiny. The mode of interpretation of a *historical poem* as 'epic' was understood after hundreds of years of imitations of and commentary upon Homer. Virgil could thus *mis*represent what he had received from earlier historical texts (such as making Dido and Aeneas contemporaries); just as famously, not only did his narrative represent historical characters and events, but the first half of his poem also referred to the literary text of the *Odyssey* as the second to the *Iliad*. As soon as the *Aeneid* was written it took its own place in the traditions of representations, and became a verbal artifact to which subsequent poems (or histories) could (and did) refer. It was the greatest secular source of, and authority for, rhetorical transformations; it was both great model text and rhetorical school.

The commentaries which 'corrected' Virgil's misrepresentations continued to offer elaborate deference to authorities which competed with his; so did other treatments of his story or his characters by other writers. The events to which the *Aeneid* referred could be the subject of narrative paraphrase, like the paraphrasal translations of the Bible discussed in the previous chapter. In the twelfth-century *Roman d'Eneas* the anonymous poet restored natural order, selected those events which accorded with his own concern with the right relations to one's polity and one's family, to war and love, and then amplified them in order to delight and instruct a secular, vernacular audience. He did not 'translate' the words of Virgil's poem, and in choosing the octosyllabic couplet, he assimilated his natural-order version to similar historical poems already familiar to his French vernacular audience.[2] In offering a redacted substitute translation, he did not replace his original; he only made some of its matter available to an audience which may

– or may not – have read Latin. Virgil's events, after all, could be extracted and discussed – as they were by John of Salisbury in his twelfth-century treatise, the *Policraticus* – for a learned Latin audience inclined to think about government and the role of the prince. In both these examples reference is directly to events, beyond Virgil's particular expression.

By contrast, one of the greatest of medieval translations, Gavin Douglas's comprehensive *Eneados* of 1513, sought to represent Virgil's words, Virgil's meaning as it had been elucidated by commentators, and Douglas's own understanding of how to read the poem, including his reservations about it.[3] In addition, Douglas intended to modify Scots English (using Chaucer's to do so), and to supply an expounding series of *accessus*, introductions to each book, which created a kind of counterpointing, an almost simultaneous voice in dialogue with Virgil and a kind of counter-poem. By adding a translation of the so-called 'thirteenth book' of Mapheus Vegius, Douglas omitted nothing traditional to reading Virgil. Within his translation he amplified in some places more than others: as one might predict, the standard *topoi* such as the great description of the storm at sea in Book VII inspired great invention by generations of imitators.

The arguments which surrounded attempts to produce some kind of substitution translation for the *Aeneid* touch most of the issues I have been considering. Above all, the *Aeneid* was taught as the secular work closest in status to the position of sacred works: its vocabulary and style, defended not only as the source of history and moral instruction, were also models of beauty. But since Virgil's version of the events at Troy was known, because of the existence of early commentaries, to be *a* version and not *the* version, there was room for revision of the events. The continuing copying of the text with its variety of commentaries supplied accompaniment texts; the same movement which led in the twelfth century to the creation of biblical translations into French also led to the *Roman d'Eneas*, and to 'epic' writing which satisfied the demand for secular history and serious entertainment.[4] The expansive vernacular inventions of the twelfth-century *Roman de Troie* were one more source text when Guido delle Colonne created his own *Historia Destructionis Troiae*, an explicitly moralized rehearsal of the story of the fall of the city in which Benoît de St. Maure (his immediate source) is never mentioned. The pre-text is potentially the whole story of the Fall of Troy and all previous treatments of it. Guido treated his vernacular source in the ways we have more commonly seen vernacular authors treating Latin sources: he discriminated examples according to his own criteria of verisimilitude and moral weight and not by comparison to other kinds of evidence for a serious historical meditation. From this widely read version descend a diverse progeny, in many European vernaculars, up to and including Shakespeare's *Troilus and Cressida*. In this genealogical tree, Chaucer's *Troilus and Criseyde* appears as a limiting case of historical translation.

The pre-text did not need to be a story as a whole, a story as already multiply represented. It could be a specific book, a linguistically represented text. To take a fifteenth-century example, Lydgate's English verse *Fall of Princes* translates Laurent de Premierfait's French translation of Boccaccio's fourteenth-century collections of Latin *exempla, De Casibus Virorum Illustrium* and *De Claris Mulieribus*. When Boccacio wrote his exemplary lives he meant them to serve moral ends as models to be imitated or eschewed. Less extended than the Encomium for Dante, they nevertheless belong in the category of works of praise and blame. Although they are taken from secular history, rather than sacred, they are historical lives, reporting what Boccaccio could discover about his subjects, that is to say, composed, perhaps compiled according to his *ingenium*, his knack for exposition, as *inventions* from the past. 'Since I have extolled with praise the deeds deserving of commendation and have condemned with reproach the crimes, there will sometimes be not only glory for the noble, but opprobrium for the wicked.'[5] The pattern is the conventional inevitability of the turning wheel of Fortune; once ambition has tempted men or women to mount Fortune's wheel, fall is unavoidable. When Laurent turned Boccaccio's Latin prose into French verse, he conflated several of Boccaccio's own works and added, according to his own invention, material which he had found elsewhere in order to amplify his model.[6] Into Boccaccio's terse Latin panegyrics and invectives Laurent inserted more material, amplifying from other historical (or pseudo-historical) sources. For example, Boccaccio allots a paragraph to the Colchian king, Aeëtes, whom he points out to the reader:

Stabet enim ante alios Aeta Colchorum rex ob insignem magnificentiam/ & diuitiarum nondum visum splendorem/ a barbaris solis creditus filius: & querula voce execrabatur/ in Colchos Thessali Iasonis aduentum: eo quod eius perfida aureum raptum sit vellus. Aegialeus filius sece flebili oppressus: & in insanam libidinem adque fugam Medea deducta: ; suum senium ex fulgore praecipuo in detestabiles tenebras deuolutum.

(There before the others stands King Aeëtes of Colchis. Because of his magnificent regalia and unprecedentedly splendid riches the barbarians thought him the son of the sun. He curses with a querulous voice that Jason of Thessaly should have come to Colchis, he by whose perfidy the Golden Fleece was stolen, Aegialeus his son mournfully cast down to die, Medea led into unclean desires and flight. And in his old age he has fallen down from the brightness he anticipated to an execrable darkness.)

(IV, p. 146)

Laurent's amplifications turn this almost iconic representation into the history of Medea's seduction and desertion by Jason, and of her murders, revenges, and eventual reconciliation to husband and father. Lydgate's rehearsal of Laurent's right so to translate and expand was quoted in the previous chapter. Where Laurent had first translated Boccaccio and then added more information, Lydgate recast the whole, so that there is only an occasional sentence which might be characterized as close correspondence to the *words* of the source text or texts. In addition, Lydgate cites classical authors he probably knew had treated Medea's story, but he did not cite Gower, his fourteenth-century predecessor, from whose (or *through* or *across* whose) citations of Ovid Lydgate may well have taken his own references, ending:

> and fynali, as writ Ovidius,
> In his tragedies makyng remembraunce,
> How Medea, lik as poetis seyn,
> Onto Jason restored was a-gayn.

> Touchyng the eend off ther furious discord,
> Poetis make theroff no mencioun
> Nor telle no mene how thei fill at accord,
> But yiff it were by incantatioun,
> which so well koude turne up-so-doun
> Sundry thunges off love & off hatreede.
> And in Bochas off hir no more I reede        (ll. 2383–94).

These amplifications nevertheless describe themselves as a translation. The multiple reference is to Boccaccio's words as conveyed by Laurent, to the historical narratives which both authors verbalize, and to the similar narratives as recorded by other authors, named or silently incorporated, which allow each new author to make of his own transformation the best equivalence, or correspondence, to past events. Re-presented in the literary/rhetorical terms and *topoi* which this book has explored, the new texts added themselves to a huge reservoir always susceptible to modification. The success of historians like Bede, and his influence on later writers, is by now a familiar example of the way that plausibility and eloquence can combine. Perhaps it will be more faithful to medieval habits of expression to think of correspondence or equivalence rather than to use that modern coinage, the seventeenth-century word, 'accuracy', which takes us back to the 'word-for-word/sense-for-sense' debate.

Multiple reference itself stimulated indeterminacies which the medieval writer could exploit. In this passage from Lydgate, poets named and unnamed become authorities to be taken, or taken issue with, or left. And where they are silent, Lydgate himself can hypothesize that some kind of magic may be the omitted explanation for the final reconciliation. Multiple reference can also help to explain why medieval authors sometimes refer to a source which they can only be reading through an unnamed intermediary: the translation of a translation may consider that its approach to the original is a kind of indirect knowledge, which resembles the indirect-knowledge saint's life quoted above in Chapter 2.

## CONVENTION AND INVENTION

What was an acceptable latitude of invention? Much must have depended upon the audience's ability to recognize allusion (either to earlier texts or the events those texts represented, or to the kinds of stylized representation I have tried to explore). Intertextuality can be a way of mediating the tensions created by a culture uncomfortable with the free-standing fiction; that is, reference to 'authority', either the authority of a particular writer or the authority of received texts, can be used to exploit that latitude. Denial of responsibility can become a way of assuming responsibility. But it can also be a way of dealing with the apparent necessity to choose between alternative, even irreconcilable, interpretations. Writers could suggest that A and not-A were authorized, or possible, and could further imply that both occupied the same space by the expedient of hypothesizing them.

No one would want to describe Chaucer's *Troilus and Criseyde* as an amplified translation so inaccurate, that is, so *bad*, as to have become an independent work. Yet that it begins as a translation, however in-etched with Chaucer's own material, must be granted. More problematic is Chaucer's attitude to its historicity, since it is also clear that his own *ingenium*

allowed him to find, amplify, and finally, to invent – in the modern sense –
many of the expansions. Although *Troilus and Criseyde* is an early example in
English of *playing* with the idea of 'authority', Italian authors such as
Boccaccio and Petrarch had played earlier in the century, hypothesizing
possible events and projecting them onto a pre-existing text, or an entirely
imagined pre-text. The insertion of a long fiction, written in middle and
high style, plausibly presented, into the historical matter of the Fall of Troy,
posed – at least in theory – both an invitation and a challenge to the medieval
author. The status of the ambitious plausible fiction was insecure; its moral
position dubious. Apparent reference to a non-existent *auctor*, Lollius,
becomes a sophisticated joke, an awareness of intertextuality in which, for
the knowledgeable, it is clear that the idea of authority is a game played for
the high literary stakes of poetic fiction, like the epic poems of Ovid, Statius,
and Virgil. Chaucer's references are in part to that poem of Boccaccio which,
although it was his major source and the basis of his translation, he never
mentions. This may itself exemplify the habits of scholarly commentators,
who did not refer by name to living or recent authorities. Were modern
editions to print the marginal glosses of medieval texts our picture of such
authority-citation might, of course, be quite different. Chaucer also refers to
the received history of the fall of the city, which he knew from a variety of
other books, from Virgil to Joseph of Exeter. His translation amalgamates
and represents many books which themselves represent what happened at
Troy. He also invented what suited him, within the generous bounds of a
historical narrative. To be more prescriptive, more exacting, about what
constitutes historical truth is to run the risk of imposing present-minded
categories (or, worse, a single present-minded definition of one thing that
counts as history) upon the range of medieval narratives which fell within
ideas of historical presentation.

   Chaucer's is one of the greatest, but by no means the first or only example,
of more or less free translations of more or less 'literary' texts. Bearing in
mind attitudes encouraged by the demands of other kinds of texts, with
other kinds of authority, the varieties of audience for whom translations
were made, and, above all, the changes that came simply with the passage of
time, it is possible to speculate about how the play of authority might have
made a space which writers could exploit in order to make room for their
own inventions. Attitudes to the original language, or languages, to be
translated changed, as did attitudes to the vernaculars into which the works
were introduced; we saw Cicero's confidence that Latin could emulate

Greek and make Roman culture equal Athens'. The argument, the competition, between the Ancients and the Moderns is always with us, and different prejudices and expectations were expressed by medieval translators and emulators of greater and less confidence in their activity. Above all, we must take into account the increased confidence that came with the passage of time and the increase in translation activity, not in any particular European vernacular, but in them all as models for each other. While 'more' does not necessarily mean 'better', 'more' is at least a legitimation and a spur.

From the fabulous, strictly defined, one can move toward the social and political criticism of the later branches of the Renart-cycle. One must say that parody is perhaps the most instant of literary reactions, and that the extension of subject is always with us. This suggests that even in the most apparently free fiction there are constraints upon the teller. Beast fables depend upon known matter conventionally interpreted, but that includes issues of surprise, in which both matter and interpretation are used in new ways. To put such characters or plots to new uses, crossing or mixing genres and styles, follows from wide understanding of old ones; new interpretations also modify those previous ones by changes of emphasis which come from alterations of style, arrangement, omission and expansion. By the late Middle Ages many of the animals have characters, and those characters restrain authors who retell or invent their inventions: foxes are clever and lions are kings of beasts, whoever the author. Among the most self-conscious and yet implicit fabulists, such as Robert Henryson, the major modification could be interpretative: by changing the *moralitas* so that it cannot be deduced from the narrative, Henryson asserted quite startling readings of his own otherwise traditional *narrationes*. This unexpected and unanticipatable allegory is a confident invitation to meditation, an invitation continually misunderstood, even suppressed, by his editors, who deleted sometimes the morality, sometimes the text.[7] For such authors what appears to begin as a reflex of modesty may be an assertion of something else.

To look back towards, even beyond, the authority of the source text, or texts, to the things, events or ideas represented in them, to consider what was represented by the languages in which the prelinguistic realities were expressed, then forward to the new audience addressed and the context of contemporary literary language, may seem not only to belabour the obvious, but to take the activity far beyond the obvious into another category yet it is precisely by assessing such relationships that I have proceeded throughout this book. For while the habits of transformation themselves became precedents which legitimated, or at least encouraged, similar treatments of existing texts, they could also provoke reactions *against* transformations perceived as beyond some undefined boundary. Some authors clearly wanted their representations to correspond as exactly as possible to the text which was their source. 'Translation' that was close and accurate was one possible transformation – but only one. At the other extreme rhetorical habits of thought encouraged new versions of old stories, either from the past, or from the thesaurus of stories. The freest fiction might be thought of as the non-verisimilar, but, as with the comparison of infinities, there is an argument that insists that one fiction is as fictional as any other.

There may be implicit signals to help the reader recognize what kind of fiction is being presented and how to read it. The inclusion of planetary gods might be thought of as a way of insisting that a fiction is non-verisimilar (and therefore not a historical re-presentation which claims to correspond to the *res gestae*, the deeds actually done in the past). Henryson's own reinterpretation, re-presentation, of the story of Troilus and Criseyde involved him in an explicit questioning of Chaucer's ostensibly historical depiction: he asks who knows whether or not Chaucer's version was true, yet alludes to his own, non-existent, textual authority for another way of telling the tale. What it is he re-presents is a fiction's relation to another fiction, where both are implicated in true tales about the remote past. The characters peripheral to the main action are the ones most likely to be developed, to tempt authors to create new adventures. The invented descendants of Aeneas who founded the European nations are a 'historical' example of a phenomenon which multiplied the kin and adventures of numerous Arthurian or Carolingian heroes.

> Quha wait gif all that Chauceir wrait was trew?
> Nor I wait nocht gif this narratioun
> Be authoreist, or fenȝeit of the new
> Be sum poeit, throw his inuentioun
> Maid to report the lamentatioun
> And wofull end of this lustie Creisseid,
> And quhat distres scho thoillit, and quhat deid.[8]

(Who knows if all that Chaucer wrote was true? Neither do I know if this narration was authorized, or newly imagined by some poet, made according to his invention to report the lament and sorry end of this lusty Cressid, both what misery she suffered and what she did.)

Implied in his choice of English vocabulary are the rhetorical labels *inventio*, *narratio*, and *planctus* (the name of a particular kind of lament) which function, like Lydgate's defence of Laurent de Premierfait's transformations, to legitimate his own fiction (a word he is the first to employ in an English poem). Henryson seems to feel no need to identify – even in pretence – the book or the language of the book from which he supposedly found his own alternate tale. He shows all the knowledgeable alertness to classical literature which liberated medieval authors to try their own hands at serious fiction. Yet liberation had to fly in the face of strong traditional arguments which disapproved such creation: that such creations are a large part of medieval writing confirms the diversity of available practice, whatever the ostensible cultural prescriptions against the free-standing verisimilar fiction.

Some of the examples discussed in previous chapters as rhetorical transformations of historiographical works crossed boundaries of language as well as of form and style. Although questions of competence arose, they were mostly questions of interpretation in the mediating sense of how the sources were understood and for what audience they were rewritten. In representing true tales about the past, including truly exemplary lives, what we might think of as the 'unit of translation' was understood to be the events themselves, the *res gestae*. This immediately modifes the authority of any exemplar, because its truth, its reliability, its authority, could be transferred beyond the pre-text incidental to transmission. That is, any interpreter could project authority beyond, or behind, the particular account to some – even some hypothesized – earlier account. Even when the original author was of the highest human status (i.e. not the Bible), he would not thereby confer upon his text the sense of crucial vocabulary, nor respect for preserving that text as intact as translation might allow. When the history represented by the Bible could be redacted by paraphrase, where events not expression were transmitted, to be turned into poetry and drama in medieval Latin or the European vernaculars, it becomes hard to recognize the new works as translations at all, because they are not necessarily translating the words, but the things represented by the words. A new kind of replacement text, for audiences incapable of direct contact with difficult originals, presents itself humbly, but still powerfully, as a representation of original events. Quite how that relation was constituted, redactors tended to leave undefined. Perhaps they themselves did not distinguish translation of the text-as-words from translation of the deeds-in-text. Tight correspondence almost necessarily depends not only upon reading, but upon a kind of accompaniment reading which is perpetually aware of the status of the words as translations, where constant reference to another language, if not specifically to the original text, can be made. Hearing (sometimes simultaneously seeing) was a different experience, and encouraged looser correspondence. The uses to which biblical historical material was put, from homily to heroic poetry, all modified the source expression, and many modified the source details, while claiming to preserve the essence.

It is time to make some allowance for incompetence and misreading. In saying this, it must also be understood that there are competent misreadings as well, where authors take what they want, or what they need, or what they think their audiences want or need, from an original text. At times it must be at least difficult, and occasionally impossible, to tell. Why did Marie de France cite an English Alured (Alfred) as the 'auctor' of her *Fables*? Was she erecting a protective screen for a woman who dared to write? If the same woman translated both the 'Espurgatoire St Patrice' and the 'Vie Ste. Audree' (Etheldreda of Ely), she was as capable of close linguistic correspondence as was Robert Wace – at will. She may also have been capable of using that same screen to defend her adaptations or inventions of Breton *lais* for her own new poems. The misrepresentation of a new text as a translation also has a claim to be considered. When Marie, in turn, became a source for translation, we find that the English and Old Norse versions are quite different from her originals. The précis of her plots which are all the Old Norse translator provided suggest this same attitude to a text as representing deeds or events which could be extracted. Much the same could be said of the Middle English 'Sir Launfal' or 'Sir Landevale', which are usually dismissed as mere popular performance material. We cannot tell if the translators saw themselves as simplifying, or manipulating in any conscious way, Marie's tales; what we do see is that turning verse into verse implies (but does not necessitate) some degree of care for the words into which the translation was put.

Here we see emerging that category of re-usable plots which is so important throughout the period, where the *Gesta Romanorum* is deliberately presented like the basic material for a rhetorical exercise of *amplificatio*, ostensibly for preachers, or, in the fourteenth century, the re-usable plots (John Bromyard's *Summa Praedicantium* might be another example) that were collected, pre-eminently by Boccaccio in Italy, but also in England by Gower and later Lydgate, as in France by Marguerite of Navarre. The distinction between translation of the words and re-presentation of the story is not in theory hard to see. Yet explaining what has become of the meaning would tax any historian or philosopher, especially in the face of the same, often-repeated prefatory statements about translation being a matter of either word-for-word or sense-for-sense. Translations are usually pendant texts, whatever our attitude to the truth-status of their contents. What they represent may be a text, or what comes prior to the text, or an amalgamation of a combination of texts, or an interpreted amplification of some kind of combination.

### TRUTH AND CONVENTION

Is there any check upon the hypotheses explored in the previous chapters which can be supplied from within medieval culture itself? I have already alluded to the importance of consulting the modes of expression manifested in legal and medical treatises. This impossible programme of comparative reading is at least a reminder that modern professional categories require constant testing. Let me end by proposing an area where intertextuality, narrative indeterminacy, range of authority, and play, sheer pleasure, intersect. Where text achieves voice is in music. That multiple interpretation was understood and used with humorous effect for sophisticated audiences who shared certain interpretative assumptions can be illustrated from the motet tradition of medieval song. By the thirteenth century it was fashionable in art-song to bring together independent tunes whose lyrics offered different versions, even competing visions, and sing them simultaneously, usually over a tenor line sung in Latin, often using a well-known tune from the chant repertory (that is, liturgical music). A French 'courtly' text could be sung at the same time as a low-style text, so that each offers its own vision, and, by offering it, also contradicts the apparent exclusivity of the paired text. Further, and to understand and situate the humour, the audience must not only supply, from their extended knowledge of liturgical music and text, the Latin lines alluded to by the tenor part, they must also recognize that the attitudes represented by the vernacular texts offer competing interpretations of the world which need not be resolved. That is, interpretation does not favour one version over another so much as recognize that the existence of each modifies the other. In the following, relatively simple example, at least three things are happening. Three melodies are sung at once: the tenor sings 'Ite Missa Est', the closing lines of the mass ('go, the mass is finished') while two equal French parts offer two different scripts of a pastourelle encounter, a standard poem-subject in which a noble man attempts (sometimes successfully, sometimes not) to seduce a peasant woman.

| | |
|---|---|
| L'autre jour par un matinet \| | Hier matinet |
| m'en aloie esbanoiant \| | trouvai sans son bercheret |
| et trouvai sans son bercheret \| | pastoure esgaree. |
| pastoure plaisant \| | A li vois ou prajolet, |
| grant joie faisant. \| | si l'ai acolee. |
| Lés li m'assis mout liement, \| | Arriere se traist |
| s'amour li quis doucement. \| | et dist: 'j'aim mieus Robinet, |
| Ele dist: 'Aymi! Sire, j'ai ami \| | qui m'a plus amee.' |
| bel et joli a mon talent: \| | Lors l'embrachai; |
| Robin, pour qui refuser \| | ele dist 'Fui de moi!' |
| voell toute autre gent. \| | Mes onc pour ce ne laissai. |
| Car je le voi et bel et gent \| | Quant l'oi rigotee, |
| et set bien muser, \| | s'mour mi pramet |
| que tous jours l'amerai, \| | et dit: 'Sire, biau vallet, |
| ne ja m'en partirai'. \| | plus vous aim que Robinet'. |

(The other day in the morning I went out wandering and I found without her shepherd (boy) a pleasing shepherdess showing great joy. I sat down beside her happily and sweetly asked for her love. She said, 'Alas, my lord, I have a handsome and cheerful friend who suits me, Robin, for whom I want to deny all other men. Because I see him as so handsome and kind, and knowing so well how to play the bagpipes, I shall love him forever and never leave him.'

Yesterday morning I found a shepherdess wandering without her shepherd. I approached her in the pasture and embraced her. She pulled back and said, 'I love Robinet better who has loved me more.' Then I kissed her; she said, 'Leave me alone!' – but I didn't let go for all that. When I had played with her she promised me her love and said, 'My lord, fair young man, I love you more than Robinet'.)

This kind of collusive, jokey, narrative indeterminacy suggests at least two possible interpretations, indeed, by giving two versions of the encounter from the same point of view (the young nobleman) in the same vocal register, it insists that we not choose between them. It implies an art-song audience, familiar enough with both the musical and the poetic contexts to enjoy complex references which play upon numerous conventions at once. This simultaneity achieves in music what even the most dialogic of sequential text presentations – even texts plus commentary – can only suggest.[9]

The reclassification of translations according to multiple reference, of translation to original text, as well as to the material represented by that text, and the expectations the authors could have for the intertextual awareness of the audience, has cut across the usual genre boundaries. It is consistent with the theme of this book that modern categories like 'history' or 'biography' or 'literature' (even its subsection, 'poetry') may subtly mislead us when modern readers attempt to understand the ostensibly true representations of pre-modern authors. Modern concepts like 'fact' and 'accuracy' need to be handled with care. The 'romans antique', like the histories of Wace and La3man with which this book began, claimed to be translations of history. They appear to be neither and both. This is perhaps easiest to see where classical historical myths, legends, and epic poems are the subject, but the implications for more contemporary historical subjects should also be considered. It was not just such European heroes as Arthur, Charlemagne, and Godfrey of Boulogne who enjoyed the transformations which the rhetorical embellishments of history invited. The panegyrics of Commynes or Froissart, or the invectives of the historians of Richard II or Richard III, combine the modern categories of fictional and historical representation in ways which make 'accuracy' problematic.

For one thing, in looking at historiographical conventions we were looking at ways of representing what had happened and at the ways rhetoric suggested manipulations of those representations. Translations claim not only to convey a true report of those things represented, but also aspects of the representation: form, content, and style. In the very act of claiming that they transmit the same prelinguistic core of reality, they enshrine through their acts an awareness of translating a certain distance from the source. Where they concentrate upon style, even if they admit defeat in the attempt to reproduce it, they turn attention to language itself. The constant effort of evocation by loan-words, doublets, manipulation of syntax, which remind the reader of the work's status as translation, turned attention from the thing expressed to the expression itself, and in the course of constant interruption modifed the new language by increasing its vocabulary, changing its style registers, and adding to its own ability to allude to earlier texts. Authors translate, but they also pose as translators in order to escape the problem of authority. Indeed, it could be argued that the daring innovations of the *romans antique* entirely failed to establish the precedent of the historical fiction as an accepted genre, and that they inspired, at two removes, Gavin

Douglas's fierce denunciations of Caxton's translation of the French prose summary of the twelfth-century *Roman d'Eneas*, which offered itself as a version of the *Aeneid*. Douglas's own practice, of course, however astringent his theories, found ways of making contemporary poetry around Virgil's model. At the same time, perhaps, in countless other studies scattered across Europe, other scholars were concentrating on making what would become something historical around that, and similar models. Within Douglas's own lifetime men like Polydore Vergil were beginning to doubt in public the historicity of the myths after Troy which had given nominal founders to the countries of Europe. They expressed their doubts in terms which changed the textual discourse of the Middle Ages, slowly (and not − or not immediately − as completely as they claimed) but in the end irrevocably. For, after all, the sixteenth century saw that masterpiece of vituperative anti-encomium, More's *Richard III*, and the recrudescence of rhetorical study encouraged historians as diverse as John Hay or Edward Hyde to imitate Latin models. The end of the Middle Ages − whenever that is deemed to be − involved the attempt to except some writers, poets or historians, depending on one's point of view, from the great mass of Gothic scribblers condemned for credulity, misrepresentation, and superstition. The Renaissance − whenever that may be deemed to have begun − also marks the beginning of forgetting how to read medieval texts.

The reacquisition of medieval habits of reading and writing can look like a Reconquista, but it can also appear to be just one more reconstruction of the past in our own image, or images. Of the painful awarenesses I mentioned at the outset of this book, one which remains to haunt its ending is an undeniable air of historical revisionism from one point of view, of canon-bashing from another. That medieval historians wrote fiction, that modern literature schools neglect medieval Latin and vernacular historians, seem to me unavoidable conclusions which thrust upon students of the Middle Ages demands which threaten − if pushed to an extreme − to collapse the difference between two healthy modern specialisms. I have not intended to argue for the discovery of 'factions' *avant la lettre*, nor to assert that no medieval historian is ever trustworthy, but to refocus the questions that we ask of such authors, such works. The limits of such ambitions have perhaps best been dramatized by the puzzle explored in Borges' short story, translated as 'Pierre Menard, author of *Don Quixote*'. In it Borges describes the way that Pierre Menard recreates, and rewrites, word-for-word, the text of Cervantes' *Don Quixote*, but because Menard's re-invention occurs three

hundred years after the original, his text cannot be identical with Cervantes',
because by now the Don has an existence of his own, more complex than the
book which once contained him. In this most intriguing of his *Ficciones*,
Borges has moved straight to the conundrum of any study of a past as distant
from us as the Middle Ages, a past which has been a palimpsest for western
culture for hundreds of years.

# NOTES

## 1 MEANING AND MEANS

1 This story is the subject of a number of studies: R. R. Bolgar, *The Classical Heritage and its Beneficiaries* (Cambridge, 1973); Fritz Saxl, *A History of Images* (London, 1970); Jean Seznec, *The Survival of the Pagan Gods* (NY, 1953); E. Panofsky, *Renaissance and Renascences in Western Art* (London, 1965) and *Studies in Iconology* (NY, 1962), intro. I shall return to some of the examples first studied by Erich Auerbach in *Literary Language and its Public in Late Latin Antiquity and in the Middle Ages*, trans. R. Manheim (Princeton, 1965). My debt throughout to Auerbach and to E. R. Curtius, *European Literature and the Latin Middle Ages*, trans. W. R. Trask (Princeton, 1963) will already be obvious. Detailed research into the history of rhetoric is in its infancy, but two collections indicate the current state of knowledge: *Medieval Eloquence: Studies in the Theory and Practice of Medieval Rhetoric*, ed. J. J. Murphy (Berkeley, 1978) and his companion volume, *Renaissance Eloquence* (Berkeley, 1983).

2 The phrase translates 'un horizon d'attente' of Hans Robert Jauss, 'Littérature médiévale et théorie des genres,' *Poétique* (1970), 79–101.

3 See Wayne Booth, *The Company We Keep* (New Haven, 1988) for a recent discussion of these problems. Defining need not delimit; innovations could be the reciprocal gift of succeeding cultures, as the Roman sense of satire as peculiarly *theirs* testifies to emulation, but also satisfaction.

4 Aristotle's *Rhetoric* is only one of many texts to open with a rehearsal of this assumption. Brian Vickers's *In Defence of Rhetoric* (Oxford, 1988) traces the debates over the ethical value of Rhetoric as a subject from the earliest attacks onwards.

5 The distinct shortage of educated women was partly due to the belief that Rhetoric was too powerful a tool to be put into frail hands. The pretence of the *public* nature of oratory as taught in the schools and practised in courts, was an obvious bar to participation in public life or high literary culture. This reinforced the view that women were incapable of rational thought or educated expression, and, concomitantly, the assumption that educated values were in essence masculine. A number of recent studies of medieval culture have addressed themselves to these issues, e.g. *Medieval Women Writers*, ed. K. M. Wilson

(Manchester, 1985); Peter Dronke, *Women Writers of the Middle Ages* (Cambridge, 1984).

6 Quintilian, *Institutio Oratoria*, ed. H. E. Butler (Cambridge, Mass., 1958–60). And for medieval knowledge of his work, P. S. Boskoff, 'Quintilian in the Middle Ages', *Speculum* 27 (1952), 71–8. For good introductory surveys of rhetorical literature see George A. Kennedy, *The Art of Persuasion in Greece* (Princeton, 1963) and *Rhetoric in the Roman World* (Princeton, 1972). M. L. Clarke, *Rhetoric at Rome* (London, 2nd ed. 1966) and *Higher Education at Rome* (London, 1971).

7 Aristotle's use of 'pathetic' in the epigraph to this book exemplifies this line of argument. The *declamationes* of the schoolroom were speeches performed in order to move in similar ways, and the preposterous 'laws' which lay behind the 'controversiae' and 'suasoriae' survived to provide plots for hundreds of years. See The Elder Seneca, *Controversiae* and *Suasoriae*, ed. Michael Winterbottom (Cambridge, Mass., 1974). Authors as diverse as the anonymous compiler of the so-called *Gesta Romanorum* and the French Romance-writer Mme de Scudéry pillaged these exercises for their own stories. The closeness between the schoolroom and the theatre, that is, the plots of New Comedy, tells us something about imaginative association.

8 Questions of oracy and literacy have concerned classical scholars of epic as well as anthropologists, and recent work suggests that writing cultures co-exist with oral cultures for a long time before the conventions of oral presentation are entirely superseded. The work of Jack Goody has been crucial: *The Logic of Writing and the Organization of Society* (Cambridge, 1986) and *The Interface between the Written and the Oral* (Cambridge, 1987). Paul Zumthor, *La Poésie et la Voix dans la civilization médiévale* (Paris, 1984).

9 Seneca's plays remained a pre-eminent source for the study of the effects of the passions; whether or not they were meant to be acted, they could be studied as examples of the high rhetorical style. That they continued to move their audiences is clear. Good translations of Seneca's plays have begun to appear and *therefore* to challenge the assumption that high rhetoric cannot move, and finally to counter T. S. Eliot's dismissal of hundreds of years of appreciation. See, for example, A. J. Boyle, *Phaedra* (Liverpool, 1987) and *Troades*, in *Imperial Latin Poetry*, ed. A. J. Boyle and J. P. Sullivan (Harmondsworth, 1991), which contains translations of Ovid, Statius, and other important Silver Latin poets.

10 In *De Copia Rerum ac Verborum* (Paris, 1512, but constantly expanded). The English translation, by D. B. King and H. D. Rix (Milwaukee, 1963) is abridged, and does not contain the variations: 'Tuae literae me manopere delectarunt' (your letters gave me great pleasure, 150 different ways) and 'Semper dum vivam tui meminero' (I shall remember you for the rest of my life, 200 different ways). The only modern equivalent is restricted to lexis, i.e. word choice: the thesaurus.

Although I did not see A. Grafton and L. Jardine's *From Humanism to the Humanities* (London, 1986) until this book was nearly completed, I was encouraged by their willingness to examine what actually took place in the classroom. On medieval education, see Nicholas Orme, *English Schools in the Middle Ages* (London, 1973) and his 'The Education of the Courtier', in *English Court Culture in the Later Middle Ages*, ed. V. J. Scattergood and J. W. Sherborne (New York, 1983). For an assessment of Carolingian use of Donatus and the advent of Priscian see Rosamond McKitterick, *The Carolingians and the Written Word* (Cambridge, 1989), ch. 1.

11 Marcia Colish, *The Mirror of Language* (2nd ed. Lincoln, Nebraska, 1983) deals in detail with the theory of language which this implies. On modistic logic see below, Chapter 4, note 2.

12 For a consideration of the traditions of epic in France, see William Calin, *A Muse for Heroes: Nine Centuries of the Epic in France* (Toronto, 1983).

13 For such surveys see, in addition to the texts cited above, n. 6, D. L. Clark, *John Milton at St Paul's School: A Study of Ancient Rhetoric in the English Renaissance* (NY, 1948); W. S. Howell, *Logic and Rhetoric in England, 1500–1700* (Princeton, 1956) and his *Poetics, Rhetoric and Logic: Studies in the Basic Disciplines of Criticism* (Cornell, 1975), ch. 2; T. W. Baldwin, *Shakespeare's Small Latin and Less Greek* (London, 1944)). C. S. Baldwin's *Medieval Rhetoric and Poetic* (London, 1928; repr. Gloucester, Mass., 1949) is still valuable. For a more recent overview, with detailed bibliographies, see *The Present State of Scholarship in Historical and Contemporary Rhetoric*, ed. W. B. Horner (Columbia and London, 1983), esp. ch. 3, by James J. Murphy.

14 Roger Ray, 'Bede and Cicero', *Anglo-Saxon England* 16 (1987), 1–15; his 'The Triumph of Greco-Roman Rhetorical Assumptions in the Pre-Carolingian History', in *The Inheritance of Historiography 350–900*, ed. C. Holdsworth and T. P. Wiseman (Exeter, 1986), pp. 67–84; Paul Mayvaert's collected essays, *Benedict, Gregory, Bede, and Others* (London, 1977); R. R. Bolgar, ed., *Classical Influences on European Culture A. D. 500–1500* (Cambridge, 1971).

15 Gordon Leff, *Paris and Oxford Universities in the Thirteenth and Fourteenth Centuries: An Institutional and Intellectual History* (NY, 1968). Many of these texts are collected in C. Halm, *Rhetores Latini Minores* (Leipzig, 1863), R. W. Hunt, 'Studies on Priscian in the Eleventh and Twelfth Centuries', *Medieval and Renaissance Studies* 1 (1941–2), 194–231 and (1950), 1–56. Priscian, *Institutio de arte grammatica*, ed. M. Hertz as vols. 2 and 3 of *Grammatici Latini*, ed. H. Keil (Leipzig, 1885–90). Donatus, *Ars Minor*, trans. W. J. Chase (Madison, 1926) and see the editions of Sedulius Scottus' commentaries ed. B. Löfstedt, *In Donati artem minorem, In Priscianum, In Eutychen* and *In Donati artem maiorem* (Turnhout, 1977). Martianus Capella, *De Nuptiis Philologiae et Mercutii*, ed. A. Dick, rev. J. Préaux (Stutgard, 1969) and trans. W. H. Stahl and R. St. C. Johnson (NY, 1977) and

their *Quadrivium* (NY, 1971). Cassiodorus, *Institutiones*, ed. R. A. B. Mynors (Oxford, 1937) and trans. *An Introduction to Divine and Human Readings*, L. W. Jones (NY, 1946). The contradictions which the texts inculcate are the subject of Wesley Trimpi, 'The Quality of Fiction: The Rhetorical Transmission of Literary Theory', *Traditio* 30 (1974), 1–118. On Merovingian and Carolingian lay literacy see McKitterick, *The Carolingians*, ch. 6.

16 See Natalie Zemon Davis, *The Return of Martin Guerre* (Harmondsworth, 1985), esp. the plate p. xiv. This text allows its author a dialogue (in the notes) with his own, apparently more 'factual' report, thus creating a voice which questions along the way.

17 *Serviani in Aeneidem, Editio Harvardiana* vols. 2, 3 (Lancaster, Penn. and Oxford, 1946, 1965); *Servii Grammatici*, ed. G. Thilo (Leipzig, 1878–83). Modern editions do not, of course, reproduce the simultaneous presentation of text and commentary which created, for earlier ages, the sense of voices in dialogue. See below, Chapter 4.

18 Ed. J. Willis (Leipzig, 1963) and *I Saturnali di Macrobio Teodosio*, ed. and trans. N. Marinone (Turin, 1967) and trans. Percival Vaughan Davies, *The Saturnalia* (London, 1969).

19 *Commentarii in Somnium Scipionis*, ed. J. Willis (Leipzig, 1963–70) and trans. W. H. Stahl, *Commentary on the Dream of Scipio* (2nd ed. NY, 1966). See Pierre Courcelle, *Les Lettres grecs en occident de Macrobe à Cassiodore* (Paris, 1943) and his 'La Postérité chrétienne du *Songe du Scipion*', *Revue des Études latines* 36 (1958), 205–34 and H. Silvestre, 'Survie de Macrobe au Moyen Age', *Classica et Medievalia* 24 (1963), 170–80.

20 Bede, for example, cites the Bible throughout his introductory textbook, *De schematibus et tropis* in about 700 A.D. Translation by G. H. Tanenhaus in *The Quarterly Journal of Speech* 3 (1962), 237–53 and excerpts in *Readings in Medieval Rhetoric*, ed. J. M. Miller, M. H. Prosser, and T. W. Benson (Bloomington, Indiana, 1973). Bede follows the order established by Donatus but changes the content of the examples. See also Curtius, *European Literature*, p. 46.

21 In the Old Testament, during the Exodus from Egypt, the fleeing Israelites are described as taking jewels and precious metals from their former masters (12.35). By putting their spoils to better, holier, use, their theft of 'Egyptian gold' was justified. So, Augustine argued, Christian writers are to be trained in classical rhetoric by which he still understands a curriculum in persuasive oratory in order to transmute this 'Egyptian gold' into a more holy word. They will take over pagan learning and redirect it to the great use of man's salvation, by creating a style and content of writing which will preserve the arguments of Christianity in forms that will appear to the highest level of literary sophistication. *De Doctrina Christiana*, ed. J. Martin (Turnhout, 1962). Translation by D. W. Robertson, Jr, *On Christian Doctrine* (NY, 1958). See especially Peter Brown, *Augustine of Hippo* (Berkeley, 1967), ch. 23 on Augustine's eloquence as a late-classical phenomenon.

22  On Theodulus see Helen Cooper, *Pastoral: Medieval into Renaissance* (Ipswich, 1977), I.i; *The Parisiana Poetria of John of Garland* is edited and translated by Traugott Lawler (New Haven, 1974), see esp. ch. 7. For the later tradition, beginning with Petrarch, see Annabel Patterson, *Pastoral and Ideology: Virgil to Valéry* (Oxford, 1988).

23  Peter Dronke, *Fabula: Exploration into the Uses of Myth in Medieval Platonism* (Leiden, 1974); Paule Démats, *Fabula: Trois études de mythographie antique et médiévale* (Geneva, 1973), ch. 1; Jill Mann, *Ysengrimus* (Leiden, 1987), intro.

24  E. Panofsky, *Renaissance and Renascences in Western Art*, esp, ch. 2.

25  *The Commentary on the First Six Books of the Aeneid Commonly Attributed to Bernard Silvestris*, ed. J. W. Jones and E. F. Jones (Lincoln, Nebraska, 1977), pp. 2–3; trans E. Schreiber and R. E. Maresca (Lincoln, Nebraska, 1979); and C. Baswell, 'The Medieval Allegorization of the "Aeneid": MS Cambridge, Peterhouse 158', *Traditio* 41 (1985), 181–237. And see B. Stock, *Myth and Science in the Twelfth Century: A Study of Bernard Silvester* (Princeton, 1972); W. Wetherbee, *Platonism and Poetry in the Twelfth Century* (Princeton, 1972), pp. 104–25. For Boccaccio, see *Genealogie Deorum Gentilium Libri*, ed. Vincenzo Romano (Bari, 1951); the last book was translated by Charles C. Osgood as *Boccaccio on Poetry* (NY, 1930). For the aesthetic categories see Edgar de Bruyne, *Études d'esthétique médiévale* (Bruges, 1946).

26  Rosamond Tuve studies the allegory of the *Ovide Moralisé* in her *Allegorical Imagery* (Princeton, 1966), ch. 4. Meg Twycross, *The Medieval Anadyomene: A Study in Chaucer's Mythography* (Oxford, 1972) considers this tradition as it affected Chaucer.

27  Quoted from *The Metamorphoses of Ovid: Translated by William Caxton 1480*, (New York, George Braziller in connection with Magdalene College, Cambridge, 1968), vol. I, ff. 13r–14r. I have punctuated and lightly modernized the orthography. Caxton gives us, incidentally and by the way, the distinctions between such different ways of writing as history and fable or poetry, and genres such as poetry, philosophy, and politics.

28  *Saturnalia*, trans. Davies, pp. 256–7. My emphases.

29  John of Salisbury, *Metalogicon* 1.24 and see R. W. Hunt, *The Schools and the Cloister* (Oxford, 1984), esp. ch. 3. G. R. Owst, *Preaching in Medieval England* (Cambridge, 1926) and *Literature and Pulpit in Medieval England* (2nd ed. Oxford, 1933) looks in detail at the religious material.

30  For the medieval Cicero see E. K. Rand, *Cicero in the Courtroom of St Thomas Aquinas* (The Aquinas Lecture 1945) (Milwaukee, 1946); Cicero includes 'Cicero', believed to have written the *Ad Herennium* as, for example, Mary Dickey, 'Some Commentaries on the *De Inventione* and *Ad Herennium* of the Eleventh and Early Twelfth Centuries', *Mediaeval and Renaissance Studies* 6 (1968) 1–41; Harry Caplan, *Of Eloquence: Studies in Ancient and Medieval Rhetoric* (Ithaca and London, 1970); J. O. Ward, 'The Date of the Commentary on Cicero's *De*

*Inventione* by Thierry of Chartres (*c.* 1095–1160?) and the Cornifician Attack on the Liberal Arts', *Viator* 3 (1972), 219–73. An adaptation of *De Inventione* is translated as *The Rhetoric of Alcuin and Charlemagne*, W. S. Howell (Princeton, 1941). In the tenth century Richer reports that his own teacher, Gerbert, employed a 'sophista' to teach eloquent debate, and there is no reason to doubt that some kind of Christian declamation is meant, but what that implies about tenth-century schools education is not clear. See Auerbach, *Literary Language and Its Public*, p. 168.

31   A manuscript in the Hunterian Library survives in which Latin poems interspersed with rhetoric texts illustrate the precepts described in the handbooks. See *A Thirteenth Century Anthology of Rhetorical Poems*, ed. Bruce Herbert (Toronto, 1975); James J. Murphy, *Medieval Rhetoric: A Select Bibliography* (Toronto, 1971); his *Rhetoric in the Middle Ages: A History of Rhetorical Theory from Saint Augustine to the Renaissance* (Berkeley, 1974). See also *Readings in Medieval Rhetoric*, ed. J. M. Miller, M. H. Prosser, T. W. Benson (Bloomington, 1973). In the Middle Ages the *ars dictaminis* become popular; see James R. Banker, 'The *Ars Dictaminis* and Rhetorical Textbooks at the Bolognese University in the Fourteenth Century', *Medievalia et Humanistica* 5 (1974), 153–68 which considers commentaries on the *Ad Herennium*, and Q. R. D. Skinner's discussion of the contents of such letters in his *The Foundations of Modern Political Thought* (2 vols., Cambridge, 1978), ch. 2. For the Renaissance, see Grafton and Jardine.

32   *Disticha Catonis*, ed. M. Boas (Amsterdam, 1952); a late Middle English dual language edition printed by Caxton is *Parvus Cato Magnus Cato*, ed. F. Kuriyagawa (Tokyo, 1974). And see Nicholas Orme, *English Schools in the Middle Ages* (London, 1973), esp. ch. 3; J. O. Ward, 'From Antiquity to the Renaissance: Glosses and Commentaries on Cicero's *Rhetorica*', in *Medieval Eloquence*, pp. 25–67.

33   Quoted from Helen Waddell, *Medieval Latin Lyrics* (London, 1929), pp. 188–91. And see Hunt, *Schools and Cloister*, pp. 4708 for Alexander Nequam's use of Cato in his Bible commentaries.

34   Caxton's translation, now available as a children's book, *Aesop's Fables: In William Caxton's Original Edition*, ed. B. and C. Gascoigne (London, 1984), was from a Dutch version. L. J. Hervieux, *Les Fabulistes latins d'Auguste à la fin du Moyen Age*, 5 vols. (Paris, 1893–9), e.g. Odo of Cheriton, vol. IV; Ben Edwin Perry, *Aesopica* (London, 1952) and *Babrius and Phaedrus* (Cambridge, Mass., 1965); see also H. J. Blackham, *The Fable as Literature* (London, 1985), esp. ch. 2 for a survey of the literature based on the earlier studies. Marie de France, *Fables*, ed. and trans. Harriet Speigel (Toronto, 1987), has a useful introduction, as has Mann, *Ysengrimus*. Dual language texts (Greek/Latin) of Aesop were early staples of humanist presses. See Grafton and Jardine, *Humanism*, p. 111. Preaching collections, like John Bromyard's *Summa Praedicantium* of the fourteenth century, often contained fables as exempla for the use of preachers.

35  *The Poems of Robert Henryson*, ed. Denton Fox (Oxford, 1981).

36  *The Complete Poems*, ed. R. A. Rebholz (Harmondsworth, 1978).

37  La Fontaine, *Selected Fables* (London, 1979).

38  Not only can there be simultaneous multiple interpretation because of audience, but the inverse also exists, with similar complexities. The allegorical sermon told by Chaucer's Pardoner exemplifies (among other things) the good argument put into the mouth of a good orator who is a bad man. The use to which the Pardoner puts his rhetorical skill is both good (because it moves men to repentance) and bad (because he uses their repentance to cheat them). Literature is more complex than rhetoric textbooks.

39  As in Aristotle, *Rhetoric*, 1393b–94a; Quintilian 1.9, v.11, 22; cp. John of Garland v (esp. p. 100); for the renaissance e.g. Francis R. Johnson, 'Two Renaissance Textbooks of Rhetoric: Aphthonius' *Progymnasmata* and Rainolde's *A Book called the Foundacion of Rhetoric'*, *Huntington Library Quarterly* 6 (1942–3), 427–44. Rainolde is available in a Scolar Press facsimile: *The Foundation of Rhetoric* (Menston, 1972).

40  Beryl Smalley's famous work on the ways that late-medieval scholars found ways to sneak their classical learning into their work is a classic: *English Friars and Antiquity in the Early Fourteenth Century* (Oxford, 1960).

41  See Hunt, *School and Cloister*, pp. 40–1. And see Cooper, *Pastoral: Medieval into Renaissance*, pp. 27ff.

42  In Roman schools these exercises led to practice *declamationes*, where 'laws' were invented to create extravagant situations for apprentice pleaders to practise their skills. The Elder Seneca is supposed to have collected, from his memory and experience of these school 'cases' and famous speeches by well-known rhetoricians, moving and persuasive examples. Ed. Michael Winterbottom, *Controversiae* and *Suasoriae* (Cambridge, Mass., 1974). See also Janet Fairweather, *Seneca the Elder* (Cambridge, 1981) and S. F. Bonner, *Roman Declamation in the Late Republic and Early Empire* (Liverpool, 1969) and his *Education in Ancient Rome* (London, 1977).

43  See, for example, O. B. Hardison, 'The Place of Averroes' Commentary on the *Poetics* in the History of Medieval Criticism', *Medieval and Renaissance Studies* (1968), 57–81; J. R. O'Donnell, 'The Commentary of Giles of Rome on the Rhetoric of Aristotle', in *Essays in Medieval History Presented to Bertie Wilkinson*, ed. T. A. Sandquist and M. R. Powicke (Toronto, 1969); Judson Boyce Allen, *The Ethical Poetic*; T. P. Wiseman, *Clio's Cosmetics: Three Studies in Greco-Roman Literature* (Leicester, 1979), ch. 1; Pierre Hadot, *Marius Victorinus* (Paris, 1971). Victorinus expanded the application of rhetorical *narratio* to history.

44  This example is expanded from a hint in C. S. Lewis's *Studies in Medieval and Renaissance Literature* (Cambridge, 1966), p. 26. For a detailed study of Wace's manipulations, see M. Houck, *Sources of the Roman de Brut of Wace* (Berkeley, 1941), esp. ch. 2. For Wace's redactive translations see below Chapter 4. For longer and more complex examples of rhetorical reinterpretation, see below.

45  See *The Historia Regum Britannie of Geoffrey of Monmouth*, ed. N. Wright
    (Cambridge, 1985), p. 113. On Geoffrey's rhetorical expansions see V. I. J. Flint,
    'The Historia Regum Britanniae of Geoffrey of Monmouth: Parody and its
    Purposes', *Speculum* 54 (1979) and Wiseman, *Clio's Cosmetics*, ch. 1.

46  *La Partie arthurienne du roman de Brut*, ed. I. D. O. Arnold and M. M. Pelan (Paris,
    1962), pp. 96–7. The poem, finished about 1155, led to a historical continuation,
    the *Roman de Rou*, written between 1160 and 1174, but never completed. Wace
    stresses his learning throughout his works, as well he might.

47  Laȝamon, *Brut*, ed. G. L. Brook and R. F. Leslie (London, 1978), p. 650–1. The
    punctuation follows the earlier edition, *Selections from Laȝamon's Brut*, ed. G. L.
    Brook (Oxford, 1963), pp. 103–4.

48  The young Macaulay 'vigorously oppos[ed] in a school debate the removal of the
    seat of the ancient Roman government from Rome to Vei; and address[ed] an
    appeal to the people of Travancore to embrace the Christian religion', records
    Macaulay's sister in a letter. This exercise survived in English schools as part of the
    training of the young men who were to run the Empire. John Clive, *Thomas
    Babington Macaulay* (London, 1973), p. 24.

49  T. Wilson, *The Art of Rhetoric*, ed. G. Mair (Oxford, 1909).

50  Robert Greene, *The Carde of Fancie* in *Shorter Novels: Elizabethan and Jacobean*, ed.
    Philip Henderson (London, 1929), p. 199.

51  See M. Lapidge, 'Gildas's Education and the Latin Culture of Sub-Roman
    Britain', in *Gildas: New Approaches*, ed. M. Lapidge and D. Dumville
    (Woodbridge, 1984), pp. 27–50, for the structure of *De Excidio Britanniae* as a
    demonstrative oration. Equally little known is John Rainolde's *Oratio in Laudem
    Artis Poeticae[circa 1572]*, ed. W. Ringler and W. Allen, Jr (Princeton, 1940).

52  The importance of imaginative writers to the advancement of rhetoric was
    remarked by Aristotle, *Rhetoric* III.i.8–9: 'The first improvement in style was
    naturally made by the poets; for words are instruments of imitation, and the
    voice is the most imitative of all our organs. Thus the arts of recitation, the art of
    acting, and more besides, were formed.' (trans. Jebb).

53  See O. B. Hardison, Jr, *The Enduring Monument: A Study of the Idea of Praise in
    Renaissance Literary Theory and Practice* (Chapel Hill, 1962).

54  Malory, *Works*, ed. Eugene Vinaver (Oxford, 1971), p. 725.

55  Quintilian, *Institutio Oratorio*, 2.1.10, 2.4.1–4, 4.2.116–20. Forensic narrative
    theory is discussed by Bonner, *Education*, pp. 261–3, 291ff. For the movement of
    the rhetorical *narratio* into historical writing see Wiseman, *Clio's Cosmetics*, ch. 2.

56  Quintilian, *Institutio Oratorio*, 4.2.88–100, 2.17.26–8.

57  On the importance of the digression to medieval historians see Bernard Lacroix,
    *L'Historien au Moyen Age* (Montreal and Paris, 1971), pp. 125–9; And see Faral,
    *Les Arts Poétiques*, p. 73; Lawler's edition of John of Garland, pp. 73–5; Michael
    Lapidge, in *Gildas*.

58 On Digression see F. W. Walbank, *Polybius* (Berkeley, 1972), pp. 46–8.

59 On plausibility see Cicero, *De Inventione 1.21.29, Ad Herennium 1.9.16, Quintilian, Institutio Oratoria*, 2.4.2–3 and Victorinus (in Halm, *Rhetores Latini Minores*, pp. 206–7).

60 Collected by C. Halm, *Rhetores Latini Minores*. The 'sentences' in printed editions of plays were often set in italic type, perhaps both as self-advertisement and defence, showing how moral they really were, how ambitious their authors.

61 'Quis, quid, ubi, per quos, quotius, quibus auxiliis, cur, quomodo, quando', are the questions confessors are instructed to ask, and this list is preserved throughout the Middle Ages. For its history and circulation, D. W. Robertson, Jr, 'A Note on the Classical Origin of "Circumstances" in the Medieval Confessional', *Studies in Philology* 43 (1946), 6–14. John of Salisbury emphasizes their importance to rhetoricians in the *Metalogicon* 1.3; see discussion in Roger Ray, 'Rhetorical Scepticism and Verisimilar Narrative in the *Historia Pontificalis* of John of Salisbury', in *Classical Rhetoric and Medieval Historiography*, ed. E. Breisach (Kalamazoo, Michigan, 1985), pp. 61–102. Further on 'conditions', see A. Minnis, *Medieval Theory of Authorship* (2nd ed. Aldershot, 1988), ch. 1.

62 Robert Greene, *The Carde of Fancie*, pp. 166–7.

63 This kind of psychomachia, or inner struggle over a decision, reached an apogee of expressive economy in French classical drama, where the soliloquy allows hero or heroine to articulate turmoil between honour and love, revenge and magnanimity. The point about time is an important one, because dramatic time is swifter, due to the exigencies of performance, than romance time, where the reader can pause at will. The application of dramatic time to the romance, which we see in the prose of Cervantes, Behn, Marivaux, or Fielding, transformed the way we habitually read, and has also made us impatient.

64 Brian Vickers, *In Defence of Rhetoric*.

65 Sister Joan Marie Lechner, *Renaissance Concepts of the Commonplace* (NY, 1962). Chapter 1 contains copious examples of classical definition and example.

66 The king then goes on to quote Euripides (in Latin translation). Thomas Gainsford, *The History of Perkin Warbeck* (London, 1618), pp. 51–2.

67 Character and expression appropriate to character will receive more attention below, Chapter 3. See also my 'Temperamental Texts: Medieval Discussions of Character, Emotion, and Motivation', forthcoming.

68 For a history of *encomium* more comprehensive than its title suggests, see O. B. Hardison, Jr, *The Enduring Monument: A Study of the Idea of Praise in Renaissance Literary Theory and Practice* (Chapel Hill, 1962).

69 Thomas Malory, *Works*, pp. 648–9. For an unusually complex example which illustrates the creative uses to which rhetorical armatures could be put, see the discussion of the pattern of *comparatio* which underlies and informs the historical narrative comparing the characters of Gilbert of Poitiers and Bernard of

Clairvaux in Ray, 'Rhetorical Scepticism'; Faral, *Les Arts Poétiques*, p. 69. On the use of a comparison (to the lilies of the field) in the *Glossa Ordinaria* see G. Evans, *The Mind of Bernard of Clairvaux* (Oxford, 1983), p. 73. In all these cases there is a possibility that only one of the terms is present, and the reader or audience are expected to recognize and supply what it is being compared to.

70　Lisa Jardine, *Francis Bacon* (London, 1974).

71　Julius Caesar Scaliger, *Poetices libri septem* (1561), ed. A. Buck (Stuttgart, 1964), and *Select Translations from Scaliger's Poetics*, F. M. Padelford (NY, 1905), discussed J. E. Spingarn, *A History of Literary Criticism in the Renaissance* (NY, 1899); Bernard Weinberg, *A History of Literary Criticism in the Italian Renaissance* (2 vols., Chicago, 1961), II.743–50; the notes to Geoffrey Shepherd's edition of Sidney's *Apology for Poetry* (London, 1965) give numerous examples of these exercises. For John of Garland, see Lawlor's edition, pp. 73, 75–7, 133 and Faral, *Les Arts Poétiques*, pp. 75–83. Grafton and Jardine, *Humanism*.

72　In *Les Arts Poétiques du XIIe et du XIIIe siècle*, ed. Ed Faral (Paris, 1971).

73　Grafton and Jardine cite a similar use of Niobe in *Hamlet, Humanism*, pp. 197–8.

74　Erich Auerbach, *Mimesis*, trans. W. R. Trask (Princeton, 1968), ch. 2.

75　This lexical imitation has often been condemned as rote copying, especially in lyric poetry, where stock phrases abound. In English, in the fifteenth and early sixteenth centuries, there is evidence that Chaucer provided vernacular writers with a style-standard which they memorized and used for their own compositions. New words, small phrases, collocations of images taken from Chaucer's poetry reappear in the poetry of his imitators. For detailed studies of this influence, see *Chaucer Traditions*, ed. R. Morse and B. A. Windeatt (Cambridge, 1990).

76　*The Poetical Works of Edmund Spenser*, ed. J. C. Smith and E. de Selincourt (Oxford, 1912), *The Shepheardes Calender*, pp. 430, 433.

77　Not that there was a single word or phrase that corresponds to our 'fiction'. 'Effictiones' or 'fabulae' carried negative, or at least potentially derogatory, connotations.

## 2　THE MEANING OF THE PAST

1　The closeness of historian and poet as fabricators is a problem frequently referred to, e.g. Aristotle, *Poetics*, 9.1451b, esp. on Epic 23.1459b; Cicero, *De Legibus* 1.1.14 and *Ad Familiares* 5.12.3, discussed at length in Michel Rambaud, *Ciceron et l'histoire romaine* (Paris, 1953); Horace, *Ars Poetria* e.g. 119ff; Quintilian, *Institutio Oratoria* 10. See also Pierre Grimal, 'Le Poète et l'histoire', *Entretiens Hardt* 15 (1968), 51–106, 108–17; T. P. Wiseman, *Clio's Cosmetics: Three Studies in Greco-Roman Literature* (Leicester, 1982); and, magisterially, F. W. Walbank's J. L. Myres Memorial Lecture, 'Speeches in Greek Historians' (Oxford, n. d.).

2 Dionysius of Halicarnassus, 'Letter to Pompey' in *Three Literary Letters*, ed. and trans. W. Rhys Roberts (Cambridge, 1901), pp. 88–127. There are important implications about genre here, since the style of history might (as Pliny insisted) at times resemble poetry or theatrical production. I discuss this at greater length in '"This Vague Relation", Historical Fiction and Historical Veracity in the Later Middle Ages', *Leeds Studies in English* 13 (1982), 85–108, citing Julian the Apostate's disgust with fictions told in the guise of history.

3 See, for example, R. R. Bolgar, *The Classical Heritage and its Beneficiaries* (Cambridge, 2nd ed., 1973). On the influence of Augustine, H.-I. Marrou, 'Saint Augustin, Orose, et l'augustinisme historique', *La Storiografia alto Medievale* (Spoleto, 1970), pp. 59–87. R. W. Southern's four presidential addresses to the Royal Historical Society form a survey of the medieval material: 'Aspects of the European Tradition of Historical Writing', *Transactions of the Royal Historical Society* 20 (1970), 173–96; 21 (1971), 159–79; 22 (1972), 159–80; 23 (1973), 243–63. Bernard Guenée, *Histoire et culture historique dans l'Occident médiévale* (Paris, 1980) and his *Politique et Histoire au Moyen Age* (Paris, 1981) addresses many of these problems.

4 Many historians accept this as 'chivalrous history' or history 'written with romance values', and think no more of it. John Taylor, *English Historical Literature in the Fourteenth Century* (Oxford, 1987) would be a recent example. Antonia Gransden's indispensable *Historical Writing in England*, 2 vols. (London, 1974, 1982) maps the terrain but limits itself to noticing the literariness of the examples. So similarly V. H. Galbraith, *Historical Research in Medieval England* (London, 1951) and Denys Hay, e.g. 'History and Historians in France and England during the Fifteenth Century', *Bulletin of the Institute of Historical Research* 35 (1962), 111–27.

5 Gransden, vol. I, pp. 215, 237, 273.

6 See M. I. Finley, 'Myth, Memory, and History', *History and Theory* 4 (1964–5), 281–302.

7 The Church's claim to power stemmed from a supposed gift by the first Christian Roman Emperor; the demonstration that the document was a forgery was one of the successes of renaissance scholarship; see, for example, R. R. Bolgar, *Classical Heritage*, p. 271; Joseph M. Levine, *Humanism and History: Origins of Modern English Historiography* (Ithaca, 1987), esp. ch. 1. On the new emphasis on literal meaning and the philological analysis of Roman law, see Donald R. Kelley, 'Legal Humanism and the Sense of History', *Studies in the Renaissance* 13 (1966), 184–99.

8 A. Momigliano, 'The Place of Herodotus in the History of Historiography', repr. in his *Studies in Historiography* (NY, 1966), pp. 127–42. *The Inheritance of Historiography, 350–900*, ed. C. J. Holdsworth and T. P. Wiseman (Exeter, 1986), esp. pp. 6–84.

9 Quintilian, *Institutio Oratoria*, x.

10 *Letters and Panegyricus*, v.viii and vii.xxxiii, ed. and trans. Betty Radice (Cambridge, Mass., 1969), pp. 356–63 and 558–63. A. N. Sherwin-White analyses this discussion in his *The Letters of Pliny: A Historical and Social Commentary* (Oxford, 1966), esp. p. 334 on ii.5.5–6. Also H. W. Traub, 'Pliny in Epistolary Form's Treatment of History', *Transactions and Proceedings of the American Philological Association* 86 (1955), 221 n. 27 on the influence of Quintilian and p. 220 on the possibility that the letter to Titinius Capito itself imitates a similar discussion in Cicero.

11 As by Moses Finley in *The Ancient Greeks* (Harmondsworth, 1966), p. 14 or Nancy Streuver in *The Language of History in the Renaissance* (Princeton, 1970), p. 24. Other influences upon late-classical historians must be taken into account: Sidonius Apollinaris declined to write history because 'to tell lies is disgraceful, to tell the truth dangerous'. See *Poems and Letters*, ed. and trans. W. B. Anderson (Cambridge, Mass., 1965), p. 148. It is too easy to impugn the honesty of the so-called 'tragic historians'; they sought to write histories which would move and persuade their audiences. This did not necessarily involve distortion of the past in order to misrepresent.

12 Some useful introductions to ideas of history include T. D. Kendrick, *British Antiquity* (London, 1950); Bernard Guenée, 'Histoires, annales, chroniques: Essai sur les genres historiques au Moyen Age', *Annales* 28 (1973), 997–1016 and his collection of essays, *Le Métier d'historien au moyen âge: études sur l'historiographie médiévale* (Paris, 1977); J. O. Ward, 'Classical Rhetoric in the Writing of History in Medieval and Renaissance Culture' in *European History and its Historians*, ed. F. McGregor and N. Wright (Adelaide, 1977); Roger Ray, 'Medieval Historiography Through the Twelfth Century: Problems and Progress of Research', *Viator* 5 (1974); *The Writing of History in the Middle Ages: Essays Presented to Richard William Southern*, ed. R. H. C. Davis and J. M. Wallace-Hadrill (Oxford, 1981), which contains an outstanding essay by Maurice Keen. For an interesting analysis of the word 'history', see K. Keuck, *Historia. Geschichte des Wortes und seiner Bedeutungen in der Antike und in den romanischen Sprachen* (Munster, 1934). Two more recent collections of essays contain helpful material: *The World of John of Salisbury*, ed. Michael Wilks (Oxford, 1984) and *Ideal and Reality in Frankish and Anglo-Saxon Society*, ed. Patrick Wormald (Oxford, 1983) (J. M. Wallace-Hadrill *Festschrift*).

13 On the exemplar theory from the mid sixteenth to the mid eighteenth centuries see George A. Nadel, 'Philosophy of History before Historicism', *History and Theory* 4 (1964), 291–315. He might have included Julius Caesar Scaliger or Sir Philip Sidney in his list of theorists. For a wider discussion than the title suggests: Peter von Moos, 'The use of Exempla in the *Policraticus* of John of Salisbury', in *The World of John of Salisbury*, pp. 207–61.

14 *The History of Rome by Titus Livius*, trans. W. M. Roberts (London, 1912), pp. 1–2. An early sixteenth-century Scots translation is in effect closer to Livy than this modern one, as well as being more oriented towards the moral/oratorical values I have been stressing: 'And þocht sic thingis (as bene schewin afore þe begynnyng of rome or sen It was biggit) be decorit mare be poeticall fabillis þan ony Incorruppit testimoniall of trew historiis, ʒit þe samyn are nouthir to be affermit nor reprevit be ws; for sic thingis suld be perdonit be ressoun of þare antiquiteis . . . Bot ʒit, in quahatsumeuir way thir and sic opiniouns are considerit or belevit, we hald þame of litil forss. Now euery redare gif his mynde with vehement attendance to knaw quhat maneris has bene afore this tyme amang þe romanis, be quhat pepill, be quhat crafty Ingynys, þe empire of romanis has be conquest and ekit baith in were and pece to þir daʒis . . . ʒit ane thing sall be richt hailsum & proffitable to þe þat happynnys to haue cognicioun of þis historie, seing þe documentis of sa mony Illuster and nobil exemplis as ar colleckit here togiddir vnder ane historie, quarethrow 8ow may do grete commodite baith to þi self & commoun wele, sum tymes lerand sic doctrynis as þow may vse eftir in þi life, And sum tymes lerand to eschew all thingis quhilkis has baith ane schamefull begynnyng & ane schamefull ending.' *Livy's History of Rome: The First Five Books Translated into Scots by John Bellenden (1533)*, ed. W. A. Craigie, STS (Edinburgh, 1901), I, pp. 8–10. Higden presents similar reports and disclaimers in his *Polychronicon* (I.i).

15 Marilyn Bendena, *The Translations of Lucan and their influence on French Medieval Literature, together with an edition of the Roumans de Jules Cesar by Jacos de Forest*, unpubl. dissertation (Wayne State University, 1976). R. W. Hunt, *The Schools and the Cloister*, p. 48. And see Gransden, *Historical Writing in England c. 550 to c. 1307* (London, 1974): Gildas (p. 5), Walter Map (pp. 243–4), Nicholas Trivet (pp. 279–80). Pierre Grimal, 'Le Poète et l'histoire', *Entretiens Hardt* 15 (1968), 51–106 and discussion 108–17, considers the *Pharsalia* and its influence, as does V. B. M. Marti, 'Tragic History and Lucan's *Pharsalia*', *Studies Ullman* (London, 1964) 1.165–204. For Sallust see for example Beryl Smalley, 'Sallust in the Middle Ages', in *Classical Influences on European Culture A. D. 500–1500*, ed. R. R. Bolgar (Cambridge, 1971), pp. 165–75; Robert Latouche, 'Un imitateur de Salluste au Xe siècle: l'historien Richer', *Annales de l'Université de Grenoble* n. s. 6 (1929), 289–306. Guibert of Nogent's description of the torturer Thomas de Marle is explicitly associated with Sallust on Catiline. See Benton, *Self and Society*, ch. 11. And for his eclipse in popularity at the end of the period, when Tacitus replaced him, see Peter Burke, 'A Survey of the Popularity of Ancient Historians, 1450–1700', *History and Theory* 5 (1966), 135–52. Myron P. Gilmore perhaps overestimates the innovations of the Renaissance, but see his 'The Renaissance Conception of the Lessons of History' in *Facets of the Renaissance*, ed. W. K. Ferguson (NY, 1959) and 'Fides et Eruditio: Erasmus and the Study of History' in *Teachers of History*, ed. H. Stuart Hughes et al. (Ithaca, 1954), pp. 9–27.

16 Roger Ray, 'Bede, the Exegete, as Historian', in *Famulus Christi: Essays in Commemoration of the Thirteenth Centenary of the Birth of the Venerable Bede* (London, 1976), pp. 125–40. See also his 'Bede's *Vera Lex Historiae*', *Speculum* 55 (1980), 1–21. Bede may have recorded the common report, but he seems to have disinguished the belief of the vulgar from that of the learned. This further suggests that the range of representation was met by a range of interpretation. See Paul Meyvaert, 'Bede the Scholar', in *Famulus Christi*, pp. 40–69, esp. n. 65. See also Peter Hunter-Blair, 'The Historical Writings of Bede', *La Storiografia altomedieavale* (Spoleto, 1970), I.197–221 and C. N. L. Brooke 'Historical Writing in England between 850 and 1150' in the same volume pp. 223–47. And Higden marked his own additions with an 'R' (see Prologue, pp. 20–1).

17 'Ad hanc formam praecipue pertinet schema [dialogismos], id est, serminocinatio, quoties uniquique sermonem accommodamus, aetati, generi, patriae, uitae[,] instituto, animo, moribusque congruentem. Nam huiusmodi sermones in historia licet affingere. Vnde tot Thucydidis, Salustii, Liuii, orationes effinguntur & epistolae & apophthegmata. Demum & cogitationes, ueluti hominis secum loquentis, quanquam hoc poetis familiarius.' *De Duplici Copia verborum ac rerum* (3rd edition, with Erasmus' final revisions, Basel, 1540). Erasmus, *De Copia*, translated King and Rix (Milwaukee, 1963), p. 53. Erasmus is one of many to insist that the characterizations enshrined in older texts must be respected, so that Odysseus remains wily. See also Janet A. Fairweather, 'Fiction in the Biographies of Ancient Writers', *Ancient Society* 5 (1974), 231–75. *A Thirteenth Century Anthology of Rhetorical Poems: Glasgow MS Hunterian V.8.14*, ed. Bruce Harbert (Toronto, 1975) contains some medieval examples.

18 Peter Burke, *The Renaissance Sense of the Past* (London, 1969) perhaps over-emphasizes the homogeneity of medieval response, but the description of Petrarch's questioning is unmatched. And see his 'Tacitism', in *Tacitus*, ed. T. A. Dorey (London, 1969). This is why medieval rhetoricians identify the historical as a style common to Tragedy, Comedy, and the Church. I have dealt with some of these issues in '"This Vague Relation"'. And see F. W. Walbank, 'History and Tragedy', *Historia* 9 (1960), 216–34.

19 The problems of combining the different claims of history, law, and philosophy are discussed in Donald R. Kelley, 'The Development and Context of Bodin's Method' in *Jean Bodin: Proceedings of the International Conference on Bodin in Munich* (Munich, 1973), pp. 123–50 where the scholastically trained lawyer approached as his 'Method of History' the art of extracting lessons. See also, on François Hotman and François de Mézeray, George Huppert, 'The Trojan Franks and their Critics', *Studies in the Renaissance* 12 (1965), 227–41; and his *The Idea of Perfect History* (Urbana, 1970).

20 Cicero's earliest exposition, in *De Inventione* I.xix, includes events which are *supposed* to have occurred.

21 F. P. Pickering, *Augustinus oder Boethius* 2 vols. (Berlin, 1967, 1976); H-I Marrou, 'Saint Augustin, Orose, et l'augustinisme historique', *La Storiografia altomedievale* (Spoleto, 1970) 1.59–87. On Isidore see further Lacroix, *L'Historien*, ch. 3.

22 *M Iuniani Iustini Epitoma Historiarum Philippicarum Pompei Trogi*, ed. F. Ruel, O. Seel (Stuttgart, 1972); trans. and revised in Elizabethan London by Arthur Goldyng (1564, 1570). *Justin, Cornelius Nepos, and Eutropius*, trans. J. S. Watson (London, 1897).

23 Ed. L. F. Flûtre and K. Sneyders de Vogel (Paris, 1937–8). See also Flûtre's *Li Fait des Romains dans les littératures française et italienne du XIIIe au XVe siècle* (Paris, 1932). Paul Meyer's 'Les Premières Compilations françaises d'historie ancienne', *Romania* 14 (1885), 1–81 is still useful. Modern editions which extract such works from their manuscript contexts ignore information about interpretative expectations. Commentaries, associated texts, and style of presentation all convey information. A survey from the German point of view is *Geschichtsschreibung*, ed. Jürgen Scheschkewitz (Dusseldorf, 1968).

24 For surveys of the historiography of Troy see Jacques Perret, *Les Origines de la légende troyenne en Rome* (Paris, 1942); his conclusions are not now thought to be correct, but his survey of the material is excellent; and my *The Legends of Jason and Medea*, unpubl. Ph.D. dissertation (Cambridge, 1978), ch. 2, pp. 36–7 nn. 25–9. For English Troy books, C. David Benson, *The History of Troy in Middle English Literature: Guido delle Colonne's 'Historia Destructionis Troiae' in Medieval England* (Woodbridge, 1980). For Spain, J. N. Hillgarth, 'Historiography in Visigothic Spain' *Storiografia altomedievale* 1 (1970), 261–311 and Ian Michael, *The Treatment of Classical Material in the Libro de Alexandre* (Manchester, 1970), esp. ch. 7.

25 Ben Edwin Perry, *The Ancient Romances* (Berkeley, 1967).

26 See the examples quoted in Omer Jodogne, 'La Naissance de la prose française', *Bulletin de l'Académie Royale de Belgique* 49 (1963), 296–308. Everyone agrees that verse requires some liberties with the material in order to fit its metre, though no one says quite why those liberties should include pure invention; nor does anyone point out the logical fallacy that even if verse is less accurate than prose that doesn't make prose accurate per se.

27 See May McKisack, *Medieval History in the Tudor Age* (Oxford, 1971); F. J. Levy, *Tudor Historical Thought* (San Marino, Calif., 1967). Eye-witness accounts had a particularly high status, though that did not protect them from rhetorical expansion, as the use of Dares and Dictys shows. The differences between them were not only a matter of degree. Epic poetry embraced gods as well as men; history tended to be more restrained. William Nelson, *Fact or Fiction: The Dilemma of the Renaissance Storyteller* (Cambridge, Mass., 1973) discusses some of these problems from the viewpoint of the writer of fictions.

28 Discussed by T. A. Shippey in his *Old English Verse* (London, 1972), pp. 185–7, with examples of other historical poems, mainly *encomia* on dead kings. Some of

the uses made of what must have been pre-existing poems were the opposite of the original intention to celebrate; Shippey remarks the pleasure poets or historians sometimes feel in the sudden downfall of the great.

29 The poem, from MS. Cotton Cleopatra c.iv. fol. 24r, names some of the nobles who fought on either side, in rhymed alliterative stanzas. See *Political Poems and Songs relating to English History*, ed. Thomas Wright (London, 1861) II.123–7. A brief extract appears below.

30 *Flowers of History*, ed. and trans. C. D. Yonge (London, 1853), II. 230, s.v. 1244.

31 Above, pp. 68–9. Gainsford introduces parallels to classical authors throughout his narrative, with no sense of anachronism, nor any worry that he is quoting Greek tragedians in Latin translation. The lessons are there, and the comparisons point them. That one of his English models is John Hayward, whose use of Tacitus is well-known, further identifies his intellectual lineage, Cp. *The First Part of the Life and Raigne of King Henrie IIII* (London, 1559).

32 *Flowers of History*, s. v. 1264, p. 418.

33 Gervase of Canterbury, *Historical Works*, ed. W. Stubbs (London, 1879–80) (R. S.). On the genres of history see Bernard Lacroix, *L'Historien au Moyen Age* (Montreal and Paris, 1971), ch. 1, esp. pp. 58–9, 71–3; B. Guenée, *Histoire et Culture Historique*, ch. 5.

34 This is one of the theses of George Steiner's *After Babel* (London, 1975). And see below Chapter 4.

35 The adventures of Hercules in Burgundy included an encounter with a legendary Burgundian princess; hence the Ducal house named Hercules among its ancestors. See my *Legends of Jason and Medea*, ch. 5.

36 *Historia Destructionis Troiae*, ed. N. E. Griffin (Cambridge, Mass., 1936) and trans. M. E. Meek (Bloomington, Indiana, 1974).

37 *Radulfi de Diceto Decani Londiniensis Opera Historica* ed. W. Stubbs (London, 1876) (R. S.) See Gransden, vol. 1, pp. 187, 259–60, 273.

38 On the growth of ambition generally, see Alexander Murray, *Reason and Society in the Middle Ages* (Oxford, 1978).

39 See my 'Medieval Biography: History as a Branch of Literature' in *The Modern Language Review* 80 (1985), 264–5.

40 See Donald R. Kelley, 'Clio and the Lawyers: Forms of Historical Consciousness in Medieval Jurisprudence', *Medievalia et Humanistica* n. s. 5 (1974), 25–50.

41 Roger Ray, 'Rhetorical Scepticism and Verisimilar Narrative in the *Historia Pontificalis* of John of Salisbury', in *Classical Rhetoric and Medieval Historiography*, ed. E. Breisach (Kalamazoo, Michigan, 1985), pp. 61–102. See further R. M. Thomson, 'John of Salisbury and William of Malmesbury: Currents in Twelfth-Century Humanism', in *The World of John of Salisbury*, ed. M. Wilks (Oxford, 1984), pp. 117–25.

42 *The Historia Novella by William of Malmesbury*, ed. K. R. Potter (Edinburgh and

London, 1955), p. 1. Now see Rodney Thomson, *William of Malmesbury* (Woodbridge, 1987), esp. Part 1 and ch. 7. This is not an announcement of objectivity, but a promise of a literary panegyric. What the editors take to be fair-minded praise of King Stephen (section 465) is, by the nature of encomiastic rhetoric, oblique criticism. There is no reason to suppose that the liveliness of William's style guarantees the truth of his depictions.

43  Eric Christianson, 'The Place of Fiction in Saxo's Later Books', in *Saxo Grammaticus: A Medieval Author Between Norse and Latin Culture* (Copenhagen, 1981), pp. 27–37 analyses the rhetorical schemes Saxo used to organize his inventions. Biblical exegetes sometimes taught their students to use the rhetorical categories they had memorized at school to classify, for example, types of prophecy. See *CHB*, pp. 173, 207. For Robert Wace's sources and imitations in the *Roman de Rou*, see the edition by A. J. Holden (Paris, 1970–3), III, pp. 99–168.

44  FitzStephen also claims that there were public *disputationes* of a classical, secular, rhetorical nature in his London. See William's 'Descriptio nobilissimae civitatis Londoniae' where the classical allusions and quotations include Virgil, Ovid, Persius, Martial, Lucan, Cicero, and, most frequently, Horace. There is evidence that John of Salisbury participated in *controversiae*. See J. O. Ward, '*Artificiosa eloquentia* in the Middle Ages', (unpub. Ph.D. diss., U. of Toronto, 1972) quoted by Ray, 'Rhetorical Scepticism'. For FitzStephen, see *Materials for the History of Thomas Becket* (London, 1877), R. S. vol. III, pp. 2–5 and F. Barlow, *Thomas Becket* (London, 1986). Dominic Mancini praised London, where he was only a diplomatic visitor: *The Usurpation of Richard III: Dominicus Mancinus ad Angelum Catonem De Occupatione Regni Anglie Per Ricardum Tercium Libellus*, ed. and trans. C. A. J. Armstrong (Oxford, 1969).

45  *Imagines Historiarum*, Rolls Series i p. 291. Alcuin's praise of York in the preface of his history of its abbots similarly belongs to the *encomium urbis*.

46  John T. Appleby, *Chronicle of Richard of Devizes* (London, 1963), pp. 64–5 *Gesta Stephani*, ed. K. R. Potter, new introduction and notes by R. H. C. Davies (Oxford, 1976), Chapter 16 contains a description of Exeter. Coggeshall's description of Constantinople is similarly derivative, *Chronicon Anglicanum*, ed. J. Stevens (London, 1875) (R. S.).

47  G. H. T. Kimble, *Geography in the Middle Ages* (London, 1938); Mary B. Campbell, *The Witness and the Otherworld* (Ithaca, 1988) contain useful surveys.

48  Lucan may also be behind the banquet at sea described by William of Poitiers. *Histoire de Guillaume le Conquérant*, ed. R. Foreville (Paris, 1952).

49  Explored at length by Robert W. Hanning, *The Vision of History in Early Britain: from Gildas to Geoffrey of Monmouth* (NY, 1966).

50  To her edition of Orderic, *The Ecclesiastical History of Orderic Vitalis* (Oxford, 1969–80) can now be added Marjorie Chibnall, *The World of Orderic Vitalis* (Oxford, 1984), and her *Anglo-Norman England* (Oxford, 1986).

51  As e.g. Higden's *Polychronicon*, ed. Churchill Babington, Rolls Series vol I (London, 1865), I.x (Paradise), I.xxvii (Poitou and Aquitaine on the authority of Isidore). John Taylor, *The Universal Chronicle of Ranulf Higden* (Oxford, 1966), ch. 3. Higden's *Ars Componendi Sermones*, ed. Margaret Jennings (Leiden, 1983), proves his rhetorical learning and commitment.

52  J. J. N. Palmer, 'The Authorship, Date, and Historical Value of the French Chronicles on the Lancastrian Revolution', *Bulletin of the John Rylands Library* 61 (1978), 145–81 and 398–421 discusses the problems this raises for modern historians.

53  Editions of Froissart are complex because he kept on revising his work. The only 'complete' modern edition is still *Oeuvres*, ed. Kervyn de Lettynhove (Brussels, 1870–7), but see the important *Chronique: Début du premier livre (dernière redaction)*, ed. G. T. Diller (Geneva, 1972). I quote from *The Chronicle of Froissart translated out of French by Sir John Bourchier, Lord Berners*, intro. W. P. Ker (6 vols. London, 1901); references are to book, chapter, and then pages of this edition: III.80, p. 451. (Oxford, 1927–8) Richer has a dialogue like this in which a wicked councillor attempts to persuade his king, Louis IV, to order a murder, *Histoire de France*, ed. Latouche, pp. 210f. Jean Frappier analysed similar techniques in Villehardouin in *Bulletin of the John Rylands Library* 30 (1946), pp. 9–11 and at length in 'Les Discours dans la chronique de Villehardouin', in *Etudes Romanes dédiées à Marion Roques* (Paris, 1946), pp. 39–55.

54  Arguments on this issue include P. F. Ainsworth, 'Style direct et peinture des personnages chez Froissart', *Romania* 93 (1972), 498–522; Jacqueline Pioche, *Le Vocabulaire Psychologique dans les Chroniques de Froissart* (Paris, 1976); G. T. Diller, 'Robert d'Artois et l'historicité des Chroniques de Froissart', *Le Moyen Age* 86 (1980), 217–31 and his edition (Geneva, 1972). Froissart attributed to Robert a desire (traditional enough from the Old French *gestes* of revolt) for revenge against the French king, who had banished him, embodying current opinion that he was responsible for beginning the war. Diller's comparison of the successive redactions shows Froissart coming to his conclusion and using the techniques common to fiction and history to dramatize it.

55  Mark Lambert, *Malory: Style and Vision in the 'Morte Darthur'* (New Haven, 1975), discusses this group narrative as it appears in Malory. It is not unique to him.

56  Froissart was not, of course, the only historian to do this. Walter of Guisborough could furnish similar examples, as Gransden, vol. 1, p. 470. *The Chronicle of Walter of Guisborough*, ed. H. Rothwell (London, 1957), pp. 198–202.

57  *Bede's Ecclesiastical History of the English People*, ed. B. Colgrave and R. A. B. Mynors (Oxford, 1969), II.16; the Penguin translation has changed the aquiline nose to 'an ascetic face'. Even here Bede defers to authority: the description of Paulinus came to him from a reliable authority, an abbot, who had himself been

told it by an anonymous very old monk. Antonia Gransden collected instances of verisimilar description, which she considered 'Realistic Observation in Twelfth-Century England', *Speculum* 47 (1972), 29ff. Her examples instantiate precisely the difficulties of distinguishing style from actual observation. For a discussion of Becket's nose see Frank Barlow, *Thomas Becket* (London, 1986).

58 *Rhetoric*, Book II; Giles Constable, ed., *The Letters of Peter the Venerable*, intro.

59 *Peterborough Chronicle*, ed. C. Clark (2nd ed. Oxford, 1970), pp. 55–6. The Welsh atrocities reported by the *Gesta Stephani* s. v. 1136 include the enslavement of the young of both sexes and public rape of women of all ages. The author makes an explicit reference to Lucan in the entry for 1142.

60 That such reports come often as the climax of a story of anarchy may be significant, as with Guibert of Nogent's version, the identification of a murdered bishop, in his *De vita sua sive monodiarum suarum libri tres*, trans. John F. Benton as *Self and Society in Medieval France* (NY, 1970), pp. 181–2 and n. 9. for similar stories of Tostig (William of Malmesbury) and Harold.

61 Sallust may have started this. Gildas and Geoffrey of Monmouth use it, e.g. effeminacy in Geoffrey x.3, XIII.19. See Hanning, *Vision of History*. Guibert of Nogent uses cross-dressing as a symbol of the anarchy caused by a popular rising in the story in which the bishop was murdered and mutilated.

62 I have dealt with this *topos* in 'Medieval Biography: History as a Branch of Literature', *MLR* 80 (1985), 257–68, where I give detailed references.

63 *La Chronique d'Enguerran de Monstrelet*, ed. L. Doüet-D'Arcq (Paris, 1858), II.338–9; and 'Medieval Biography', 265f.

64 Discussed at length by Beryl Smalley, *English Friars and Antiquity in the Early Fourteenth Century* (Oxford, 1955), ch. 1.

65 Froissart, I.130, pp. 298–9. Tradition has exaggerated the king's handicap: Berners translates 'nyghe blynde'. The king's behaviour fits conventional report, though of course it may be true that he first asked after his son before launching himself into the thick of the battle. Froissart leaves until later the report that his son had made a timely withdrawal. The irony which arises from this near juxtaposition depends upon recognition of convention and contrast.

66 *The Carmen de Hastingae Proelio of Guy Bishop of Amiens*, ed. C. Morton and H. Muntz (Oxford, 1972), pp. 12–15. They point out the reminiscence of Lucan, *Pharsalia* I.145 in the couplet which begins 'Milicie . . .'

67 For Henry V see C. L. Kingsford, *The First English Life of Henry V* (Oxford, 1911), which is still valuable, as is his *English Historical Literature in the Fifteenth Century* (Oxford, 1913). Wright, *Political Poems and Songs*, p. 124. A. M. Kinghorn, *The Chorus of History: Literary-Historical Relations in Renaissance Britain 1485–1558* (London, 1971) is useful in this context, as is V. J. Scattergood.

68 *Gesta Henrici Quinti: The Deeds of Henry the Fifth*, trans. F. Taylor and J. S. Roskill (Oxford, 1975), p. 79.

69 Holinshed, *Chronicles*, III.553, quoted from *Henry V*, ed. J. H. Walter (London, 1954), p. 162.

70 Monstrelet, *Chroniques*, ch. 146. Richard of Hexham reports fasting before the Battle of the Standard, pp. 160–2, and see also Henry of Huntingdon on the same battle, *Historia Anglorum*, ed. T. Arnold (London, 1879), p. 262.

71 *Froissart*, I, 130, p. 297.

72 Renate Blumenfeld-Kosinski, 'Old French Narrative Genres: Towards the Definition of the Romans Antique', *Romance Philology* 34 (1980–1), 143–59 emphasizes their bookishness.

### 3    LET US NOW PRAISE FAMOUS MEN

1 Surveys of biography concentrate on the modern period, but see Harold Nicolson, *The Development of English Biography* (London, 1928), for a graceful survey of some biographical texts and an anachronistic approach to 'a' genre; Donald A. Stauffer, *English Biography Before 1700* (Cambridge, Mass., 1930), esp. pp. 36–7; and his *The Art of Biography in Eighteenth-Century England* (Princeton, 1941), which contains a useful bibliographical supplement; Warren Ginsberg, *The Cast of Character: The Representation of Personality in Ancient and Medieval Literature* (Toronto, 1983), which is largely a sequence of essays on individual works. For an excellent study with comprehensive bibliographical coverage, beyond its notional dates, see Judith H. Anderson, *Biographical Truth: The Representation of Historical Persons in Tudor-Stuart Writing* (New Haven, 1984). Autobiography inspired a number of studies, of which the most famous is the great survey by Georg Misch, of which the early volumes, translated into English, are *A History of Autobiography in Antiquity* (London, 1950) 2 vols.; Paul Lehmann, 'Autobiographies of the Middle Ages', *TRHS* 5th series 3 (1953), 41–52; Elizabeth Bruss, *Autobiographical Acts* (Baltimore, 1976) begins with essential definitions relevant to the modern period; Georges May, *L'Autobiographie* (Paris, 1979) and Philippe Lejeune, *L'Autobiographie en France* (Paris, 1971), *La Pacte Autobiographique* (Paris, 1975), and *Je est un Autre: l'autobiographie, de la littérature aux médias* (Paris, 1980) concentrate on modern French material; Wm. C. Spengemann, *The Forms of Autobiography: Episodes in the History of a Literary Genre* (New Haven, 1980) jumps from Antiquity to Dante to the modern period. A good collection of essays is *Autobiography: Essays Theoretical and Critical*, ed. James Olney (Princeton, 1980).

2 The Theophrastan 'character' is important in this context. Two good introductions are Warren Anderson, *Theophrastus, The Character Sketches* (Kent State, Ohio, 1970); Benjamin Boyce, *The Theophrastan Character in England to 1642* (Cambridge, Mass., 1947). The roots of the 'character' go back to Aristotle's *Rhetoric*, discussed in Chapter 1 above.

3  The phrase is Judson Allen's. See his *Ethical Poetic* (London, 1982).

4  A. Momigliano, *The Development of Greek Biography* (Cambridge, Mass., 1971) is far more than a survey of the Greek material. For the essential questions see esp. pp. 15–16. In addition, see Duane Reed Stuart's Sather Classical Lectures, *Epochs of Greek and Roman Biography* (Berkeley, 1928), esp. ch. 7.

5  See Elizabeth Rawson, *Cicero: A Portrait* (Harmondsworth, 1975).

6  See Baldwin, p. 31. Aphthonius' scheme is also analysed by T. C. Burgess in *Epideictic Literature* (University of Chicago Studies in Classical Philology, 3, 1902).

7  Geoffrey Chaucer, *The Works, 1532: With Supplementary Material from the Editions of 1542, 1561, 1598, and 1601* (Menston, 1969), f.b.i.r.

8  E.g. the distinction between panegyric (other historians) and history (his own work) in VIII.10. On Polybius see F. W. Walbank, *Polybius* (Berkeley, 1972), pp. 38–40; and his 'Tragic History', *Bulletin of the Institute of Classical Studies* 2 (1955), 4–14. On Lucan see Pierre Grimal, 'Le poète et l'histoire', *Entretiens Hardt* 15 (1968), 57–106 and the discussion, 108–17; V. B. M. Marti, 'Tragic History and Lucan's *Pharsalia*', *Studies Ullmann* (1964) I, 165–204. on Plutarch, P. De Lacy, 'Biography and Tragedy in Plutarch', *American Journal of Philology* 73 (1952), 159–71; E. R. Dodds, 'The Portrait of a Greek Gentleman', *Greece and Rome* 2 (1933), 97–107. The argument throughout refers not only to reader- or audience-awareness of other genres (viz., tragedy) which influence presentation, but also to the ability of interpreters of the text to discriminate 'decorative' rhetoric from the essence of the narrative. Cp. Arnaldo Momigliano's *The Development of Greek Biography* ch. 3 on late Greek biography and on the establishment of Roman forms.

9  Translated and discussed by James Robinson Smith, *The Earliest Lives of Dante* (NY, 1901). and, more recently, by David Wallace, in *Medieval Literary Theory and Criticism c. 1100–c. 1375*, ed. A. J. Minnis and A. B. Scott (Oxford, 1988), pp. 492–519.

10  In 'Sallust in the Middle Ages' Beryl Smalley traced the history of his influence upon historians and life writers in both Latin and the vernacular. See *Classical Influences on European Culture A. D. 500–1500*, ed. R. R. Bolgar (Cambridge, 1971), pp. 165–75. For a particular application see Robert Latouche, 'Une Imitation de Salluste au Xe siècle: l'histoire de Richer', in *Annales de l'Université de Grenoble* n.s. 6 (1929), pp. 289–306 and his edition of Richer's *Histoire de France (888–995)* CFMA (Paris, 1930), esp. pp. 27–9, 83–5 and the 'characters' of Charles the Simple and Gilbert, pp. 39, 73–5.

11  Ed. Henri Ailloud (Paris, 1931–2); for a historical study, Clare Stanfield, *St Martin and His Hagiographer: History and Miracle in Sulpicius Severus* (Oxford, 1983). And G. K. van Andel, *The Christian Concept of History in the Chronicle of Sulpicius Severus* (Amsterdam, 1976), esp. pp. 70–4 on Catiline as a model for

Priscillian. On Gildas' use of Jerome and Sulpicius see N. Wright, 'Gildas's Prose Style' in *Gildas: New Approaches*, ed. M. Lapidge and D. Dumville (Woodbridge, 1984), pp. 109–11.

12   Sulpicius Severus, *Vie de Saint Martin*, ed. Jacques Fontaine Sources Chrétiennes, 133, 3 vols. (Paris, 1967–9), ch. 2, esp. pp. 101, 105–6, 111–12. See also Andrew Wallace-Hadrill, *Suetonius* (London, 1983), ch. 3. It must be recalled in this context that other lives, particularly of the Desert Fathers, were also important. Benjamin Kurtz looks at one instance of transmission in *From St Anthony to St Guthlac*, University of California Publications in Modern Philology 12 (1926). *Early Christian Biographies*, ed. R. J. Deferrari (NY, 1952). Also discussed in Richard Southern, *Saint Anselm and his Biographer: A Study of Monastic Life and Thought* (Cambridge, 1962), esp. pp. 320–8. For a study of St Denis and the 'historical' additions to his Lives by Hilduin and Hincmar, see Gabrielle M. Spiegel, 'The Cult of St. Denis and Capetian Kingship' in *Saints and their Cults*, ed. Stephen Wilson (Cambridge, 1983), pp. 141–68.

13   The Alexander Romances have been mapped by G. A. Cary, *The Medieval Alexander*, ed. D. J. A. Ross (Cambridge, 1956); Ross, *Alexander Historiatus* (London, 1963); *The Romances of Alexander*, trans. D. M. Kratz (NY, 1989); and Robin Lane Fox, *Alexander the Great* (London, 1973) discusses the sources pp. 499ff.

14   See Momigliano, *Greek Biography*, ch. 1 and 3.

15   Although Plutarch's parallel lives and moral essays were inaccessible through the main medieval period, their rediscovery in the Renaissance and their translation into the vernaculars has been well documented. See for example the reactions to the work of Philemon Holland, whose translation of the moral essays appeared (from the French) in *Plutarch's Moralia: Twenty Essays* (London, 1603, revised 1657; repr. of 1603 ed., 1911), intro.

16   Considered, from the Freudian point of view, by Otto Rank, *The Myth of the Birth of the Hero: A Psychological Interpretation of Mythology*, trans. F. Robbins and S. E. Jelliffe (NY, 1952), which analyses fifteen 'heroes' (including Judas), pp. 12–61. The description of the standard form is 'explained' by the Family Romance; rhetoric is not mentioned, pp. 61–94.

17   For classical precedents see J. A. Fairweather, 'Fiction in the Biographies of Ancient Writers', *Ancient Society* 5 (1974), 231–75. Boccaccio's *Dante*, ch. 2; Bernard of Clairvaux's mother is discussed in G. Evans, *The Mind of Bernard of Clairvaux* (Oxford, 1983), p. 37; for Christina's mother, *The Life of Christina of Markyate: A Twelfth Century Recluse*, ed. and trans. C. H. Talbot (Oxford, 1987); for Becket see Garnier de Pont-Sainte-Maxence, *La Vie Saint Thomas le Martyr de Cantorbie*, ed. E. Walberg (Oxford, 1922), II. 166–205 and trans. Janet Shirley, *Garnier's Becket* (London, 1975), pp. 6–7. F. Barlow, *Thomas Becket* (London, 1986), p. 282 n. 10; for Gregory of Nyssa's mother before the birth of her

daughter, Peter Brown, *The Cult of the Saints: Its Rise and Function in Latin Christianity* (Chicago, 1981), pp. 57–8. For a more positivist reading of the biographies of Becket, see Dom David Knowles, 'Archbishop Thomas Becket: A Character Study' in his *The Historian and Character and Other Essays* (Cambridge, 1963), pp. 98–128. The dream or vision as a floating *topos* is the subject of Jacques Le Goff, *The Medieval Imagination*, trans. Arthur Goldhammer (Chicago, 1988), part V and see esp. pp. 220–32 on Sulpicius and Gregory of Tours. Peter Brown's Stenton Lecture on Gregory, collected in *Society and the Holy in Late Antiquity* (London, 1982) has been absorbed in his *The Cult of the Saints*.

18 *The Apocryphal Gospels*, ed. M. R. James (Oxford, 1924).

19 The idea of the Life of Christ as a model to be lived is perhaps nowhere so famously imitated as in the reports of the life of St Francis, which manage to credit him with humility for refusing to appear to compete with Christ (as in the forty days' fast) by throwing the match in sight of victory, or manifesting (but hiding) stigmata.

20 *Encomium Emmae Reginae*, ed. Alistair Campbell, Camden Third Series, 72 (London, 1949), p. 5. The author's literary self-consciousness is manifested not only in such topics as group dialogue urging the king to war (p. 11) and a set-piece description of the navy (1.4), but also by his references to Virgil, Lucan, and Sallust. He is unusually interested in motive.

21 *Pagan and Christian in an Age of Anxiety: Some Aspects of Religious Experience from Marcus Aurelius to Constantine*: (Cambridge, 1965) collects a number of essays on this period by E. R. Dodds. See also Peter Brown, *The Cult of the Saints*.

22 These lessons – for Martin's status as bishop could also be described as the culmination of a meteoric rise – contradict the ostensible message of humility, contempt for the things of this world, and utter reliance upon God: although he values his success only as testimony to God's goodness, Martin is depicted as an effective administrator. There is an underlying message of recruitment to the religious life in this story of the rise of a poor boy in a society in which social mobility was rare that no doubt increased its popularity. So, too, exhortations to the single life for women include the paradoxical offer of the highest-status married life, with God Himself as the spouse, which also offer male patterns of independence from family and even the possibility of dominance and power.

23 C. W. Jones, *Saints Lives and Chronicles* contains extremely useful material and traces lines of influence. Herbert Paulhart discusses Odilo's use of Sulpicius for the *Epitaphium Adelheide* in 'Die Lebensbeschreibung der Kaiserin Adelheid von Abt Odilo von Cluny', *Festschrift zum Jahrtausendfeier der Kaiserkrönung Otto des Grossen* (Graz-Koln, 1962), esp. pp. 11–12 for emulation of Cicero and Suetonius. For Higden's use of Sulpicius see John Taylor, *The Universal Chronicle of Ranulf Higden* (Oxford, 1966), ch. 3.

24 Gregory of Tours, *The History of the Franks*, trans. O. M. Dalton (Oxford, 1927)

vol. 1, intro. See also his saints' lives, e.g. *De Miraculi sancti Juliani* and above all his *De Virtutibus sancti Martini* in *Les Livres des Miracles et Autres Opuscules*, ed. H. L. Bordier, vol. 2 (Paris, 1860), which stresses Martin's status as an eye-witness to the miracles, though not to the life; discussed by Peter Brown, *Cult of the Saints*, chs. 3 and 4.

25  *The Blickling Homilies*, ed. R. Morris *EETS* o. s. 58, 63, 73 (repr. London, 1967), pp. 210–27.

26  Edmond Faral, 'Sidoine Apollinaire et la technique littéraire du Moyen Age' in *Miscellanea Giovanni Marcati* II (i.e. *Studi et Testi* 122) (Vatican City, 1946), 567–80 considers the importance of Sidonius' portraits for the later middle ages. Matthew of Vendôme, Guillaume de Blois, and Geoffrey of Vinsauf used what Sidonius offered. The Letters are edited in the Loeb series. Another late-classical Christian trained in rhetoric, Sidonius was connected with the court of Theodoric II before becoming a bishop in southern France. He had some facility as a poet, though his lines are rhetorical in the unfortunate sense of substituting decorative formulae for inspiration. He was a prolific writer of letters, which he collected and published at the end of his life, and which survived as model letters throughout the Middle Ages. In one of these he includes a description of Theodoric (*Epistulae*, 1.ii).

27  That there was a manuscript of Sidonius available to Einhard is confirmed by my colleague, Rosamund McKitterick. See now her *The Carolingians and the Written Word* (Cambridge, 1989), pp. 154, 251. Einhard's use of Suetonius has long been known, but see esp. G. B. Townsend, 'Suetonius and his Influence' in *Latin Biography*, ed. T. A. Dorey (London, 1967), pp. 79–111 and Richard Southern, *Saint Anselm and his Biographer*, p. 327n. On John of Salisbury's use of Suetonius see Roger Ray, 'Rhetorical Scepticism'.

28  Of course, they may also indicate, often by *occupatio*, a reference to topics the particular life will omit, an attitude to Life-writing itself. More's *Picus* argues, by just such omission, that true nobility is earned not inherited. Reversing an expectation, too, is a reactionary interpretation. More's *Life* is available in facsimile in the series The English Experience, no. 884. More opens with the briefest of references to Pico's ancestry, though he assures us that it was worthy, 'But we shal let his auncestres passe to whome (though they were ryght excellent) he gaue agayne as moche honour as he receyued' (Aiii). Chapter titles like 'Of his parentes and tyme of his byrth' and 'Of the wondre that appered before his byrth' indicate the traditional topics. The latter chapter includes references to the frequency of prognosticating events, and specifies St Ambrose and the bees which surrounded the future saint's cradle. Behind the *occupatio* lies the assumption of mind encouraged by the school-exercise, *comparatio*, which encouraged arguments on either side of the question of the sources of true nobility, enjoying the process of debate as much as the search for an answer. Plays like *Fulgens and Lucrece* stem from the same preoccupations.

29 Ruotger, *Vita Brunonis*, ed. I. Ott, MGH n.s. 10 (Weimar, 1951). *Vita Mahthildis reginae antiquior*, ed. R. Koepke, MGH 10 (Hanover, 1852). See E. Auerbach, *Literary Language and its Public in Late Latin Antiquity and in the Middle Ages*, trans. R. Manheim (London, 1965), ch. 2, pp. 156–64; Georges Duby, *Medieval Marriage: Two Models from Twelfth-Century France*, trans. Elborg Forster (Baltimore, 1978), ch. 3 on the biographies of the Counts of Guines and extensive bibliography. And Adam of Eynesham, *Magna Vita Sancti Hugonis: The Life of Hugh of Lincoln*, ed. D. L. Douie and D. H. Farmer (Oxford, 1985), pp. xiv, 43, 123. The editors remark in passing Adam's realism, but it arouses no scepticism. Adam's literary effects include quotations of Ovid and Virgil as well as the Bible.

30 Recorded by A. Poucelet in *Analecta Bollandiana* 12, pp. 422–40.

31 C. W. Jones, *Saints' Lives and Chronicles* (Ithaca, 1947), p. 61.

32 See my 'Biography' and Jones, *Saints' Lives*.

33 See Hippolyte Delehaye, *The Legends of the Saints*, trans. Donald Attwater (London, 1962 [from 3rd ed., 1955]), p. 77.

34 The text survives imperfectly in a single copy which is defective throughout as a result of the fire in Cottonian Library which destroyed so many medieval books. It is ed. and trans. C. H. Talbot, *The Life of Christina of Markyate: A Twelfth-Century Recluse* (Oxford, 1987).

35 Not, of course, that this proves that she could read the book if she owned it. See Talbot, *Life of Christina*, pp. 25–7.

36 For a discussion of types of text for another period, see Michael Goodrich, 'Politics of Canonization in the Thirteenth Century' in *Saints and their Cults*, pp. 169–87.

37 On the bookishness of Margery Kempe, the fifteenth-century 'mystic', see the Introduction to *The Book of Margery Kempe*, trans. B. A. Windeatt (Harmondsworth, 1985).

38 *Bedas metrische Vita S. Cuthberti*, ed. W. Jaager (Leipzig, 1935) and *Two Lives of St Cuthbert*, ed. B. Colgrave (Cambridge, 1940).

39 *Bede's Ecclesiastical History of the English People*, ed. B. Colgrave and R. A. B. Mynors (Oxford, 1969); trans. Leo Sherley Price (Harmondsworth, 1955), p. 252. A similar analysis might be made of the contrast between the mission to Britain (1.23–30), i.e. the deeds, and the life of St Gregory. The manipulations are recognizable. See Paul Mayvaert, 'Bede and Gregory the Great' in his *Benedict, Gregory, Bede, and Others* (London, 1977), VIII. The idea of two texts as twinned works is explored in *Aldhelm: The Prose Works*, ed. and trans. M. Lapidge and M. Herren (Cambridge, 1979), pp. 14 and 185 n. 11.

40 *Ecclesiastical History*, IV.27–32.

41 See Jones, *Saints' Lives*, pp. 54, 215 and for Felix of Croyland's use of this life for his own life of Guthlac, see p. 55. For Aldhelm's influence, perhaps confirmed by Bede, see Lapidge and Herren, *Aldhelm*, p. 2.

42  Alcuin's *Vita S. Willibrordi* in prose and in verse is ed. P. Jaffé, *Monumenta Alcuini* (Berlin, 1973), pp. 35–79.

43  This may appear to import a Whig theory of historiographical progress, but a reminder that 'success' also includes the influence of Froissart on the shape and style of history should help emphasize the literariness of the idea of 'success'; that Bede's historical judgement also coincides with a line of astringent belief is another matter.

44  Ed. and trans. Bertram Colgrave (Cambridge, 1956), intro., e.g. pp. 18–19. There are useful annotations to the abridged translations included in *Anglo-Saxon Saints and Heroes*, trans. Clinton Albertson (n.p., Fordham University Press, 1967).

45  *The Life of Ailred of Rievaulx*, ed. F. M. Powicke (London, 1950), intro.

46  Garnier, *Vie de Thomas*, II. 3611–35.

47  See C. H. Talbot, *The Anglo-Saxon Missionaries in Germany: Being the Lives of SS. Willibrord, Boniface, Sturm, Leoba and Lebuin, together with the Hodoeporicon of St Willibald and a Selection from the Correspondence of St Boniface* (London, 1954), p. 30. This life contains the wonderful report of a martyrdom in which the saint and all his companions were killed, despite which claim Willibald gives their dying words.

48  *Vita Wulfstani*, ed. R. R. Darlington (London, 1928), and *Life of Wulfstan*, trans. J. H. F. Peile (Oxford, 1934). See D. H. Farmer, 'Two Biographies by William of Malmesbury', in *Latin Historians*.

49  Peile, p. 12.

50  I, 16 (Peile, p. 35). Some of these caveats may be due to his sense of audience. Later he addresses them as learned men who would not need to have instances spelled out for them (II.15, Peile, p. 56).

51  See Southern, *Saint Anselm and his Biographer: A Study of Monastic Life and Thought* (Cambridge, 1963), pp. 320–8 on genre.

52  As in the famous story (recounted below) told of William Rufus's chamberlain. *De Nugis Curialum* is only one repertory of such anecdotes. On the literary form of William's Lives, and the influence of Suetonius, see Marie Schütt, 'The Literary Form of William of Malmesbury's *Gesta Regum*', EHR 46 (1931), 255–60. Suetonius is also discussed by Janet Martin, 'John of Salisbury as a Classical Scholar', in *The World of John of Salisbury*, ed. M. Wilks (Oxford, 1984), pp. 184–5.

53  May McKisack discusses the 'restorations' made by the scribes in Archbishop Parker's library, which in effect rewrote some Anglo-Saxon texts, in her *Medieval History in the Tudor Age*. This is as true of biographical as of historical writing. Eustace, who compiled the Life of St Edmund of Abingdon, adapted in turn material from John of Salisbury's Life of Beckett as well as the (by now almost predictable) Life of St Martin. The variety of potential interpretation for

each incident created important narrative latitude: what might be perceived as an uncertainty principle freed writers to say what needed to be said. Their own concerns with the truth of what they wrote were no bar to expressing that truth in many garbs. Implicit allusion is one of the most frequent. A recognizable allusion to St Thomas in the Life of St Edmund probably constituted Eustace's claim that the martyred archbishop's mantle had fallen upon his own hero, as discussed by S. H. Lawrence, *St Edmund of Abingdon: A Study in Hagiography and History* (Oxford, 1960), intro, esp. p. 34. Despite the ostensible strictures of the canonization process, the Life by Eustace borrows from John of Salisbury on Becket and Sulpicius on Martin (p. 34). Lawrence points out that in the anonymous lives one is arranged chronologically, the other by topics (pp. 56–7). See also 'La Vie St Edmund', *Romania* 55 (1929), 332–81 and E. Walberg, *La Tradition Hagiographique de St Thomas Becket avant la fin du XIIe siècle* (Paris, 1929).

54  On Lupus's own classicizing, especially his imitations of Sulpicius, see Auerbach, *Literary Language and its Public*, ch. 2, pp. 123–5. The changes that come with the sense of a community of like-minded readers and writers require no expansion. See McKitterick, *Carolingians*, pp. 158, 251.

55  Discussed in several of the essays in *Latin Biography*, e.g. G. B. Townsend, 'Suetonius and his Influence' (pp. 79–91) and T. A. Dorey, 'William of Poitiers: "Gesta Guillelmi Ducis"', in his *Latin Biography* (London, 1967), pp. 139–56.

56  *Alfred the Great: Asser's Life of King Alfred and Other Contemporary Sources*, ed. and trans. S. Keynes and M. Lapidge (Harmondsworth, 1983). For direct borrowing from Einhard see nn. 35, 139, 194. There may also be the adoption of what amounts to a scholar's *topos* in which a king tempts a man of learning to his court, imitated from the anonymous *Life of Alcuin*; see n. 195. See also James Campbell, 'Asser's *Life of Alfred*', in *The Inheritance of Historiography 350–900*, ed. C. Holdsworth and T. P. Wiseman (Exeter, 1986), pp. 115–35.

57  *De gestis regum Anglorum*, ed. W. Stubbs (London, 1887–9) (R. S.). Marie Schütt, 'The Literary Form of William of Malmesbury's *Gesta Regum*', *EHR* 46 (1931), 255–60. D. H. Farmer, 'Two Biographies by William of Malmesbury' in Dorey, *Latin Biography*, pp. 157–76, notices that Einhard's Charlemagne has also been put to use. Three articles by R. M. Thomson consider William's reading: 'The Reading of William of Malmesbury', *Revue Benedictine* 85 (1975), 362–402 and, as 'Addenda and Corrigenda', *Revue Benedictine* 86 (1976), 327–35, and 'William of Malmesbury as Historian and Man of Letters', *Journal of Ecclesiastical History* 29 (1978), 387–413, now collected in his *William of Malmesbury* (Woodbridge, 1987). William wrote 'declamatio' in the margin of his copy of Orosius to mark certain speeches (p. 404).

58  Conveniently edited in *Historiens et Chroniqueurs du Moyen Age*, ed. A. Pauphilet (Paris, 1952) which does not, however, distinguish genres. Trans. René Hague

(London, 1955) and on style see Paul Archambault, *Seven French Chroniclers* (Syracuse, NY, 1974). Further on anecdotal method, see Peter von Moos, 'The Use of Exempla in the *Policraticus* of John of Salisbury', in *The World of John of Salisbury*, pp. 256–61.

59 See Dorey, 'William of Poitiers' in his *Latin Biography*.

60 *The first part of the Life and Raigne of King Henrie IIII* (London, 1559) includes 'characters' (Bolingbroke when Earl of Derby), *chrias*, and at one point in a speech has a debater remark that something is 'profitable to be done' (John Holland, p. 113).

61 *Histoire de France*, ed. Latouche, pp. 210ff.

62 Dorey, 'William of Poitiers', p. 144. Townsend, 'Suetonius', p. 321.

63 See, in addition to Marjorie Chibnall, *The World of Orderic Vitalis* (Oxford, 1984), her monumental edition with translation in the Oxford Medieval Texts series, *The Ecclesiastical History of Orderic Vitalis*, (Oxford, 1969–80).

64 *De Gestis Mirabilibus Regis Edwardi Tertii*, ed. E. M. Thompson (London, 1899), R. S., p. 414.

65 For Eadric, William of Malmesbury, *Gesta Regum* II.181 (R. S.), and Freeman, *The History of the Norman Conquest* (Oxford, 1867–79) I, appendix II. For William of Newburgh's criticism of Hugh de Puiset see G. V. Scammell, *Hugh de Puiset* (Cambridge, 1956).

66 *The History of Richard III*, ed. Richard Sylvester in *The Complete Works of St Thomas More* (New Haven, 1963) vol. 2., discussed by L. F. Dean, 'Literary Problems in More's *Richard III*', in *Essential Articles for the Study of Thomas More*, ed. R. S. Sylvester and G. P. March'hadour (Hamden, Conn., 1977), pp. 315–25. See also Judith Anderson, *Biographical Truth*, Part II, esp. ch. 6.

67 This is not to suggest that 'anxiety of influence' exhausts the categories, since the idea of precedent could have such an encouraging effect in a culture that was supposed to be dedicated to individual salvation.

68 Perhaps, if more records survived of the relations between penitents and skilled confessors, there might be similar, similarly conversational and interactive texts, but it would be hard to imagine anything as *mutual* as these exchanges. In the Inquisition records, where we do have something like a record of conversation (if we can call it that), there is no parity, only an Inquisitor and a witness whose actual words were almost undoubtedly spoken in another language than that of the Latin transcript. Some of the issues will be raised in the next chapter. Discussed by E. Le Roy Ladurie, *Montaillou: village occitan de 1294 à 1324* (rev. ed. Paris, 1982), e.g. p. 190, 201, 314–15.

69 The sense of Heloise as a rhetorician of skill co-existed with more romantic interpretations, and in the eighteenth century, when the view of the pair as 'tragic lovers' reached new heights, Alexander Pope could see her as a self-tormented and self-deceived figure unable to accept her vocation because of her unwilling-

ness to give up her love for Abelard; on balance, Pope condemns her out of her own mouth, loving the sinner, but hating the sins.

70  Translated as *Self and Society in Medieval France: The Memoirs of Abbot Guibert of Nogent* by John F. Benton (NY, 1970).

71  C. C. Willard, 'The Franco–Italian Professional Writer: Christine de Pizan', in *Medieval Women Writers*, ed. K. M. Wilson (Manchester and Athens, Georgia, 1984), pp. 333–64.

72  *La Male Regle in Selections from Hoccleve*, ed. M. Seymour (Oxford, 1981); and intro. pp. xvi–xviii. The *Regiment of Princes*, ed. F. J. Furnivall (London, 1897). For Hawes, *The Pastime of Pleasure*, ed. W. E. Mead (London, 1928); A. S. G. Edwards, *Stephen Hawes* (Boston, 1983).

73  Ed. P. Démats (Paris, 1968).

74  For Opicinus see Ernst Kris, *Psychoanalytic Explorations in Art* (London, 1953), pp. 118–27 and the edition of R. Salomon (London, 1936). Otloh has been the subject of many discussions, e.g. Misch, *Autobiographie*, III.1.7. See also A. Sachs, 'Religious Despair in Medieval Literature and Art', *Medieval Studies* 26 (1964), 231–56. Depression is also the subject of M. M. McLaughlin, 'Abelard as Autobiographer: The Motives and Meaning of his Story of Calamities', *Speculum* 42 (1967), 463–88. Eric Auerbach discusses Rather's style as a kind of tenth-century egotistical self-expression in *Literary Language and Its Public*, pp. 136–52.

75  Analysed by, for example, Peter Burke, *Montaigne* (Oxford, 1981).

76  See J. B. Bamborough, *The Little World of Man* (London, 1952).

77  Studies of these problems include Colin Morris, *The Discovery of the Individual 1050–1200* (NY, 1972); R. W. Hanning, *The Individual in Twelfth-Century Romance* (New Haven and London, 1977), esp. ch. 1; see also W. C. Calin, *The Old French Epic of Revolt: Raoul de Cambrai, Renaud de Montauband, Gormond et Isembard* (Paris and Geneva, 1962).

78  See Gransden, vol. 1, pp. 189–191.

## 4  TRAITOR TRANSLATOR

1  Modern scholarship on the theory and practice of translation probably begins with the preface to the King James Bible. Early considerations of the problems include A. F. Tytler, *Essay on the Principles of Translation* (London, 1907) which prints the addresses the author, Lord Woodhouselee, gave the Royal Society of Edinburgh in 1790; F. R. Amos, *Early Theories of Translation* (NY, 1920); Justin Bellanger, *Histoire de la Traduction en France (auteurs grec et latin)* (Paris, 1903); P. H. Larwill, *La Théorie de la Traduction au début de la Renaissance: (d'après les traductions imprimée en France entre 1477 et 1527)* (Munich, 1934); S. K. Workman, *Fifteenth-Century Translation as an Influence on English Prose* (Princeton, 1940). Theodore Savory's essay for the general reader, *The Art of Translation* (2nd ed.

London, 1968), contains much common sense for modern translation. T. R. Steiner, *English Translation Theory 1650–1800* (Amsterdam, 1975) has useful material but is mainly concerned with poetry. More recent – and more sophisticated – scholarship includes George Steiner, *After Babel: Aspects of Language and Translation* (London, 1975); Eugene Nida, *Toward a Science of Translating* (Leiden, 1964) used the advances of linguistics to further the cause of Bible translation; J. C. Catford, *A Linguistic Theory of Translation* (Oxford, 1965) also takes accuracy as its starting point, sharing the view that the intention of translators is to produce a fluent new text. L. G. Kelly, *The True Interpreter: A History of Translation Theory and Practice in the West* (Oxford, 1979) begins from the 'word-for-word sense-for-sense' dichotomy. For a study of Chaucer with some reflection on translation, Tim Machin, *Techniques of Translation: Chaucer's Boece* (Norman, Oklahoma, 1985). Susan Bassnet-McGuire, *Translation Studies* (London, 1980) surveys the linguistic and philosophical literature. Bibliographies can be found in these works and in *The Science of Translation: An Analytic Bibliography*, ed. K.-Richard Bausch, J. Klegraf, W. Wilss (Tübingen, 1970) and *Translation Theory: A Comprehensive Bibliography* (Arust, 1978).

2  E.g. Pseudo-Albertus Magnus, *Quaestiones Alberti de Modis Significandi*, ed. L. G. Kelly (Amsterdam, 1977). The literature on the Modistic Logicians considers their language theories, which attempted to understand the processes by which interior thought became ideas and then words which could be spoken, but the students of the history of linguistics who have worked on these figures sometimes treat their work anachronistically. R. H. Robins, *Ancient and Medieval Grammatical Theory in Europe: With Particular Reference to Modern Linguistic Doctrine* (London, 1951) initiated the discussion. *History of Linguistic Thought and Contemporary Linguistics*, ed. H. Parret (NY, 1976) contains a broad selection of essays with excellent bibliographies; see esp. pp. 85–101, 164–88, 254–78. G. L. Bursill-Hall's introduction to Thomas of Erfurt, *Grammatica Speculativa* (London, 1972), pp. 1–127 is a useful study as are his *Speculative Grammars of the Middle Ages: The Doctrine of the Modistae* (The Hague, 1971) and 'The Middle Ages' in *Current Trends in Linguistics*, ed. T. A. Sebeok (The Hague, 1975), vol. I, pp. 179–230.

3  Quoted as the epigraph to this chapter from the translation by A. W. Haddan, rev. W. G. T. Shedd, in *Select Library of the Nicene and Post-Nicene Fathers of the Christian Church* (Grand Rapids, Mich., 1956), p. 209. *De Trinitate*, in Sancti Aurelii Augustini, *De Trinitate Libri XV*, ed. W. J. Mountain and Fr. Glorie (Turnholt, 1968), XV.10.19. The famous quodlibetal discussion of Duns Scotus (1.3.57–61) linked 'word' to 'memory' in the Augustinian sense. See the translation by F. Alluntis and A. B. Wolter, *God and Creatures* (Princeton, 1975), and their glossary, pp. 521–2.

4 John of Salisbury, *Metalogicon* I.19 (p. 56), III.1–3. Discussed also by William of Moerbeke; see *Dictionary of Scientific Biography* IX.436. Chaucer laments the lack of English vocabulary several times, though he makes it appear that it is his characters who are in part lamenting their own lack of skill which makes it impossible for them to say what they want to say in language as dignified as would be appropriate, e.g. the Squire, disclaiming the ability to describe the beauty of Canacee:

> But for to telle yow al hir beautee,
> It lyth nat in my tonge, n'yn my konnyng;
> I dar nat undertake so heigh a thyng.
> Myn Englissh eek is insufficient.
> It moste been a rethor excellent
> That koude his colours longynge for that art,
> If he shoulde hire discryven every part.     (V.34–40)

In *The Book of the Duchess* 896ff the Man in Black complains that he lacks both the requisite English and the wit to describe White.

5 There is a sensitive discussion of some of these issues in the postscript to Pope's *Odyssey*. See *The Prose Works of Alexander Pope*, ed. R. Cowler (Oxford, 1986), II.58–9 and notes 74–5.

6 e.g. Walter Hamilton, 'Classical Prose at its Extremes', in *The Translator's Art: Essays in Honour of Betty Radice*, ed. W. Radice and Barbara Reynolds (Harmondsworth, 1987).

7 *Cambridge History of the Bible: The West from the Fathers to the Reformation*, ed. G. W. H. Lampe (Cambridge, 1969), sect. VI.5. (Hereafter cited as *CHB*.)

8 *The Orations of Marcus Tullius Cicero*, trans. C. D. Yonge (London, 1876), IV.530–1. Discussed, briefly, by R. L. Enos, in *The Present State of Scholarship in Historical and Contemporary Rhetoric*, ed. W. B. Horner (Columbia and London, 1983), ch. 1.

9 *The Romans of Partenay or of Lusignan*, ed. W. W. Skeat (London, 1899), II. 6553–73.

10 Some acknowledgement of particular difficulties, especially those posed by rhyme, metre, and paucity of vocabulary or style registers regularly appears in translated texts, often as a defence for choices taken to make the translation more like the original than its language currently appears to allow.

11 *The Fall of Princes*, ed. H. Bergen, (London, 1924–7), 1.8–42.

12 *Caxton's Own Prose*, ed. N. F. Blake (London, 1973), p. 105.

13 Augustine, *De Trinitate* xv. Smalley, *The Study of the Bible in the Middle Ages* (3rd ed., Oxford, 1983).

14 Analysts of Bible translation often assume that the ambition of all such work must be a sequential and independent text. See, for example, Werner Schwarz,

'The Meaning of *Fidus Interpres* in Medieval Translation', *The Journal of Theological Studies* 45 (1944), 73–8 and his *Principles and Problems of Biblical Translation: Some Reformation Controversies and their Background* (Cambridge, 1955).

15 Discussed at length in Beryl Smalley, *The Study of the Bible in the Middle Ages* (3rd ed. Oxford, 1983), e.g. 103ff. See also Gilbert Dahan, 'Les Interprétations juives dans les commentaires du pentateuque de Pierre le Chantre', in *The Bible in the Medieval World: Essays in Memory of Beryl Smalley*, ed. Katherine Walsh and Diana Wood (London, 1985), pp. 131–55. For Rashi, see the monumental edition, ed. W. Rosenbaum and A. M. Silbermann, 5 vols. (London, 1929–34).

16 See the chapter on Jerome in *CHB* and Peter Brown, *Augustine*, pp. 265–6; *Select Letters*, ed. and trans. F. A. Wright (London and NY, 1933), p. 124.

17 Smalley, *Bible*, II.2, V.1; *Bible in the Medieval World*, xi–xiii; *CHB*, pp. 147–8.

18 Smalley, *Bible*; Gillian Evans, *The Language and Logic of the Bible* (2 vols. Cambridge, 1984, 1986).

19 There are exceptions to this generalization; the *Saturnalia* of Macrobius disguises its function as a commentary by appearing to be a Dialogue in which a number of speakers discuss the *Aeneid*, calling each other's attentions to its beauties.

20 Beryl Smalley, 'Two Biblical Commentaries of Simon of Hesdin', *Rech. Théol. anc. med.* 13 (1946) and her *Bible*, pp. 321ff. See Caxton on glossing Cicero's *De Senectute* in *Caxton's Own Prose*, pp. 120–3 on improving the original while preserving it. See also René Sturel, *Jacques Amyot* (Paris, 1908), pp. 221–2 on Laurent de Premierfait and, on the whole question, pp. 187–267.

21 See Smalley, *Bible*, p. 321. Modern interpretation has not resolved the issue. The Douai Bible called the weed 'cockles', the New English Bible 'darnel'. For a homely example which would compel instant recognition in the pastoral audience, this has generated self-defeating quantities of scholarship.

22 Discussed, for example, by George Campbell in *A Translation of the Four Gospels with Notes* (London, 1789), p. 346.

23 That this is a remarkably tendentious defence of pagan literature which merely asserts the identity of the 'Israelites' as well as their failings should not escape notice, but it may be taken as evidence of the extremity of the need to legitimate the reading of pagan literature. Roger Ray, 'Bede and Cicero', *Anglo-Saxon England* 16 (1987), 2–3. 'The smiths are those who produce secular literature. Israel possesses only divine literature . . .', *CHB*, p. 183.

24 Rivkah Zim, *English Metrical Psalms* (Cambridge, 1987) discusses translation as imitation, chs. 1 and 2. This is also the case with Douglas's translation of the *Aeneid*, as Priscilla Bawcutt shows in her *Gavin Douglas: A Critical Study* (Edinburgh, 1976), chs. 4 and 5.

25 Sed voces significant res intellectus, id enim voce significamus quod intelligimus, Q85.art.2.obj.3.

26  Discussed by M. Nims, '*Translatio*: "Difficult Statement" in Medieval Poetic Theory', *University of Toronto Quarterly* 43 (1974), 215–30.

27  'Sed non tantum debemus inhaerere improprietati verborum veritatem tegenti, quantum inhiare proprietati veritatis sub multimodo genere locutionem latenti', where the Latin uses technical language of interpretation which the English disguises (to use the same metaphor). *De Casu Diaboli*, in S. Anselmi Cantuarensis Archiepiscopi Opera Omnia 1 ed. F. S. Schmitt (Edinburgh, Nelson, 1946), p. 235; trans. Jasper Hopkins and Herbert Richardson, *Truth, Freedom, and Evil: Three Philosophical Dialogues by Anselm of Canterbury* (NY, Harper Torchbooks, 1967), p. 149. When Anselm quotes the Bible in his prayers and meditations, apparently from memory, he seems unconcerned to quote exactly, and the quotations become a tissue of allusion, as if in some instances, like praying from the heart, the actual words did not matter. See *The Prayers and Meditations of St Anselm*, ed. and trans. B. Ward (Harmondsworth, 1973), intro.

28  'Et par mon conseil, tant que tu pourras tu liras les livres en latin, car tu es aucunement fonde en clergie. Et soies certains que se tu te delicteras a lire le latin, une hystoire ou enseignemens te plairont mieulx au cuer que dimie dozeime d'ystoires en francoys. Car la saincte escripture, escripte et dictee par les sains en latin et depuis translatee en francois, ne rent pas telle substance aux lisans es ruisseaux comme elle fait en sa propre fontayne. Quel Merveille! car il y a en la sainte escripture certains et plusieurs motz en latin qui du lisant percent le cuer en grant devocion, lesquel translatez en francois se treuvent en vulgal sans saveur et sans delectacion.' Philippe de Mézières, *Le Songe du Vieil Pelerin*, ed. G. W. Coopland (Cambridge, 1969), II.222–3. The translation into English hides the casually sensual metaphors for pleasure that the French uses.

29  'On n'extirpe pas ces qualitez originelles, on les couvre, on les cache. Le langage latin m'est comme naturel, je l'entens mieux que le Francis; mais il y a quarante ans que je ne m'en suis du tout poinct servy à parler, ny à escrire; si est-ce que à des extremes et soudaines esmotions où je suis tombé deux ou trois fois en ma vie, et l'une, voyent mon pere tout sain se renverser sur moy, pasmé, j'ay tousjours eslancé du fond des entrailles les premiers paroles Latines; nature se surdant et s'exprimant à force, à l'encontre d'un long usage.' Michel de Montaigne, *Essais*, III.ii (Du repentir) (Paris, Garnier Flammarion, 1969), p. 26. The following quotation appears on p. 21. Montaigne presents himself, in his private state, as an example of the whole human condition. He contrasts himself to 'autheurs', that is, authorities, who premise what they have to say upon marks of something exceptional or strange; only his articulateness about himself singles him out. His sense of himself as an example which can be interpreted, read, itself exemplifies the application of an old technique to a new subject. This kind of personal testimony is rare, as Montaigne knew perfectly well, and delighted in reminding his readers, as when, at the beginning of this essay, 'On Repenting' ('Du

repentir'), he describes his intention to present himself as himself rather than as a grammarian, poet, or legal philosopher ('par mon estre universel, comme Michel de Montaigne, non comme grammarien, ou poete, ou juriconsulte').

30 'Langagis, whos reulis ben not writen, as ben Englisch, Frensch, and manye othere, ben chaungid withynne ӡeris and cuntrees, that oon man of oon cuntre, and of oon tyme, myӡt not, or schulde not kunne undirstonde a man of the othere kuntre, and of the othere tyme; and al for this, that the seid langagis ben not stabili and foundamentali writen', Reginald Peacock, *The Book of Faith*, quoted J. F. Patrouch, Jr, *Reginald Peacock* (NY, 1970), pp. 47–8.

31 *De finibus* I.ii; II.iv; III.ii, iv, xii and *Tusculan Disputations* IV.v–vi. Cicero often refers to Greek literature and assumes that the interlocutors of his Dialogues (and by implication his readers) know the references in the originals; he frequently discusses particular Greek words.

32 See 'Maistre Nicole Oresme, *Le Livre de Yconomique d'Aristote*', ed. A. D. Menut, *Transactions of the American Philosophical Society*, n. s. 47 (1957), 781–924, intro.; Reginald Pecock, *The Folewer to the Donet*, ed. E. V. Hitchcock, *EETS*, o.s. 164 (London, 1924), p. 220. As soon as familiarity with the source language is lost these references also lose their force, and decline from deliberate 'referring' oddities of style to normal expressions with no value as signals to another language or another text. We might adduce as a parallel the absorption of loan words, where *successful* innovation, whether at the word or phrase level, rapidly ceases to call attention to itself. Success is perhaps never so subjective a measure as it is in aesthetic matters.

33 This is probably an audience-centred humility topos which tacitly defends both the existence and style of the translation. That is, by posing as intended for readers as simple and ignorant as women, much of its own simplicity becomes defensible. By the same token, this made it an important target for manipulation of its glosses for Lollards who had tendentious views of what the text really meant.

34 *The Psalter or Psalms of David and Certain Canticles with a Translation and Exposition in English*, ed. H. R. Bramley, (Oxford, 1884), pp. 4–5. I have lightly modernized and punctuated. Note the rhetorical stress on profitability. For a medieval German dual language text of *The Song of Songs* see *CHB*, 424. For an Occitan example, Albert Henry, 'Traduction en oil du troisième sermon sur le *Cantique des Cantiques*', in *Medieval French Textual Studies in Memory of T. B. W. Reid*, ed. Ian Short (London, 1984), pp. 54–64. *Art in Plantagenet England*, ed. Jonathan Alexander and Paul Binski (London, 1987), p. 236 for a bilingual mass book. See also A. Grafton and L. Jardine, *From Humanism to the Humanities* (London, 1986), chs. 1 and 3. In what follows I am grateful to my colleague, Dr David Pearl, for interpreting and translating the original Hebrew texts.

35 Wyatt's Psalm translations also imbed the psalm in a narrative voice which explains how to read them. See Zim, ch. 2.

36  Oresme emphasizes, however, that ignorance of Latin did not mean stupidity, and justifies his own Bible translating for intelligent secular readers. See Monfrin, 'Humanisme et Traduction au Moyen Age', *Journal des Savants* 148 (1963), 173 and similarly on Aristotle's *Ethics*, quoted pp. 175–6. For another approach, using the idea of the 'service' translation, see Peter F. Dembowski, 'Learned Latin Treatises in French: Inspiration, Plagiarism, and Translation', *Viator* 17 (1986), 255–66 and his 'Two Old French Recasting/Translations of Andreas Capellanus's *De Amore*' in *Medieval Translators and their Craft*, ed. Jeanette Beer (Kalamazoo, Michigan, 1989), pp. 185–212.

37  See *Aurora: A Twelfth-century Latin Poem by Petrus Riga, Canon of Reims* (Notre Dame University Press, 1965). A verse adaptation by Macé de la Charité has been published by a team of editors under the direction of J. R. Smeets, *La Bible de Macé de la Charité* (Leiden, 1982– ). No doubt authors were moved by more than one ambition, and a motive to outdo secular vernacular poetry on its home ground was one of them. See Smalley, *Bible*, pp. 179–80 for Peter's translation of earlier Bible glosses as part of his own text.

38  *La Bible de Jehan Malkaraume*, ed. J. R. Smeets, 2 vols. (Amsterdam, 1978). This is a late thirteenth- or early fourteenth-century verse adaptation of the Bible stories organized on the model of the universal chronicle, that is, it treats the Bible as a historical narrative. Jehan adapts speeches just as any historian might, including putting a version of Ovid's monologue for Medea (*Metamorphoses* VII.9–89) into the mouth of Potiphar's wife (vv.2705–2898), pp. 32ff and notes pp. 265–71; he uses the fountain of Narcissus for the well at which Rebecca met Abraham's messenger (pp. 45–6). Jehan is also one of the adapters of Benoît's *Roman de Troie*, which suggests that he was a vernacular popularizer of history.

39  *CHB*, 425–6. Vernacular saints' lives which translate Latin originals show similar patterns. Robert Wace's twelfth-century *La Vie de Sainte Marguerite*, ed. E. A. Francis (CFMA.) (Paris, 1932) prints the French and Latin texts in parallel and offers a convenient comparison. Wace's *La Conception de Notre Dame* is a more ambitious redaction-translation; see Francis, pp. xiv–xvi. There is a survey of some late German translations in Patricia A. McAllister, 'Apocryphal Narrative elements in the *Genesis* of the Middle Low German *Historienbibel* Helmstedt 611.1', in *Medieval Translators and their Craft*, ed. Jeanette Beer (Kalamazoo, Michigan, 1989), pp. 81–92.

40  Cotton Nero A.x, the manuscript in which the four poems appear, contains numerous pointing hands to alert readers to important moments, The addition of 'nota' or 'nota bene' signals is common. See, for example, Jill Mann, *Ysengrimus* (Leiden, Brill, 1987), p. 53 for manuscripts which call attention to extractable proverbial wisdom.

41  For an extreme case see the discussion of the 'cento' of Lipsius in Grafton and Jardine, *Humanism to Humanities*, pp. 196–9.

42  Jacques Monfrin, 'Humanisme et Traduction', 161–90. This article was followed by 'Les Traducteurs et leurs public en France au Moyen Age', 149 (1964), 5–20. Together they form an excellent survey of the translations made and some of the problems which arose from them. There is a chapter on the law and literacy in R. McKitterick, *The Carolingians and the Written Word* (Cambridge, 1989) which provides a reminder that Germanic law had first to find its way *into* Latin.

43  Herbals had been translated into Italian in the mid-sixteenth century by Pietro Andrea Matthioli many times and in many editions, as, indeed, was the case with Culpeper.

44  *The Cambridge History of Renaissance Philosophy*, ed. C. B. Schmitt et al. (Cambridge, 1988), e.g. pp. 394–402, 777–8.

45  *Cambridge History of Renaissance Philosophy*, pp. 88–90, 108.

46  'Priscian says in a little book that he made about the poetry of Terence, that of all the languages in the world Latin is the most skilful to express his thoughts best and most nobly . . . and as it happens that at the present time Latin is a more perfect and more copious language than French, by the strongest reason one cannot correctly translate all Latin into French, as may appear from among many examples this proposition: homo est animal . . . therefore I must be excused if I do not speak of this matter as well, as clearly, or as ornately as was his craft.' Quoted by G. W. Coopland, *Nicole Oresme and the Astrologers* (Liverpool, 1952), p. 182 n. 14. Bert Hansen, *Nicole Oresme and the Marvels of Nature* (Toronto, 1985). Oresme was by no means alone as a translator of the *Ethics*; there is a partial translation inserted in Brunetto Latini's *Tresor* about 1268 which adapts Hermannus Alemannus' *Translatio Alexandrina*. And see Monfrin, 'Traduction'.

47  See Monfrin, 'Traduction', p. 173.

48  This manner of treating vernacular translations spread. Douglas's translation of Virgil's *Aeneid* mimics this presentation as a commented text divided into *distinctiones*. So Laurent de Premierfait divides Cicero into *distinctiones*. It amounts to a claim that difficulty is appropriate. Similar claims have been made for Chaucer, as by Judson Boyce Allen and T. A. Moritz in their *A Distinction of Stories: The Medieval Unity of Chaucer's Fair Chain of Narratives for Canterbury* (Columbus, Ohio, 1981), where the main model cited is Ovid's *Metamorphoses*. Jacques Bauchant, translator of Seneca, complained, 'Ja soit ce que ce livre soit petit en escripture, toutefois il m'a esté assez duret en translation, tant pour ce que je n'ay peu trouber vrais exemplaires ne du tout semblables mais les uns plus contenans et autrement que les autres, tant pour ce que le stile est grief et estrange quant a moy . . .', quoted by Monfrin, 'Traduction', pp. 18–19.

49  'To your royal majesty, very noble prince, by the grace of God king of the French, Philippe the fourth, I Jean de Meung, who once in the Romance of the Rose where Jealousy put Good Welcome in prison, taught how to take the castle and pluck the Rose and translated from Latin into French Vegetius's book of

Chivalry and the Book of the Marvels of Ireland and the Life and Letters of Peter Abelard and his wife Heloise, and Alfred's Book of Spiritual Friendship, now send the Consolation of Boethius which I have translated from Latin into French. Although you understand Latin well, nevertheless it is much easier to understand French than Latin. And since you have said to me – which I take as an order – to take the meaning of the author without following the words of the Latin too closely, I have done it according to my small skill just as your grace commanded me to. So I beg all those who will see this book, if it should seem to them that in some places I have gone too far from the words of the author, that they will forgive me. For if I had fitted the French word for word to the Latin, the book would have been too obscure to lay men and clerks, even the least learned, would not easily have been able to understand the Latin by the French.' V. L. Dedeck-Héry, ed., *Boethius' De Consolatione by Jean de Meun*, in *Mediaeval Studies* 14 (1952), 168. And see A. J. Minnis, *Medieval Theory of Authorship* for analysis of this kind of preface and its relation to the problem of authority.

50 See Fabrizio Beggiato, ed., *Le Lettere di Abelardo ed Eloisa nella traduzione di Jean de Meun* (Modena, STEM-Mucchi, 1977), 2 vols. The Introduction (vol. II) gives numerous examples of Jean's amplifications.

51 As analysed by Richard A. Dwyer, *Boethian Fictions: Narratives in the Medieval French Versions of the Consolatio Philosophiae* (Cambridge, Mass., Medieval Academy of America, 1976). See also *The Medieval Boethius: Studies in the Vernacular Translations of* De Consolatione Philosophiae, ed. A. J. Minnis (Cambridge, 1987).

52 From the Epilogue to *The Boke of the Consolacion of Philosophie*, quoted from *Caxton's Own Prose*, ed. N. F. Blake (London, 1973), pp. 59–60. On the difficulty of Livy see Jean Rychner, 'Observations sur la traduction de Tite-Live par Pierre Bersuire (1354–56)', *Journal des Savants* 148 (1963), 257. Rychner accuses Bersuire of incompetence.

53 Blake, *Caxton's Own Prose*, p. 121.

54 Modern editions have until recently suppressed the accompanying glosses in medieval and early modern books. The Ellesmere Manuscript of Chaucer's *Canterbury Tales* contains detailed glosses which comment on the text while appearing often simply to supply the sources of quotations and references. For a detailed survey of the arguments, see Susan Schibanoff, 'The New Reader and Female Textuality in Two Early Commentaries on Chaucer' in *Studies in the Age of Chaucer* 10 (1988) 71–108.

55 Discussed by George Steiner, *After Babel*.

56 Francis Kynaston translated Chaucer's *Troilus and Criseyde* into Latin and produced an accompanying commentary for it. See Richard Beadle's essay in *Chaucer Traditions*, ed. R. Morse and B. A. Windeatt (Cambridge, 1990).

57 Jacques Monfrin quotes a number of these prefaces. And see Glending Olsen, *Literature as Recreation in the Later Middle Ages* (Ithaca, 1982).

58 J. Monfrin, 'Humanisme et Traduction', pp. 173–5. For a more detailed
   examination of Raoul's work and his use of commentators, see C. C. Willard,
   'Raoul de Presles's translation of Saint Augustine's *De Civitate Dei* in *Medieval
   Translators*', pp. 329–46.

59 Richard Copley Christie, *Étienne Dolet: The Martyr of the Renaissance 1508–1546*
   (London, 1899). Etienne Dolet, *La Manière de Bien Traduire d'une langue en autre*
   (Paris, 1540). Dolet's five requirements were that the translator must first
   understand the original text extremely well, next that he must have perfect
   command of both languages, third that although he must not translate word-for-
   word he must preserve his author's word and idea order in so far as possible,
   fourth that he must find words already existing in the target language and adapt
   from the source language only when absolutely necessary, fifth that he must
   imitate the original style. While this contains good sense about accuracy, it begins
   from the modern perspective that 'accuracy' entails close adherence to words and
   sense, without thinking about the problems of text-and-gloss. Nor does it
   consider the relation between the new and the old texts as one of constant
   reference.

60 'Because the rhymed romance of Troy contains many things which are not to be
   found in the Latin (because he who made it could not otherwise beautifully have
   made his rhymes), I, Jean of Flixecourt, translated without rhyme the history of
   the Trojans and of Troy from Latin into romance word for word just as I have
   found it in one of the books of the library of my lord St Peter of Corbie', *Li
   Romans de Troies: A Translation by Jean de Flixcourt, 1262* ed. G. Hall (University
   of London unpublished Ph.D. dissertation, 1951), p. 2. The late-thirteenth-
   century translation made by the learned Dominican Geoffrey of Waterford with
   the help of Servais Copale survives, like Jean's, in only one manuscript, and seems
   to have had no circulation. Scholarly objections to popular work seem to have
   had as little effect on stopping sales in the Middle Ages as they do now.

61 For a more detailed study see C. David Benson, *The History of Troy in Middle
   English Literature* (Woodbridge, Suffolk, 1980).


## 5   TEXTS AND PRE-TEXTS

1 For a detailed survey of the legends of Aeneas in the Middle Ages, see Jerome E.
  Singerman, *Under Clouds of Poesy: Poetry and Truth in French and English
  Reworkings of the* Aeneid, *1160–1513* (NY, 1986).

2 *Eneas: Roman du XIIe Siècle*, ed. J.-J. Salverda de Grave, CFMA, 2 vols. (Paris,
  repr. 1964); see now the essays collected in *Relire le 'Roman d'Eneas*, ed. Jean
  Dufournet (Paris, 1985).

3 *Virgil's Aeneid Translated into Scottish Verse*, ed. D. F. C. Coldwell, STS, 4 vols.
  (Edinburgh, 1957–64). I have discussed Douglas in greater detail in 'Gavin

Douglas: Off Eloquence the flowand balmy strand' in *Chaucer Traditions* ed. Ruth Morse and B. A. Windeatt (Cambridge, 1990), pp. 107–21.

4 See Nancy Partner, *Serious Entertainments* (Chicago, 1977).

5 *Concerning Famous Women*, trans. G. A. Guarino (London, 1964), p. xxxviii.

6 *De Casibus Virorum Illustrium libri novem* (Vienna, 1544) [and many later editions]. *De Claris Mulieribus* (Uln, 1473) [but many later editions]. Laurent de Premierfait's *De Cas de Nobles Hommes et Femmes*, Book I, ed. P. M. Gathercole (Chapel Hill, NC, 1968). *Lydgate's Fall of Princes*, ed. H. Bergen, *EETS* e. s. 121–4 (London, 1924–7) contains extracts from both the Latin and French sources. (References to these volumes will be in brackets in the text.)

7 Extreme examples of this impulse, like Bersuire's extravagant multiplication of interpretations in the moralized Ovid, have tended to be seen as part of a purely allegorical impulse, and restricted to the literature about allegory.

8 *The Testament of Cresseid*, in *The Poems of Robert Henryson*, ed. Denton Fox (Oxford, 1981), ll.64–70.

9 The song texts are slightly adapted from Hans Tischler, *The Manuscript Montpellier H 196. A New Transcription, I–III* (Madison, Wisc., 1978), p. 85. I owe this reference — and the careful *explication d'intertextualité* which accompanied it — to Professor Wulf Arlt.

# INDEX

Abelard, Peter, 116, 168, 170
Abingdon Chronicler, 89
*Ad Herrenium*, 24
Aesop, 18, 40
Ailred of Rievaulx, 89
Alcuin, 154
allegory, 4, 31–2, 36, 42
anecdotes, 163
Anglo-Saxon Chronicle, 99
Anselm, *De Casu Diaboli*, 200
Aphthonius, 20, 129
Apocryphal Romances, 148
Aquinas, Thomas, 199, 217
Aristotle *Rhetoric*, 15 translations of, 217
Arthur, King, 6, 71
Asser, 162
audience, 65, 103–4, 148, 182, 188, 190, 202, 209, 238, 255
Augustine, 8, 86, 193, 196
   *De Civitate Dei*, 226
   *Confessions*, 29
   *De Doctrina Christiana*, 27
   *De Trinitate*, 179
Augustine, influence of, 170
Austen, Jane, 85
authority, 3, 15, 40, 42, 102, 105, 139, 144, 156, 207, 212, 216, 231, 233, 238, 242, 243
   attitudes to, 1, 7, 281
   deferral, 108
   invented, 197, 239
autobiography, 43, 149, 170

Bacon, Francis, 23, 65, 71
Becket, Thomas, 36, 109, 155, 176, 275
Bede, 10, 47, 76, 90, 94, 113, 114, 137, 139, 151, 161, 180, 203, 238, 262

influence of, 155, 157
   Lives of Cuthbert, 152, 153
Beethoven, 81–2
Benoît de Ste. Maure, 52, 103, 227, 235
Bernard of Chartres, 38
Bernardus Silvestris, 31
Bible, 16, 22, 36, 99–100, 165, 184–5, 233
   Apocryphal Gospels, 185, 209
   as referring text, 185
   Chronicles, 107
   Exodus, 198
   Genesis, 28
   Glossed, 28, 195, 196, 223
   Jeremiah, 153
   Matthew, 197
   Psalms, 68, 198
   Psalter, 8, 37, 204–6
   Samuel, 198
   Septuagint, 194, 203
   Song of Songs, 33
   Talmud, 26
   translations of, 12, 191, 193, 202, 209–10, 216
biography, 6, 92, 125 (*see encomium*)
biography (defined), 128
Blake, William, *Marriage of Heaven and Hell*, 21
Boccaccio, Giovanni, 55, 102, 132, 159, 180, 189, 191, 227
Boethius, translations of, 218, 219
Borges, 247
Bromyard, John, 243, 254

Calque, 204
Capgrave, John, 1
*Carmen de Hastingae Proelio*, 120
*Carmina Burana*, 39

Cassiodorus, 24
Cato, *Distichs*, 38–40, 179
Catullus, 18
Caxton, William, 191
  Preface to Chaucer, *Boece*, 220
  Preface to moralized Ovid, 32
character, 51, 61, 151, 155
  ages of man, 176
  as argument, 57, 74
  depression, 277
  passions, 15, 19, 33, 34, 73, 93, 99,
    100, 112, 165, 174, 174, 177
  reported speech, 121
  rhetorical *ethos*, 21, 57, 62, 100, 109,
    123, 141, 160, 174, 176, 177
  vices, 163, 176
  virtues, 140, 143
  works, 160, 162
character (defined), 174
character of a great man, 127, 128,
    133, 136, 144, 161, 171, 174, 176,
    269, 176 physical description, 113,
    114, 133
Charlemagne, 6, 145, 159, 160, 161
Charles I, King of England, 138
Chastellain, Georges, 88
Chaucer, Geoffrey, 131, 171, 241, 255,
    258
  *Boece*, 220
  *Book of the Duchess*, 26
  *Knight's Tale*, 35
  *Nun's Priest's Tale*, 39, 41–2
  *Parlement of Fowles*, 55
  *Troilus and Criseyde*, 56, 63, 67, 197,
    236, 238, 239
  *Wife of Bath*, 74
Chrétien de Troyes, 73, 177
Christina of Markyate, 136, 149–51,
    171
Christine de Pizan, 171
chronicle (*see* history), 33
Cicero, Marcus Tullius, 7, 23, 26, 38,
    53, 63, 185, 186, 188
  *Ad Atticam*, 58
  *De finibus*, 204
  *De legibus*, 86
  *De optimo genere oratorum*, 187
  *De senectute*, trans. of, 221
  Fourth *Tusculan*, 187, 204
  *Pro Milone*, 56, 129

*Cloud of Unknowing*, 116
commentary, 24, 26, 27, 31–34, 36,
    76, 180, 193, 225, 234
Commynes, Philippe de, 118
complexion, *see* character, 175
*Croyland Chronicle*, 118
Culpeper, Thomas, 216

Daniel, Walter, 155
Dante, 24, 133, 221
Dares, 97, 98
depression, 172
*descriptio*, 72
desire, as metaphor, 173
dialogue, 113, 153, 172, 174, 203, 229,
    232 sayings, 140
*diglossia*, 204
*dispositio*, 154
disposition, (*see* character), 175
distinctiones, 184
Dolet, Etienne, 226, 230
Donatus, 20, 24, 27
Douglas, Gavin, 27, 224, 235
dreams, 26, 55, 172, 211

Eadmer, 157
*ecphrasis* (*see descriptio*), 71
Edward I, King of England, 119
Einhard, 145 *Life of Charlemagne*, 158,
    160–2 preface 159
Eliot, T. S., 18, 207
Elizabeth I, Queen of England, 123, 130
embellishment (*see* rhetorical
    invention)
*encomium*, 159, 160 (*see* genre,
    rhetorical genres) works, 133
  *Encomium Emmae Reginae*, 139
  funeral oration, 128
  schema for, 129–31
Erasmus, 20, 38, 53, 63, 69, 96

Fantosme, Jordan, 89
Felix of Croyland, 155
fiction, 5
  dangers of, 10, 27, 92, 93, 180
Froissart, Jean, 88, 112, 113, 123, 124,
    177, 180 trans. Lord Berners, 111

Gainsford, Thomas, 68
genre, 11, 15, 30, 45, 75, 81, 104, 240, 246

biography, 12
complaint, 71
*consolatio*, 169
De Casibus, 167, 236
debate literature, 56, 70
*demande d'amour*, 54
dialogue, 26, 200
encomium, 82
epic, 22, 46, 91, 98, 116, 148, 234
essays, 116
fable, 33, 40, 41, 44, 80
fabliau, 5
history, 23, 33 chronicle, 100
history (defined), 6
letters, 78, 96, 113–16, 168, 170, 254
Lives, 12, 92
lyric poetry, 78
pastoral, 29, 45, 46
Planctus, 58, 119, 242
romance, 5, 15, 88, 92, 148
saint's life, 5, 128, 138, 141, 147
sermon, 82
tragedy, 91, 98
Geoffrey of Monmouth, 47, 48, 63,
    89, 100, 103, 110, 226, 267
Gervase of Canterbury, 89, 101
*Gesta Stephani*, 117
Gibbon, Edward, 144
Gildas, 261, 267
gloss, 192, 197 authorial, 221, 224 (*see*
    commentary)
*Glossa Ordinaria*, 28, 195
Greene, Robert, 55, 56
Guerre, Martin, and commentary, 24
Guibert of Nogent, 170, 261
Guido delle Colonne, *Historia
    Destructionis Troiae*, 52, 103, 105,
    227, 228, 235

hagiographies, 164
Heliodorus, *Aethiopica*, 15
Helisenne de Crenne, 172
Heloise, 116, 168, 170
Henry I, King of England, 162 *anti-
    encomium of*, 1
Henry IV, King of England, 118
Henry of Huntingdon, 1
Henry V, King of England, 120, 121
Henry VII, King of England, 68, 100
Henryson, Robert, 240, 241 *Fables*, 41, 44

Herodotus, 86, 91, 93, 94, 97, 98
Higden, Ranulph, 262
*Historia Ecclesiae Dunhelmensis*, 117
history, 1, 2, 5, 6, 7, 11
    closeness to poetry, 96
    model texts, 89, 90
    sources common report, 95, 96, 110,
        154 (*see* rhetorical exercises)
history, model texts, 164, 165
Hoccleve, Thomas, 171, 172
Holinshed, 121
Holinshed, Ralph, *Chronicles*, 121
Homer, 17, 22, 98
Horace, 31, 110
Hugo, Victor, *Quatrevingtreize*, 54

Interpretation, 9, 10, 27, 36, 44, 170,
    180, 181, 194, 198, misreading,
    211, 243
Isidore of Seville, 97

Jean de Flixecourt, 228
Jean de Meung, 116, 218
Jerome, 8, 27, 86, 135, 147, 193, 196,
    270
John of Garland, 29
John of London, *Commendatio
    Lamentabilis*, 119
John of Salisbury, 36, 38, 90, 107, 275
Johnson, Samuel *Lives of the English
    Poets*, 126 *Rambler*, 125, 126
    *Rasselas*, 134
Joinville, *Life of St Louis*, 164
Jonson, Ben, 54
Julian of Norwich, 211
Juvenal, 18

Kempe, Margery, 171, 176
Kipling, Rudyard, *Just So Stories*, 64

La Fontaine, Jean, 40
Laȝman, 50
Langland, Will, 211
Laurent de Premierfait, 167, 189, 236
Lefèvre, Raoul, 191
lexis, 183, 194, 206, 213
*L'Histoire ancienne jusqu'à César*, 227
*Li Fet des Romains*, 97, 98
*Liber Eliensis*, 117
literature, 80

Livy, 91, 93, 94, 106 translations of, 261
Louis XI, King of France, 106, 118
Lucan, 98, 165, 261, 265, 267
    Pharsalia, 110, 116
Lucan, influence of, 117
Lydgate, John, 167, 189, 190, 236, 237

Macaulay, Thomas Babbington, 7
Machiavelli, 106
Macrobius, 34
    Saturnalia, 26, 33
Malkaraume, Jehan, 209
Malory, Thomas, 58, 70, 71
Map, Walter, 261
Marche, Olivier de la, 88
Marie de France, 211, 220 Fables, 41, 43
Martianus Cappella, 24
Matthew of Vendôme, 72
Matthew of Westminster, 100, 101, 103
Melusine, translation of, 188
metaphor, 173, 225 spatial, 3, 5, 33, 75, 192, 193, 199, 201, 210
Mézières, Philippe de, 200
Milton, John Areopagitica, 56
    'L'Allegro', 70 Paradise Lost, 21, 57
mimesis (see representation)
Mirror for Magistrates, 167
model texts, 16, 17, 19, 29, 45, 84, 116, 144, 180
modistic logicians, 278
Monstrelet, Enguerrand de, 119, 123, 124
Montaigne, Michel de, 172, 175, 201
More, Thomas, 165, 166, 167, 176, 215
mores (see character), 128
motive (see character, rhetorical ethos)

narrative, verisimilar, 149, 150, 151, 152
narrative indeterminacy, 53, 80, 98, 102, 149, 171, 232, 233, 245, 275 ethos, 139
narrative voice, 87, 95, 139, 143, 149, 154, 156, 168, 187, 206

'Nennius', 110
Notker, 162

Opicinus de Canistris, 172
oration, 54-4, 132, 133
    demonstrative, 57
    epideictic, 59
    judicial, 55
    parts of an, 59–62
oratory, 9, 18–9, 34, 42, 47, 65, 129, 130, 156, 186, 187
Orderic Vitalis, 1, 110, 165
Oresme, Nicole, 215, 217, 226
Ormulum, 209
Orwell, George, Animal Farm, 41
Otloh, 172
Ovid, 7, 18, 19, 29 Heroides, 34 Metamorphoses, 31
Ovide Moralisé, 32

panegyric (see rhetorical exercises, encomium)
Persius, 18
Peter Comestor, 209
Peter Lombard, Sentences, 27, 205
Peter of Langtoft, 89
Peter of Riga, 209
Peterborough Chronicle, 117
Petrarch, 86, 102, 262
Phillipe de Commynes, 106, 130
Piccolomini, Aeneas Silvius, 172
Plato, 16, 136 Apology, 41 Republic, 93
Plutarch, 59
Polybius, 130
Priscian, 20, 24, 27, 43
Progymnasmata see rhetorical exercises, 96, 97

Quintilian, Institutio Oratorio, 7, 18, 53, 60–1, 91

Ralph Diceto, 89 109
Raoul des Presles, 226
realism, 152
realism (see style, representation), 12
reality, prelinguistic, 3, 83, 179, 181, 183, 232
reference, 5, 17, 18, 20, 83, 99, 170, 180, 187, 190, 198, 231, 232, 282

audience, 181 intertextual, 3, 4,
11, 16, 39, 95, 108, 151, 152, 238
Reginald of Canterbury, 147
Reginald of Durham, 145
representation, 2, 64, 83, 99, 134, 231
deliberate misrepresentation, 234
fabulous, 4 plausible, 257
verisimilar, 86, 92, 95, 101, 232,
267
rhetorical *ethos*, 15, 84, 87, 148
rhetorical *ethos* (*see also* character), 101,
172 (*see also* rhetorical genre), 5
rhetorical exercises, 16, 97
*amplificatio*, 78, 243
*chria*, 65–7, 69, 132, 140, 153, 276
commonplace, 170
*comparatio*, 70, 74, 202, 257, 272
*confirmatio*, 69
*controversiae*, 47, 110, 250, 265
declamation, 19, 47, 250, 254, 255
*descriptio*, 145, 158, 176 of a person,
145
*destructio*, 69
*digressio*, 154, 257
disputation, 265
*encomium*, 127, 160, 190, 272
description of a city, 158
fable, 18, 40, 41
*legislatio*, 74
*narratio*, 60, 64
*progymnasmata*, 64
*sententiae*, 140
*suasoriae*, 22, 47, 52, 110, 111, 250
rhetorical genre
*controversiae*, 54
*declamatio*, 275
*encomium*, 1, 8, 57, 59, 69, 106, 125,
130 132, 144, 146, 147, 153, 162,
263, 265
epideictic speeches (*see encomium*),
129
*ethopoeia*, 73
judicial oration, 56
*prosopopeia*, 73
*suasoriae*, 54
rhetorical invention, 1, 2, 4, 7, 9, 11,
85, 86, 87, 88, 92, 96, 98, 99, 101,
103, 108, 139, 140, 238
rhetorical style, 8 low (pastoral), 4

rhetorical terms
*amplificatio*, 63
anaphora, 50
commonplace, 68, 104
*descriptio*, 271
*digressio*, 61, 70, 162
*dispositio*, 132, 160, 169
*divisio*, 131, 143, 149
enthymeme, 61, 139
*ethos*, 63
exclamatio, 34, 132
hyperbole, 34
irony, 34
metaphor, 8
occupatio, 101, 132, 160, 272
paronomasia, 13, 59
parts of a spech, 56, 59, 62, 63
*pathos*, 62, 91, 126
*peroratio*, 133
schemes, 7, 20, 76
sententiae, 62, 67, 100
tropes, 7, 20, 76
rhetorical *topoi*, 11, 69
cannibalism, 117
catalogues, 116
claim to be eye-witness, 105
cross-dressing, 267 hair, 73, 118, 162
crossing a river, 52, 108
death, 106, 116, 160
holy, 118 kings, 118
*descriptio*, 72 description of a city, 8,
71, 109, 265 description of a
person, 72, 73 description of a
place, 109, 110 acquisition of
name, 110
dreams, 271
eve of battle, 119, 124, 268
good death, 8
group dialogue, 271
hagiographical, married celibacy,
150 mortification by cold water,
155 torture, 118
humility, 43, 105, 106, 282
incest, 117
inexpressibility, 156
infant hero, 137
marriage, 52
memory of ancestors, 105, 106, 142
mutilated corpse, 118

rhetorical *topoi* (*cont.*)
  mutilation of pregnant women, 117
  parents of hero, 136, 137
  praise of ancestors, 272
  prefaces, 94, 107, 142, 188, 205, 215,
    218, 219, 225 need to eschew
    idleness, 105 writing at
    command, 105
  prophecy, 118 prophetic dream,
    132, 136
  rape, 117, 267
  royal invitation to scholar, 275
  speech before a battle, 119, 120, 123
  storm at sea, 8, 116
  superiority of prose to verse, 98, 99
  works, 153, 171
Richard II, King of England, 110, 113
*Richard II, Traison et Mort de*, 177
Richard III, King of England, 104,
  118, 166
Richard of Devizes, 109
Richer, 164, 165, 261, 266
Robert Manning of Bourne, 89
Robert of Gloucester, 89
Rolle, Richard, 205, 206, 208
*Roman de Renart*, 240
*Roman d'Eneas*, 235
Ruotger, 146

Sallust, 91, 98, 103, 107, 135, 141, 165,
  267, 269 translations of, 227
Satan, as rhetorician, 21, 62
Scaliger, Julius Caesar, 72
Scott, Sir Walter, 7
Seneca, 19, 116, 250 translations of,
  218
Servius, 24
Shakespeare, 54
  *2 Henry IV*, 119
  *Coriolanus*, 42
  *Hamlet*, 68, 73, 174
  *Henry V*, 121–4
  *Julius Caesar*, 59, 60
  Sonnets, 52, 53
  *Troilus and Cressida*, 236
Sidney, Philip, 56 72
Sidonius Apollinaris, 145, 160, 260
Skelton, John, 166
*Song of Roland*, 52

speeches, 5, 8, 9, 33, 47, 52, 55, 57, 73
Spenser, Edmund, 223 *Shepheardes
  Calender*, 24, 42, 76–7 *The Faerie
  Queene*, 57
Statius, 7 *Thebaid*, 35
Stephen, King of England, 117
style, 2, 15, 17, 29, 30, 43, 44, 45, 46,
  70, 71, 80, 95, 106, 107, 137, 170,
  244, 279
  archaizing, 22, 76, 84, 213, 217
  aureation, 78
  calques, 214
  crucial vocabulary, 183, 196, 214
  epic similes, 35
  fabulous, 42
  high, 100
  historical, 91–2, 259
  low, 150
  referring register (*see also* reference),
    226, 230
  register, 171, 183, 204 social status, 75
  verisimilar, 12, 35
Suetonius, 118, 135, 274
Suetonius, influence of, 159, 160
Sulpicius Severus, 135, 140, 142, 143,
  144, 146, 153, 270, 275 influence
  of, 145 *Vita Martini*, 141
Susenbrotus, Johannes, 79

Tacitus, 165, 261, 262 *Agricola*, 129
  annals, 52 *Germania*, 123
Thebes, history of, 6
Thegan, 162
Theodulus, 29 *Eclogue*, 45, 46
Theophrastan characters, 174
Thucydides, 92
translation, 5, 20, 76, 158, 283
  accompaniment, 36, 205, 207
  as interpretation, 30
  fluent-text, 186
  narrative paraphrase, 209
  redaction, 210
  replacement, 215
  substitute, 36, 205
  unit of, 206, 242
  word-for-word debate, 186–7, 197,
    199, 218–9, 228, 230, 244
translation (schema for medieval), 181,
  182

translation *see also* interpretation, 102
translation, inertia in, 183, 193, 216
Trivet, Nicholas, 107, 261
Trojan War, 98
Troy, history of, 6
tyranny, 166

Villehardouin, 266
Virgil, 7, 8, 16, 26, 29, 38, 43, 45, 46,
    80, 98, 165, 223, 233 *Aeneid*,
    24–5, 31, 33, 36, 234 *Aeneid*,
    trans. of, 224, 234 *Georgics*, 196

Wace, Robert, 49 *Roman de Brut*, 48,
    51 *Roman de Rou*, 89, 99
Wakefield Master, 210

Webster, John 57
Will, 176
'William FitzStephen', 109
William of Malmesbury, 1, 90, 107,
    117, 139, 162, 163, 165, 180, 267
    *Life of Dunstan*, 157 *Life of
    Wulfstan*, 156
William of Moerbeke, 217
William of Poitiers, 164, 165
William Rufus, King of England, 118,
    162, 163
William the Conqueror, 1, 164
Wilson, Thomas, *Art of Rhetoric*, 52
Wyatt, Thomas, 41, 43, 198

Xenephon, 136 *Anabasis*, 123